AN

UNSPEAKABLE

SADNESS

The
Dispossession
of the
Nebraska
Indians

T0317156

DAVID J.
WISHART

University
of Nebraska Press

Lincoln & London

© 1994 by the University of Nebraska Press

All rights reserved

Manufactured in the United States of America

♾ The paper in this book meets the minimum requirements
of American National Standard for Information Sciences–
Permanence of Paper for Printed Library Materials, ANSI
z39.48-1984

First paperback printing: 1997

Library of Congress Cataloging-in-Publication Data

Wishart, David J., 1946–

An unspeakable sadness: the dispossession of the Nebraska
Indians / David J. Wishart.

p.   cm.

Includes bibliographical references and index.

ISBN 0-8032-4774-5 (cl.: alk. paper)

ISBN 0-8032-9795-5 (pa.: alk. paper)

1. Indians of North America—Nebraska—Removal.

2. Indians of North America—Nebraska—Land transfers.

3. Nebraska—History—19th century. I. Title.

E78.N3W57 1994

978.2´ 00497-DC20

94-4611

CIP

Now the face of all the land is changed
and sad. The living creatures are gone.
I see the land desolate, and I suffer
unspeakable sadness. Sometimes I wake in
the night and feel as though I should suffocate
from the pressure of this awful feeling of
loneliness.

White Horse, Omaha
August 13, 1912.

Contents

Illustrations

TABLES

Preface

In 1800 there were at least 14,000 American Indians living in what is now the eastern half of Nebraska. These included, at a minimum, 10,000 Pawnee, 2,000 Omaha, 900 Ponca, and 1,000 Otoe-Missouria. These nations, or tribes, held sway over more than thirty million acres of land. One hundred years later, of these original Nebraska Indians, only 1,203 Omaha and 229 Ponca remained in their homelands, and their combined estate was little more than two hundred thousand acres. The others, including most of the Ponca, had been excised from their reservations and moved to Indian Territory (now Oklahoma). They had received an average of ten cents an acre for the land that became Nebraska. American and European immigrants—almost one million of them by 1900—filled the vacated lands, fenced the open prairie, plowed over the topsoil, laid down railroads and towns, and in countless other ways metamorphized the landscape to such an extent that it was barely recognizable to the old Indians who had lived through it all.

This book tells the story of this century of dispossession. The study begins around 1800, with the Nebraska Indians living in traditional ways and still relatively unscathed by the external colonizing forces that would rapidly push them to the brink of destruction. It ends in the final two decades of the nineteenth century with the Indians living poorly on allotments—individual parcels of land—in Indian Territory and Nebraska. This was not the end of the dispossession, because most of those allotments also ended up in American hands, but it was in the nineteenth century that the great losses of land, traditions, and population occurred. A twentieth-century postscript is added, partly to emphasize that these nations have endured, and so triumphed over acculturation, and partly to use claims-case findings as a means of determining the justness, or lack of justness, of the United States' treatment of the Indians.

Acknowledgments

I **owe many** institutions and individuals thanks for their assistance in the production of this book. A substantial grant from the National Endowment for the Humanities reduced my teaching load and greatly facilitated the research and writing. Smaller grants from the American Council of Learned Societies, the American Philosophical Society, the University of Nebraska Research Council, and the Center For Great Plains Studies also assisted in many ways. I am particularly grateful to Jeanne Kay for getting this project out of first gear, to Sharon Valencia for her care in producing successive drafts, and to the Map Press of Lincoln, Nebraska, for taking my rough hand-drawn maps and turning them into electronic works of art. John Ludwickson saved me from making mistakes on early Indian locations; any remaining mistakes are my own. The staff on the front line at the Nebraska State Historical Society also deserve my thanks. Less directly, but nonetheless important, was the example set by the senior historical geographers in my department, Dr. Leslie Hewes and Dr. C. Barron McIntosh, and the contributions made by students in my seminars in Indian dispossession over the past ten years. Last, but certainly not least, I'd like to thank my family and friends for patiently listening to this story in the making, especially my wife, Sarah Disbrow, who edited the manuscript.

AN
UNSPEAKABLE
SADNESS

CHAPTER ONE

Lands and
Lifestyles of the
Nebraska
Indians at the
Beginning of the
Nineteenth
Century

In July 1804 the expedition led by Meriwether Lewis and William Clark inched its way up the Missouri River along the eastern border of what is now Nebraska. The explorers were two months and 630 miles into a journey that would take them to the Pacific and back by late September 1806. President Jefferson's instructions had been explicit: Lewis and Clark were to explore and survey the newly acquired Louisiana Territory and beyond to Oregon, find a "direct and practicable water communication" across the continent to the "Western ocean," assess the potential of the area for the fur trade, gather scientific information on all aspects of the environment, and, in general, assert the American presence in the trans-Missouri West.[1]

The American Indians were central to all of these objectives: not only did they inhabit the country, but also, under U.S. law, they remained owners of the land, subject only to the recently imposed sovereignty of the United States. Consequently, Jefferson's instructions concerning the Indians were particularly specific, and, in carrying them out, Lewis and Clark made the first systematic survey of Indian populations, territories, and lifestyles in the western United States. They recorded languages, estimated the numbers of villages, lodges, warriors, and total populations, described the territory claimed by each Indian group, their role in the fur trade, and their animosities and alliances. Significantly, given the turn of events after 1820, they also investigated whether the Indians on the lower reaches of the Missouri (Osage, Kansa, Otoe-Missouria) would be willing to move in order to make room for relocated Indians from the increasingly populated eastern United States.[2]

By the time the expedition passed the mouth of the Platte, the explorers were becoming concerned that the local Indians, the Otoe-Missouria, had not put in an appearance. They would be aware, from discussions with St. Louis traders like Jean Pierre Chouteau, and from the seasoned frontiersmen—Francois Labiche, Pierre Cruzatte, Pierre Dorion, and George Drouillard—who had signed on as guides and interpreters, that the eastern Nebraska Indians (the Omaha,

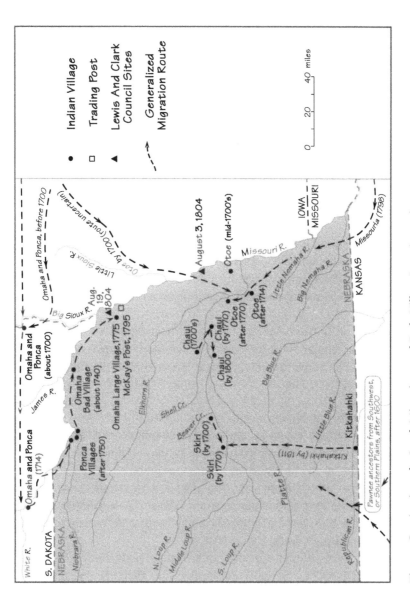

Fig. 1 Coming into the Land: Migrations and Early Village Locations, circa 1800

Pawnee, and Ponca, in addition to the Otoe-Missouria) would be out on the plains on their summer bison hunts. They had hoped, perhaps, to make contact when the Indians returned from their summer bison hunts to their villages for the early, or green, corn harvest which took place in July. Lewis and Clark wanted a council: eastern Nebraska was to be the testing ground for Jefferson's Indian policy and for their own diplomatic skills.

On July 22 the expedition set up camp on the Iowa side of the river, about ten miles up from the mouth of the Platte. Drouillard and Cruzatte were sent to the Otoe-Missouria village, located eighteen miles to the west near the confluence of the Elkhorn and Platte rivers. They found the village empty, and the route of departure concealed so that hostile Indians (most likely the Kansa, Omaha, or Pawnee) could not follow them on their hunt.

The explorers' luck changed on July 28 when Drouillard brought a lone Missouria into camp. Drouillard had been hunting elk along the Missouri with about twenty families who lacked the horses to join the main party on the distant bison range.[3] Lewis and Clark immediately dispatched a scout to find the Indians and bring them in for a council to be held further up the river a few days later.

The council took place August 3 on a "hansom elevated" site overlooking the Missouri, near present-day Fort Calhoun, Nebraska (fig. 1).[4] There were six headmen of the Otoe-Missouria in attendance, but the principal chiefs, Little Thief (We-'ar-ruge-nor) and Big Horse (Shon-go-ton-go) were not present. The council was marked by the strained protocol and diplomatic maneuvering that would characterize treaty councils for the remainder of the century. Meriwether Lewis made a forceful speech (one he probably repeated many times during the next two years) filled with references to the "Great Father" in Washington, D.C., and his "suffering" Indian children. He promised the Indians a dependable fur trade and a post at the mouth of the Platte if they maintained peace with their neighbors and did not obstruct American navigation on the Missouri. He stressed the power of the United States and invited the chiefs and warriors to Washington to see it for themselves. Finally, on a more ominous note, he warned the Indians not to listen to the "councils of bad birds" or they would be destroyed "as the fire consumes the grass on the plains." Presents (clothes, flags, and medals) were then handed out to the Indians "in perportion to their Consiquence," and they were asked to return any French or Spanish emblems because, as Lewis explained, only the United States mattered now.

Seemingly pleased with the way the council had gone, Lewis and Clark scheduled another meeting with the Otoe-Missouria to be held further up the Missouri, this time with the Omaha invited. Their objective was to mend the rift that had developed between the Otoe-Missouria and the Omaha as a result of mutual raiding activities and reprisals. But the Omaha were nowhere to be found, and their village on Omaha Creek was deserted and in ruins (fig. 1).[5]

On August 18 a party of nine Otoe-Missouria chiefs and warriors, including Little Thief and Big Horse, rode into the explorers' camp. The council took place the following day. Lewis repeated his speech explaining the conditions of the new American order. Then Little Thief and Big Horse made their replies. Immediately it was evident that the Indians had their own pressing agenda. They were concerned that their strategic position in the St. Louis fur trade would be undermined if the United States established closer ties with the Omaha, Ponca, and other Indians further up the Missouri. They were also, as William Clark reported in his journal, "not well satisfied with the presents given them."[6] So the council closed on a sullen note, the Indians asking for more gifts, especially whiskey, the captains angry because their solemn speeches appeared to have made no impression on the Indians. This is hardly surprising, because they had been hearing similar speeches promoting the "Spanish Father" for more than a decade.

The expedition resumed its journey upstream the next day, passing by the Ponca village near the mouth of the Niobrara on September 5, then moving beyond the borders of Nebraska into the relatively uncharted reaches of the northern Great Plains. Lewis and Clark had made contact only with the Otoe-Missouria, but they had amassed considerable information on all of the indigenous Indians of eastern Nebraska. Who were these peoples, how did they live their lives, and how resilient were their societies on the eve of the American takeover?

Before Lewis and Clark

Of the five Indian nations living in eastern Nebraska in 1800 only the Pawnee could claim deep historical roots. The others—Otoe, Missouria, Omaha, and Ponca—were eighteenth-century immigrants. Nevertheless, like the cottonwood tree that is native to the area, these late arrivals quickly and firmly attached themselves to the land. By the beginning of the nineteenth century, eastern Nebraska was the center of their universe, the place where the practicalities of everyday living were connected to the eternal rhythms of life.

Both the Skiri (Loup) and Chaui (Grand) bands of the Pawnee were direct descendants of the Lower Loup peoples who lived in villages on the banks of the Loup and Platte rivers from about 1600 to 1750 and who had, in all probability, originally migrated from the Southwest or from the southern plains. The ancestors of the Pawnee in Nebraska may go even further back, to what has been called the Central Plains tradition (900 to 1450), but this remains unproven. Archeological evidence reveals that by 1700 the Skiri were living in a large number of small villages along the north side of the Loup while the Chaui lived further east on Shell Creek, then later on the south bank of the Platte and along its Skull Creek tributary.[7] By 1750 Kitkahahki (Republican) and Pitahawirata

(Tappage) bands had separated from the Chaui. The specific causes of these schisms are buried in the past, but such splits often involved factional disputes over leadership or policy. Decentralization into separate villages might also have been a rational decision to optimize the use of scarce and scattered resources, such as timber, by a large population.

By the late eighteenth century, eastern Nebraska had become a dangerous place to live, as the westward penetration of Europeans and Americans into the interior compressed Indian space all the way from the Appalachians to the Great Plains. The Pawnee bands sought the protection of larger settlements. By 1800 the Skiri were living in a large village or town (twenty to forty acres in extent) on a terrace of the Loup near what is now Palmer, Nebraska; the Chaui occupied two villages on the south side of the Platte near Bellwood and Linwood; and the Kitkahahki lived to the south on a terrace overlooking the Republican River between Red Cloud and Guide Rock (fig. 1). By 1811, under pressure from the Kansa, the Kitkahahki had moved north to the Loup. The location of the Pitahawirata village, if indeed it was separate from the Chaui sites, is unknown.

The archeological evidence is partly substantiated by Pawnee traditions. One tradition maintains that the "South Bands" (Chaui, Kitkahahki, and Pitahawirata) were offshoots of the Skiri and originally formed a single band, the Kawarahki.[8] In fact, the Skiri had more in common with the Arikara, who had separated out after 1600 and occupied the Missouri valley in South Dakota, than with the nearby South Bands. Other traditions, barely remembered when they were related to ethnologist George Bird Grinnell in the 1870s and 1880s, told of a prehistoric Pawnee origin with the Wichita in the southwestern United States, and then a slow migration north, leaving the Wichita behind on the southern plains.[9] Linguistic analysis supports this oral tradition, dating the Wichita-Pawnee split in the first few centuries A.D.

At about the same time that the Skiri and Chaui separated, the Otoe (members of the Chiwere group of Siouian speakers) were being forced westward across southern Minnesota and northern Iowa from an original homeland near the Great Lakes by the well-armed and hostile Dakota (Sioux) peoples. The Dakota, in turn, and south of them the equally militant Sauk (Sac) and Fox, were moving west toward the rich bison range of the Great Plains under pressure of white encroachment and the resulting diminution of game.

The Otoe, repeatedly buffeted from the east, successively occupied villages on the Iowa and Blue Earth rivers until, by 1700, they had reached the Little Sioux River and the east bank of the Missouri.[10] There they once again fell victim to the Dakota, and they fled south. In 1714 the French explorer Etienne Veniard de Bourgmont located their village on the Salt Creek tributary of the lower Platte, about thirty miles to the east of the Chaui settlements.[11] The Otoe continued to occupy the vicinity near the mouth of the Platte for the remainder of the century (fig. 1). They were joined there by their close relatives, the Missouria, in 1798, after the Sauk and Fox had made living in their previous homeland of western Missouri an exercise in terror. From that time on, the Otoe and Missouria were essentially "one nation," though this overlooks the persistence of the Missouria as a band for much of the nineteenth century.[12]

Like the Otoe, the Omaha and Ponca were driven into eastern Nebraska from the northeast by the Dakota. They were originally members of a single Dhegiha division of Siouian-speakers that also included the Kansa, Quapaw, and Osage. Even in the late nineteenth century, long after this division had fragmented, similar dialects, traditions, and social organization pointed to a common origin for all of these peoples. Their place of origin, according to Omaha tradition, was in wooded country, "near a great body of water," probably the Great Lakes.[13] Over the course of centuries they migrated down the Ohio River to the Mississippi, where segments pulled away to form the Quapaw, Osage, and Kansa.

The remnant of the group, the ancestors of the Omaha and Ponca, continued up the Mississippi until, in the late seventeenth century, they were driven across Iowa to the eastern side of the Missouri.[14] For much of the eighteenth century the Omaha and Ponca together occupied a territory stretching from western Iowa to eastern South Dakota. Both Omaha and Ponca traditions describe frequent contacts with the nearby Arikara, from whom they adopted the earth lodge and, possibly, corn. At an unknown time, probably in the early 1700s, the Ponca separated from the Omaha, and after a period of wandering that took them as far west as the Black Hills, they established a village near the mouth of the Niobrara around 1750. The Ponca maintained this general location for the remainder of the century, building their villages along Ponca Creek and the lower Niobrara (fig. 1).

The Omaha continued south along the west side of the Missouri into what is now Nebraska. Their first village, on Bow Creek near the present-day town of St. James, was quickly abandoned and christened Bad Village (To^{n}iwo^{n}pezhi) because it was the scene of internal conflict among Omaha families. With the shadow of the Dakota looming over them, the Omaha moved south by 1775 to Omaha Creek where they built Large Village (To^{n}iwo^{n}to^{n}ga) (fig. 1). It was near there in 1795 that the Scottish-born Spanish explorer John Mackay built a trading post, and the Omaha were pulled conclusively into the orbit of external economic and political systems.

Although the Indians of eastern Nebraska were in continual contact with Europeans only after 1790, they had felt reverberations from the European presence in North America since the seventeenth century. At its worst this contact brought disease, especially smallpox, which, as Mackay wrote in 1795, struck an otherwise healthy people with a "Mortality as frightful as Universal."[15]

At the time of Lewis and Clark all five nations had been drastically reduced in numbers, power, and confidence by recurring waves of epidemics that had swept through the area since at least 1750. The explorers estimated that there were 6,850 Indians left in eastern Nebraska in 1804: 500 Otoe and 300 Missouria, 900 Omaha, 250 Ponca, and 4,800 Pawnee.[16] They understood that this was a sparse population for a country that impressed them as fertile, teeming with game and fish, and endowed with numerous species of wild fruits. The cause of this underpopulation, as they realized, was smallpox.

Lewis and Clark found the Nebraska Indians reeling from the smallpox epidemic of 1800–1801, an epidemic which devastated Indian nations from the Columbia River to the Gulf of Mexico.[17] The disease was so virulent among the Otoe-Missouria, Omaha, and Ponca that in 1801 the Spanish authorities in St. Louis ordered all traders returning from these nations to undergo quarantine on an island one mile from the city and to "pass their furs through smoke" to purify them.[18]

The record of the epidemic is most complete for the Omaha. Lewis and Clark, probably relying on the figures of James Mackay, claimed that the Omaha had "boasted 700 warriors" in 1795, which translates into a total population of more than two thousand people. Then smallpox struck in the winter of 1800–1801. The Omaha were not simply out on their summer bison hunt when Lewis and Clark passed by. With their population reduced by more than one-half, they had burned and abandoned their fated village and become a "wandering nation" living off the land along the Niobrara and Loup rivers.[19]

The damage wrought by smallpox and other epidemic diseases was multifaceted. Smallpox, for example, brought headaches, fever, muscular pain, vomiting, and eruptions of pustules on the face, hands, and feet which left lasting scars if the afflicted person was fortunate enough to survive. The death rate of unimmunized victims (immunization came from previous exposure or, after 1830 in eastern Nebraska, from inoculation) could run as high as 70 percent. High mortality rates hindered the Indians' ability to carry out subsistence activities, and diseases of undernutrition and malnutrition killed many more, especially children. Lacking labor and energy, the Indians could not participate in the fur trade. The Omaha, Lewis and Clark explained, were "deserted by the traders," and the "consequent deficiency of arms and ammunition" left them vulnerable to attack.[20] As a result, their numbers fell even more drastically. The deaths of Indians, especially chiefs, priests, and doctors, eventually left holes in the cultural memory—visions were no longer explicated, ceremonies no longer practiced, knowledge lost.

The depth of the trauma is evident from the Omaha's reaction to the 1800–1801 scourge. According to their traditions, when they saw the disfigured appearance of the survivors (believing that this disfigurement would be passed on to their children) they decided to launch a war party and die with some glory in a way that they understood. The tradition holds that the Omaha war party (which included all the survivors of the epidemic) fought with the Ponca, Cheyenne, Pawnee, and Otoe until finally they returned to their Omaha Creek site to sow life again in the ashes of their past.[21]

There is less documented evidence concerning the impact of the 1800–1801 epidemic on the Otoe, Missouria, Pawnee, and Ponca. All of these nations, however, had been decimated by smallpox in the decades preceding Lewis and Clark. The once-powerful Missouria had been forced to join with the Otoe by "repeated attacks of the small pox" together with constant pressure from the Sauk and Fox. Similarly the Ponca were described by Lewis and Clark as a "remnant of a nation once respectable in point of numbers."[22] Pierre Tabeau, one of the most experienced traders on the river, attributed the Ponca's decline to smallpox, as well as warfare with the Brulé band of the Teton Dakota. Tabeau noted that the Ponca were forced to seek refuge with the Omaha in the winter of 1804–5 "in order to escape entire destruction."[23] First-hand information is less available for the Pawnee, but in 1831 their agent John Dougherty, who was witnessing the terrible impact of yet another smallpox epidemic, reported that the last time the disease had struck was in 1798, which may have been a mistaken reference to the 1800–1801 scourge or an indication that such epidemics were by then endemic.[24] Lewis and Clark's estimate of four thousand eight hundred Pawnee in 1804 may well be only one-quarter of the population they had sustained in the mid-eighteenth century.

The European impact, though disastrous, was not without its compensations. At best, Europeans provided horses, which were diffused by trading and raiding from Santa Fe after 1600.[25] The Pawnee had horses by 1714, and they subsequently supplied them at great profit to the Omaha and Otoe to the east. The Ponca first got their horses from the Comanche, trading them for bows and arrows.[26] Horses increased the Indians' range of hunting, trading, and raiding, and in general made life much easier by providing a means of haulage that was far more efficient than the previously used dog. Moreover, horses, being self-propagating, did not establish a dependency on Americans and Europeans. Of course, horses also increased the striking range of enemies like the Dakota, and villages in eastern Nebraska became more vulnerable to attack.

Imported trade goods also made life easier, especially for Indian women, who bore the burden of daily chores. Less time was needed for pottery making, for example, when copper and brass kettles were available. Time saved in this sector, however, was quickly filled by the additional labor required to process the extra robes. Kettles, cloth, blankets, vermillion, blue beads, knives, and tobacco were exchanged for furs, or given as gifts—a reluctant concession to the Indians' traditional trading rules. Alcohol was also a major trade item, especially at the easily reached Omaha and Otoe-Missouria villages. The powerful Omaha chief Blackbird, for example, was known to have a "great passion" for brandy, and the traders willingly supplied it, along with flags and medals, in order to keep his favor.[27] The Pawnee chiefs, on the other hand, realizing the social disruption that came with alcohol, kept it out of their people's lives for much of the nineteenth century.

What the Indians wanted most, however, was guns—British guns—not (as the Omaha specified to James Mackay) the "French ones which burst in their hands."[28] The trade in guns started a minor arms race in the late eighteenth century, shifting the balance of power among the Indians and complicating the traders' operations. Each Indian group tried to exclude its rivals from the fur trade and thus cut them off from the source of guns. During the 1780s the Kansa attempted to prevent Spanish traders from penetrating up the Missouri and supplying their enemies, the Otoe and Pawnee. The traders eventually bribed their way upstream with gifts in the 1790s, only to find first the Otoe, then the Omaha and Ponca, trying to block the river and monopolize the gun trade. In 1800 the trader Jacques Clamorgan complained to his superiors of having to make "considerable sacrifices" not only to the chiefs of the Omaha but also to the "entire nation" just to keep the river open.[29] To avoid this expense, traders tried to sneak upriver, but the Indians were vigilant and demanded their toll. Hostilities often erupted, as in the smallpox winter of 1800–1801, when the Omaha attacked a party of Spanish traders, leaving people dead on both sides.

The Omaha may have been encouraged by the British to attack Spanish traders (Spanish officials in St. Louis certainly believed so): like the Indians, the Europeans were using the fur trade to further their political ambitions. Operating out of St. Louis, the Spanish viewed their expansion up the Missouri after 1790 as a defensive strategy to counterbalance the activities of the British. British traders based at Prairie du Chien and Mackinac visited the Omaha, Otoe, and Pawnee villages annually in the early 1790s (fig. 2). Otoe Indians even journeyed east to trade at the British posts on the Mississippi in 1791. The British were also in regular contact with the Mandan and Arikara Indians of the upper Missouri from Brandon House and other posts on the Souris, Assiniboine, Qu'Appelle, and Red rivers in Canada. The Spanish feared that the British, with their cheaper and better goods, would capture the trade of the Missouri River and eventually penetrate to Santa Fe, right into the heart of their North American possessions. They were also increasingly concerned by the rapid rise in American population and the movement of their frontier (that is, the front waves of Euro-American settlement) west into Illinois and Missouri.[30]

The geopolitical picture changed radically in April 1803, when France, having acquired Louisiana from Spain in 1800, sold the vast territory to the United States. From that time on, although French and Spanish traders continued to populate the St. Louis fur trade, and British explorers and traders still interfered on the upper Missouri, the United States would be the arbiter of Indian fortunes in eastern Nebraska.

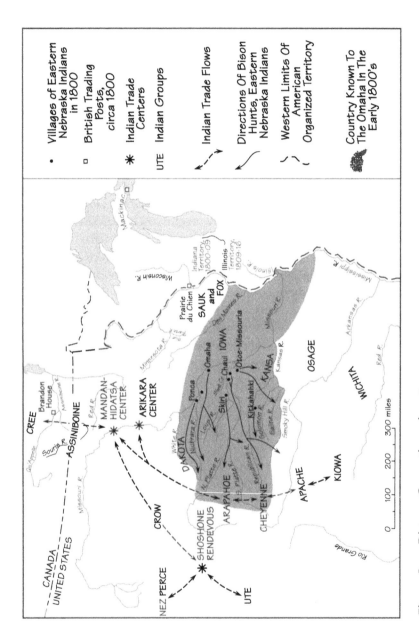

Fig. 2 Long Distance Connections, circa 1800

Traditional Ways of Life

Religion, Place, and Environment

Religion was the well-spring of traditional Indian life; everything else, from the structure of society to the performance of everyday tasks, flowed from that source. For example, Wakon'da, the mysterious, all-pervading force in the Omaha's creation story, began the process of life by arranging the sexual union of the male sky and the female earth. This dualism was represented in the division of Omaha society into two parts, the Sky people (I^{n}shta'cu^{n}da) and the Earth people (Ho^{n}igashenu). The two sacred pipes of the Omaha represented this dual organization. In theory at least, members married outside of their division but within the village, thus replicating the first union of sky and earth as well as maximizing biological diversity in a relatively small group. Even the spatial organization of the *hu'thuga,* the camp on the bison hunt or for cere- monial occasions, reflected the Omaha's cosmology. The *hu'thuga* was always arranged in a circle, with the door symbolically or actually facing east. There was a strict cosmic regulation of every aspect of life, from the spatial arrange- ment inside the lodge to the procedures of farming, warfare, and the bison hunt.[31]

There were, of course, significant differences in religious emphasis and cere- monial expression among the Indian nations of eastern Nebraska. The most striking differences were between the Pawnee and the others, reflecting their different linguistic affinities (Caddoan as opposed to Siouian) and geographical backgrounds (Southwest or Great Plains versus Midwest). The Pawnee bands, with a long tradition of Plains farming behind them, venerated corn above all else. The Omaha, Otoe-Missouria, and Ponca, on the other hand, had gradually subordinated corn to the bison in their ceremonies as they moved west and placed more emphasis on hunting. The Ponca's religious life was truncated when they separated from the Omaha, leaving behind sacred icons and vital ceremonial knowledge. However, the Ponca did adopt the Sun Dance (probably from the Dakota), a ceremony to bring rain and grass that was practiced by none of the other Nebraska Indians. There is less known about the religious system of the Otoe-Missouria, because many of their traditions have been forgotten. When the anthropologist William Whitman visited their reservation in Oklahoma in 1935, he was told by an old man, "You have come to us fifty years too late." Still, the evidence that does survive reveals a people who were close, in both society and religion, to their fellow Siouian-speakers, the Omaha and Ponca. Richard Shunatana, chief of the Buffalo Clan of the Otoe, recalled in 1922 that in days gone by his people "remembered their Maker daily and always called on Him for guidance and protection."[32]

There were even distinct differences in religious belief among the Pawnee bands. The Skiri had one of the most complex religious systems of all Native

Americans, a system founded on the belief that the stars were transformed gods and dead heroes. Every ceremony of the Skiri took its cue from the movement of the heavens. The South Bands took their authority more from animals, who were seen to possess supernatural powers and to have a direct link to Ti-ra'wa, the Pawnee name for the mysterious life force (literally "this expanse").[33] Moreover, the Skiri opened up their ceremonies to any interested onlookers, while the South Bands excluded everyone but initiates. Finally, of all the Indians of Nebraska, only the Skiri traditionally practiced human sacrifice (the Morning Star Ceremony).[34]

Despite many differences, the religions of the Nebraska Indians shared certain root themes; they were all "dialects of a common language of the sacred."[35] The Indians believed in the great unifying power of the life force, which they saw manifested all around and felt within them. They believed that this life force was responsible for the order and rhythms of day and night, winter and summer, and that this order had to be recognized and reinforced through ritual and ceremony. In other words, the Indians saw themselves as participants in an ongoing creation. They believed that everything in the creation was connected, a web of life reaching from the individual through the family and band and out into nature. They believed that their own position in this scheme was a humble one, and they viewed nature with a respect bordering on fear and a sympathy born of consideration for the welfare of all living things. Finally, they invested the places where they lived, farmed, and hunted with sacred meaning, blending the practical and spiritual into a successful strategy for life.

Although the environment as a whole was revered for what it provided and represented, certain landmarks stood out on the sacred map of eastern Nebraska. Burial grounds were holy places where the spirits of the dead lingered and affected human fortunes. Even an outsider like the English naturalist John Bradbury understood the Indians' reverence for their burial grounds. On May 11, 1811, after climbing the bluff behind the Omaha village to gain a better view of the settlement, he found himself in a burial ground with "heaps of earth, some of these recent" all around him. He left quickly, in consideration of their "veneration . . . for the graves of their ancestors."[36]

Certain physical features, such as caves, springs, rivers, and hills, were prominent in the Indians' sacred geography. These were often seen as supernatural places, and they were approached with trepidation, if at all. Spirit Mound, for example, in Clay County, South Dakota, was avoided by the Dakota, Omaha, and Otoe because it was thought to be the "residence of Deavels" who could afflict death from a great distance.[37] The Pawnee's sacred sites—fourteen sites have been identified, though the locations of only five are known—contained the lodges of the *nahu'rac*, supernatural animals that were the representatives of the gods on earth. These animals were fearsome and had the capacity to kill, but they could also bestow the power to cure disease, perform magical feats, and inflict injury. These were the skills of the doctors, who were organized into secret medical societies named after the animal, or group of animals, from which their power was derived. The sacred sites were places of pilgrimage, where visions were sought and offerings were made to Ti-ra'wa. The most renowned site, the home of the most powerful of the *nahu'rac*, was Pa:haku, located in the bluffs opposite the present-day town of Fremont, where the Platte River begins its wide bend to the south. All the Pawnee's sacred sites except for one—Spring Mound (Kicawi:caku) on the Solomon River in Kansas—were located between the Republican and Loup rivers, adding yet another connection to the homeland of eastern Nebraska.[38]

Lewis and Clark were unable to appreciate this symbiotic relationship with nature. (Perhaps they were exhibiting a degree of wishful thinking, because even in 1804 President Jefferson harbored the idea of transferring eastern Indians into the Great Plains.) They concluded that the Indians of eastern Nebraska had "no idea of an exclusive possession of any country."[39] This was largely accurate in a Euro-American sense of individually owned land, but it misses the point that each of the Indian nations had an intense attachment to specific homelands which they identified as their own. Their history was etched in the landscape in place-names commemorating people, deeds, visions, and disasters. Unlike many of the settlers who later came in and frequently moved on, the Nebraska Indians were deeply committed to place. The names for their months were not abstract terms applicable everywhere but descriptions of changes in the local environment over the course of each year (table 1).

Traditional Homelands

The home territories claimed by the Indians of eastern Nebraska in the early nineteenth century overlapped each other and extended into lands claimed by surrounding Indian groups (fig. 2). According to Howard's informants, the Ponca claimed as their own the country stretching from the White River on the north to the Platte on the south. The eastern boundary of this claimed homeland ran south from the Missouri near present-day Sioux City to the Platte; the western limit was nebulous, but the Ponca believed that it was beyond the Black Hills.[40]

This extensive claim was disputed by the Omaha and the Pawnee, as well as by the Teton Dakota to the north. The Omaha considered that most of northeastern Nebraska was their domain. A map drawn in 1816 from the notes of the St. Louis trader Auguste Chouteau shows the Omaha in control of the land from the Missouri to the Loup, or "Potato," River (fig. 3).[41] Later, Fletcher and La Flesche maintained that Omaha territory was defined on the east by the Missouri River from the mouth of the Niobrara to the mouth of the Platte, on the south by the Platte and its Shell Creek tributary, and on the west by a straight line drawn from Shell Creek back to the mouth of the Niobrara.

Table 1 Omaha, Otoe-Missouria, and Ponca Calendars

Month	Translation of Omaha Name	Translation of Otoe-Missouria Name	Translation of Ponca Name
January	When the snow drifts into the tents of the Ho^{n}/ga	Mating of the raccoon	Snow thaws
February	The moon when the geese come back	Month of the waterfrog	Moon when the ducks come back and hide OR Water stands in ponds moon.
March	The little frog moon	Month of doing nothing	Sore eyes (because of snow glare)
April	The moon in which nothing happens	Plow month	Rains
May	The moon in which they (the tribe) plant	Sprouting month	Summer begins
June	The buffalo bulls hunt the cows	Cultivating month	Hot weather begins
July	When the buffalo bellow	Mating of the bison	Middle of summer
August	When the elk bellow	Bellowing of the elk	Corn is in silk
September	When the deer paw the earth	Deer's wallow frosted	Moon when the elk bellow
October	When the deer rut	Mating of the deer	They store food in caches
November	When the deer shed the antlers	Buck's horns broken	Beginning of the cold weather
December	When the little black bears are born	Bear getting down	Beginning of cold weather with snow

Sources: Howard, *The Ponca Tribe* 73–74, Fletcher and La Flesche, *The Omaha Tribe*, vol. 1, 111, and Shunatona, "Otoe Indian Lore" 62

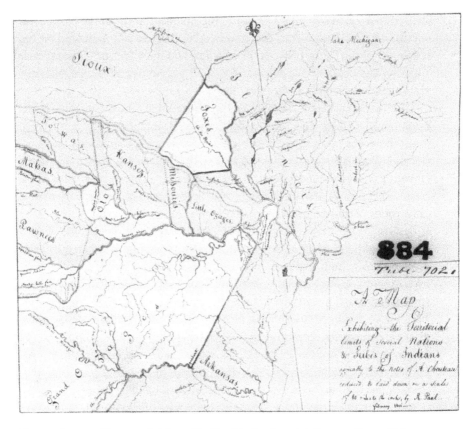

Fig. 3 Auguste Chouteau's Map of Indian Territories, 1816. Source: Central Map Files, National Archives, RG 75, No. 884

Gilmore, drawing his information from elderly Omaha people in the early twentieth century, argued that this territory extended much further west to the headwaters of the North Loup and then was demarcated by a line of boulders reaching north to the Niobrara.[42]

This Sand Hills country was also claimed by the Pawnee, though they seem to have acknowledged the Omaha's superior right to the land. Omaha officers directed the proceedings on occasions when the Pawnee bands joined with the Omaha to hunt bison in the Sand Hills (which, according to Fletcher and La Flesche, they did "frequently" in the first half of the nineteenth century). As a more powerful people, the Pawnee could have easily challenged this Omaha claim, but their sights were set more to the south. Chouteau's map shows that they claimed the plains almost all the way to the Arkansas, a claim bitterly disputed by the Comanche, Cheyenne, Arapahoe, and Kiowa. The Otoe-

Missouria, hemmed in by the Omaha, Pawnee, and Kansa, were largely restricted to a heartland lying east of the Big Blue and north of the Nemaha in southeastern Nebraska. They did, however, lay claim to a strip of land on the north side of the Platte, between the Missouri and the Elkhorn.[43] It is not clear why Chouteau showed the Missouria in their old homeland in 1816, eighteen years after they had joined the Otoe (fig. 3).

All four nations were claiming as their own some lands that were shared bison range. As long as population density was low and the extensive land base intact there was room to accommodate the overlapping claims, and the question of boundaries was irrelevant. But when the Indians' lands were sold to the United States government later in the nineteenth century, and when these cessions became the subject of claims cases in the twentieth century, the precise dimensions of traditional territories became a contentious issue.

Because of the overlapping nature of the claimed homelands, it is wise to forget about the concept of hard boundaries and to consider Indian territories as grading out from a village core, through a hunting range, to a far-flung trading and raiding periphery. Expressed this way, territory and occupancy (that is, where the Indians lived during the course of a year) were synonymous. The cores, containing the villages, farming areas, and main sacred sites, were discrete, though by no means immune to enemy raids. The hunting ranges overlapped, were sometimes shared, and were frequently contested. And trading and raiding activities took the Indians of eastern Nebraska deep into other peoples' heartlands, from the Spanish settlements on the Rio Grande to the Arikara villages on the upper Missouri. There was little extension of territory and activity to the east of the Missouri after 1800, although the Omaha and Otoe-Missouria did assert historic claims to parts of western Iowa and occasionally hunted there. In general, the cardinal directions out from the villages were south and west.

Village Life

At the center of Indian territories and Indian social organization lay the village. Villages were generally located on river terraces, above flood level yet within reach of rich bottomland soils, timber, and water. The river on one side and the bluffs on the other afforded protection. Some of the villages—the Ponca's, for example, and most of the Pawnee sites—were enclosed by earth walls as an additional precaution against enemy raids. Burial grounds were on the high land overlooking the settlements. Villages were moved, generally short distances, every ten to twenty years as the local timber was depleted and as their sites became unsanitary.[44]

There was "little of the picturesque" in the village landscape, to use Fletcher and La Flesche's words.[45] The scene was dominated by scores of circular earth lodges rising like hummocks from the ground. The dun-colored landscape was relieved only by the decorations on occasional tipis interspersed among the lodges. Dwellings were not arranged in any fixed order, although close kinfolk and friends tended to build homes near each other. There was, however, a definite orientation to each lodge: the door, leading out along a corridor from the dome, faced east. This certainly had sacred significance, because east was the direction of the day's rebirth, and the first light to penetrate the lodge fell on the altar near the western wall. But the east-facing door also had the practical advantage of catching the warmth of the morning sun and facing away from the prevailing winds, as the old Ponca tribal historian Peter Le Claire told ethnologist James Howard in the early 1950s.[46]

One of the best early descriptions of an earth lodge village was made by John Bradbury. In early May 1811, Bradbury and the trader Ramsey Crooks (who wanted to collect furs that were owed to him), visited the Otoe-Missouria village near the junction of the Platte and Elkhorn rivers. The village was situated on a "declivity" near the Platte, and the entire riverbank was "wholly divested of timber." The Indians were out on their bison hunt, so Bradbury walked into an empty village. He counted fifty-four lodges, each about forty feet in diameter and with projecting corridors about twelve feet in length. The doorways to the lodges had been blocked with sticks arranged in precise order, so that any intrusion would be noticed. Finding one lodge with the doorway unsealed, Bradbury entered through a passageway that declined to a dug-out floor. The lodge was supported around the outside by fifteen posts which were connected by rafters to four large posts set near the center. Layers of smaller sticks, sod, and then earth made up the roof.[47]

The Otoe-Missouria earth lodge described by Bradbury was essentially the same as those used by the other nations of eastern Nebraska.[48] The large posts were cut from elm trees. Elm bark, stripped and soaked, was used to fasten sections together. The thatch on the roof was big bluestem grass laid on a frame of willow withes.[49] Like the settlers' sod houses half a century later, the lodges were practical and efficient homes, but they were quickly infested with fleas and other vermin, and their life span was brief.

The Indians lived in their earth lodge villages for less than half of the year, the rest of the time being spent on the summer and fall-winter bison hunts. Still, the village was where the most important ceremonies took place, where a large proportion of year's food was procured, and where the ancestors were buried. The village was also the primary social unit, a "large extended family, geographically localized."[50]

The village social unit was held together by webs of family connections, by mutual obligations and responsibilities, by common traditions, customs, and speech, and by a united stance against the rest of the world. In the case of the Omaha, for example, both divisions of the village (Sky and Earth peoples) contained five clans which were descended through the father. Both divisions (and their sacred pipes) had to be represented at any council or treaty negotiation. Each clan had its own subdivisions, food avoidances, rites, and special functions in the operation of the annual cycle, and each was distinguished by a special haircut given to boys at an early age. All were integrated through the practice of exogamy into a "great kinship community." Regulations governing marriage among the clans were strict and intricate, and designed to keep kindred at a distance. The Ponca had a similar social structure, with seven to ten clans. Similarly, the Otoe were not "one tribe," according to Whitman's informants, but rather "a confederation of ten clans, each with its own privileges, its own institutions and its own supernatural origin." All the clans, however, were braided together in the functioning of the village.[51]

Religious icons such as the Pawnee's village bundles and the sacred pipes and sacred pole of the Omaha also focused the identity of each group of Indians. The village bundles were portable shrines consisting of ritual and symbolic items contained in a rolled bison hide. Each one—there were twelve bundles in the Skiri band alone—was kept on the west wall of a chief's lodge, where it was carefully looked after by one of the chief's wives. The bundles represented the covenant between the people and their gods, recalling the original encounter with the supernatural that gave each village its unique history. Throughout the year every significant activity was sanctioned by the power of a specific bundle. This ceremonial authority was alternated from one bundle, and hence one chief, to another, so that a balance of political power and responsibility was maintained.[52]

The bundle system was present, though probably less developed, in Omaha, Ponca, and Otoe-Missouria societies. But to a similar end, the two sacred pipes and the sacred pole of the Omaha allowed access to divine power while giving the chiefs their authority and the people their own particular identity. The sacred pole, especially, a slender two-and-one-half-meter hewn cottonwood tree, symbolized the unity of the Omaha people: according to their legends, it was "a gift from Wakon'da . . . the thing that would help to keep the people together." In one of the most important ceremonies of the Omaha calendar, taking place in late summer, the sacred pole was anointed with bison meat as a commemoration of its authority and a thanksgiving for the success of the hunts.[53]

These were stratified societies, characterized by class distinction and aristocratic rule. At the top of the social scale were the hereditary chiefs and priests, the former concerned with the smooth operation of worldly affairs, the latter in charge of the ceremonies and the harnessing of divine power. Others of high status included warriors, doctors, and arrow makers. The rest of the men (and their families), about half the population, were commoners who by birth, choice, or lack of skills, had little status or power.[54]

In most portrayals by early nineteenth-century observers, Indian women of

Nebraska were depicted as mistreated, overworked, downtrodden, and power-less. Indian men were characterized as living lives of "extreme indolence," while all the "domestic drudgery" was undertaken by the women.[55] Even long-term residents with the Indians, such as the Reverend John Dunbar (who lived with the Pawnee from 1834 to 1846) considered the women to be "mere slaves" and the men to be "abominably lazy." Dunbar claimed that the "life . . . of constant toil" left the women old before their time and that few lived past the age of sixty. To Americans at the time this alleged mistreatment of women was confirmation of the Indians' uncivilized state, and changing the respective roles of Indian men and women was a major thrust of federal policy throughout the nine-teenth century.

This prevailing American image of the role and status of Indian women was distorted by two major preconceptions. First, early travelers (at least the edu-cated ones who wrote down their ideas) were blinded by their own cultural assumption that women were to be cloistered and protected: placed, as Alexis de Tocqueville observed of American society, in a "situation of extreme depen-dence."[56] The understanding was that women were the weaker sex, both men-tally and physically. The second, connected, preconception was the equating of hard physical work with low status, and nobody worked harder than Indian women. Belief in Indian women's low status was also confirmed by the men's domination of the political and religious spheres.

There is no doubt that Indian women's lives were hard, a repetition of arduous daily tasks.[57] The women erected and dismantled the tipis, built and repaired the lodges, produced the staple crops, collected wild plants, hauled fuel and water, dug and transported salt, processed skins and furs, bore and raised children, and in general looked after the household (table 2). In fact, this heavy work load actually increased in the early nineteenth century, as the fur trade raised the demand for dressed skins. It is equally true that Indian women lacked societywide political power and played a subordinate role in ceremonial life. They did not hold public office, and though they did participate in secret societies, they did so to a lesser degree than men. Only one Pawnee ceremony—the Corn Planting Ceremony of the Skull Bundle—included women directly in a major role, and even in this ceremony male priests were in charge of the proceedings. Indian men, not women, represented their societies in dealings with the American government through treaties, annuity payments, and even in the allocation of allotments. This role, of course, reveals as much about American norms as it does of Indian priorities.

Yet, in the lodge, and in other contexts too, women had positions of author-ity and respect. Women in all of the Indian societies of Nebraska owned the lodge, the tipi, and most of its contents, a right of ownership that American women did not have until after the middle of the nineteenth century. The women also owned the fields, seeds, and implements of production. They often

Table 2   Men's and Women's Responsibilities and Activities

Men	Women
Political decision making (chiefs)	Day-to-day decision making in lodge.
Sacred matters (priests)	Child-rearing (mothers and grandmothers)
Medical/supernatural matters (doctors)	Ownership of lodge, tipi, and household property
Military protection and raiding (warriors)	Assistance in ceremonies
Hunting	Care of religious items
Manufacture of weapons	Virtually all farming (clearing the fields, planting, hoeing, harvesting) Virtually all wild plant collection
Minor assistance in fields	Food storage and processing (care of cache pits)
Care of horses (mainly by boys)	Hide and skin processing and manufacture (clothes, tipi cover, etc.) Construction and dismantlement of tipi Construction and repair of lodge Household maintenance (cooking, dishes, haulage of water and fuel, etc.) All household crafts except weapon making (quill work, pottery, stonework, and woodwork) Haulage of possessions, including sacred items, on bison hunts and, occasionally, on raids

determined where to camp on the bison hunts and where, specifically, to pitch the tipis in relation to other members of the clan. The senior wife was the main decision maker in the lodge and controlled the distribution of food. A woman had the right to refuse to marry a man selected by her parents, and she also had the right to divorce. Women were held in high esteem for the elemental role they played in the functioning of village life, including the production of food surpluses. They were often largely responsible for their husband's status (and hence the family's) because they manufactured the garments, skins, pipe stems, and other products that were traded or given as gifts to attain or consolidate social position. Some women were especially esteemed for their craftwork skills, including the production of wooden bowls and spoons and tipi covers. They earned additional wealth for the family in the form of fees for imparting knowledge of such skills. Women also played a role in healing, especially in problems associated with childbirth. Among the Otoe-Missouria, at least, women could become members of the doctors' societies. Finally, they had the responsibility of taking care of the religious items, an obligation of the highest importance.

Men were mainly responsible for hunting, defensive and aggressive warfare, manufacture of weapons, and most ceremonial and societywide political decisions. The division of labor had some flexibility: men would help with heavy tasks such as lodge construction or clearing the fields for cultivation, and there were many instances of women aiding in the defense of the village. The complementary nature of the roles, and the high status that went with being a skillful farmer as well as a successful hunter, was missed by the early nineteenth-century travelers.

Later in the century, when the first professional ethnographers studied the Nebraska Indians, a much more balanced picture emerged. James Owen Dorsey, for example, who lived and worked with the Ponca and the Omaha in the 1870s, concluded that "a woman had an equal standing in society as a man" and "always did her work of her own accord." He added that the "husband had his share of the labor, for the man was not accustomed to lead an idle life." This balance of obligation and status is also evident from the hard facts of Indian demography. Because of the dangers of hunting and raiding, men died in greater numbers than women and often at an early age, resulting in a wide gender gap that persisted for much of the century. There were single men in these societies, but there were no unmarried adult women because, as Dorsey put it, the "demand [was] greater than the supply."[58]

The class system was expressed on the landscape in the morphology of the village. The explorer Stephen Long noticed that at the Pawnee villages in 1819 lodges were "similar in structure but different in size."[59] Only the chiefs and other leaders could command the respect to mobilize the large labor force that was needed for major lodge construction. Chiefs' families, generally including many wives and children, as well as grandparents and various transitory occupants, also tended to be larger than average (perhaps as many as forty people), so they needed a sizable lodge. Those of lesser social status lived in smaller lodges or tipis. People with no status at all, including those who had violated the rules of society, such as murderers, and those who had been scalped and were therefore shunned, were relegated to the outskirts of the village where they lived in tipis or dugouts.[60]

Despite these class differences, there was a genuine safety net in village societies which ensured that no one went without food when any was available. Everyone was enmeshed in a kinship network whose inner circle was the lodge and whose outer limit was the village. This was a mutual support system whereby people of wealth redistributed food and other goods at ceremonies and on less formal occasions to those who were without. Anyone—even an enemy—who entered the lodge at mealtime would receive a share of the food. This sharing strengthened the security of the entire group and also enhanced the status of the donors. Generosity, after all, was one defining quality of a chief. In turn, commoners who were anxious for enhanced status would donate gifts—eagle feathers, quivers, buffalo robes, horses, and so on—to chiefs or priests in public ceremonies. Payments were also demanded by doctors as entrance fees into their societies and in return for knowledge. In general, to give a gift or share some food was a payment on future security. The expectation was that a "return gift would be made with interest."[61]

At the villages, the Indians' lives revolved around farming, the chores of daily maintenance, and ceremonies that lifted these activities above the mundane. The agricultural cycle began in April with ceremonies connected with the consecration of corn seeds and the preparation of the ground for cultivation. The fact that none of the other crops were featured in these ceremonies is a measure of corn's symbolic and practical importance. The Skiri's Corn Planting Ceremony celebrated fertility in songs and dances that mimicked women hoeing and planting. The Omaha's Maize Ritual song transformed corn into a human persona that urged its own growth, stanza by stanza, from seed to harvest. Every Omaha clan had its own particular role in the planting ceremonies, a balance of responsibility that bound each family to the fortunes of the group as a whole. One clan kept the sacred ears of red corn, another distributed four sacred kernels to each family to vivify their own seeds, while others, by virtue of their own taboos and rites, were charged with invoking supernatural power to bring bountiful rain or to protect the crops from insects.[62]

By early May the women would be clearing and burning the vegetation, and smoke would rise in plumes from the scattered plots and hang in the sky over the valleys. The fields were located along the floodplain, especially at the edges of the bluffs where erosion had already removed the tough mantle of prairie sod.[63] They ranged in size from half an acre to three acres and were often enclosed by a willow fence or an earth ridge capped with sunflowers. This served to keep the horses out and also denoted a woman's ownership of the land for as long as it was used. The Pawnee chiefs allocated the fields to their followers, and proximity to the village was roughly proportionate to social status. Commoners were relegated to the less convenient—and more dangerous—distant fields. It was not unusual, however, for a family to have a field near the village and another further out. With this "agricultural sprawl" extending for several miles from each village, and with well-traveled footpaths linking all the settlements and fields together, the north side of the Loup valley seen by Stephen Long in the summer of 1820 was a completely humanized landscape.[64]

Working cooperatively, the women of the household completed their planting in about a week. They used digging sticks and bone hoes to mound the earth into closely spaced hills. Corn was planted first, four kernels to a hill for the Pawnee, seven to a hill for the Omaha. Beans were interplanted with the corn so they could later use the cornstalk for vertical support. Finally, pumpkins, beans, and squash were planted in separate patches between the different strains of corn to maintain the purity of the breeds. The Indian women were expert farmers and accomplished geneticists: the Pawnee alone had ten pure varieties of corn, seven of pumpkins, and eight of beans.

In the weeks following the planting, the hills were kept carefully weeded and hoed twice to give the corn a head start on the encroaching vegetation. The villages were abandoned for the bison hunt in late June or early July, and the crops matured untended in the simmering heat of the Nebraska summer.

In late August, when the prairie goldenrod bloomed on the western plains, the Indians knew that the corn was ripening and it was time to return to the villages. After a ceremonial burning of bison meat in the fields and an offering of newly picked corn to the bundles, the harvest commenced. Some of the corn was picked green and sweet and eaten fresh, or boiled, dried, and stored for the winter. Bean, pumpkin, and squash harvests followed, and finally, in early October, came the mature corn harvest. The harvest scene was one of great activity and rejoicing, of both men and women in the fields, of corn roasting on willow pyres or strung like necklaces on scaffolds to dry, of women sitting in circles scraping the corn from the cob with clamshells, of feasting and the ceremonies which closed the agricultural cycle by replacing the sacred ears of corn in the bundles.

By 1800 bison meat was displacing corn as the Indians' main source of food. Horses had enlarged the scale of hunting and transportation, and bison meat was generally plentiful and preferred. Corn and other vegetables became a delicacy to be eaten fresh at harvest time, or else stored for future use as an accompaniment to meat, as a buffer against famine, or as a trade item. Visitors who were graced by the Indians' hospitality in the early nineteenth century were generally served corn soup enriched with bison meat, pumpkins, salt, and various herbal flavorings, or cornmeal mixed with honey and bison marrow. In most years food was plentiful. In 1834, for example, an emaciated John Dunbar was told solicitously by his Chaui hosts that he would "become fat after living with them awhile and eating their good, fat buffalo meat."[65] But the bison herds sometimes stayed distant, and drought, grasshoppers, and rival Indians sometimes ravaged the crops, so there was probably considerable variation in food supplies from year to year. Hence, Zebulon Pike's statement in 1806 that the Kitkahahki Pawnee raised only enough corn to "afford a little thickening to their soup."[66]

When the harvests did fail, and when bison were scarce, the Indians fell back on their final dietary recourse of collected fruits, nuts, and vegetables. Even in good years, however, wild plants were a vital part of the food supply, adding variety and nutritional balance as well as substance. The most important collected food was the Indian potato, which grew in abundance in the river valleys, especially on the sandy soils along the Loup and on Grand Island in the Platte. The women collected hundreds of bushels of this tuber as soon as the ground thawed in spring, and they continued to collect it well into the fall after the bison hunt had started. Some plants, such as wild plums, grapes, and gooseberries, were ubiquitous in the river valleys of eastern Nebraska; others, like the wild rice of the Sand Hills and the crab apples of Otoe-Missouria country, were localized points of attraction for the food gatherers. Altogether, according to Gilmore's inventory, more than a hundred varieties of plants were regularly used by the Indians of eastern Nebraska for food, medicine, ceremonial purposes, aphrodisiacs, and, in the case of the down of the cattail as an effective diaper.[67]

Food gathering, like most matters pertaining to plants, was the women's domain. Men contributed to the food supply at the villages by local hunting. Deer and elk were abundant in eastern Nebraska, and they were best taken in winter when they were fat. Small game, like rabbits and squirrels, were hunted only when food supplies were low, because the amount of meat garnered was hardly worth the effort. The men would also keep their eyes open for delicacies like sand cherries while they were out hunting. Men, women, and children fished, which was not a difficult procedure because the rivers teemed with trout, pickerel, buffalo fish, salmon, pike, and many other varieties.[68]

There was a tangible security afforded by drawing food from such a broad spectrum of the environment, and the Indians seemed to have thrived on their traditional diet. John Mackay was certainly impressed by their stands of crops and by their healthy constitutions.[69] All of this, of course, would be changed by smallpox and other imported diseases. Less dramatic than smallpox, however, but perhaps equally damaging in the long run, was the steady erosion of the Indians' health by malnutrition as their traditional food base collapsed and was replaced by the starvation diet of government rations and annuities.

The Indians were astute managers of their local environments. Fields were left fallow when their fertility declined, until the natural decomposition of vegetation restored vitality to the soil. Plum seeds were thrown (or possibly excreted) on the outskirts of the villages, creating semidomesticated orchards. Prairie grasses were burned in the fall to produce a rigorous growth in the early spring, when forage was desperately needed for the horses. And the continued abundance of Indian potatoes and wild onions in the vicinity of the villages suggests that care was taken not to overcollect.[70]

Still, even with this stewardship, it was inevitable that so many people and so many horses (the Pawnee had six thousand to eight thousand horses in the early nineteenth century) would strain the local resource base to its limits. There was a heavy demand for wood for construction and fuel, and early travelers, like Bradbury and Long, remarked on the denuded appearance of the valleys near the villages. Moreover, despite the management of the grasslands through burning, the horses could not be sustained near the villages for much of the year. By early fall the tall-grass prairie had become parched and deprived of its nutrients, and the problem of feeding the horses became pressing. This is why the bison hunts were so vital and such a logical adaptation to the environmental conditions: not only did the hunts provide food, clothes, and other resources, but they allowed the Indians and their horses to live for seven months of the year away from the strained environs of the villages, extending the subsistence base onto the mixed prairie beyond the ninety-eighth meridian.[71]

The Bison Hunts

The Nebraska Indians were absent from their villages on their bison hunts from late June to early September, and again, after the harvest, from early November to March. The summer and winter hunts had much in common in terms of general location, organization, and religious significance, but there were some important seasonal differences. In summer the bison scattered on the abundant buffalo grass plains of west-central Nebraska and Kansas. The Indians usually attacked in late morning, when the bison returned from drinking at the river to graze on the uplands. When they had enough meat, they returned to their villages. In winter, particularly if the season was cold and the snow deep, the bison sought refuge in timbered river valleys like the upper Republican, where they could be taken almost at will by the Indians who sought the same ecosystems for their own (and their horses') survival.[72] The summer hunt yielded most of the year's meat and also supplied *teshna'ha*, the Omaha term for "hide without hairs," which would be tanned on both sides and made into moccasins, leggings, and tipi covers. The winter hunt furnished *meha*, the heavy robe of the bison cow, which not only served to protect from the cold but also reminded the Indians of the close relationship between animals and humans, the one giving life to sustain the other.[73]

The bison hunts provided at least 50 percent of the Indians' food. This included the large amounts of dried meat that were consumed at feasts associated with religious ceremonies.[74] The consecration of bison meat to the gods through bundle ceremonies was an indispensable part of Indian religious life, a part that could not be severed without destroying the whole. Each year, the meat from hundreds of bison was given to the priests for this purpose. On one occasion, Samuel Allis, a missionary associate of John Dunbar who lived with the Skiri in the late 1830s and 1840s, tried to dissuade the Indians from offering "eighteen of the fattest of the buffalo" to Ti-ra'wa, arguing that they would need the meat for food in the future. To this they logically replied that "if they made great sacrifices to him he would give them good luck in hunting, and they would not come short of provisions."[75]

The bison was also the Indians' basic industrial raw material, furnishing essential products for shelter, clothing, utensils (such as horn spoons), tools (for example, shoulder blade spades), and weapons (as in the sinew bow-strings). Finally, the hunts were, for the men and boys at least, a time of great excitement and sport, eagerly anticipated as a break from monotonous village life. The women, on the other hand, must have viewed the hunting seasons with more ambivalence, because for them these were periods of exacting labor.

Preparation for the hunts began weeks before the actual departure. Hunters had to make sure that they had at least twenty arrows, and specialist arrow makers worked day and night to meet the demand. Woman dug deeply into their storage pits for food to send on the journey—corn, beans, pumpkins, fruits, slabs of bison meat, all dried to last longer and facilitate transportation. Horses had to be carefully tended and rested. The Pawnee, for example, would send their horses to Grand Island in late September, where they fattened on prairie cordgrass. Healthy horses were a prerequisite for a nineteenth-century bison hunt: a chief might be able to harness as many as twenty, so that his entire extended family could be transported; most families possessed only one or two, which meant that the women walked and carried a heavy load. Families who were without horses were obliged to stay at the village with the old, the sick, and those who for reasons of their own had decided not to participate.

Also in the weeks prior to departure, the power structure of the hunt was organized. In all of the Indian societies of eastern Nebraska, a man of integrity and courage was given responsibility for the direction of the hunt, and soldiers were appointed to preserve order. Even the Pawnee bands, which retained their individuality on the hunt, recognized a single leader who was appointed by a council of chiefs from all of the villages. Similarly, the Council of Seven, the governing body of the Omaha, appointed a single leader, the *watho^{n}i*, who was drawn from the Black Shoulder clan and who decided on every detail of the march and hunt. This was a mechanism to divert blame from the chiefs and priests in the event that the hunt failed. It was also a means of maintaining order and eliminating factional contention when the Indians were away from their stable village environments. There was even a mechanism for protecting the *watho^{n}i* if there was internal disorder, or in case luck was bad and the wind always blew toward the herds, warning them of impending danger. The *watho^{n}i* appointed a scapegoat (necessarily a man of good humor) who bore the brunt of criticism when things went wrong.[76]

The hunts could not begin, of course, without the necessary ceremonies that celebrated the great gift of the bison and called upon godly powers to aid in the hunt. The dramatic Omaha ritual of the White Buffalo Robe recounted in nineteen songs the creation of the bison and every stage of the hunt, each song proclaiming the connection between prescribed human actions and divine ordinance. The Pawnee prepared for their hunts with the pageant of the Great Washing Ceremony, which was carried out under the auspices of the meteoric star bundle, the bundle which controlled the coming of animals. The ceremony took the form of a footrace from an appointed lodge to the river, with each runner carrying an object from the bundle. These sacred objects were cleaned in the water to ensure that the bison herds would not scatter when the Indians approached.[77] Once the ceremonies and organizational meetings were completed, the lodges were closed, the storage pits sealed, and the hunt would begin.

Each of the Indian groups had its own customary western hunting range, which William Clark identified quite accurately in the inventory he made at Fort Mandan in the winter of 1804–5.[78] The Ponca hunted along the Niobrara River toward the Black Hills, one of the richest bison ranges on the Great Plains (fig. 2). The Omaha also hunted in the Niobrara country, and south from there into the Sand Hills and down to the Platte. The Otoe-Missouria headed southwest for their hunts, moving up the Saline and Smoky Hill river valleys to the High Plains. The Pawnee worked the range between the North Platte and the Solomon River of western Kansas. The Skiri, in keeping with their independent stance, often hunted alone on the North Platte; at other times they joined the South Bands, though at night they always made the westernmost camp, just as they always occupied the westernmost villages. No bison hunting was done east of the Missouri after 1800, but small parties of Omaha, Otoe, and Missouria sometimes ventured across the river for elk and deer.

The geography of the hunting range was etched in the Indians' minds "like a series of vivid pictorial images, each a configuration where this or that event had happened in the past to make it memorable."[79] They knew the best camping grounds, where wood and water were available, and they knew the shortcuts across the dry uplands between these places. They traced maps on the ground with sticks, showing the trails and fords and the anticipated location of the herds. Journeys were oriented to take in stands of potatoes, or herbs, like sweet cicely, that could not be found near the villages.

The Indians also knew where they were likely to meet their enemies on the bison range. The Pawnee had to contend with the Comanche, Cheyenne, and Arapahoe on the upper reaches of the Platte and Republican rivers, and the Ponca were often harassed by the Brulé Dakota along the Niobrara. The Otoe-Missouria periodically clashed with the Kansa and Osage on their hunts, and, as Lewis and Clark had discovered, the Nebraska Indians often clashed with each other. Still, at the beginning of the nineteenth century the bison hunt was a less hazardous operation than in later years. The Dakota had not fully expanded into the Nebraska Indians' bison range, and the very size of the herds created a resource buffer between the various groups.

The movement of the Indian encampments toward the bison range was slow and methodical. Six to ten miles a day was good progress when it took three hours to break camp in the morning and another three to reestablish it in the evening. The exact route of the hunt depended largely on the movements of the bison, and this in turn depended upon the vagaries of the weather and the availability of forage. During cold winters the bison would be encountered further east, sheltering in the timbered bottoms of rivers like the Loup. In warm winters the herds stayed to the west, and the Indians faced a long journey through country where timber and water were scarce and enemies plentiful.[80]

The migration to the hunting grounds was particularly onerous on the women. They were the first to rise in the morning, making breakfast, then scrubbing the dishes clean with false indigo. While some of the women dismantled the tipis and packed the horses, others started on foot for the next camping ground, where wood and water would be secured and the evening meal started. The size of the load carried by the women was inversely proportionate to the number of horses in the household. In addition to the stocks of food and utensils, women often carried the sacred items. The *washa'be*, for example, the decorated staff which symbolized the authority of the *watnon'* on the Omaha hunt, was always carried by a virgin, and the sacred bundles of the Pawnee were strapped to women's backs. The men rode horses and carried little, ostensibly because they needed their hands free for their weapons in case of attack.[81]

Human organization could only accomplish so much, and at every stage of the migration and hunt the assistance of the gods was respectfully requested. The *watho^ni* observed a code of behavior called *non'zhinzhon*, which rendered him oblivious to the everyday world and put him in communication with the supernatural and the power of Wakon'da. He achieved this state by fasting, walking barefoot, living apart from his family, and praying continually. When the herds were reached, the director of the hunt appointed marshals to regulate the process of the kill and to punish anyone who violated the rules. These marshals relied on the assistance of mythic animals, especially the crow and the wolf, who were called upon to bring the herds close. This was seen as a form of mutual aid, and after the kill the hunters made sure to leave flesh on the ground so that the wolf and crow could feast.[82]

The Indians killed only bison cows and calves because the meat of the bulls was tough and their hides hard to tan. Contemporary estimates from observers like Dunbar and Allis suggest that in a successful attack the Pawnee would kill as many as four hundred or five hundred bison.[83] Counting four formal hunts twice a year, as well as the smaller-scale informal hunts that followed, the

Pawnee probably killed four thousand to five thousand bison annually. Despite the fact that the Indians' selective killing of cows and calves would seem to have damaged the reproductive capacity of the herds, the vast numbers of bison seen by early nineteenth-century travelers indicates that this mortality rate could be sustained.[84]

In winter the Indians would camp near a large herd for weeks on end. Allis spent fifty-six days in the same general locale near the forks of the Platte with the Skiri in the winter of 1834–35. The same camps were returned to year after year. In contrast to the monochromatic landscape of the earth-lodge village, the tipi encampment on the hunts was a spectacular sight. Hundreds of white tipis, their covers tanned to transparency decorated the prairie. There was an atmosphere of frenzied activity, the men riding out to hunt each day, the women pounding and drying meat or stretching and scraping hides. Everywhere there was feasting, generally accompanied by offerings of bison hearts and tongues to the bundles. No one lacked food, because even a man without a horse could obtain his share of meat and hides by helping to butcher a dead animal.

The journey back to the villages was slower than the journey out because there was the extra burden of meat and hides to carry. Transporting the products of the hunt presented problems, especially in winter when the attrition rate on horses was high. In the absence of horses, dogs were used in the traditional way to haul the meat, but again much of the carrying was done by the women. By the time the hunting party reached the villages in spring, they had been on the move for five months and had covered more than five hundred miles.[85] Soon the stars and animals would indicate that the time for planting was again upon them, and the entire round of ceremonies and subsistence activities would begin anew.

The Peripheries of the Indians' World

The main circuit of the Indians' lives year in and year out reached from their villages to the hunting grounds and back. Beyond, in country claimed by other Indians, were lands less intimately known to the Nebraska Indians through trading and raiding, from an association at some time in the past, or from the travels of individuals who were driven by curiosity to see what lay beyond the horizon.

The world known to the Omaha in the early nineteenth century reached east to the Mississippi and west to the Black Hills (fig. 2). The Ponca, more footloose than the Omaha, knew the Rocky Mountains well and had names for, and had probably met, the Nez Perce of Idaho and the Blackfeet of Montana.[86] The Pawnee were known, and feared, at the Spanish settlements on the Rio Grande and throughout the southern plains. Also, by the early nineteenth century, the horizons of a few Indians were once again widening to the east. In 1806 the explorer Zebulon Pike was accompanied to the Pawnee villages by two Pawnee youth who were returning from an unsanctioned visit to Washington, D.C.[87] Trips to St. Louis were quite frequent: Big Elk, chief of the Omaha, had been there five times by 1813.[88] Whereas a trip to the eastern United States would impress upon the Indians the power of the burgeoning white population, the frontier town of St. Louis may have had little impact. After all, with a population of only 2,780 in 1804, St. Louis was considerably smaller than the combined Pawnee villages.

The Nebraska Indians were localized participants in an age-old trading network that spanned the continent. The network consisted of numerous regional systems integrated through strategic trading points. On the Great Plains the main axis of trade arced around eastern Nebraska, linking the bison hunters of the west and south (Crow, Dakota, Cheyenne, Arapahoe, and Kiowa) to the Mandan-Hidatsa and Arikara villages on the upper Missouri (fig. 2). These villages were the control points in the trade, also attracting Cree and Assiniboine hunters from Canada. In its traditional form—the trade has been traced back to prehistoric times—products of the hunt (dried meat, fat, robes, dressed skins, and manufactured articles such as moccasins) were exchanged for products of the soil, especially corn. After 1700, guns filtered into the system from the north, and horses were driven up from the southwest. These two expanding frontiers converged at the Mandan-Hidatsa and Arikara villages by 1750. As middlemen in this trade, marking up prices by as much as 100 percent each time an item was passed on, the village Indians of the upper Missouri accumulated a wealth hitherto unknown on the Great Plains.[89]

Why, then, were the village Indians of Nebraska rather marginal to this lucrative trade? First, despite their success as farmers, they did not produce the consistently large surpluses that were available at the Mandan-Hidatsa and Arikara villages. Second, they had few guns, and it was guns, along with corn, that the nomads wanted. Even the reputedly well-armed Pawnee had only one gun for every two warriors in 1806.[90] Third, the Pawnee, especially, were constantly at war with the western Indians, perpetuating an animosity that not even elaborate trading rituals could overcome. Finally, the Indians of eastern Nebraska could largely provide for themselves, not only because they had convenient access to European and American manufactured products via the British and St. Louis traders, but also because they had their own horse dealers, the Pawnee.

Much of the eastern Nebraska Indian trade was a localized affair.[91] The Omaha regularly bartered corn to the Ponca in exchange for bison products. The Ponca, of course, grew their own corn, but they preferred to emphasize the hunt and to get their grain by trade. This was also an example of "redundancy trading," whereby two parties would exchange products to which they already had access. This served to keep trading channels in place in the event that the harvests failed at one village and corn was in short supply. For the same security

Table 3 Estimated Dollar Value of Furs and Consumption of Goods, 1804

Indian Group		Goods Consumption		Fur Production
Otoe-Missouria		$4,000		$6,000
Omaha		$3,000		$5,000
Ponca		$1,000		$2,000
Pawnee Total		$8,800		$13,500
Skiri	$2,400		$3,500	
Chaui	$3,200		$5,000	
Kitkahahki	$3,200		$5,000	

Source: Moulton, *The Journals of the Lewis and Clark Expedition*, vol. 3, 388–400. See pages 398–99 for discrepancy in the Ponca estimates. Note: The value of the merchandise consumed includes transportation costs, which averaged about one-third of the whole amount. The value of furs produced was estimated by the "peltry standard" in St. Louis, which was forty cents a pound for deer skins, with all other furs being valued against this standard (389–90)

reasons, the Pawnee traded corn with the Arikara and the Mandan-Hidatsa. Corn and other provisions were also bartered to travelers through eastern Nebraska. In the summer of 1811, for example, Bradbury found a "considerable number" of Omaha waiting near their village who set about exchanging corn, bison meat, and tallow for tobacco, vermillion, and blue beads.[92]

The bands of Pawnee were the main long-distance traders in the region. In addition to trading with their relatives—the Arikara to the north and the Wichita to the south—they also sent large trading expeditions to Santa Fe about once every three years.[93] They obtained horses and blankets from the Spaniards. The Pawnee also got their horses from the Ute, possibly at the Shoshone rendezvous, the trade assembly that was held annually in spring at various sites in southwestern Wyoming (fig. 2). The Ute received guns in return. The Pawnee traded some of the horses to the Omaha in exchange for their superbly crafted arrows.[94] Horses were also sold to travelers passing through Pawnee country: on October 6, 1806, for example, Pike paid what he considered to be "exorbitant prices" for a few "miserable horses" that were needed for his western expedition.[95]

All eastern Nebraska Indians were engaged in the St. Louis fur trade by the first few years of the nineteenth century. Pike considered this trade to be of little account, but Lewis and Clark's figures suggest a substantial exchange (table 3). The Indians supplied mainly bison robes, but also deer, otter, racoon, and beaver skins; the traders paid with the usual manufactured products: blue beads, vermillion, knives, axes, guns, ammunition, and alcohol. The Indians could easily have dispensed with these trade goods, with the possible exception of guns and ammunition, which were increasingly necessary for successful warfare. But the traders were creating needs, not least of which was alcohol. As Pierre Tabeau perceptively noted in 1803, once the needs were created the goods became essentials. Lewis and Clark realized this too and advocated the construction of a trading post near the mouth of the Platte as the focal point of an expanded fur trade, anticipating that the Indians would "always consume as much merchandise as they [could] pay for."[96]

American traders would subsequently find that they had to fit into the Indians' trading routines and rituals. Traditionally, trading could take place at any time of the year, depending on needs and circumstances. The most important seasons, however, were spring, when the thick winter bison robes were ready, and fall, when the crops were harvested and meat was plentiful from the summer hunt. Indian trading parties were of varying size but were often very large, involving entire villages. Both men and women traded, generally with members of their own sex and generally in items of their own production: women, for example, did much of the corn trading, while men bartered horses and guns. Profit was the main motivation, but, as American fur traders learned, the Indians were discriminating in their tastes for goods, and they drove a hard bargain.

Much of the trading was actually reciprocal gift-giving associated with the calumet ceremony. This ceremony—the Hako to the Pawnee and the Wa'waⁿ to the Omaha—was widely practiced throughout the Great Plains and beyond. It was the means through which otherwise hostile bands could preserve peaceful relations for the duration of the trading. The calumet was a wooden pipe stem (the Omaha used ash) with a catlinite bowl, that was used to establish fictive relationships between the trading parties. The person, or party, presenting the pipe became "father" and the recipients, "son." As Lewis and Clark explained, "The party delivering generally Confess their Errors and request a peace, the party receiving exult in their Suckcesses and receive the Sacred Stem."[97] A large number of gifts—eagle-feather bonnets, bows and arrows, skins, robes, food, and guns—accompanied the pipe ceremony, given back and forth as mutual courtesies and as a means of gain. The calumet ceremony was also used *within* specific societies to cement ties: the Pawnee bands, for example, used it to solidify their confederation, and the Omaha had originally adopted the ceremony at a time deep in the past when they were threatened by disintegration.[98]

Raiding was the men's avocation, their main route to success, the focus of their ambitions.[99] It was the primary means by which commoners advanced by acquiring wealth and status. Some raiding involved revenge, perhaps a retaliation to an enemy's previous attack, but the prime motivation by 1800 was profit, especially in the form of horses. When the war party returned to the village, the spoils might be given as gifts to the village chief or to the priest who, as representative of the war bundle, had sanctioned the raid. By such displays of courage and generosity a man might rise through the ranks of warriors to achieve a position of high standing, below only the hereditary leaders. Even in the 1860s this route to success was still mapped ahead for Pawnee youth: at that time Lone Chief, son of a deceased Kitkahahki chief, was advised by his mother that "it is not the man who stays in the lodge that becomes great; it is the man who works, who sweats, who is always tired from going on the warpath."[100]

For the Indians of eastern Nebraska in 1800 the warpath led in most directions. Lewis and Clark, hoping to establish peace among the Indians to allow for a more successful fur trade, made particular note of their enmities.[101] The Otoe-Missouria were at war with "all nations generally," though they were "partially at peace" with the Pawnee and Kansa. The only nations the Pawnee were not consistently antagonistic toward were the Arikara and the Omaha. The Omaha and Ponca were in conflict with the Otoe-Missouria and with all the bands of the Dakota except the Yankton. During the summer of 1804, for example, sixty Omaha were killed or captured in a raid by the Brulé Dakota. Even alliances were brittle: the Pawnee raided, as well as traded with, the Wichita, and in the famine summer of 1802 the Omaha attacked their relatives, the Ponca, looking for food.

Raiding took place throughout the year whenever opportune. The wide-ranging nature of the raiding is exemplified by the small Otoe party that struck an Arapahoe camp on the upper Arkansas in 1825 (fig. 4). Often a war party would take off from the returning bison hunt on foot, walking the divides between the streams, hoping to return on stolen horses. Generally only eight or ten men were involved: a small mobile unit of hunters, moccasin carriers, kettle carriers, and camp keepers. Warriors seldom went on raids alone unless seeking to kill a stranger who would then become a "spirit companion" for a loved one, especially a child, who had just died.[102] Sometimes large parties left on raiding expeditions: Pike noted, for example, that the Pawnee commonly sent two hundred or three hundred men to the southern plains.[103] Large expeditions included women who took care of the moccasins, did the cooking, and shared in the gains.

Every war party had to be authorized by the chiefs and priests. Warriors who returned from unauthorized raids were severely punished. Authorization involved passing on the responsibility for the success of the raid to cosmic forces. In Omaha society, for example, warfare was controlled by rites associated with the four sacred packs of war (*wai^ni waxube*). These packs contained the remains of birds that were regarded as the special messengers of Thunder, the god of war. Once the authorization was given, the outcome of the raid was in the hands of cosmic forces, and the leader could not be blamed for failure.

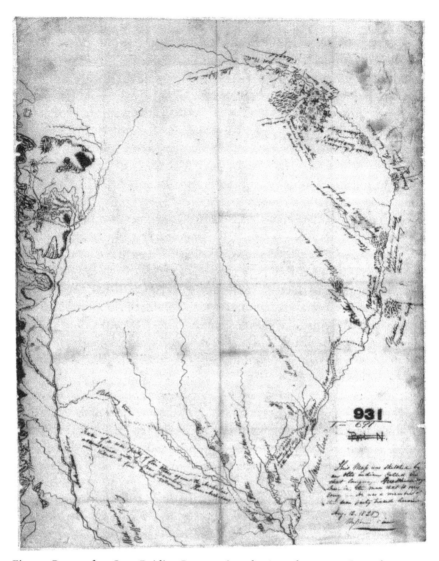

Fig. 4 Route of an Otoe Raiding Party against the Arapahoe, 1825. Central Map Files, National Archives, RG 75, No. 931

Open warfare was generally avoided, and in 1800, territories were generally not fought over or patrolled. The objectives were to display courage, to acquire horses and other goods, and to damage the economic base of the enemy by destroying their crops or food stores. A successful raiding party returned home to great celebration and ceremony. Standing in front of the sacred packs of war, the Omaha warriors recited their deeds: to have struck an unwounded enemy with a hand or bow was the highest honor; to kill an enemy ranked fourth on the honors' table; and to decapitate a dead body was the sixth, and lowest, grade of honor. Through an accumulation of honors a warrior earned the right to wear symbolic war decorations that marked him as a man of courage and achievement. A successful warrior was also a man of wealth, with ample horses and goods to donate to chiefs, priests, and ceremonies. To restrict raiding, therefore, as the American government strove to do in the nineteenth century, was to cut right to the heart of the man's role in society by blocking his access to wealth, status, and self-esteem.

Stability and Instability

The world of the Nebraska Indians had never been stable, but before 1800 change had generally been slow enough to accommodate without major disruption. By the beginning of the nineteenth century, however, the changes were occurring virtually overnight, and the shock waves were increasingly difficult to absorb.

All the changes can ultimately be traced back to the European and American presence in North America: horses were diffused from the Spanish in the Southwest, trade goods of all kinds flowed from St. Louis, and disease swept in from every direction. The migration across the Missouri of powerful nomadic hunters like the Cheyenne and Dakota peoples, under pressure from Europeans and Americans to the east, added to the competition for horses and trade goods and increased the likelihood of meeting enemies on the bison range. Defensive warfare became more common, putting the lives of the chiefs in jeopardy and causing villagers to erect fortifications around their settlements. Attacks on villages had to be avenged, and so an endless cycle of defense and retaliation was set in motion. Such was the strained relationship between the Otoe-Missouria and the Omaha when Lewis and Clark passed through the area.

Intensified warfare, together with disease, placed great stress on the traditional village way of life. Population loss and the need for protection resulted in the amalgamation of Pawnee villages during the eighteenth century. "Consider," writes Holder, "the unenviable position of a chief with the remnants of his own people joining an established village."[104] How could he preserve his status? How could he maintain his share of goods when the established chief would demand his due? How could the different families meld into the functioning unit of the village?

Rivalries among chiefs and their retinues were also exacerbated by access to new wealth through the fur trade. For example, Blackbird, the despotic chief of the Omaha in 1800, used the fur trade as a springboard to power. He imposed himself upon the traders, supplying them with furs in return for goods, and, reputedly, poisons which he used to eliminate his rivals. The Spanish trader Jean Baptiste Truteau estimated that Blackbird took at least one-third of all the merchandise coming into the village and controlled the redistribution of the rest. Through this accumulation of wealth, Blackbird, who had started his career as a warrior, was able to elevate himself to the "highest place of authority" in Omaha society.[105]

Blackbird's ascent to power is an example of the deepening class struggle taking place in the Indian societies. The established leadership was being challenged by young men who had increased opportunities for aggrandizement through war and trade. Factions—leaders and their followers—appeared as fissures in the superstructure of village life, and in this context it is worth recalling that the villages were only "voluntary associations of families."[106] Societies could split apart as readily as they could amalgamate, as the Ponca and Omaha had done at some time before 1800.

With all these pressures, internal and external, it is remarkable that the Indian societies of eastern Nebraska held together for as long as they did in the nineteenth century. There are a number of reasons for this resilience. The most practical was that their way of life worked and had endured for many hundreds of years. The combined hunting, farming, and gathering cycle spread their subsistence base over a wide area and was a successful ecological adaptation to the transitional tall-grass and mixed-grass environments of the Great Plains. Daily life was hard and often dangerous, but the production cycle was sustainable and, unless disrupted by environmental disaster, war, or disease, yielded sufficient food. By 1800, with more horses available and with economic specialization made possible by long-distance trading, there was an incentive to give up farming and live off the bison herds. The Ponca, at least, periodically did this, and the Cheyenne and Arapahoe had made the transition from sedentary to nomadic life in less than a generation. But the vital importance of corn, in both their diet and their cosmology, would have made this transition difficult for the Nebraska Indians, particularly for the Pawnee. Moreover, the villages were their homes, the places where their ancestors were buried, and only in the most dire circumstances (as when the Omaha fled their smallpox-ridden village in 1801) were they abandoned.

The resilience of village life also owed a great deal to the many institutions and procedures that had been devised over centuries to minimize disputes and promote stability. The Omaha's Council of Seven Chiefs, for example, was a political innovation instituted at an early date to preserve order and to bind the various clans together. The calumet pipe was a specific instrument of peace and unification. Ingeniously conceived offices, such as those of the director of the bison hunts and his unfortunate scapegoat, functioned to deflect conflict. Finally, in 1800, and for a few more decades in the nineteenth century, the class system, with its entrenched hereditary leaders, also contributed to the short-term stability of village life.

The most intrinsic strength of village life was its firm grounding in religious beliefs and rituals. Religious rites worked to control the actions of members of society, especially the energetic young men. Rites were, to use Fletcher and La Flesche's words, "a means to augment in the popular mind the importance of self-control, of composure, and of submission to authority."[107] The strict, religiously defined code of behavior on the bison hunt, for example, and the sanction of raiding parties by the sacred packs or war bundles, allied these activities to cosmic forces and made any infractions of the rules a transgression against the gods themselves.

Religion also gave the people their identity, drawing them together under a canopy of shared beliefs. This identity was encapsulated in icons like the sacred pole and the village bundles, which were essentially charters of existence given to the people by the gods. In the broadest sense, religion provided the purpose behind the Indians' traditional way of life. The world all around expressed the mysterious life force, and through conscientious practice of rituals and proper conduct the Indians could come into relation with this force and so find success in their endeavors.

All these foundations of life were gradually undermined in the half-century between the acquisition of Louisiana Territory and the opening of Nebraska Territory to American settlers. Fur traders came seeking Indian labor and pelts, missionaries strove to save Indian souls, and government agents tried to tie Indian men down to farming and started the process of buying their lands. The outside world closed in, as Indians were uprooted from the eastern United States and resettled on the margins of the Great Plains, and hundreds of thousands of migrants to Oregon, California, and Utah cut a swath across Nebraska. The Dakota closed in too, sweeping down on the villages in a war of intended extermination.

CHAPTER TWO

Forces of Intervention

1800–1854

The Americans who filtered out from the settled areas to live with the Nebraska Indians in the first half of the nineteenth century were either fur traders, missionaries, or Indian agents and their employees. Often the fur traders were also, eventually, Indian agents. Numerically they were insignificant: a few hundred traders, fewer than thirty missionaries (their families included), and eleven Indian agents and various agency employees over the course of half a century. Each group, however, had behind it the force of powerful American cultural, political, and economic agencies. Each had its own uses and plans for the Indians, designs that were not always in accord.

Fur Traders and Economic Dependency

When Lewis and Clark glided past the mouth of the Niobrara on September 1, 1806, heading rapidly downstream, they found the lower Missouri much more heavily trafficked than it had been in 1804. Just below the mouth of the James River lay the ruins of one of the earliest American posts in the area, built by Robert McClellan in the fall of 1804 for the Yankton's winter trade. Further down, near the mouth of the Vermillion, the explorers met James Airs, a Scottish trader working out of Prairie du Chien who was licensed to trade with the Dakota for a year. Passing the Omaha village, they encountered a boat from the trading house of Auguste Chouteau, the dominant early St. Louis entrepreneur, heading for the James River and the Yankton's trade. South of the mouth of the Platte they came across two separate French trading ventures, one bound for the Skiri, the other for the Omaha. South again, heading toward a triumphant return to St. Louis, Lewis and Clark met yet another Chouteau boat, this one destined for the Mandan villages.[1] Lewis and Clark's discoveries, news of which had been relayed back regularly to St. Louis, had sparked an explosion of economic activity on the Missouri. The Nebraska Indians were no longer at the far borders of the fur trade.

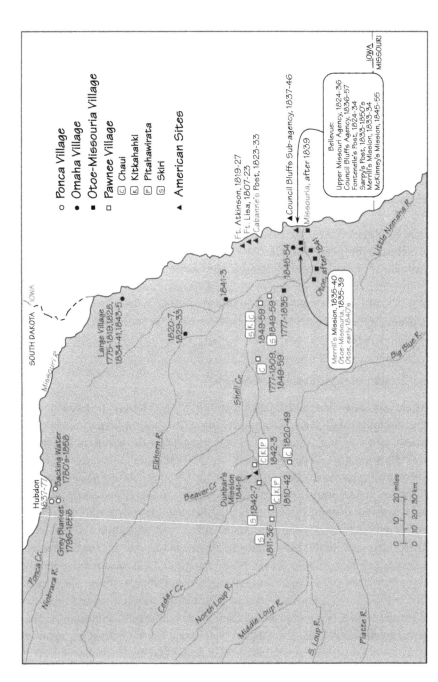

Fig. 5 Indian and American Sites, 1800–1854

Even in 1806 the sights of the St. Louis traders were set on Crow and Blackfeet lands at the headwaters of the Yellowstone and Missouri rivers, where Lewis and Clark had seen streams that were "richer in beaver and otter than any [other] country on earth."[2] From 1807 to 1826, first Manuel Lisa, then his successor as head of the Missouri Fur Company, Joshua Pilcher, developed a two-tier strategy to get at these furs. They built a series of trading posts from the mouth of the Platte to the Mandan villages. These posts were important production sites in their own right, but more crucially their establishment served to placate the Indians by providing them with access to trade goods, and so the river was kept open to its upper reaches. Lisa's and Pilcher's men tried to trap this upper country but were driven out, virtually empty-handed, by the Blackfeet. After 1826 the American Fur Company, with its western operations eventually under the control of Pierre Chouteau, Jr., solved this problem of access by extending the trading post network into Crow and Blackfeet territories and encouraging the Indians to do the trapping themselves. Thereafter, the American Fur Company, legally known as Pierre Chouteau, Jr., and Company, virtually monopolized the upper Missouri fur trade until it was swamped by the arrival of the settlement frontier and the railroads in the 1850s.[3]

The Nebraska Indians were one regional cog in this extensive network. Their trade—beaver, otter, raccoon, and muskrat pelts, deer skins, and bison robes—funneled to various posts located mainly between Council Bluffs and Bellevue, just above and below the present site of Omaha (fig. 5). During the early stages of the American fur trade Fort Lisa at Council Bluffs was the dominant post, especially from 1812 to 1819 when the war with Great Britain and its unsettled aftermath disrupted operations on the upper river. In 1823 Pilcher moved the post down to Bellevue, where it was run by Lucien Fontenelle (when he wasn't trapping in the Rocky Mountains). The St. Louis firm of Bernard Pratte and Company, which was closely associated with the Chouteau family and American Fur Company interests, operated a rival trading post at Council Bluffs from 1823 to 1833 that was managed by the French-born trader John Cabanné. This post was also relocated to Bellevue after 1833, with Peter Sarpy serving as resident trader until 1854.

Many other posts, most lasting only a season or two, were established between Council Bluffs and the mouth of the Platte in the first half of the nineteenth century for the Otoe-Missouria, Omaha, and Pawnee trade.[4] The Pawnee never merited a post of their own because of the difficulties of land transportation (the braided Platte being, for all practical purposes, unnavigable), but traders visited their villages each year in fall and spring and often accompanied the bands on their winter hunts. Trading outfits were also dispatched to the Omaha, Otoe-Missouria, and Ponca winter camps. Cabanné even sent traders to the Dakota.[5] Traders often set up temporary quarters at the Omaha village to take their furs directly, but the Omaha were too close to

Council Bluffs to justify a separate permanent post. The Ponca, more distant and within easy reach of the Missouri, were periodically served by a small post near the mouth of the Niobrara.

Although some traders—Cabanné and Fontenelle, for example—clearly enjoyed living on the fringe of their own society, the primary motivation was profit. The fur trade was a risky business, plagued by cutthroat competition, but for shrewd dealers profits were there for the taking.[6] William Gordon, another St. Louis-based entrepreneur, estimated that the exchange of goods for furs gave the trader a "great ostensible profit upon primary cost, say from 200 to 2,000 percent."[7] This estimated rate of profit was "ostensible" because it did not take into account transportation costs. Much of the profit came via the credit system. In the fall, after the corn harvest and before the departure for the hunt, trade goods—blankets, red and blue stroud and cloth, rifles, powder and flints, vermillion, knives, copper, brass and tin kettles, traps, looking glasses, beads, needles and thread—were distributed to the Indians on credit against furs to be delivered in spring. A gun that cost twelve dollars in St. Louis was worth the equivalent of thirty dollars in furs, a one-pound bag of gunpowder bought for twenty cents and given on credit in the fall earned four dollars in furs in the spring, and a three-point blanket costing less than four dollars could be bartered for at least ten dollars' worth of furs. At such inflated prices, even if the Indians did not deliver enough furs to cover the debt (which was frequently the case) the trader still made a handsome profit.[8]

The Indians were also in the fur trade for profit; otherwise they would not have participated. A hardworking hunter and his wife—or wives, because polygyny became more common under the impetus of raised labor demands—could accumulate trade goods to donate up the social hierarchy, so enhancing the family's prestige.[9] New products such as broadcloth and, later, calicos, sewn into clothes and decorated with beads, became ostentatious status symbols, supplementing the traditional skin garments and their quill adornments. A warrior's status and potential were enhanced by the possession of a gun, and on raids his life was threatened without one. As warfare intensified during the first half of the nineteenth century, the fate of entire Indian societies hinged on access to guns, and access to guns was contingent on production of furs.

In times of heated competition, like the 1790s and early 1820s, the Indians could obtain favorable rates of exchange by playing the traders off against each other. Gifts also flowed freely during these times. But under monopoly, which was virtually the prevailing system after 1826, the Indians were caught in a buyer's market and received less for their work. Gift giving was cut back as the traders felt less obliged to conform to Indian customs. The exchange rates the Indians received for their furs were also affected by conditions in distant fur markets, such as London and Leipzig. If, for example, the Hudson's Bay Company swamped the European market with beaver pelts, then the Indians of eastern Nebraska felt the repercussions in reduced demand and lower prices for their product. Gradually, therefore, the Indians surrendered their economic autonomy and became dependent on the traders for the flow of goods and the lifestyles they were creating.

The dependency was most advanced among the Otoe-Missouria and Omaha, who lived close to the major trading posts. The Pawnee maintained a more independent stance, partly by choice because, even in 1830, they were still a powerful people who could obtain goods and horses by raiding on the southern Great Plains, but also because their relative remoteness from the Missouri insulated them from American contact. This remoteness was not only a matter of distance but also of accessibility, because the small, incised creeks in eastern Nebraska were very difficult to cross, especially in spring and early summer when they were likely to be swollen.

The Ponca were also less acculturated through the fur trade than the Otoe-Missouria and Omaha, but this was probably through no decision of their own. Repeated attacks by the Dakota and Pawnee in the 1820s had driven them from their villages and forced them into a nomadic life on the Niobrara. They wanted American trade goods, but socially they were too fragmented to produce the furs. This situation was explained through an exchange which took place between Kenneth McKenzie, the dynamic head of the American Fur Company's Upper Missouri Outfit, and the Ponca chief Shudegacheh on board the steamboat Yellowstone near the mouth of the Niobrara in the summer of 1833. McKenzie told Shudegacheh that the Ponca did not furnish enough furs or grow enough corn to merit a post. To this Shudegacheh responded that "there was no unity among his people; that they lived too scattered, and, therefore, he could not superintend them and keep them to work."[10]

The trading posts were more than centers of economic exchange; they were also points of cultural convergence. This was particularly the case at Bellevue, where the Upper Missouri Indian Agency was also located after 1819, and near where Moses Merrill operated his Baptist mission after 1835 (figs. 5 and 6). Omaha, Otoe-Missouria, and Pawnee converged on Bellevue, not only in the spring and fall trading seasons, but throughout the entire year. There they saw the steamboats heading upstream in early summer laden with trade goods, and watched them return in the fall with their cargoes of furs. They met exotic travelers like Maximilian, Prince of Wied, and his artist companion Karl Bodmer, who had come to study and paint the equally exotic Indians of the upper Missouri. The Indians came to beg or dance for food and alcohol, or simply to watch and learn about this external world that was seeping into their lives.

Cultural convergence is, of course, a two-way process, and many of the traders became partially integrated into Indian communities. At Bellevue and Cabanné's post in 1833 the dominant population was the mixed-blood offspring of company employees and their Omaha or Otoe-Missouria wives.[11]

Fig. 6 Bellevue Agency, Post of Major Dougherty, May 1833, by Karl Bodmer. Courtesy Joslyn Art Museum, Omaha, Nebraska. Gift of the Enron Art Foundation

Both Pilcher and Fontenelle had Indian wives. Traders and Indians alike benefited from these unions. The traders gained companionship in an area where few white women ventured. They also forged links through marriage to prominent Indian families, getting exclusive access to their furs and up-to-date information on which trade goods were in demand. Traders also married Indian women to get a share in the annuities which were dispensed to the Indians in payment for their lands. Some Indian women, in turn, were attracted to trader marriages because their lives were easier at the posts than in the villages, and they had the novelty of dressing in American clothes. Often they had little say in the matter, because the marriages were arranged by ambitious fathers who wanted first pick of the traders' goods.[12]

The offspring of these "country" marriages played important roles in the subsequent relations between the United States and the Indian communities. Logan Fontenelle, for example, the son of Lucien Fontenelle and an Omaha woman (possibly Bright Sun [Me-um-ba-ne], the daughter of the Omaha chief Big Elk) was born at Bellevue in the 1820s. He subsequently became a chief of the Omaha and an interpreter on treaty negotiations. Joseph La Flesche, the son of a French trader of the same name and an Omaha or Ponca woman, was even more influential in shaping the future of the Omaha. Mixed-bloods like Fontenelle and La Flesche formed a bridge between the two cultures, but it was a bridge across which power and mandate moved mainly in one direction—from American to Indian societies.[13]

Trading posts were also points of diffusion for the two most damaging imports from the outside world, alcohol and disease. Despite progressively more rigorous federal efforts to control the importation of alcohol into "Indian country"—specifically the Intercourse Acts of 1802, 1822, 1832, and 1834—whiskey flowed freely in the fur trade along the Missouri River.[14] Licensed traders brought in large amounts of whiskey to exchange for furs under the pretense that it was for their own use (private use was allowed under the 1802 and 1822 acts); unlicensed traders, already operating illegally, needed no pretense to use whiskey in their drive for quick profits. The Otoe-Missouria even imported it themselves. For example, the Reverend Dunbar, on his way to the Pawnee villages in 1834, encountered a party of Otoe who were returning from Fort Leavenworth, their horses packed with kegs of whiskey. The Otoe had bartered furs for the alcohol with Americans at the fort, or obtained it through Kickapoo and Shawnee middlemen who lived nearby.[15] The Otoe-Missouria and Omaha also traded horses and guns to the Iowa for whiskey, which they in turn obtained from traders whose cabins lined the east bank of the Missouri opposite Bellevue. The Ponca had easy access to alcohol via the Missouri River, but their consumption was probably limited by their low production of furs and by their long absences on the western plains. Only the Pawnee, whose chiefs refused to be subordinated to the traders, chose to exclude alcohol altogether: "I am pleased," wrote missionary Samuel Allis, that "the Pawnees have no desire for the taste of whiskey, neither is it brot among them."[16]

Alcohol wreaked havoc in Indian communities that were already reeling from the impacts of disease, resource depletion, and increased warfare. Family or village rivalries that might have lain dormant, or been accommodated through traditional channels, now erupted in frequent acts of violence. Allis was staying with Merrill at Bellevue in the summer of 1835 when an Omaha woman, bearing a long-standing grudge, took advantage of an Iowa man's drunkenness and split his head open with an axe as he lay on the floor. This act would inevitably have to be avenged, and so the violence became self-perpetuating. Dougherty also witnessed the escalating violence at Bellevue. Writing to the secretary of war in 1827, he recounted how two brothers, both Otoe chiefs, had become intoxicated with whiskey, that "blackest of poisons." They argued, then fought, one biting off the other's nose before being shot dead by the injured party. This was only one episode among many, Dougherty added.[17]

Such incidents of drunkenness and violence were also common among

Americans on the frontier, and they were the Indians' models concerning alcohol use and subsequent behavior. Both Fontenelle and Sarpy, for example, had bad drinking habits, and in the eyes of the missionaries at least, the traders and other "abominable whites" who populated the frontier were much less principled than the Indians.[18] The significant difference is that alcohol was new to the Indians, not an established way of life, and its impact on their lives at a time of great instability was all the more traumatic.

The situation was worst at Bellevue, where the independent traders Jean Baptiste Roy and Joseph Robideaux used whiskey as a weapon to compete with the American Fur Company.[19] By the early 1830s many Otoe men were staying for extended periods of time near the trading post, dealing and begging for whiskey when they should have been hunting. "They are complaining of starvation," Merrill wrote in his diary, "and at the same time leave their families to give away their little means of subsistence for whiskey at an extravagant price." Merrill considered the Indians to be victims of the traders; so too did Ietan, the principal Otoe chief, who lamented (after a night of drinking) that it was Americans, not Indians, who manufactured the alcohol and brought it into their country.[20]

The congregation of Indians from different societies at the trading posts, where they also came into contact with traders and travelers from St. Louis and beyond, facilitated the diffusion of contagious diseases. The smallpox epidemics of 1800–1801 and 1837–38 spread in this way; so did the terrible cholera epidemic of 1849. In the summer of that year cholera was transported upriver from the stricken town of St. Louis on board the American Fur Company's steamboat, the Amelia. The traders knew cholera was on board, but they did not want to lose the season's trade. At each trading post cholera was unloaded with the cargo. The Omaha and Otoe-Missouria evaded the worst effects of the disease by leaving early on their summer hunts, but it was carried west along the Platte by immigrants and traders, and one-quarter of the Pawnee were "swept off like chaff in the wind."[21]

Even discounting epidemic disease, which could as easily have been spread by missionaries as by traders, the fur trade was disastrous for the Indians of eastern Nebraska. Fletcher and La Flesche summarized its impact on the Omaha, and the same would apply for all of the Indians in the area, though probably at a later date for the more removed Pawnee.[22] The gradual loss of skills like quill working, pottery, and arrow making (to be replaced by beads, metal products, and guns, respectively) in itself did not deplete Indian cultures, because new skills, such as metal working, were learned in their stead. But the loss of rituals associated with these traditional skills "made pointless some of the old teachings to the young" and broke the continuum of knowledge that had been passed on from generation to generation. The increased emphasis on hunting, under the stimulus of the fur trade, "weakened the influence of the old village life, created different standards of wealth . . . and greatly increased the labors of women in preparing pelts and skins for the market." Alcohol worked like ice in the crevices of Indian societies, expanding the level of pressure until fragments broke away.

The traders also caused fragmentation by meddling in the power hierarchy of Indian communities. They enriched Indians who were accommodating to their demands and undermined the influence of chiefs who opposed them. For example, during the winter of 1843–44, A. L. Papin, Roy's equally unscrupulous partner, handed out medals to young Omaha braves in order to secure their trade. The traditional chiefs, feeling that their authority was being challenged, complained to their agent David Miller that Papin was "making chiefs in their nation." One of the two principal chiefs, Big Elk, told Miller that he felt displaced and humiliated, "like an old scabby Buffalo Bull who had got separated from his herd on the Prairies."[23]

Finally, and most disastrously, the fur traders co-opted the Indians in the destruction of their own resource base. The increased market demand, and possibly a relaxation of cultural restraints on hunting, resulted in a rapid depletion of fur-bearing animals. The beaver, with its low rate of reproduction, was the first animal to disappear. By 1833, according to Maximilian (who heard this from the traders) beavers had been "extirpated" from the streams of eastern Nebraska.[24] It should not have been difficult for the Indians to adjust by raising their output of bison robes—robes could be easily obtained within their traditional annual cycle, whereas trapping beaver was a new task that had been introduced by the traders. But, in a short period from about 1818 to 1822, the bison were driven out of much of Nebraska. The young naturalist Paul Wilhelm, Duke of Wurttemberg, who traveled overland through eastern Nebraska in 1822, was told by traders that the bison herds were rarely seen along the Missouri below the mouth of the Niobrara and that their first occurrence to the west was "a hundred hours distance." The Duke attributed this depletion to increased Indian hunting to supply the fur trade.[25] Like the Indians, the traders were only interested in the robes of cows, and this additional kill seems to have been critical in impairing the herds' capacity to sustain their numbers. By 1831, according to Dougherty, bison and other game had been largely exterminated from the country lying between the Kansas River, Ponca Creek, and the forks of the Platte. The bison herds would push east periodically in subsequent years, driven by snow or Dakota, but these were only temporary reversals of a general retreat westward.[26]

The consequences for the Indians, especially for the Omaha and Otoe-Missouria, who were most distant from the herds, were widespread starvation and loss of trading power. By 1830, the Omaha and Otoe-Missouria were starving for at least half of each year. Big Elk blamed the traders for this situation. Speaking at a large council at Fort Leavenworth in 1828, he complained that the traders kept his people "scouring the country in search of skins," but they could find only "the licks which [the bison] had visited."[27] Even the Pawnee, who, like the Ponca, still had relatively easy access to the bison herds in the 1830s, complained that they had to travel further to hunt because large parties of trappers bound for the Rocky Mountains and caravans of traders on the Santa Fe trail had driven off the game.[28]

As the eastern Nebraska Indians traveled further west on their hunts, they came into more frequent contact with hostile bands of Cheyenne and, especially, Teton Dakota. Unlike the village Indians, the Dakota, living on the abundant bison plains between the Black Hills and the Missouri, benefited from an expanding robe trade from the 1820s until at least the 1860s. The Rocky Mountain traveler William Marshall Anderson was told by Lucien Fontenelle that the Dakota bands traded fifty thousand robes to the American Fur Company in 1831.[29] Meanwhile, Cabanné's post was bringing in only four thousand robes a year. So the Dakota were well supplied with guns and ammunition at a time when the Nebraska Indians could not produce enough furs to obtain the weapons. The Duke of Wurttemberg understood the reasons for this changing balance of power: "It is evident," he wrote in his diary, "that the Omahas and Poncas are at a disadvantage when compared with the Sioux, in that they have fewer firearms than the latter, insomuch that the returns of the hunt are much smaller than those of the Sioux." As the Duke correctly concluded, "Clearly, the wealth of the Indians depends on the returns of the hunt."[30]

When the fur trade gave out in eastern Nebraska, the St. Louis merchants simply moved their operations to new frontiers, specifically to the northern Great Plains. Some local traders, like Sarpy, adjusted to the changing times and new opportunities by diversifying their enterprises and supplying military posts and emigrants. Others, like Pilcher, parlayed their profits and influence into Missouri politics. The Nebraska Indians had none of this flexibility. They were tied to their impoverished homelands and their increasingly strained cycle of hunting and farming. Left behind like detritus when the fur trade moved on, their options were being foreclosed, while those of the Dakota and Americans were opening up.

Missionaries and Americanization

The missionaries who lived with the Nebraska Indians after 1833 were representative of the outpouring of proselytizing zeal which swept the country after the Second Great Awakening, beginning in the 1790s. After the war of 1812 this religious mission was fused with a nationalistic drive, and Christianization became synonymous with Americanization. The missionaries were Protestants of various denominations who were sponsored by east coast societies such as the American Board of Commissioners for Foreign Missions. Despite doctrinal differences, their programs for the Indians were essentially the same: to spread the Gospel and thereby gain conversions to Christianity. But to achieve this, either the missionaries had to know Indian languages in order to preach, or the Indians had to know English in order to read the Bible. Consequently, teaching English, using the Scriptures as texts, became an integral part of the program. Moral training was also part of the program, and this involved instilling in the Indians the basic values of American society, such as the work ethic, individualism, a sense of private property, and monogamy. The missionaries themselves and their families would be models of this American ideal. Their thinking was that these traits were so self-evidently superior that the Indians only had to be exposed to them to achieve mass conversions.[31]

The missionaries came to Nebraska full of optimism that they could "remove the darkness" from these "superstitious" and "benighted" people. Most left disappointed, weary from the hardships they had endured, and not a little afraid. Baptists Moses Merrill and his wife were the first to arrive, transferring from the Chippewa to the Otoe-Missouria mission in the fall of 1833. For the first one and a half years Merrill preached out of the Bellevue agency, or the lodge of Ietan at the Otoe-Missouria village. From 1835 until his death in 1840 Merrill and his wife were based at the newly constructed mission, located on the north side of the Platte, eight miles from Bellevue and six miles above the confluence with the Missouri (fig. 5). After Merrill's death the mission was vacant until August 1845, when the Presbyterians Edmund McKinney and his wife transferred from the Iowa mission to administer to the Otoe-Missouria and Omaha. McKinney worked at the mission until the early 1850s.[32]

The year after Merrill's arrival at Bellevue, the Presbyterians John Dunbar and Samuel Allis were sent by the American Board of Commissioners for Foreign Missions to live with the Pawnee. Allis went to the Skiri band, Reverend Dunbar to the Chaui. From 1834 to 1839 the missionaries lived as welcomed guests in the Pawnee lodges and accompanied the Indians on most of their hunts. By 1837 they had both traveled back east and married, bringing their wives back to Bellevue and later to Pawnee country. In 1840 they built their mission on the north side of the Loup near the junction with Plum (Council) Creek (fig. 5). The mission consisted of three log houses covered with sod, which made for rough living; but as Dunbar explained to his sponsors, "After camping out about nine weeks my family think they have a pretty good home."[33] They were joined in the summer of 1845 by the Puritans Timothy and Charlotte Ranney, who were also sponsored by the American Board of Commissioners for Foreign Missions. In June of the following year, after repeated Dakota raids, the missionaries abandoned their station, grateful to be alive. Thereafter the Pawnee mission was amalgamated with that of the Otoe-Missouria and Omaha and run by McKinney.

All of the missionaries were offended by the Indians' way of life. They were

appalled by the men's apparent idleness and by the women's seeming enslave-
ment, by the practice of polygyny and the quick recourse to warfare, and even
by the Indians' eating habits. They were particularly contemptuous of the Indians' religious ceremonies, which were dismissed as mere superstition and occasions for gluttony. The priests and doctors came in for severe criticism: they
were "imposters," wrote Dunbar, "who exert a great and pernicious influence
over the people." Dunbar could have been speaking for all the missionaries
when, after leaving the Chaui's Spring Renewal Ceremony in April of 1835
"perfectly disgusted," he wondered: "When shall these dark minds be enlightened by the bright beams of the gospel's light, and serve God in sincerity and
truth?"[34]

Despite this shared denunciation of Indian lifestyles and beliefs, the missionaries varied greatly in their capacity for compassion. The Ranneys marked the
hostile end of the spectrum. Writing soon after she had arrived in Nebraska,
Charlotte could not help expressing (as if with a shudder) how it was "revolting
to see the degrading and filthy habits of these children of nature." She added,
with the resignation of a martyr, that "nothing but the hope of elevating them
would induce us to stay among them." At the sympathetic end of the spectrum
was John Dunbar, who cared deeply for the Pawnee and who, like Merrill,
considered the Indians to be far more civilized than the traders and other
frontiersmen who came in contact with them. But even Dunbar, who knew the
Pawnee to be a "liberal, kindhearted people," could not get around his conviction that they were "heathen, darkminded heathen."[35]

All the missionaries set about saving the Indians by preaching the gospel.
Immediately they ran into problems. First there was the language barrier. None
of the missionaries initially knew the Indian languages, and there were no
translations of the Scriptures into any of the local tongues. Dunbar, with characteristic determination, spent his first two years learning the Chaui dialect of
Pawnee. By 1836 he could "converse with them on most subjects" and had
started preaching to them in their own language. By 1845, with the aid of a
Canadian-born interpreter who had lived with the Pawnee for twenty-five
years, he had translated St. Mark's Gospel and other parts of the Scriptures into
Pawnee. Merrill was slower in picking up the Otoe-Missouria language. There
was only a French-speaking interpreter available at Bellevue, and Merrill didn't
speak French. Four years after his arrival Merrill still did not have a good
knowledge of the local language, but four hymns had been translated into
Otoe-Missouria and were featured in his services.[36]

Beyond the problem of communication, there was the Indians' lack of interest in abandoning their own religions for Christianity. Most of the Indians
welcomed the missionaries and treated them well. Dunbar was particularly
esteemed as a holy man, because soon after he arrived in the winter of 1834–35,
the bison herds came as far east as the Pawnee villages, which had not happened

in at least twenty years. The Pawnee "repeatedly" told Dunbar that Ti-ra'wa had sent back the bison because a man of God had come to live with them. Many of the Indians listened carefully to what Dunbar and the other missionaries had to say. They saw some commonality in the belief in a supreme being, whether Ti-ra'wa or God. Some attended services and enjoyed singing hymns, though Merrill and McKinney wondered if this was less for spiritual sustenance than for the food which was dispensed: "It is very evident," McKinney wrote with uncharacteristic humor, "that their expectations of good are not from what comes out of our mouths but from what goes into theirs."[37]

Whatever their motivations—and a major one seems to have been intellectual curiosity—the Indians showed a theological open-mindedness in considering the missionaries' preaching. But very few, if any, were converted to Christianity by 1850. "They are so tenacious in their religious rites," wrote Allis, though here he was describing the Skiri, who were the most overtly religious (or as Dunbar put it, the "most superstitious") of all the bands.[38] The general attitude was that Christianity was the "whites'" religion and should be respected, but that it had little to do with the Indians' world. Proselytizing was hard for them to comprehend. Big Elk of the Omaha tried to explain this to McKinney, telling him that he "had long heard of the gospel and attempted to come near to it, but like the dawn of the day the more he approached it the more distant it seemed to be." Big Elk continued, arguing that "if his forefathers had known how to make a bible, they doubtless would have made one and handed it down." Instead, they made "a sacred pipe with which to worship God, which has been presented for many generations, and which they use upon every solemn and important occasion."[39]

Not surprisingly, the greatest opposition came from the doctors and priests who saw their positions threatened by the missionaries. A Skiri priest candidly admitted his vested interest in the continuation of traditions to the Duke of Wurttemberg in 1822. The Duke had asked him if the ceremonies he conducted to protect the fields had any real effect. "Great father," the priest replied, "if the enemies and the boys did not believe in that, the old men would starve and the priests perish."[40]

Because of the general intransigence of the adults, the missionaries focused their attention on the Indian children, hoping to shape their ideas and behavior from an early age. They strove to get the children into their schools and houses, where they could be taught the English language and American cultural values. In the 1830s and 1840s these endeavors met with little success. The missionaries quickly found that the children were no less attached to traditional lifestyles than were their parents. On February 23, 1833, for example, Warinase, an "Otoe chief of distinction," brought his son to stay with the Reverend and Mrs. Merrill at Bellevue. The boy quickly fell into a deep depression and refused to eat. On March 8 he left and did not return.[41]

By the 1840s, however, as missionary efforts continued and living conditions deteriorated, more Indians brought their children to the missions to be fed, clothed, and taught the new ways. In 1849 McKinney reported that as many as seventy scholars had attended classes at the Bellevue mission school during the course of the year, including twenty-four Otoe-Missouria, twenty-four Omaha, thirteen Pawnee, and nine mixed-bloods. Some who had been in attendance for eight or nine months could read English and "write a legible hand."[42] Unless they were desperate, however, and unable to provide food, parents understandably were unwilling to be separated from their children, and the children were reluctant to give up the adventures of the hunt for the discipline of the mission.

The traders also worked hard to prevent the missionaries from achieving their goals. For their own selfish reasons, the traders wanted the Indians to continue in their traditional lifestyles: Indians who were settled down on farms would not make good robe producers. Dunbar's efforts to attract the Pawnee bands to the mission were constantly thwarted by traders who insisted on doing their business only at the villages. Merrill was even more plagued by the traders' interference. Not only did Roy, Robideaux, and Sarpy undermine his civilization program by importing whiskey and encouraging the Indians to continue hunting, but they also campaigned against him, telling the Otoe-Missouria that he would take their children away. They also pointed out that, unlike the traders, the missionaries did not supply presents. This was a convincing argument, and Merrill admitted to his superiors that he could not win the Indians' confidence the way the traders did by handing out gifts. At both Bellevue and the Pawnee mission, traders stoked up animosity against the missionaries and were partly responsible for the escalation of violence which complicated, and endangered, the missionaries' lives.[43]

Within a few years of residing with the Indians, the missionaries realized—and admitted as much to their superiors—that they were not achieving their goals. As long as the Indians were starving, teaching the gospel to them was a wasted effort, Dunbar wrote in 1843.[44] The missionaries' problem was larger than this, however. Their goal was simply too ambitious. By linking Christianity to American ideas of civilization, success could only be achieved if the Indians rejected their entire way of life and settled down on individual farms where the men labored from dawn to dusk. Even by 1900 this had not been completely accomplished.

So the missionaries found themselves, as Dunbar put it, doing little for the "spiritual good" of the Indians, but having some success in "relieving their temporal wants."[45] In this respect many of the missionaries showed great compassion for the Indians and served as a buffer against the forces of the outside world.

As living conditions deteriorated, the missions became a last resort for health care and food. Merrill recorded in his diary in 1834: "I am repeatedly called to try my skill in medicine."[46] Indians were frequently treated for wounds inflicted in fights and for diseases like measles, malaria, and cholera. This attentiveness had its costs. The missionaries themselves often contracted diseases. Mrs. Merrill, for example, was generally ill, and on September 5, 1837, Allis and his wife buried their "only child, a boy of 13 months," the victim of a fever.[47]

When starvation became the normal condition of life, particularly in the 1840s, groups of Indians camped near the missions and begged for corn and potatoes. Often they helped themselves from the mission gardens. One episode, involving Dunbar and the Pawnee in the desperate year of 1844, illustrates how far Dunbar had come in understanding Indian culture and recognizing the limits of what he could achieve. The spring of 1844 found all the Pawnee bands without food. The Indians living around the mission had raised a good crop of corn the previous fall, but in their eagerness to leave on the winter hunt they stored it before it was dry, and the entire harvest rotted. The Skiri had been so harassed by the Dakota that they were not able to work in the fields and had raised no corn at all. The Dakota also preyed on the Skiri and Pitahawirata while they were out on the winter hunt and prevented them from getting any meat. None of the Pawnee bands had a good hunt that winter, and when those who continued to live south of the Platte returned to their villages in the spring, they found that their caches had been plundered by the Otoe-Missouria. Dunbar was surrounded by more than three thousand starving Indians who begged for corn during the day and stole it at night.

The missionaries had three hundred to four hundred bushels of corn stored for their own future use. "The dictates of benevolence" made it mandatory for Dunbar to give the corn to the starving Pawnee. But he was in a quandary about how to achieve this. He considered giving the corn to the chiefs, who would then have the responsibility to dispense it to their followers. This course, Dunbar realized, would have made him "very popular with the principal men of the nation," but he doubted that much food would filter down to the ordinary people. He next considered handing the corn out to everyone, but he didn't know how to accomplish this without strife. Moreover, he opposed the entire concept of gratuities as contrary to the missionaries' goal of making the Indians self-sustaining through farming. He also understood that a gift of corn one year would set a precedent for future years. Finally, "after much reflection," he chose the course which seemed to present the "fewest evils": he decided to trade the corn to the Pawnee and then return the items traded to their owners over a period of time. The trade was accomplished, starvation was held at bay, and Dunbar was elevated even higher in the Pawnee's estimation. The only problem was that, as an unlicensed trader, Dunbar had broken the Intercourse Laws, but by that time he felt little but contempt for government laws and officials.[48]

Dunbar and the other missionaries strove to protect the Indians from others who populated the frontier. They envisioned themselves to be a race to civilize the Indians—specifically to turn them into Christian farmers living on individual holdings—before they were engulfed by the tide of settlement. This protective attitude is vividly illustrated by an incident involving Dunbar and Major Clifton Wharton's First Dragoons which took place near the Skiri village in August 1844. The dragoons had been sent to impress the Pawnee with the power of the United States, to reiterate the necessity that the Indians should settle down to farming and urge them not to retaliate against the Dakota (despite the obvious fact that the Pawnee were only defending themselves). Major Wharton delivered these messages in a council held at the Chaui village. The troops then traveled from the Platte through the mud and mosquitoes to the south bank of the Loup, opposite the Skiri village, where the council was to be repeated (fig. 5). Wharton sent a message ahead to Dunbar asking for assistance in crossing the treacherous Loup. Dunbar ignored the message and stood on the opposite bank, watching impassively as the soldiers floundered in the quicksand. Finally some Skiris came down from the village and guided the troops across. Dunbar gave the visitors a cool reception and offered them no information.[49]

The missionaries' kindness and dedication won them the support of many of the Indians at a time when their distrust of Americans in general was growing. Merrill, for example, was known to the Otoe-Missouria as The One Who Always Speaks The Truth, no doubt in sharp contrast to negligent government agents and self-serving traders.[50] Dunbar and Allis, who were threatened with expulsion by the government for opposing unscrupulous agency employees, also gained the confidence of the Indians. "We have their sympathies," wrote Dunbar, "and they were hoping to live a long time with us."[51]

Still, particularly at Bellevue, where social collapse was most advanced, Merrill and his family found themselves caught in a vortex of violence. The Otoe-Missouria, afflicted by famine, sickness, and death, and worked up by the traders' machinations, began to focus their anger against Americans in general, and on the missionaries in particular. On September 15, 1838, they complained to Merrill that they had "listened to the whites and now they are dying off." Moreover, they continued, because of Merrill's opposition, the traders were not bringing as much whiskey to their village. On May 30, 1839, while Merrill was at the agency, a party of Otoe-Missouria, masquerading as Dakota, threatened to rob the mission and terrorized Mrs. Merrill. Reverend Merrill blamed these depredations on "impudent and troublesome" young men who could no longer be controlled by the chiefs, and he began to fear for his family's safety.[52]

At the Pawnee mission the danger came not so much from the local Indians as from Dakota and Ponca, who became increasingly bold in their attacks during the 1840s. At first the raiding Indians avoided conflict with the missionaries, understanding the serious implications of killing Americans, as opposed to Pawnee. But by 1845 they were also threatening the missionaries, so much so that Dunbar no longer felt that it was safe to shelter Pawnee children in his mission. In the summer of 1846, after waiting in vain for the government to offer some protection, Dunbar, Allis, the Ranneys, and their families retreated to Bellevue. "They will doubtless feel bad when they come to know we have left them," Dunbar wrote, adding, "their prospects are dark and as we turn away from them we commend them to Him. . . ."[53]

This was only the beginning, however. Individual missionaries like Dunbar left, thinking themselves to be failures, but as a group the missionaries were there to stay. The seeds that were sown in those classes at the missions in the 1830s and 1840s took root in the second half of the nineteenth century when missionaries dominated Indian education and were appointed as Indian agents. They were unwavering in their dedication to the civilization program and, together with the agents, they would dismantle Indian cultures piece by piece, until only kernels of traditions remained intact.

Indian Agents and Federal Indian Policy

The most powerful and pervasive intervention in Indian lives was the agent: the representative of the federal government and enactor of its policies. Agents were charged with maintaining peace among the Indians and between Indians and Americans, with enforcing the Intercourse Laws which regulated the fur trade, with arranging for the sale of Indian lands as needed for frontier expansion and dispensing the cash or annuities that were payments for these lands, and with promoting the civilization program. Agents varied as much in character and ability as did any other segment of American society. If the Nebraska situation can be accepted as typical, some were committed to their jobs and strove under difficult circumstances to shield the Indians from the destructive impact of the frontier; others saw the job as an easy way to earn a salary of fifteen hundred dollars a year (or more, if they embezzled), or as a convenient stepping-stone to higher office in government service. Whatever their motivations, they did little to alleviate the stress on the Indians: inefficiency was inherent in the administration of Indian affairs, programs were always inadequately funded, and in practice, if not in rhetoric, the Indians' welfare was always subordinated to the process of acquiring their lands.

The administrative structure of Indian affairs was pyramidical in shape. At the apex was the commissioner of Indian affairs, who managed Indian relations under the direction of the secretary of war until 1849, and thereafter under the secretary of the interior.[54] The commissioners were political appointees who generally rode the wave of patronage into office, and for this reason their terms of tenure were generally no longer than those of the presidents who sponsored them. Some of the commissioners, like Thomas McKenney (1824–30), were sincerely concerned about the fate of the Indians; others, like Elbert Herring (1831–36) and Carey Harris (1836–38), paid only lip-service to protecting their "wards" and pushed hard for the acquisition of Indian lands; all were convinced, like other Americans of the time, that the Indians had to give up their traditional lands and lifestyles, or else be crushed under the "westward march of progress."[55]

The second level of the administrative hierarchy was staffed by a small number (four in 1830) of superintendents who were responsible for large regions and several Indian groups. The superintendents oversaw agents who were assigned to a single group of Indians or a few closely related communities (geographically or culturally). The bottom of the pyramid consisted of blacksmiths, teachers, farmers, interpreters, and other poorly paid employees who were charged with giving the Indians the basic skills to compete in an American world.

From 1822 to 1851 the Nebraska Indians fell under the jurisdiction of the St. Louis superintendency. For more than half of that time (1822–38) William Clark was in charge of the St. Louis office. Locally the Otoe-Missouria, Omaha, Pawnee, and Ponca were administered by the Upper Missouri Agency from 1824–36, with its headquarters at Bellevue. After 1836 the Upper Missouri Agency was moved up river to the vicinity of the Big Bend of the Missouri, where it continued to oversee the Ponca and also had authority over the Dakota and Cheyenne. The Omaha, Otoe-Missouria, and Pawnee were assigned to the Council Bluffs Agency from 1836 to 1857, also located at Bellevue. From 1827 to 1839 the Bellevue agency was run by John Dougherty, the veteran fur trader and interpreter. Thereafter there was a rapid turnover of agents up until 1854. In the second half of the 1850s, when separate reservations were created for the eastern Nebraska Indians, each group was assigned its own agent.

The agents at Bellevue did their jobs with varying degrees of ability and commitment. Dougherty was, intrinsically, the most capable of the group, but he was also one of the least committed. He knew the Nebraska Indians well and spoke their languages fluently. He also had their trust: "We have known him since his boyhood," Ietan told William Clark in 1830, in an expression of confidence.[56] But by the late 1820s Dougherty had had enough of frontier living. He had married a Missouri woman in 1823 and wished to live in "a situation less exposed" than Bellevue.[57] Dougherty did not want to give up his agency, however, because he had his sights set on Clark's job when it fell vacant.[58] Consequently, from 1827 on, Dougherty ran the agency from the relative comfort and security of Fort Leavenworth, visiting Bellevue only occasionally to hold councils or dispense annuities. In his absence, conditions at Bellevue went from bad to worse as traders plied the liquor trade with impunity. The empty and decaying agency building stood as a symbol of this neglect. When Dougherty's successor Joseph Hamilton took over in 1839 he found the building in a "shocking condition, fit only for rats and bugs."[59] The agency employees had abandoned their posts, and the Otoe-Missouria, Omaha, and Pawnee were not able to avail themselves of services that were due under the terms of their treaties.

Even conscientious agents, however, could do little to improve the living conditions of the Indians. John Miller, for example, who ran the Council Bluffs Agency from 1846 to 1849, found himself surrounded by starving Indians. His letters to his superiors took the form of pleas—to control the liquor trade, to dispatch troops to protect the Nebraska Indians from the Dakota, to issue emergency rations, and to send supplies of quinine to control the autumnal outbreaks of "chills and fevers" (malaria).[60] Emergency rations of beef, bacon, and corn were sent in 1849, but this was only a palliative. The high-flown rhetoric of the civilization program had little to do with the stark realities of Indian life on the frontier.

The main goal of federal Indian policy, underpinned by the civilization program, remained remarkably consistent throughout the nineteenth century; only the circumstances in which it was applied changed.[61] From the time of Jefferson through the imposition of allotments in severalty on the Indians in the last quarter of the nineteenth century, the objective was to break up the communal organization of Indian societies and settle individuals on their own pieces of private property. Dougherty, who was often drawn upon for reports on Indian affairs, outlined the details of this standard policy to Senator Thomas Hart Benton in 1829. He proposed that the Indians should be placed on a small tract of land which could be farmed and where there was no game, "in order to wean him from his favorite pursuit and thereby prepare his mind to encounter the laborious duties of domestic life." Blacksmiths, farmers, laborers, and implements should be furnished, so that in time the Indians would be able to "clothe and subsist themselves by individualized exertions." Once settled down, the Indians should be "taught to read, use figures, divide the year into months and days, so that they could undertake domestic manufacture." Agriculture was the key, Dougherty concluded, to raising the Indian "one grade higher in civilization," and self-sufficiency would reduce the sums of money needed for their support when the game gave out.[62]

With a few variations—Dougherty thought that it was "worse than useless" to introduce religion until the Indians were settled down to farming, whereas many others, including Thomas McKenney, thought that Christianization and individualization should go hand in hand—his letter was a blueprint for federal Indian policy in the nineteenth century. In essence, civilization would be offered in exchange for the Indians' lands. Both humanitarians and expansionists could support that plan, the former because they believed that they were rescuing the Indians from a condition of savagery, the latter because they saw no reason why the Indians should be allowed to occupy so much land and obstruct the ordained westward expansion of Americans.

The optimistic expectations of men like McKenney that the Indians could be assimilated within a generation were dashed by events on the frontier. The Indians were not willing to jettison their lands and lifestyles for duties which, to the men, especially, seemed arduous and unexciting. They were, in any case, convinced of the rightfulness of their own way of life. Moreover, contact with frontier Americans clearly led to the Indians' debasement, not to their "improvement." So while the ultimate goal remained assimilation, in practice federal policy makers fell back on the expediency of temporary segregation. Indians were repeatedly moved away from the frontier and restricted to smaller and smaller tracts of land where the civilization program was applied with increasing intensity. First, in the 1820s and 1830s, the Indians of the eastern United States were coerced into relocating west of the Mississippi, where they were guaranteed new, permanent homelands. But within two decades Americans had caught up, and this "permanent Indian frontier" was fragmented into numerous reservations. Finally, after about 1870 (and culminating in the Dawes Act of 1887) the Indian Office made a concerted push for assimilation by settling the Indians on allotments and opening up the remaining reservation lands to settlers. At each stage the frontier of settlement enveloped the Indians before they could make the social and cultural adjustments that were being demanded of them.

One of the problems was that there existed an inherent contradiction in federal policy: the civilization program was never given the necessary funds to have even a chance of success. A civilization fund was established in 1819 and used to support educational activities by missionaries like Dunbar and Allis. But ten thousand dollars a year for all American Indians did not go very far. The main funding for the program throughout the nineteenth century came from the Indians' own money, which they received for the sale of their lands. However, Congress was always niggardly in funding the Indian Office. Requested appropriations were invariably cut by congressmen who, reflecting their constituents' views, regarded any payments to the Indians—even payments owed for the sale of Indian lands—as a form of welfare. Always short of funds and constantly pressured to facilitate frontier expansion, the Indian Office obtained cessions at the lowest cost possible, then used the payments to try to make the Indians self-sufficient so that they would not need support in the future. The result was that the Indians' land base rapidly diminished, but the civilization program stalled for want of funds.[63]

There was also a massive assumption underlying federal Indian policy which ensured that there were no legal constraints on the taking of Indian lands. Following the example of the colonial powers, especially Spain and Britain, the United States recognized the Indians as "legal occupants" of the land but maintained that their title of ownership had been "impaired" by the "right of conquest." This presumed sovereignty, also known as the "Doctrine of Discovery" gave Congress "plenary" (or absolute) power over the American Indians, including the right to take their traditional lands and even to abrogate former treaties without agreement by the peoples involved. The Doctrine of Discovery thus accomplished through treaties and laws what had previously been accomplished by war, namely colonization and displacement of native populations. It has been argued that the United States wielded this assumed power more humanely than many other Western nations (for example, the British in Australia) by extinguishing Indian title through treaties. But, in the final analysis, it was a compulsory purchase: negotiations did take place, the Indians did have their say in councils, but it was the United States that set the conditions of the divestiture.[64]

The first federal acquisition of the Nebraska Indians' land came in 1830 with the Treaty of Prairie du Chien. This was one of the largest treaty councils held in the first half of the nineteenth century, involving delegations from the Sauk and Fox, eastern bands of the Dakota (Sisseton, Wahpeton, and Medawakonton), Iowa, Menominee, Winnebago, Omaha, and Otoe-Missouria. The Yankton and Santee bands of the Dakota were also subject to the treaty, although they did not attend the council. The delegations met with Colonel Willoughby Morgan and William Clark over the course of a week in mid-July. Dougherty served as interpreter for the Omaha and Otoe-Missouria. Morgan and Clark forcefully presented their argument that it was time for the Indians to "bury the war tomahawk deep in the earth," or else face the U.S. army.[65] The main issue of contention among the Indians was the right to hunt on the territory between the Missouri and Des Moines rivers, essentially the western third of the present state of Iowa and the northwestern part of Missouri. The Sauk and Fox, Yankton and Santee Dakota, Iowa, Otoe-Missouria, and Omaha peoples all claimed parts of this territory, though in the case of the Nebraska Indians the claim was more historical than possessive.

On July 10, Clark secured the signatures of all the delegations on a treaty of peace, although Big Elk of the Omaha let it be known that he doubted that many of the Indians believed "in their hearts" that peace was possible. In an effort to secure the peace, Clark persuaded the Indians to relinquish their claims to the disputed territory, which would subsequently serve as a common hunting ground for all involved in the treaty.

According to the terms of the Treaty of Prairie du Chien the Omaha and Otoe-Missouria gave up their "title and claim" to their traditional lands east of the Missouri (fig. 7). They retained the right to hunt there. In return they were each given an annual annuity of twenty-five hundred dollars for ten years, to be paid either in cash, merchandise, or domestic animals. They were also each provided with the services of a blacksmith and five hundred dollars worth of farming equipment. An annual educational fund of three thousand dollars was set up for all of the signatories of the treaty. Ietan, of the Otoe, pleaded with

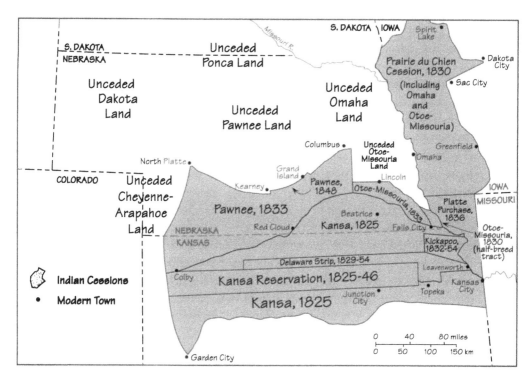

Fig. 7 Land Cessions in the 1830s and 1840s

Clark to extend the annuity to twenty years because game was scarce and his people could not yet support themselves by farming. Clark replied that he was sorry that the compensation disappointed them, but it was as much as the "Great Council of the Nation" (that is, Congress) would give.

There was more than a little deception involved in this treaty. Clark had placated the Indians by assuring them that "we don't purchase those lands with a view to settling the white people on them" and "we think you are more bene-fitted by it than the Government." Yet a week later he was writing to commis-sioner McKenney that the government "will have a disposable country of the best lands on the Missouri. . . ."[66] The hunting rights were simply allowed to lapse. In 1835, bands of the Potawatomie, Chippewa, and Ottawa were removed from Illinois and Indiana into western Iowa and took over the hunting grounds that the Otoe-Missouria and Omaha believed were still theirs. Dougherty wrote to Commissioner Harris on behalf of the Omaha and Otoe-Missouria, stating that he, like the Nebraska Indians, had not understood from the treaty negotia-tions that other Indians could be settled in the ceded area. There had been subtle alterations of the text of the treaty, he maintained, "which changed and perverted the true meaning" as he had understood it, and as he had explained it to the Indians.[67] Dougherty tried to get extra compensation for the ceded lands, but to little avail. A small sum of money ($3,320) was appropriated for the Omaha and Otoe-Missouria in 1836 for the formal extinguishment of their title to the northwestern part of Missouri (the Platte Purchase). But when the Potawatomie, Chippewa, and Ottawa ceded their claim to western Iowa in 1846, the Omaha and Otoe-Missouria were not even mentioned in the treaty.[68]

There was a second cession of land involving the Otoe-Missouria which stemmed from the Treaty of Prairie du Chien. According to Article 10, the Omaha, Otoe-Missouria, and Iowa had "earnestly requested" that their mixed-bloods (together with the mixed-bloods of the Yankton and Santee nations) be given a separate homeland. This triangular homeland was carved out of southeastern Nebraska and named the Nemaha Half-Breed Reservation (fig. 7). In return for this 138,000-acre cession, the Otoe-Missouria were given an annual annuity of three hundred dollars for ten years, or 2.2 cents an acre. This money was not actually paid by the federal government, but by the Omaha, Iowa, Yankton, and Santee out of their Prairie du Chien annuities. In 1833, according to Prince Maximilian, about one hundred twenty to two hundred mixed-bloods were eligible for settlement in the tract, but none had done so. The boundaries of the tract were surveyed in 1838, but it was not until 1860 that mixed-bloods were actually settled in the area. In that year, 389 descendants of Americans (mostly fur traders) and Indians were issued patents for individual allotments. These were the first allotments assigned to Indians in the United States. They were almost all sold to white settlers within a decade.[69]

The next two cessions of lands of the Nebraska Indians were made in 1833, and both were connected with the relocation of eastern Indians into what is now northern Kansas. In 1832 the Kickapoo were moved out of Missouri into northeastern Kansas, just north and west of Fort Leavenworth (fig. 7). This was land that the Otoe-Missouria still claimed; in fact, they had driven the Kansa out of the area in the late 1820s and forced them to rebuild their villages sixty to eighty miles to the west up the Kansas River. A second conflict developed between the Pawnee and the Delaware. In 1829 the Delaware were moved from the Sandusky River in Ohio to the "Delaware Outlet," a ten-mile-wide strip of land which extended for an indeterminate distance west from the Missouri River, just south of Fort Leavenworth. This was land that the Kansa had ceded in 1825, but which the Pawnee regarded as their own. Immediately Delaware and Pawnee hunting parties clashed, and hostilities culminated in the burning of the Chaui's village in 1832 by the Delaware.

In an attempt to quell this escalating violence, the Indian Office dispatched Henry L. Ellsworth to negotiate treaties with the Otoe-Missouria and Pawnee. The objective was to extinguish the Indians' claim to their southern lands, thereby creating a buffer between them and the immigrant Indians.

In the late summer of 1833 Ellsworth traveled up from Fort Leavenworth with a small party that included Washington Treat Irving, the twenty-year-old nephew of Washington Irving. They reached the Otoe-Missouria village on the Platte on September 23. The treaty council was held in a crowded, stifling lodge where the chiefs sat "like statues" at the front while the warriors, women, and children craned to see from the back and even peered down through the smokehole in the roof.[70] Ellsworth argued that now the game was gone the Otoe-Missouria must "cultivate the ground or starve." He promised the Indians all the help they needed to make the transition to sedentary life. The Otoe-Missouria chiefs were willing to agree to just about any terms the United States proposed, as long as they resulted in better living conditions. Ietan responded to Ellsworth, promising him that they would indeed give up "the chase." It seemed to Irving, however, that Ietan was speaking less to Ellsworth than to his own warriors, urging them to accept the conditions of the treaties. Dougherty and Papin, who were doing the interpreting, told Irving that the gist of Ietan's speech was that "the less difficulty they made in agreeing to the terms of the treaty, the greater would be their share of the presents." The treaty was signed, and on the next day Ietan and the subsidiary chiefs, Big Kaw and The Thief, sat in the middle of a large circle of expectant men, women, and children and handed out four hundred dollars' worth of presents.

The Otoe-Missouria treaty of 1833 set the general pattern for the following treaty with the Pawnee and for subsequent treaties with all the Indians of eastern Nebraska in the 1850s. They ceded their lands between the Great and Little Nemaha rivers and as far west from the headwaters of the Little Nemaha as they "have, or pretend to have any claim."[71] In return they were given an annual annuity of twenty-five hundred dollars for ten years, starting in 1840 when the previous annuity from the Treaty of Prairie du Chien expired. They were also given five hundred dollars worth of agricultural equipment to be delivered annually for five years or longer, at the discretion of the president. This too was a continuation of the terms of the Treaty of Prairie du Chien. In addition they were to receive five hundred dollars a year for five years for education purposes, one thousand dollars worth of cattle and other stock, and the service of two farmers for at least five years. As their first task, the farmers were to build a horse mill for grinding corn. These agricultural and educational provisions would only be fulfilled if the Otoe-Missouria agreed to give up the hunt and remain at their village year-round, thus providing protection for the farmers. In total, the Otoe-Missouria were given almost forty thousand dollars' worth of goods and services for relinquishing their title to about one million acres of land, or 4.1 cents an acre (fig. 7).[72] Thus began in earnest the process whereby the Nebraska Indians sold their lands for a living.

While Ellsworth was at the Otoe-Missouria village, a party of Omaha led by Big Elk came in from their village on the Elkhorn for a meeting. Ellsworth explained to the Omaha chiefs that he wanted nothing from them (their lands not being involved in the resettlement of immigrant Indians). He did, however, urge them to settle near the Missouri and farm year-round. In such a location, Ellsworth argued, their annuities (from the 1830 treaty) could easily be delivered, and their surplus agricultural products marketed by water. Big Elk agreed that they would "stay home" if they were provided with farmers, teachers, seeds, and cattle.[73]

Ellsworth's small party then traveled the eighty miles to the Chaui village on the Platte, which had been rebuilt after the sacking by the Delaware. Ellsworth was weak, barely recovered from the cholera that was raging on the frontier. The Pawnee were in even poorer shape. Smallpox had torn their society apart in 1831, reducing their population by half and turning their villages into open graveyards where the dogs were left to dispose of the bodies.[74] The Pawnee were, in the words of the Chaui chief Shah-re-tah-riche, "sick, weary and dying" and looked "like persons who have passed through a burning prairie."[75] Ellsworth repeated the speech he had made to the Otoe-Missouria to the assembled chiefs of the four Pawnee bands. Desperate for assistance and protection, they agreed to every condition that was proposed. Irving noticed, however, that only the chiefs and older men participated in the council. The young warriors kept their distance and seemed defiant.[76]

The terms of the Pawnee treaty differed only in detail from that of the Otoe-Missouria. They relinquished their "right, interest, and title" to all of their lands to the south of the Platte.[77] They would still be allowed to hunt there, along with other Indians, "during the pleasure of the President." It was stipulated that the Chaui, in keeping with the treaty terms, would have to relocate to the north of the Platte. In return the Pawnee were given an annual annuity of forty-six hundred dollars for twelve years, divided proportionately among the four bands. Like the Otoe-Missouria, each Pawnee band was provided with five hundred dollars' worth of agricultural equipment for five years. The four bands in total were supplied with an educational fund of one thousand dollars and the services of two blacksmiths and two strikers for ten years. A farmer would be assigned to each band, and a horse mill would be built at each village. The United States would bear the expense of breaking the prairie near each village for the first year and would also provide one thousand dollars of stock for the bands collectively. In an interesting clause, the United States also promised to furnish the farmers with twenty-five guns and ammunition to help protect the Pawnee from the Dakota and other hostile Indians. None of these funds would be appropriated unless the Chaui moved north of the Platte and unless all of the bands located themselves in "convenient agricultural districts and remained in these districts the whole year, so as to give protection to the teachers, the farmers, stock and mill." In one six-hour council, therefore, the Pawnee signed away their title to thirteen million acres of land and received, in return, goods and services amounting to $148,200 or 1.1 cents an acre.[78]

Ellsworth and his small party then traveled to the other Pawnee villages, which lined the Loup, and explained the new conditions to those chiefs and warriors who had not attended the main council. Finally, in this round of negotiations, Ellsworth returned to Fort Leavenworth, accompanied by delegations from the Omaha, Otoe-Missouria, and Pawnee. There, from November 8 to December 4, 1833, he presided over a series of councils which established, in theory at least, peace among the Nebraska Indians, the Delaware, Shawnee, Kickapoo, Ottawa, Wea, Peoria, Sauk and Fox, Iowa, Piankeshaw, and Osage. His mission had been successful. He had secured a vast area of good land for the United States at little cost to the government.

At the Leavenworth councils Ellsworth had argued that both the indigenous and immigrant Indians now had a "separate country" where they could feel secure in their ownership and make the transition to sedentary life in peace.[79] But, for the Nebraska Indians especially, these were empty words. Ever since William Ashley had forged the supply route to the Rocky Mountain fur trade rendezvous in 1824–25, the Platte flood plain had become the major arterial of western travel. Each summer during the late 1820s and the decade of the 1830s, large caravans of traders traced the Platte and Sweetwater rivers to the central Rockies. The Rocky Mountain fur trade gave out by 1840, victim of ruthless competition and resource depletion, but the traffic along the Platte route only increased. In 1840, the year of the last rendezvous, thirteen emigrants crossed Nebraska to Oregon. By 1845 this trickle had swelled to 5,397 emigrants. The Mormons added to the flow in 1847, and three years later, after the discovery of gold in California, 98,297 emigrants made the journey west. The emigrants cut the timber, depleted the grass, and eliminated what little game was left. The Indians, especially the Pawnee who lived along the trail, were reduced to begging and stealing from the travelers. Sporadic violence erupted, especially at the Shell Creek ferry where the Pawnee tried to levy a fee for the right of passage through their lands.[80]

At the same time that Americans were encroaching upon the "separate country" of the Nebraska Indians from the east, the Dakota were invading from the north and west. The Pawnee, Omaha, and Otoe-Missouria were caught in a tightening vise. The Ponca avoided the situation only by throwing in their lot with the Dakota. The United States did nothing to curb the raiders. This was partly because the U.S. Army was incapable of suppressing the estimated twenty-five thousand Dakota, but it was also a result of deliberate policy. The Indian Office continued to supply the Dakota with guns as a form of appeasement, while denying the Nebraska Indians any weapons. Less directly, guns continued to flow to the Dakota from the United States via the fur trade, an exchange that was sanctioned, through licensing, by the government. Meanwhile, guns promised to the Pawnee through the treaty of 1833 were not delivered because some of the bands continued to build their villages to the south of the Platte, using the river as a protective moat against the Dakota. In 1843 the Pawnee chiefs pleaded with Agent David Miller for the weapons, saying that if the "Great Father had done as he promised by giving us guns and ammunition we would have been able to protect our wives and children from slaughter." But the guns and protection were not forthcoming; in fact, that same year Miller wrote to superintendent David Mitchell that "it would not seem to be advisable for the Government to commence hostilities against the Sioux at this time, which might lead to protracted difficulties between the Sioux and the citizens of the United States." So the Dakota continued to prey on the Nebraska Indians, and the Pawnee were reduced to begging from the emigrants.[81]

Finally, in 1845, after years of vacillation, the United States decided to build a fort on the Platte and mobilize troops to ensure the "safety of the emigrants and the tranquility of the Indians." The following year, Thomas Harvey, super-intendent of Indian affairs at St. Louis, wrote to Commissioner Medill propos-ing the purchase of a "path through Pawnee lands" and a site for a fort. The right of way and land, Harvey suggested, could be obtained for a "trifling consideration."[82]

In March 1847 an army survey team and escort of seventy men was dis-patched across southeast Nebraska to Grand Island, in the Platte. Lieutenant D. P. Woodbury reported back that Grand Island, with its abundant timber and grass, was an excellent site for a post. The fort—first named Fort Childs, but subsequently known as Fort Kearney—would be appropriately placed, Wood-bury wrote, to "overcome the audacity" of the Pawnee. The soldiers would be able to intercept the Pawnee between their villages and hunting grounds. With their "incumbrances" of women, children, and baggage, Woodbury conjec-tured, the Pawnee would be no match for the mounted dragoons.[83]

On August 6, 1848, a battalion of Missouri Mounted Volunteers under the command of Lieutenant-Colonel Ludwell E. Powell met with the assembled chiefs of the four Pawnee bands near the head of Grand Island.[84] This was another case of a land cession made against the backdrop of starvation. In the previous March, sixty Pawnee, including all the chiefs, had straggled into Belle-vue in a "wretched condition."[85] The entire nation was starving to death. Only one hundred fifty bison had been killed on the winter hunt, there was no corn left, and the Indians had been living on roots, which were also almost gone. Under the circumstances, the Pawnee had no option but to sell Grand Island and the adjacent floodplain of the Platte (fig. 7). They also gave the United States the right to cut timber on Wood River, a north-bank tributary of the Platte. In return for this 110,000-acre strip of land and river they were given two thousand dollars' worth of merchandise, or 1.8 cents an acre.[86]

When Agent John Miller learned of the purchase he complained to Harvey that the land was worth ten times what the Pawnee were given. Moreover, he added, the Pawnee had no idea what they were ceding, "as they know nothing about the length of a mile."[87] The Pawnee continued to use Grand Island for late-summer pasture for their horses, but after 1848 this area, like all their lands south of the Platte, was American property.

The 1848 Pawnee cession was the last sale of Indian lands before the Kansas-Nebraska Act of 1854 opened the floodgates to settlers. As the Indians' ability to support themselves through their traditional cycle failed because of depletion of game, intimidation by the Dakota, and rapidly decreasing populations, they came to rely increasingly on the government for food, clothing, and other necessities. No one recognized the radical change that was taking place more clearly than Big Elk, the chief of the Omaha. In a poignant speech to Henry Ellsworth at the 1833 council, he acknowledged that the Omaha could no longer continue to live as they had done, but must put their faith in the "Great Father." Big Elk compared his people to a "canoe gliding swiftly down the swift waters; now, they go on beautifully, but in a moment they touch some concealed object and are bottomed out. But you—*you* are a great thick iron spike deeply driven in the ground. We can lean against it and know ourselves to be safely supported."[88]

Big Elk's faith was misplaced. An analysis of the funds made available through the land sales of 1830 and 1833 reveals just how infirm this "iron spike" was. Every year from 1834 to 1840 the United States was obligated, under treaty stipulations, to spend twenty-one thousand dollars on behalf of the Pawnee, Otoe-Missouria, and Omaha (table 4). The Ponca, having made no cessions of land, received no annuities. The Omaha had only annuities from the 1830 treaty of Prairie du Chien, and from these funds they were obliged to pay the Otoe-Missouria one hundred dollars a year for ten years as their share of purchasing the Nemaha Half-Breed Tract. The Omaha were also provided with an educational allowance of four hundred dollars through the civilization fund. The Pawnee bands received their basic annuities from the 1833 sale of land, but none of the educational and agricultural aid earmarked in that treaty was delivered because they would not stay at their villages year-round. For the same reason, the promised guns were withheld. The Otoe-Missouria had the most sustainable annuity because they had made two cessions (1830 and 1833) of land. Funds from the 1830 treaty expired in 1840 for both the Omaha and the Otoe-Missouria. The latter continued to be supported for another ten years under the terms of the 1833 treaty, but the Omaha were left to fend for themselves. They repeatedly petitioned the government to buy their lands and give them an annuity, but even though Harvey advised Commissioner Medill that the Omaha would accept any offer, their lands were not sold, and they starved.[89] The Pawnees' annuities expired in 1844. So by 1850, none of the Nebraska Indians were receiving aid from the government, except for emergency rations and discretionary assistance in farming and education.

The terms of the government assistance looked better on paper than they

Table 4 United States Treaty Obligations to the Omaha, Pawnee, and Otoe-Missouria, 1839

Synopsis of treaty stipulations with the Ottoes & Mifsourias, Omahas & Pawnees not yet fully executed.

Ottoes & Mifsourias.

1. Annuity $2500 in money or goods at their option until 15 July 1850.

2. Agricultural Impl^ts, $500 per annum _____ until 15 July 1850.

3. 1 Blacksmith & tools _____ until 15 July 1840.

4. Schools in Nation, $500 pr. ann. at discretion of the President.

5. 2 farmers _____ at discretion of the President.

6. Share of $3,000 education _____ until 15 July 1840.

7. Horse Mill for grinding corn

8. $1000 in Stock

($300 pr an. from ann^t of Omahas, Ioways, & Yanetons, Santie Sioux $100 each.)

Omahas.

1. Annuity $2500 in money or goods _____ until 15 July 1840.

2. 1 Smith & tools _____ Do.

3. Agric^l Impl^ts, $500 _____ Do.

4. Share of $3000 for education _____ Do.

5. 100 acres land to be broken & fenced

($100 of their ann^t to be p^d to Ottoes until July 1840.)

Pawnees.

1. Annuity $4,000 in goods _____ until 1846.

2. Schools. $1000 _____ until 10 years.

3. 2 Bl^ths & strikers, shop, tools & iron _____ 10 years (1844).

4. 4 Farmers _____ 5 years.

5. Oxen & c. $1000. when Pres^t thinks best.

6. 4 Horse mills for grinding corn.

All but the 1st & 3^d items not to be furnished until the Pawnees locate in convenient agricult.^l districts.
U.S. will break up a piece of land one season.
25 guns & ammunition to be given to farmers, in case Pawnees remain at home all the year.

Sources: LR, Council Bluffs Agency, 1839. Courtesy of Nebraska State Historical Society, RG 508

were in reality. The Indians of eastern Nebraska did not receive their annuities in cash, though they frequently asked for them in that form. Cash payments were opposed by agents and superintendents alike on the grounds that they would quickly disappear into the traders' pockets. Instead, the Indians received cloth, food, utensils, and other items which the government considered to be useful for them. Big Elk was concerned that his people were not receiving the full amount of their annuities, because they did not understand the money value of the goods. He also believed that they were being overcharged for transporting the goods from St. Louis to Bellevue.[90] It is more than likely that both concerns were warranted.

The annuities were delivered under contract by St. Louis merchants, and often they were of poor quality or useless: "See what our Great Father sends us to fight the Sioux with," the Pawnee chiefs disdainfully told David Miller in 1844 after receiving a shipment of combs and forks.[91] The annuities were supposed to be delivered at Bellevue in the late summer, before the Indians left on their bison hunts. But there were frequent delays, and often the Indians had to wait at Bellevue until late fall, which cut into their hunts and strained their resources. In 1847 the Otoe-Missouria had to butcher some of their stock to sustain them until the annuities arrived. Some provisions of treaties were not fulfilled for years after the official starting date. In 1834 the Omaha still had not received the funds for a teacher allocated under the Prairie du Chien treaty. Finally, any "depredations" committed by the Indians on Americans or other Indians were paid for by deductions from the annuities.

The failure of the annuity system to support the Indians until they could support themselves was not all the government's fault. Despite avowals to the contrary, Indian men resisted farming; this, to them, was women's work, and dull by comparison to hunting. In the spring of 1847, for example, John Miller had fifty acres of land plowed up for the Otoe-Missouria and obtained a promise from their chiefs that the young men would stay home and work the field. But by June the young men had left to visit the Iowa, and the field was being reclaimed by the prairie.[92]

At Bellevue, annuities were often traded for liquor or other prized items. In 1839 an amazed Samuel Allis watched the Pawnee trade all but six of their fifty-two plows "before the Agt.s eyes."[93] Finally, the actual distribution of goods to the Indians posed a problem. The chiefs of the Omaha, Pawnee, and Otoe-Missouria insisted that they should receive all of the annuities, then allocate to the heads of families, and so on down to individuals.[94] This was in keeping with the traditional mode of wealth distribution, but it became clear that the best goods remained at the top of the hierarchy, and commoners often received nothing. During the 1840s and 1850s federal policy on annuities swung back and forth, from distribution via the chiefs to per capita payments, from annual to semiannual delivery, from goods to cash, and all versions posed problems.

At midcentury, then, after twenty years of government support and substantial sales of land, the Indians of eastern Nebraska were worse off than ever before. Moreover, according to Superintendent Mitchell, no progress at all had been made in implementing the civilization program. A major reason for this was the Indians' insecurity and lack in faith in government promises. When asked to farm, Mitchell explained to Commissioner Luke Lea in 1852, the Indians replied, "What is the use of it? In a few more years we will be driven back into the plains, or the Rocky Mountains, and what will our knowledge of agriculture, or the mechanic arts, avail us then?" According to Mitchell, the Indians fully realized that "there is no resting place for them under the existing order of things."[95]

They were correct. The prevailing American attitude, whether posed from the humanitarian or the racist end of the spectrum of opinion, was that the Indians had no real alternative but to Americanize: "It is by industry or extinction," Commissioner Lea grandly wrote in his 1852 report, "that the problem of their destiny must be solved."[96] With the American population expanding to the Pacific, the concept of a separate Indian country—a "permanent barrier"— was no longer tenable. By the late 1840s the Indian Office was advocating the removal of the Pawnee, Omaha, Ponca, and Otoe-Missouria to the southern plains "so as to leave an ample outlet for our white population to spread and pass towards and beyond the Rocky Mountains."[97] By the early 1850s the idea of the reservation had crystallized: the Indians would be placed on small areas with well-defined boundaries where the civilization program would be applied with intensified effort.[98] By 1858 all four Indian societies had sold the last of their ancestral lands except for small reservations.

CHAPTER THREE

Twilight of Independence

1800–1854

Against the backdrop of American encroachment, the Nebraska Indians lived in a fading twilight of independence. They remained traditional in their ways and beliefs, but the age-old cycle of hunting and farming could no longer reliably support them. Their deteriorating standards of living are expressed on the graphs of population change (figs. 8 through 11). The first twenty years or so of the nineteenth century were spent rebuilding families and communities after the trauma of the 1800–1801 smallpox epidemic. The initial success of this recovery is testimony to the continued viability of their established way of life, which flourished while game was plentiful. It also suggests a hiatus in the flow of disease epidemics. Then, smallpox appeared again in 1831; thereafter, the waves of epidemics—influenza, whooping cough, malaria, and cholera, in addition to smallpox—landed on the Indians like breakers on a beach, with little time for recovery before the next one struck. The weakened Nebraska Indians were no match for the better-armed and more numerous Dakota, and war was brought to the doors of their lodges. Famine became the norm of daily life, and communities broke apart from the stress. For all four societies these were some of the worst years in a bad century.

Recovery and Reversal, 1802–40

It is more than likely that the Nebraska Indians doubled their numbers in the twenty years following the 1800–1801 epidemic. Demographically this is feasible. High death rates caused by epidemics and warfare were offset by high birth rates. Smallpox carried off the weaker members of society, especially children who had no immunity from having survived earlier epidemics. The years following an epidemic were probably characterized by lower than average death rates (because the vulnerable had already died), as well as by higher than average birth rates, as individuals tried to restore their families, and societies

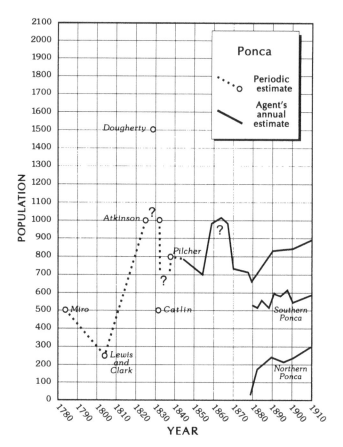

Fig. 8 Ponca Population, 1780–1910

strove to regain their strength.[1] This could only happen, however, if the population was well fed and relatively free from subsequent epidemic diseases.

Even in times less stressful than the aftermath of an epidemic there was a
strong desire to have many children. Children brought aging parents security—
labor in the fields, assistance on the hunts, defense from attack. They were also
treasured for their own sakes as additions to the close and enduring families,
which were the foundation of Indian society. The loss of entire generations of
children from epidemic disease only made this natural tendency for high birth
rates all the more imperative. The birth rate was kept in check by the practice of
breast-feeding children for three or four years (breast-feeding delays, or in-
hibits, ovulation). But even taking this natural check into account, and allowing
for the high infant mortality rates that characterize all premodern societies, a
woman who began child-bearing at the age of fifteen (by which time most
Indian women were married) could raise four children within twenty years.

And, indeed, the average number of children in Pawnee and Omaha families was four to six; in some families there were as many as ten.[2]

Not surprisingly then, the Indians of eastern Nebraska were increasing their populations by 1804. Lewis and Clark specifically noted this for the Otoe and Pawnee, but other early nineteenth-century accounts indicate that the same was true for the other nations. In 1811 John Bradbury estimated that the Omaha could "muster about two hundred warriors," fifty more than Lewis and Clark's total. Bradbury was particularly impressed by the great number of children at the Omaha village, and he concluded that the Omaha were "again increasing." This was despite a savage attack by the Brulé in 1803 that destroyed the village and left seventy-five inhabitants dead. The Ponca were also badly hit by the Brulé in 1803 and forced to abandon Backing Water Village (fig. 5). But again this short-term loss was quickly recouped through high birth rates. Henry Brackenridge, a colleague of Bradbury's, found Backing Water Village rebuilt in 1811 and reoccupied by a Ponca population that was "rapidly increasing."[3]

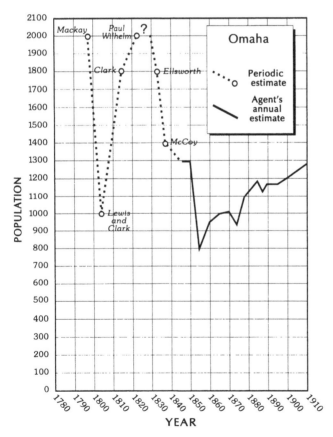

Fig. 9 Omaha Population, 1780–1910

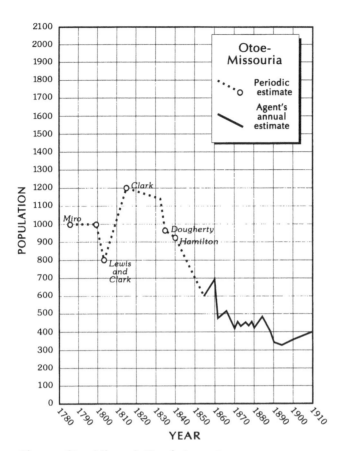

Fig. 10 Otoe-Missouria Population, 1780–1910

According to various estimates, derived mainly from fur traders and Indian agents, the population increase was sustained into the 1820s, when there were as many as one thousand Ponca, about two thousand Omaha, twelve hundred combined Otoe-Missouria, and at least ten thousand Pawnee.[4] This evidence is fragmentary but it suggests populations on the rebound.

The trend of increasing population was reversed during the decade from the early 1820s to the early 1830s. This was a period of transition from the relative security and independence of traditional life to a "dark ages" of fear and uncertainty. A concatenation of disasters struck the Nebraska Indians and sent their populations on a protracted decline. There were brief periods of recovery following the worst disasters, but the general deterioration of living conditions assured that the long-term population trend was downward. For all four nations the population totals reached in the 1820s or early 1830s were the peaks for the entire century (figs. 8 through 11).

By the 1820s the Ponca were increasingly dominated by the Teton Dakota. In one brief battle in October 1824 they were stripped of their leadership. Peter Wilson, on his way to his new post at the Mandan subagency, came across the distraught survivors of this battle near the mouth of the Niobrara. He was told that thirty Ponca, including all of their chiefs, had been returning from a friendly visit to the Oglala when they were attacked by another band of the Teton Dakota. The chiefs, all old men, were unable to flee and were easily killed. Among the dead was the Ponca's principal chief, Smoke Maker (Shu-de-gah-he). Wilson, asserting his new authority, appointed Smoke Maker's son as the new chief, but, in effect, Ponca society had been decapitated.[5]

The Ponca continued to occupy villages near the mouth of the Niobrara during the 1820s. In 1825, for example, Brigadier Henry Atkinson and Benjamin O'Fallon negotiated a treaty of peace with them at Backing Water Village on Brazille Creek, just downstream from where the Niobrara joins the Missouri. At that time there were an estimated one thousand Ponca at the village.[6] But

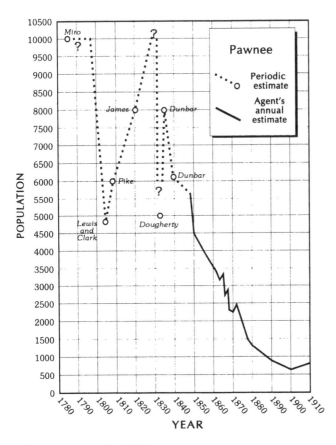

Fig. 11   Pawnee Population, 1780–1910

increased hostilities with the Brulé and Pawnee, together with smallpox in 1831, made living in fixed villages precarious. When Prince Maximilian passed by Brazille Creek in 1833, the only remaining evidence of the Ponca was nine or ten tipis near the mouth and many graves further up. As Maximilian explained, the Ponca had been forced to abandon their settlements and to scatter in small bands along the valley of the Niobrara: "They formerly lived, like the Omahas, in clay huts, at the mouth of the river, but their powerful enemies, the Sioux and the Pawnees, destroyed their villages, and they have since adopted the mode of life of the former, living more generally in tents made of skins, and changing their place from time to time."[7]

Even this drastic measure did not bring the Ponca security. Caught as they were in a shatterbelt between the feuding Teton Dakota and Pawnee, they could find no peace. Finally, in the early 1830s, they sided with the Dakota, and thus against the Pawnee. A Ponca chief who was visiting the Omaha in the summer of 1834 explained the reasoning behind this strategy to Dougherty, who subsequently passed on the information to Clark: "He stated that living as they did, near-neighbors to the Sioux and being few in numbers they would be necessarily obliged to war against the Pawnees, as long as the Sioux did."[8] Thereafter, the Ponca lived for the remainder of the 1830s "exclusively by the chase," according to Joshua Pilcher, gathering only infrequently at the mouth of the Niobrara to plant a little corn or to trade.[9]

At least the Ponca, by virtue of their understanding with the Teton Dakota, still had relatively easy access to the bison, which remained abundant in the region north of the Niobrara and between the Missouri River and the Black Hills. But this access to game, and also government vaccination efforts in 1832 and 1838–39, could not forestall a drop in the Ponca's population to a lower plateau in the 1830s. Following a possible dip to about five hundred people after the 1831 epidemic, their population recovered and remained constant at about 775 to 800 for the remainder of the decade (fig. 8). The most detailed estimate, made by Pilcher in 1837, reveals 800 Ponca, including 300 women, 240 men, and 260 children.[10] The large number of children indicates, of course, the high birth rate. The demographic imbalance between men and women reflects the high mortality rate of the warriors and was the norm in all four Indian societies of eastern Nebraska for much of the troubled nineteenth century.

By the second half of the 1820s, the Ponca's relatives, the Omaha, found themselves surrounded by hostile forces in a country largely depleted of game, and their numbers diminished rapidly (fig. 9). There were two main reasons for this decline. First, the Dakota and other hostile Indians turned the Omaha into refugees by keeping them from their homes on Omaha Creek for much of the 1820s and 1830s. Second, even as early as 1823, as a result of game depletion and disrupted farming, the Omaha were stalked by the specter of famine. These two factors were interconnected. Dougherty understood this when he reported to

Commissioner McKenney in 1827 that the Omaha's lack of food was causing warfare by forcing them to "prowl over the country like so many hungry wolves."[11] The further afield they were forced to travel for bison, the more likely they were to clash with the Dakota on the hunting grounds. Famine was also connected to disease, because poorly fed and inadequately clothed Indians had little resistance.

The Omaha were initially driven from Large Village by the Sauk and Fox in 1820, and they were prevented from returning there until 1833 by the Yankton and Brulé Dakota, who established a suzerainty over northeastern Nebraska by 1830. One portion of the Omaha did attempt to resettle Large Village in 1828–29, but again they were expelled by the Yankton and Sauk. For most of the years in exile they lived in an earth-lodge village on the Elkhorn, near a shallow crossing not far from the modern town of Stanton (fig. 5). In some years in the 1830s, some of the Omaha, at least, may have retreated as far south as Bellevue. Even in exile, however, the Omaha never gave up the hope of returning to their homes on Omaha Creek.

Their main challenge was obtaining sufficient food. Life was too unstable on the Elkhorn to do much farming. They hunted west into the Sand Hills and along the Niobrara in summer, but because of the Dakota threat and the sheer distance to the herds, they were unable to stage large winter hunts. Instead, winters were often spent on the bottomlands along the Missouri, where fuel, small game, and fish were available. The Omaha also hunted to the east of the Missouri in 1828 and 1832, but there they had to contend with the Yankton, Sauk and Fox, and more than two thousand transplanted Potawatomie, Ottawa, and Chippewa. They did raise crops successfully at Large Village. In 1836 they had an estimated 250 acres under cultivation and produced ten thousand bushels of corn, as well as a "large quantity" of beans and pumpkins. The following year the Omaha harvested an estimated twelve to fourteen thousand bushels of corn from three hundred acres. But, according to Dougherty, "breadstuff" was all they had, because the local game was completely depleted, and the distant game was too dangerous to obtain.[12]

Like the other Nebraska Indians, the Omaha were struck by smallpox in 1831–32 and 1837–38, with unknown losses. In 1835 cholera took at least 180 Omaha lives. In addition to mortalities from disease and the conflicts with the Dakota and Sauk and Fox, the Omaha also suffered losses in a "serious war" with their erstwhile friends, the Pawnee, in the fall in 1831. This was a war started and prolonged by young men from both nations.[13] Petty disputes with the Iowa and Otoe-Missouria added to the turmoil.

By 1833, according to Prince Maximilian, this attrition through war, famine, and disease had left the Omaha "quite powerless and insignificant."[14] Their population of at least two thousand in 1823 was reduced to eighteen hundred in 1833 and fourteen hundred in 1836 (fig. 9).[15] The Omaha's main advantage in surviving these dark days was their chief, Big Elk, a paternal leader who held office from about 1811 to 1843. "I must take care of my people," Big Elk told Henry Ellsworth in 1833, adding, "They are factious without me."[16] There were signs of divisiveness among the Omaha, mainly over the question of where to live. Ellsworth noted this in his letter to Commissioner Herring in 1833, for example. But Big Elk retained respect and control, and the Omaha, unlike the other Nebraska Indian societies, did not cleave apart by 1840.

Big Elk was recognized by American authorities as the "most progressive" of the Nebraska Indian chiefs. He had visited Washington, D.C., in 1837–38, and on his return he warned his people of the changing world that confronted them. He urged the Omaha to prepare for these changes by settling down to permanent farming. He even told Ellsworth that the "Great Father" could choose the place for them, as long as he furnished "cattle, potatoes, implements, and teachers." Because of this compliant attitude, the Omaha early gained a reputation with Americans as a "well disposed little tribe," a reputation that endured. The same compliance, however, earned the Omaha a quite different (and undeserved) reputation with their neighbors: "Among the other Indians," the Duke of Wurttemberg wrote, "the Omaha are reputed to be cowardly."[17]

There was no such cohesion in Otoe-Missouria society, which lost its leadership and splintered into a number of different factions by 1840. The main stresses were lack of access to food and too easy an access to Americans. Like the Omaha, the Otoe-Missouria were cut off from their sources of meat by 1830. Their options were to travel far to the west and face the danger of the Dakota, Cheyenne, and Arapahoe, to range south for elk and deer and risk clashing with the Kansa and Osage, or to compete with the Potawatomie for what was left of the game to the east of the Missouri River. Scarcity of meat was compounded by inconsistent agricultural production. Potentially, the Otoe-Missouria could raise twelve thousand bushels of corn a year, as well as beans, squash, and pumpkins.[18] But life at the village was too disrupted by the ravages of poverty and alcohol for there to be any assurance of a stable supply of crops. An ongoing enmity with the Osage and the two smallpox epidemics of the 1830s added to the turmoil. In most years after 1830 a large proportion of the Otoe-Missouria's food came from gathered roots and plants, government donations of corn, and thefts of potatoes and other vegetables from the mission garden.

The year 1836 was typical. There was no carry-over of food from the previous year, and the spring found the Otoe-Missouria "destitute of provisions." Crops were planted, and at the end of May the Indians scattered in search of game. Most went west to the bison range, some went south to hunt deer and elk, and "a few" crossed the Missouri to look for deer. The parties came in at the end of July with "little or no meat." In August the cattle that had been issued in accordance with the 1833 treaty destroyed most of the corn crop, and the

Indians starved for the rest of the year. Meanwhile, on at least four occasions in the late summer and fall, Iowa Indians crossed the river and traded whiskey for horses, which only further impaired the Otoe-Missouria's ability to conduct successful hunts.[19]

Under these constant pressures of famine, disease, war, and social chaos, the population of the Otoe-Missouria dropped from about 1,200 in the 1820s to 964 in 1836 (fig. 10). Although there is a dearth of reliable estimates from Clark's enumeration in 1816 until Dougherty's "Statistical Return" in 1836, it is reasonable to assume a gradual decline in numbers during the late 1820s as food became scarcer, and a significant drop in 1831–32 as a result of smallpox. The rather slow decline from 1836 to 1840, when Agent Joseph Hamilton reported 943 Otoe-Missouria, reflects the Indians' high birth rate and, perhaps, the measure of protection afforded by the smallpox vaccination in 1832 and 1839.[20] In the latter year 575 Otoe-Missouria, including 455 children, were inoculated.[21] This figure indicates that almost half of the population were children.

The stress of such wretched living conditions widened the divisions within Otoe-Missouria society. The most serious division was between the Otoe and the Missouria. The United States' policy was to blend these two peoples. In 1819, for example, at a council attended by the explorer Stephen Long and Agent Benjamin O'Fallon, only the Otoe were recognized as chiefs of the nation: "No chief was acknowledged among the Missourias," Long explained, "as it is the wish of Major O'Fallon to extinguish as much as possible national prejudices between the two nations or tribes."[22] Financial considerations were no doubt part of this strategy, because it was less costly to deal with one nation than with two.

But this was an inherent societal fault line, and it widened in the 1830s. Amid escalating violence in 1837, Merrill wrote in his diary, "It appears that a grudge has long subsisted in the breasts of some against that part of the tribe called Missouri." In particular, Nehlhunca, the second chief of the Otoe, opposed the Missouria. By late winter of 1839, the schism was complete, and the Missouria withdrew to form a separate village on the south side of the Platte, near its junction with the Missouri.[23]

Lines of fracture also ran through the Otoe. As early as 1823 the Duke of Wurttemberg observed that the Otoe chiefs could not control their people. The Duke's party was continuously harassed by beggars and thieves, and the Duke also noted that whiskey was readily available at the village.[24] This collapse of authority came to a head on April 28, 1837, with the death of the principal chief, Ietan. A few weeks previously, two young Otoe had absconded with two of Ietan's five wives. Ietan swore revenge. On April 28 the two young men returned to the village, singing a war song as a challenge. In the ensuing battle, which involved allies on both sides, fourteen shots were fired. Ietan and his two rivals died that night.

The society was cleaved to its very roots: "One part are eager to revenge the death of their chief," Merrill wrote, "the other part are equally eager to revenge the death of the young men." It was more than a factional feud, he added, because "in some instances the same family are divided on the subject."[25] Two of the three remaining chiefs tried in vain to restore order, and many people fled to avoid death. Ietan had never been a leader of Big Elk's caliber, and he probably owed his preeminent position to the traders, but his death marked the end of any semblance of unity among the Otoe-Missouria. They entered the decade of the 1840s without effective leadership, and with little else to hold them together as a nation.

Unlike the other Nebraska Indians, the four bands of the Pawnee remained powerful and confident throughout the 1820s. Dougherty, writing to the secretary of war in 1827, described them as "without doubt the most powerful and most important tribes that inhabit our frontier." Their attacks on the Santa Fe Trail and the Mexican settlements on the upper Rio Grande were so frequent in the early 1820s that the governor of Santa Fe threatened to declare war if the United States did not restrain them. The attacks continued. In 1828 Dougherty informed Clark that the Pawnee were becoming "daily more and more outrageous" along the Santa Fe Trail. Dougherty added, "they have great confidence in their own strength, believing themselves to be more numerous, warlike and brave than any other nation on earth." Expressing the same self-assurance, the Kitkahahki chief Schak-ru-leschar told the Duke of Wurttemberg that his nation "numbered as many heads as the stars in the sky."[26]

This all changed in the smallpox winter of 1831–32. The Pawnee population was halved, to about five or six thousand people (fig. 11). Young people under the age of thirty-three died in disproportionately high numbers because smallpox had not struck the Pawnee since 1798 (or 1800), and those born since then had no immunity.[27] The Dakota immediately took advantage of the Pawnee's misfortune. The first raid on a Pawnee village was made on the Skiri in the fall of 1832. With only seven guns between them, the Skiri were no match for the well-armed raiders. Nineteen Skiri were killed and many possessions stolen.[28] From this time on, until they were forced from Nebraska to Indian Territory in 1874–75, the Pawnee lived in fear of Dakota attack.

The attacks came on two fronts. Oglala and Brulé raiding parties struck the Pawnee villages whenever opportune. Women working in distant fields were particularly vulnerable. The Pawnee's horses—Dunbar estimated that there were six thousand of them in 1835—were a major attraction for the Dakota and their subordinated allies, the Ponca.[29] In 1836, for example, Dougherty reported that the Dakota and Ponca were "constantly hanging around the Pawnee villages taking or losing a scalp." Since the previous fall twenty Pawnee had been killed in these raids and two hundred horses stolen.[30]

The second front was the western bison range. After 1830 the Oglala made a concerted effort to wrest control of the North Platte hunting grounds from the Pawnee, most specifically from the Skiri, who customarily wintered there. "They are crowding in on their buffalo lands, above the Platte," Dougherty wrote in his 1838 report. The Pawnee, Dougherty continued, were determined to "contend for every inch of ground" because they understood that it was a fight for survival. By 1839, however, the Pawnee had effectively surrendered the North Platte bison country to the Dakota. Meanwhile, to the south, the Cheyenne, Kansa, and Delaware were contesting for the bison range along the upper Republican and Smoky Hill rivers.[31]

The Dakota's greatest ally in their territorial war was disease, particularly smallpox. The Dakota actually had lower immunity to smallpox than the village Indians, because they had been afflicted less in the past, but their mobile and decentralized existence meant that when epidemics did strike, the effect was likely to be localized. The Pawnee, on the other hand, with their densely populated villages, were ripe for disease. Influenza and whooping cough were prevalent at the villages in the mid-1830s; then in the winter of 1837–38 smallpox struck again. The Skiri brought the disease back to their village with twenty captive Oglala women and children. Within days all but three or four of the captives were dead from smallpox. The disease spread to the Skiri children who had been born after the 1832 epidemic. Soon "multitudes of children" in all of the villages had smallpox, and, in Dunbar's opinion, "the greater part of them died with it."[32] In the following October, a Doctor John Gray vaccinated 870 Pawnee, including 460 infants. Gray found that virtually every child over three and all the adults showed signs of having had the disease.[33]

These recurring epidemics and the constant warfare brought the Pawnee's population down from about 8,000 in 1835 to 6,244 in 1840 (fig. 11). The latter figure is an actual count taken by Dunbar, who also gave a demographic breakdown of the population. The profile was skewed, with about three females for every two males over the age of ten and a preponderance—fully 45 percent of the total—of children (table 5). Presumably, most of those children would have been born after the 1837–38 epidemic, and there would have been a lost cohort of three- to eight-year-olds.[34]

The Pawnee were in a terrible quandary. The United States was insisting that they should move north of the Platte, in compliance with the 1833 treaty; but north of the Platte they were particularly vulnerable to Dakota attack. Moreover, the government's injunction that they should live in peace with their neighbors placed them in an impossible position. Dunbar observed that the Pawnee men felt worthless because they were being restrained from their "proper business" of raiding and hunting. A Skiri chief, visiting Bellevue to collect annuities in 1834, expressed his people's frustration: "How can they

Table 5 Pawnee Demography, 1840

Band	Males over 10	Females over 10	Males under 10	Females under 10	Population of each Band
Skiri	469	598	367	472	1,906
Kitkahahki	404	609	371	439	1,823
Chaui	330	563	416	472	1,683
Pitahawirata	246	315	134	137	832
Totals for all Bands	1,449	2,085	1,288	1,520	6,244

Source: Dunbar to Greene, July 13, 1840, *The Dunbar-Allis Letters* 700

be peaceful," he asked Dougherty, "when immigrant Indians and Sioux are raiding?" Pleas for peace were "very useless" in those circumstances, he told Dougherty.[35]

The dilemma over whether to accede to government demands or stay south of the Platte, using the river as protection against the Dakota, left the Pawnee chiefs divided. Some of the Pitahawirata even wanted to move one hundred miles further up the Platte, presumably to be nearer the bison herds. Dunbar was given the responsibility of arranging the relocation to the north bank of the Loup, where there was adequate, if not abundant, timber and good soils. The Skiri and some of the Pitahawirata were already there, and most Chaui supported the move. Some of the Chaui, however, chose to stay at their long-established and well-defended village on the south bank, opposite the present-day site of Clarks, Nebraska. Moreover, a segment of the Kitkahahki under the leadership of Capot Bleu had only just built a "fine village" of twenty-nine lodges on the south side of the Platte, four miles up from the Chaui village. Under the circumstances, Dunbar wrote, it was "not strange" that Capot Bleu did not want to move again.

By 1839, according to a map drawn by Dunbar, the Pawnee had splintered into six villages in two general locations (fig. 12). Four of these villages were populated by factions of the Kitkahahki. This decentralization may have been in response to diminishing timber supplies around their old village on the Loup, but the Kitkahahki also seem to have been the most volatile of the Pawnee bands, with a warlike coterie of young men, so the conditions were there for the development of factions.[36] This tension between the impetus to divide into smaller villages because of social or ecological stress, and the need to congregate in fewer, larger villages for the purposes of defense, would only increase in the 1840s as the Pawnee were beleaguered from all sides.

The Dark Years, 1840–54

In 1847 or 1848 an Omaha chief lamented to the Reverend McKinney: "We have had a dark time. The clouds came down alone to us. They pressed on our heads."[37] This heartfelt sorrow was not limited to the Omaha but shared by all the Indians of eastern Nebraska. Since 1840 the old pressures had intensified, and new ones, including the swelling stream of emigrants along the Platte, had been added. The trend of population for all four societies was relentlessly downward, but the specific impact varied as each nation coped in its own way with the accumulating stress.

As the Ponca dispersed west along the Niobrara in the 1840s, living on bison, smaller game, and collected fruits, roots, and plants, so they virtually disappear from the historical record.[38] Reports from the Upper Missouri Agency, a vast jurisdiction which also supervised the several bands of the Dakota, Crow, and

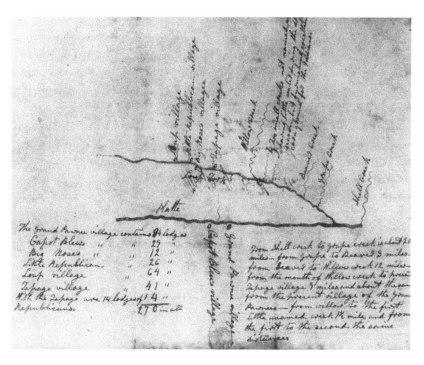

Fig. 12   Dunbar's Map of the Pawnee Villages, 1839. From Dunbar to Joseph Hamilton, October 1839, LR, Upper Missouri Agency, 1836–51. Courtesy of Nebraska State Historical Society, RG 508

Blackfeet, rarely mentioned the Ponca. Fur trade licenses that had previously been issued for the accessible mouth of the Niobrara now bore the general description "Niobrara," suggesting that the traders rendezvoused with Ponca at various distant points along the river. The traders, mostly illiterate and more interested in profits than ethnography, left few records. Ponca country remained remote from the main thrust of the American frontier, which was spearheaded in northwestern Missouri and funneled west along the Platte, more than one hundred miles to the south. The Ponca attracted few visitors; they did not even see a missionary until 1848 when the "Black Robe," Father Pierre-Jean De Smet, briefly visited and baptized their children.[39]

The sparse and contradictory data that do exist suggest that the Ponca's population fell from about eight hundred to seven hundred people from 1837 to 1855 (fig. 8). The relatively gradual population loss among the Ponca indicates that they fared better than any of the other Nebraska Indians during this period. The population decline was probably most evident after 1845, when the Ponca found it increasingly difficult to get access to the bison herds. Under pressure of the fur trade, the herds were thinning on the formerly abundant range along the Niobrara. More than one hundred thousand robes were traded each year in the 1840s by the Indians of the Upper Missouri Agency. In 1853 alone, according to Agent A. J. Vaughan, four hundred thousand bison were killed on the northern Great Plains. Increasingly the bison were also being killed by Americans who often took only their tongues (considered a delicacy) and left the rest of the animal to rot.[40] For the Ponca, therefore, like the Omaha and Otoe-Missouria before them, the bison became a progressively scarcer, more distant, and more keenly contested resource.

The Ponca's access to the herds was contingent on the Dakota. The various bands of the Dakota were autonomous groups, aggregates of closely related families whose attitudes to the outside world were set by their leaders, men who earned their positions through war. To be tolerated by one band did not necessarily mean acceptance by another. So the Ponca's relationship with the Dakota was capricious: at various times during the 1840s Ponca warriors joined Dakota parties to raid the Pawnee and Omaha; at other times the Ponca themselves were targets of Dakota aggression.

Their relationship seems to have deteriorated in the early 1840s. By 1842 the Ponca had reactivated their village near the mouth of the Niobrara.[41] Most likely, the Dakota had cut them off from the bison range and forced them to turn back to corn farming for their food. This would have been a reluctant concession to necessity, because, as Father De Smet later observed, the Ponca were "by taste attached to the wandering life." Further evidence of their hostilities came in April 1843, when a Ponca chief, visiting Bellevue, told Daniel Miller that his people wanted to sell some of their land for guns and ammunition so that they could fight the Dakota. Miller also learned from the chief that the Omaha and Ponca were considering a union, "to live together as one people." No doubt this was a defensive strategy against the Dakota. Within a few years, however, plans for the union (or reunion, as it would have been) were forgotten, and the Ponca again joined the Dakota to raid the Omaha.[42]

Sometimes in the company of Dakota, sometimes alone, the Ponca frequently raided Pawnee villages. In the summer of 1845, for example, while most of the Pawnee were away on their bison hunt, Ponca raiding parties struck several times, stealing horses, killing cattle, destroying fields. One Ponca warrior even took a shot at Mrs. Allis. As the Reverend Dunbar well understood, in the chaotic years of the 1840s when starvation confronted all the Indians, warfare became the primary means of spreading the subsistence base.[43] It was a way to get horses so that increasingly distant bison hunts could be made and a method of obtaining corn when life was too disrupted to grow it. Warfare was also, of course, a means of destroying the enemy's subsistence base by pillaging their caches and burning their lodges, thus impairing their ability to compete for the bison.

By the second half of the 1840s the Ponca were again spending more time in tipi encampments and earth-lodge villages near the mouth of the Niobrara. According to De Smet, this was their "favorite haunt during the fruit season and the gathering of the corn harvest," which implies a return to their earlier, dual economy of farming and hunting.[44] The Ponca, or at least two hundred of them, spent the winter of 1846–47 in several camps located between the Niobrara and Brazille Creek (fig. 5). Again, this immobility at a time when they would usually have been out on their winter hunt was probably in response to Dakota competition on the bison range. The Ponca used a clever strategy to secure their encampments during that winter. They persuaded two hundred Mormons, whom they had met near the Pawnee villages, to stay with them on the Niobrara. As the Ponca agent pointed out, the Mormons provided a measure of protection against Dakota war parties. Their possession of a small canon seems to have been particularly influential in the Ponca's decision to extend the invitation. For their part, the Mormons were pleased to be able to winter in what they considered to be a "country of verdure" with plenty of feed, timber, and (surprisingly) game.[45]

Even though the Ponca's position, hemmed in as they were between the powerful forces of the Dakota and Pawnee, was precarious, it does not seem to have cowed them. They had a reputation as a "brave, warlike people" and were considered to be among the best hunters and horsemen on the Plains. Their warlike attitude was also extended to Americans. In the spring of 1848, for example, a party of Ponca came into Bellevue full of bravado and boasting that if troops were sent to keep them in order they would "take their [the troops'] pants off."[46]

By the early 1850s a schism had developed among the Ponca. In the spring of

1852 Charles Larpenteur, a veteran of the fur trade, was sent to manage Peter Sarpy's trading post ("a very poor establishment," he called it) at the junction of the Niobrara and Missouri rivers. Used to "large tribes of Indians and to big trades," Larpenteur was dismissive of the Ponca, "a small tribe who made but few robes," and he stayed only one year. During that time, however, he made important observations on Ponca life on the eve of the Kansas-Nebraska Act. The Ponca were divided into two groups, each with its own village. The villages were differentiated by clan affiliation, which ran like a grain in wood through the population. One settlement, Grey Blanket Village (Wáin-xùde) was located on the northwest bank of the Niobrara (fig. 5). The principal chief there was The Whip (Wégasàpi). The second was Fish Smell Village (Húbdon), located near the mouth of Ponca Creek and reputedly so called because its inhabitants relied so much on fish for food that they smelled of it. The chief at Fish Smell Village was The Drum. The two chiefs were jealous of each other, and hostility was simmering between the two divisions. Larpenteur also noted that the Ponca were no longer remote from the frontier. By 1853, settlers were "coming in fast" to the adjacent country to the east of the Missouri, in the recently created state of Iowa (1846) and territory of Minnesota (1849).[47]

The Omaha continued to live as refugees during the 1840s and early 1850s. In the decade and a half preceding the Kansas-Nebraska Act, they managed to live on or near Omaha Creek for only brief periods in 1841, 1843–44, and 1846–87. Each attempt to return to their homeland was thwarted by the Dakota, who, in an avowed war of extermination, took every opportunity to kill the Omaha and destroy their lodges and cornfields. The Ponca joined the Dakota war party that killed seventy-three Omaha in the winter of 1846–47. Despite the hazards, the Omaha never gave up on their attachment to Large Village. It was home: the hills above were the resting place of their ancestors, there was plenty of timber in the Blackbird Hills and on the Missouri flood plain, and there was easy access to the river for the purposes of trade. By comparison, their alternative settlement sites left much to be desired.

When the Omaha were driven from Omaha Creek in the spring of 1841, they retreated to the Elkhorn, though further south than their customary refuge (fig. 5). But they were too unsettled there to put down roots; they continued to live in tipis rather than build earth lodges, and they grew no corn.[48] Moreover, even on the Elkhorn, only fifty miles from Bellevue, they were vulnerable to Dakota attack. So they retreated further south and in 1845 established a tipi and earthlodge village on a hill between the forks of Papio (Papillion) Creek, about six miles west of Bellevue. Except for the abortive attempt to return to Omaha Creek in 1846, they occupied the village on Papio Creek (Pathúthoudathon) until 1854. This site was more secure, and in some years (1849, for example) they managed to grow a good corn crop, but there were problems. The Omaha suffered badly from homesickness, and influenza and malaria were endemic, the former particularly in the winter, the latter in late summer and early fall. They were close to the whiskey dealers, and drinking became widespread. The Reverend McKinney, who ran the Omaha mission at Bellevue, was told by the Omaha that they were drinking "to forget their sorrows." Finally, the Otoe-Missouria objected to the Omaha settling on land which they regarded as their own, and threatened to expel them. Superintendent Harvey held a council with the Omaha and Otoe-Missouria in 1846, and the Omaha were allowed to remain in the disputed territory, but it is evident that they never felt at home there.[49]

In most years they were unable to get sufficient meat to sustain them. Superintendent Mitchell was of the opinion that their country was "more destitute of game than any other."[50] The thousands of Mormons who passed through and camped on their land after 1847 depleted any game that was left. But even when the bison herds did come close, as in the winter of 1846–47, the Omaha were too afraid of the Dakota to venture out for the hunt. Most of their horses had been stolen, which cut down on the distance they could travel and the amount of meat and robes they could haul back. They traded few robes and furs, so they had no guns or ammunition. They hardly had any robes for themselves, and often went virtually unclothed. Their only known successful bison hunts during this period were made through temporary alliances: they hunted with the Skiri in 1842 with some success, and in 1844, the year they broke off plans to unite with the Ponca, they established a brief truce with the Brulé or Yankton and hunted in Dakota country. All this time they pleaded with the United States to protect them from the Dakota, or at least to give them guns and ammunition so that they could defend themselves. The United States offered plenty of sympathy to this "well-disposed little tribe" but nothing more substantial.[51]

Their day-to-day living conditions were abysmal. After the Dakota drove them from the Blackbird Hills in the summer of 1845, they survived on roots with "now and then a stray racoon or muskrat."[52] In 1847–48 they were again living on roots, and Harvey told Commissioner Medill that if emergency rations were not sent, the Omaha would soon be "extinct." They were hit badly by smallpox in 1851, venereal disease was rife, and many of the old people were blind. Sick, hungry, and afraid, the Omaha's distress was unremitting. Their population fell drastically, from fourteen hundred in the late 1830s to eight hundred in 1855 (fig. 9). A large proportion of their people were children, suggesting a continued high birth rate, but the women's fertility was probably being impaired by disease and malnutrition, so the ability to recoup losses was fast disappearing.[53]

The Omaha continued to petition the United States to buy their lands so that they could have an annuity, guns, and farming equipment. They made this request in 1842, 1843, 1845, and again in 1847, pleading that they could not "exist as a nation without assistance from their Great Father." In 1845, Superintendent

Harvey recommended that the government purchase the disputed territory north of the Platte, between the Elkhorn and the Missouri, to furnish funds for the Omaha's support.[54] Nothing came of this plan, and the Omaha continued to live in abject poverty, without annuities or any other government support. Finally, in 1853, the Indian Office authorized five thousand dollars' worth of emergency funds for farming. That year the Omaha raised a good corn crop, enough to get them through the winter, and Agent James Gatewood reported that they were doing "moderately well considering their circumstances." For the Omaha, the worst years of the century were almost behind, and the gradual process of rebuilding their population lay ahead.[55]

The fact that Omaha society did not splinter into factions under all this stress can again be attributed to strong leadership. Big Elk was succeeded by his son (also named Big Elk) possibly in 1843. The son seems to have emulated his father in ability and attitude. Shortly before his death in 1853, he visited Washington, D.C., and returned with the pragmatic view that they must prepare for the "coming flood." This flood, he sadly told his people, would sweep away everything they had known, and he urged them to accept the new order, but to do so with dignity and in unity: "Speak kindly to one another," he urged. "Do what you can to help each other, even in the troubles with the coming tide."[56] The Omaha would divide into factions in the years to come, but Big Elk had charted a course toward accommodation with the United States, and the "progressive" element remained a significant force in the society. Consequently, the United States continued to regard the Omaha favorably; as Harvey put it in 1845, "They have ever been friends of the whites."[57]

The Otoe-Missouria, on the other hand, were regarded quite differently by Americans. They were, as Lieutenant Henry Carlton wrote in 1844, "considered to be the most rascally Indians in the West."[58] Their agent, Daniel Miller, was of the same opinion. Their abject poverty and social disintegration (following Ietan's death) produced a state of lawlessness at their villages and a hostility toward Americans. In 1843 two Otoe fired on an American boat on the Missouri, severely wounding one man. The culprits were taken to Leavenworth in chains, where one escaped and the other was killed in the attempt.[59] The Otoe were reprimanded in council and told that any further depredations would be penalized by deductions from their annuities. But they remained hostile throughout the 1840s. Even the missionaries were not able to live among them: "It would be the next thing to madness," McKinney wrote in 1847, "to put yourself in the power of the tribes."[60]

The chaos at the Otoe village and the Indians' antagonism toward Americans were products of a lacerating poverty which had deepened steadily since the 1820s and which had torn the society to pieces. A dramatic incident which took place "on about the first of February, 1841" reveals the extent of their desperation. According to David Miller, some Otoe, "in a moment of drunkenness and riot," set fire to their village and "reduced it to ashes." The government field, adjacent to the village, was similarly destroyed. The Otoe withdrew to the south side of the Platte, where they split apart into four groups, each with its own village (fig. 5). Miller tried to persuade them to return to the old site, but they refused, because they believed that an "evil spirit hovered over and around them" at the tainted village where Ietan had been killed.[61] It is possible that this division was a logical decentralization, an attempt to allocate their population out to scarce resources like timber; but it is much more likely, given the factionalism which had surfaced in the late 1830s, that the society was breaking apart under the various pressures of American contact.

Alcohol was both a symptom and a cause of this decline: a symptom because of the temporary escape it offered, a cause because the Otoe-Missouria continued to trade their meager wealth for it. Consequently, they had few horses and virtually no guns and ammunition. Without horses they could not hunt; without guns and ammunition they were unable to survive by raiding their neighbors' supplies, and they were easy targets for Dakota or Osage attack. Their lives were so disrupted, and their energy so low, that they were unable to make up for the lack of meat by raising agricultural production. Natural disasters, like the floods of 1844 and 1849, which washed out their crops, also conspired against them. Malaria ("autumnal fevers"), influenza, and, in 1851, smallpox, raged among the weakened Indians.[62] Their population, never large, continued on its steep decline, from 940 in 1840 to 600 in 1855 (fig. 10).

The years 1842 and 1843 were typical. The harvests in 1842 did not produce enough food to see the Otoe-Missouria through the winter. Heavy snows fell in November and prevented them from leaving for their winter hunt. By December they were reduced to eating the thatch off their lodges to stay alive (presumably big bluestem hay, boiled into a thin soup). Large numbers of people, especially children, died of starvation. In the spring of 1843, Agent Miller obtained emergency rations—22 barrels of pork, 995 bushels of corn, and 15 barrels of flour—but these only lasted until June. The Indians' hostility seethed, and the agency's blacksmith and his assistant fled the vicinity "in fear for their lives."[63]

More than any of the Nebraska Indians at this time, the Otoe-Missouria relied on the United States for their survival. They still received the annual annuity payments from the 1833 treaty, and would continue to do so until 1850, and they were given more gratuitous support, in the form of emergency food, than the Ponca, Omaha, or Pawnee. But this support was a poor substitute for their former, now depleted, resource base. The provision that they would receive five hundred dollars a year for ten years to assist agriculture (Article 5 in the 1833 treaty) was never carried out, nor was the promised corn mill erected. Efforts to teach them farming, according to Agent Gatewood in 1853, had been "misdirected."[64] Moreover, the government, in its drive to make the Otoe-

Missouria into self-sufficient farmers, was concerned about sending too much emergency aid. Superintendent Harvey, asking for rations to keep the Indians alive in 1844, felt obliged to assure Commissioner Crawford that the amount of the relief was not so much as to produce an overreliance on the government.[65]

The society remained fragmented into at least four units, each with its own village, for the remainder of the 1840s. By 1847, according to Agent John Miller, three "bands" were living together in a single village on the north side of the Platte, near the site of the old village. Each of these bands had its own chief, but they all recognized Big Kaw as the principal chief and rightful successor to Ietan. Three other divisions, one of them Missouria, occupied separate villages on the south bank of the Platte. The south bands were jealous of Big Kaw's village because they too wanted the government services (farmers, blacksmiths, and equipment) that were provided north of the river. In the late summer of 1847, however, three hundred to four hundred Dakota swept down on Big Kaw's village, burning it to the ground, and leaving twenty-eight Otoe dead. The frightened survivors once again retreated across the river.[66]

In 1853 the Otoe and Missouria were still living on the south side of the Platte, just up from where it joins the Missouri. It was no longer possible for them to survive by hunting, and their farming output was going down, contrary to the government's hopes and plans. They had sold everything—guns, horses, robes—for food, and they had nothing left to sell.[67] Their population was declining so rapidly that it seemed likely they would become extinct. Meanwhile, only a few miles away on the east side of the Missouri, settlers' cabins nestled in the bluffs, looking out over the deforested flood plain to the next available land.[68]

The frontier also caught up with the once-remote Pawnee in the 1840s, in the form of the burgeoning stream of emigrants along the north and south sides of the Platte, right through the heart of their country. The trails became lines of friction between starving Pawnee and nervous, often contemptuous, emigrants. The Pawnee gained a reputation, widely published in the emigrant guidebooks, as a hostile and treacherous people. In actuality, they were too ravaged by poverty to be a serious threat. Most incidents were minor, involving begging or thefts. The few fatalities that did occur were mostly after 1850, when the volume of the migration increased, and they all seem to have been Pawnee. In one incident in 1852, for example, Charachaush, the aged head chief of the nation, was seriously wounded, and his wife killed, by emigrants, as they approached to beg for food.[69]

The Pawnee most involved in "depredations" along the Oregon Trail were the Kitkahahki and Chaui living south of the Platte. Siracherish's band of Chaui was particularly notorious.[70] These Indians were, in Dunbar's estimation, the "ill-disposed and unmanageable part of the tribe," meaning that they refused to settle down near his mission on the Loup and continued to raid widely.[71] They chose to stay south of the Platte, in contradiction to the 1833 treaty and despite the lack of trees, for a number of reasons: it was convenient for launching raids on the Santa Fe Trail and Indian settlements on the southern plains; it was closer (with two fewer rivers to cross) to the still viable bison range along the upper Republican, Solomon, and Smoky Hill rivers; and it was a little removed from the regular orbit of Dakota raids. Moreover, for many of these Indians, opposition to American policy was a motivation in itself. The warriors did not want to give up hunting and raiding, the very activities which gave them their wealth and status. Like Wild Warrior, a Kitkahahki brave, they "thirsted for the blood" of their enemies, and would not be restrained by American mandate from taking it.[72]

The south bank Pawnee also engaged in an "unhappy feud" with those bands which had, at Dunbar's exhortation, built their villages on the Loup.[73] The South Bands raided the mission village twice in 1845, killing stock. By 1847, employees at the mission and nearby farm were almost as afraid of the South Bands as they were of the Dakota. Dunbar attributed their hostility to jealousy, because government services and annuities were only delivered to the north of the Loup: "They do such mischief from spite," he wrote, though he conceded that perhaps the raids were also caused by hunger.[74] They were probably also related to the south villagers' contempt for those Pawnee who were willing to accede to American demands. This division, a geographical and social expression of different responses to violent change, persisted at least until all the Pawnee bands were driven south of the Platte in the late 1840s and forced to coalesce.

By the summer of 1843 more than half of the Pawnee were living on the north bank of the Loup (fig. 5). The mission, built at the mouth of Plum (Council) Creek in 1840–41, was the focus of the new settlements. A new village of combined Chaui, Pitahawirata, and Kitkahahki bands was built only one mile away. Important leaders like Charachaush, Big Axe of the Pitahawirata, and Capot Bleu of the Kitkahahki moved with their followers to the Plum Creek village from 1842 to 1843. Three miles further up the Loup, at the mouth of Willow (Cedar) Creek, sat the large and heavily fortified Skiri village. A few lodges of Kitkahahki lived with the Skiri. Dunbar hoped that these settlements would become the nucleus of a changed Pawnee society—a Christianized, sedentary, farming community. And indeed, in the spring of 1843 the Pawnee women, and even some men, commenced farming with what was said to be "great zeal."[75]

Then, in one single, bloody attack, the Dakota virtually put an end to the Plum Creek village and to Dunbar's acculturation program. On June 27, 1843, as many as five hundred mounted and well-armed Dakota attacked the village just before dawn. The massacre took place in full sight of Dunbar and others at the mission. The poorly armed Pawnee retreated and took refuge in one section of the village, while Dakota burned the lodges behind them and drove off the horses. The Skiri, afraid for their own lives, stood and watched the drama unfold, a betrayal that was not forgotten for generations. At eleven o'clock a detachment of Chaui from south of the Platte rode in to help, their deep animosity toward the Dakota clearly overriding any ill feelings to other Pawnee. The battle raged for another hour, the Pawnee retaliating against the mounted warriors from the tops of their lodges. When the fighting ended at noon, sixty-seven Pawnee were dead, many more wounded, and two hundred horses lost. The dead included the "best and bravest men of the tribe," among them Big Axe and Capot Bleu. Also in this number were many women and children, killed in flight from the lodges to the river.[76]

The Pawnee hastily buried the dead and withdrew to the south of the Platte. Some moved into the south Chaui village, others eventually returned to live with the Skiri on Willow Creek. Capot Bleu's band, especially, "became scattered by mingling with the other branches of the tribe." During the following year, the dislocated Indians returned to the destroyed village to salvage possessions, and, perhaps, to harvest the untended crops. But to Dunbar they seemed "wonderfully timid," afraid of both the Dakota and of a place so steeped in death. When Wharton's expedition passed through the village in 1844, the lodges had almost disappeared into the earth, and the once-busy streets were clogged with grass and sunflowers.[77]

A few years later, in 1846 or 1847, the Dakota attacked the Skiri village, and they and the other bands at Willow Creek also scattered in tipi encampments along the south side of the Platte. The abandonment of the mission in 1846, because of escalating violence, signaled the end of this phase, at least, of the Loup resettlement plans.

But not even the south side of the Platte was safe from the Dakota. In the summer of 1849, about the same time that cholera struck, they attacked and burned the south Chaui village. Now all the Pawnee were homeless. By 1851, when the Moravian missionaries Gottlieb Oehler and David Smith visited the Pawnee to offer their services, the Indians had regrouped into two villages (fig. 5). The Skiri and Pitahawirata were living in an eighty-lodge village on the south side of the Platte, near their Pa:haku sacred site. Within a year of the missionaries' visit a second Skiri village, along with communities of Kitkahahki and Chaui, had been built nearby. The largest Pawnee village in 1851 was on the old eighteenth-century Skull Creek site, and was occupied by Chaui and Kitkahahki.[78] Ironically, and tragically, the Pawnee had been driven eastward toward the American frontier, just as the area was about to be opened to settlers.

Starvation and disease stalked the Pawnee to all their locations. The disasters piled up on each other, interacting to produce an accumulating poverty. Any succession of seasons from the 1840s and early 1850s could be chosen to show the depth of the Pawnee's distress. For example, from 1847 to 1850, the Pawnee not only saw their villages destroyed, but also experienced severe famine, violence on their hunts, and a terrible epidemic.[79] On their winter hunt in 1847–48 the Skiri were attacked by Dakota at the forks of the Platte, and thirty-two Skiri were killed. Only 150 bison—barely enough for the ceremonial feasts—were taken by all the bands that winter. There were no stores of corn to fall back on, because the Indians had been too unsettled to see a harvest through to fruition. So the spring and summer of 1848 found the Pawnee living on roots. The women's time and energy was spent collecting wild potatoes to fend off starvation in the short run, so there was no opportunity to plant crops and thereby ensure a future supply of food.

The disasters continued. On their summer hunt in 1848, Pawnee clashed with Potawatomie and Kansa, with more deaths. Unknown numbers died of starvation in the following fall and winter. Just as the weather ameliorated in the spring of 1849, cholera struck and raged through the summer. When Subagent John Barrow arrived at Bellevue to take up his new post in June, he found Pawnee lying all around the agency in a "dying condition" brought on by "absolute starvation" and cholera. The Indians were so afraid of the disease, with its violent vomiting and diarrhea, that they refused to bury their dead. The bodies had been partially eaten by wolves and other animals. Barrow moved the surviving Pawnee to higher ground, probably to avoid an outbreak of malaria. In a brief period of six months 1,234 Pawnee died. The following year all the Pawnee's crops failed because of drought.

As a result of these dreadful, continuous reversals, the Pawnee population fell to forty-five hundred in 1850 and four thousand in 1855 (fig. 11). Their lopsided and bottom-heavy demographic structure bespoke the tragedies and traumas that had struck them over the previous years. Carlton noted the shortage of men at the south Chaui village in 1844, the result of constant warfare. Carlton also saw children everywhere: "on the lodges, on the plazas, in the cornfields, on the bluffs, besides swarms of them swimming in the river, boys and girls together, all about four years old, and just three feet high." These were the children who had been born since the 1837–38 smallpox epidemic. There was also, Carlton noticed, a lack of teenagers, which reflected the deaths of infants and young children in the 1831–32 smallpox epidemic.[80]

Apparently, despite the feasible reduction of fertility by disease, the Pawnee's birth rate remained high through the 1840s. John Barrow, in his annual report for 1850, commented on the "almost astonishing number" of Pawnee children. By his estimation, at least twelve hundred from the total population of forty-five hundred were under the age of twelve (that is, Carlton's four-year-olds grown into teenagers). Oehler and Smith were also "struck with the large proportion of children" at the Pawnee villages in 1851.[81] Clearly the Pawnee were striving to maintain their population through high birth rates; but it is equally clear that they were failing to offset the soaring death rates. Pawnee population continued on this steep decline for the rest of the nineteenth century.

Persistence and Change in Everyday Life

How much persisted, and how much had changed, in the Indians' lives by mid-century? Despite the traumas and disruptions, their annual cycle went on largely as before: the signal to plant was still given by the first thunder of spring; barring disasters, the bison hunts were still made twice a year; and the repeating round of ceremonies still gave cohesion and meaning to their lives. Even in the 1860s, according to Weltfish, the Pawnee "retained their old social forms and independent polity, and a traditional rhythm of life throughout the year."[82] The same could be said of the Ponca, Omaha, and Otoe-Missouria. All four peoples continued to hunt and raid until the 1870s, despite concerted efforts by the United States to stop them. Only after the last, sad bison hunts was the age-old cycle broken and the harmonious coordination between religion and everyday life destroyed.

From the mid-1820s on, however, it had become increasingly difficult to survive in traditional ways. Resource depletion, warfare, disease, hunger, and government injunction intervened to destabilize the Indians' lives. More and more, men did not return from hunts and raids, women were struck down in the fields, and children were swept away by epidemic disease, or else died a lingering death from starvation. Government annuities and rations, issued as poor payments for lands or occasional beneficencies, could not replace bison meat and agricultural self-sufficiency. The severe population losses from 1825 to 1855—at least 50 percent of the Pawnee and Otoe-Missouria, about 60 percent of the Omaha, and 33 percent of the Ponca—are graphic evidence that the major change in the Indians' lives was their deepening impoverishment.

The Indians' cultures had also been changed in other ways by contact with Americans. The changes in material possessions are the most evident. From the beginnings of the fur trade in the eighteenth century, the Indians had welcomed imported manufactured products. Government annuities kept these new items coming, even after the Indians were too poor to obtain them through trade. Blankets, strouding, calicos, guns, powder, ammunition, hoes, axes, knives, looking glasses, paints, beads, and tobacco were among the introductions. The advantages of the new products were readily acknowledged by the Indians. Charachaush, for example, told Carlton and Wharton that the new tools had made their lives easier: "Before we were obliged to use flint for arrow heads and for lances, and, likewise vessels made of clay. We are now blest with iron spears and with kettles in which to cook our food."[83]

As the new goods filtered in, old skills and practices fell by the wayside.[84] The quality of pottery declined steadily over the first half of the nineteenth century as the Indians relied more on durable brass and copper kettles. The Pawnee had lost the art of pottery making altogether by 1846. Pawnee, Omaha, Otoe-Missouria, and Ponca archaeological sites from after 1850 yield very little pottery and increasing amounts of European and American metal products. Flint arrowheads were abandoned by the Pawnee as early as the 1830s, and the art of chipping stones died out with the advent of metal blades. Although at the south Chaui village in 1844, Carlton had noticed only moccasins and robes, and no blankets or shoes, by 1850 it appears that blankets, strouds, and calicos were being increasingly worn by the Indians in place of, or in combination with, traditional skin clothing.[85] This was not necessarily a case of superior products replacing lesser ones: dressed bison and deer skins were simply worth too much in trade value to be used as everyday clothing. For the same reason, canvas and muslin had begun to replace bison hides as tipi covers. New foods—wheat flour, coffee ("black medicine" to the Omaha), sugar, and beef—became commonplace.

Because of the Indians' reduced purchasing power, following the local decline of the fur trade, and because of the paucity and poor quality of annuity goods, the imported items were not abundant, and the old and new often coexisted. Most tellingly, guns and ammunition were in short supply, and the bow and arrow (albeit with metal point) remained the primary weapon in hunting and war. Metal cooking pots were few enough to be shared by many families. Other metal goods were remodeled to serve the Indians' own uses: iron hoops from traders' barrels were taken to the agency blacksmith, who beat them into arrow heads; hoes were also cut up into arrow heads and scrapers, clearly showing where the Indians' priorities lay; and gun barrels, long silent for want of ammunition, were used as tent pins and stakes. Horses, the earliest and most vital introduction from the outside world, became harder to hold onto, and their numbers, like the numbers of the Indians themselves, plummeted from the 1820s to the 1850s.

Despite the loss of some skills, and possibly of important religious rites that were associated with them, the new tools and other goods (with the notable exception of alcohol) were incorporated into Indian cultures without significantly disturbing the cadence of everyday life. These were voluntary assimilations, and new items were often given the names of the artifacts they replaced, suggesting a smooth transition: to the Omaha, canvas was *ti'ha,* as was the traditional skin tipi cover, and the metal axe (*mon'cepe*) and knife (*monhi^n*) also took the names of their flint and stone predecessors. But flint knives continued to be used in the Omaha's ceremonies, such as the ritual cutting of a boy's hair, and for bleeding and other curative purposes. And spears persisted as the standard of Ponca warrior societies long after guns had replaced them in war. Imported goods were certainly useful, but in these cases at least, they were not allowed to invade the sanctums of ceremonial life.

The main problems with the new goods were their unobtainability, given the poverty of the Indians, and the dangerous reliance on undependable outside suppliers. As Lewis and Clark had anticipated, the Indians of Nebraska did furnish a market (and a labor force) for external economies; but this situation was short-lived, and within a few decades of the first American contact they were left dependent, but unable to satisfy their new needs.

Changes in social organization were not voluntary, but were forced adaptations to population loss, escalating violence, and other ailments that stemmed, directly or indirectly, from contact with the United States and its frontier populations.[86] The changes were significant enough to call into question Welt-fish's claim that the "old social forms" persisted in the 1860s. The most dramatic social shifts were the coalescence of depopulated bands and villages for the purposes of defense and the related, but countervailing, trend of social fragmentation that occurred when leaders and their followers were thrown together in the same settlement.

This tension between "fusion" and "fissuring," which resulted in rapid changes in village locations and compositions, is most apparent from the experiences of the Pawnee.[87] Before 1830, each of the four Pawnee bands had preserved its separate identity, partly by enforcing endogamy, or marriage within the band. In fact, to marry outside one's village was an affront to the cosmic order.[88] By the late 1830s, however, such stability was a thing of the past. Fragmentation first occurred among the Kitkahahki, who splintered into several settlements (fig. 12). This fragmentation was probably the result of disputes over whether to live on the Loup or south of the Platte. The same dispute led to divisions within the Chaui and Pitahawirata in the early 1840s, when some members from each band chose to move to the mission village at Plum Creek, while others stayed south of the Platte. The old order was breaking down, and the pieces were being patched together in different combinations. Intermarriage among the bands increased, especially between the Chaui and the Pita-hawirata. After the destruction of the mission village in 1843, the Kitkahahki also merged more with the other bands. Only the Skiri remained endogamous, though even they shared their village sites with the others. By the late 1840s, the depopulated Pawnee bands had sought refuge in the two large composite villages on the south bank of the Platte. The split of the predominantly Skiri village into two settlements in the early 1850s (a division that continued on the reservation after 1859) was possibly caused by jealousies between two Skiri chiefs, Siskatuppe and Gatarritatkutz, as noted by Oehler and Smith in 1851.[89]

The rivalries in the amalgamated Pawnee villages were not only "horizontal," involving chiefs and their extended families, but also "vertical," indicating a widening generation gap between chiefs, who tended to be more pacifistic, and young warriors, who wished to follow the warpath to wealth, glory, and status. Charachaush told Carlton in 1844 that the young men of his band no longer paid any attention to his council.[90]

The Otoe-Missouria and Ponca were also plagued by divisions at mid-century. The fragmentation of the Otoe-Missouria into as many as five settlements by the early 1840s is the most dramatic example of the consequences of jealousies and rivalries that festered in composite villages. Similar jealousies kept the Ponca divided into two villages in the early 1850s. There were disputes among the Omaha too, particularly differences of opinion over where to live, but the leadership of the two Big Elks and the compelling need to take a united stand against the Dakota continued to prevent serious factionalism before 1850.

These conflicts were intensified by American agents, traders, and missionaries. Coalescence was promoted by the Indian Office, primarily as a money-saving device. Hence in 1845, Superintendent Harvey advocated merging the Omaha with the Otoe-Missouria on the grounds that they were already "a good deal connected by marriage and in everyday intercourse." Two years later Harvey brought up the subject again, recommending that the Omaha be amalgamated with the Otoe-Missouria or the Kansa: moving them would cost nothing, Harvey wrote, because they "had nothing left to move." Then in 1851, Superintendent Mitchell proposed merging the Otoe-Missouria with the displaced Winnebago, using the strained logic that they "got along well" and "are, or at least were, the same people."[91] Missionaries like Merrill and Dunbar also wanted to combine bands in a single village where old allegiances and practices could be broken and American ideals instilled in their place. Traders, on the other hand, encouraged factionalism, using alcohol and other inducements to play chiefs off against each other to gain the maximum commercial advantage.

Other social changes were forced on all four societies as the traditional structures of life were shaken. Indian women became even more essential to family and band survival when the bison hunts became a less dependable source of food. Food gathering, in particular, absorbed great amounts of time and energy. Polygyny increased, initially in response to labor demands from the fur trade, then later because of the scarcity of men. Carlton described in crass terms how, in the aftermath of a war, Pawnee society was "overstocked with young widows" who could be obtained for a mule or a donkey.[92] Carlton also observed that wives welcomed the extra women (generally younger sisters) into the lodge as a way to share the onerous work load. Class distinctions may have been accentuated by the differential accumulation of wealth through the fur trade and monopolization of the most prized annuities by a few leading families.

The most difficult changes to assess involve the beliefs of the Indians, their image of themselves, and their attitudes toward nature and the outside world. It is impossible, for example, to identify how much the Indians' conception of the bison hunt was corrupted by commercial motivations stimulated by the fur trade. Feasibly, as long as the proper ceremonies and practices were followed, it was irrelevant whether the hides were being taken for themselves or for the traders. Some erosion at the core of the Indians' belief systems had taken place by 1850, however, including the loss of ceremonies and societies. The Indians must also have experienced a certain loss of confidence in their ways of doing things, the result of repeated disasters, efforts by outsiders to transform them, and the recognition by some members of each society that their lives were bound to change in the face of indomitable American pressure.

Although the great decay of ceremonial life and traditional beliefs did not occur until the last quarter of the nineteenth century, some rituals were defunct by the 1850s. Reasons for these losses include direct suppression by the United States and the ending of knowledge with the deaths of priests, doctors, and other important carriers of culture. If there was any possibility that a ceremony could not be performed correctly, down to the last detail, it would not be done at all. Moreover, the elaborate cycle of ceremonial life had simply become difficult to sustain: bison meat, often large quantities of it, was needed for every ceremony, and bison meat was frequently scarce; also, hypothetically, how could gift giving, another essential part of every ceremony, go on when people had nothing to give?

The Skiri's Morning Star Ceremony, which involved the ritual killing of a captive girl, was an early extinction. The last sacrifice took place on April 22, 1838, with the killing of Haxti, a fifteen-year-old Oglala girl. The United States had tried to stop this ceremony on a number of occasions, including in 1833 when Dougherty, aided by the Skiri chief Big Axe, escorted the captive from the village, only to see her shot and sacrificed on the prairie.

To the Skiri, the Morning Star Ceremony was not a matter of choice. It was not part of the regular cycle, but rather an awesome event that took place when a man, through a vision, was commanded by the morning star to make a sacrifice. The power of the ritual was that it provided for success in war and for fertility, which explains the timing of the 1838 event, coming as it did on the heels of the smallpox epidemic and the Dakota's expansion. The subsequent cessation of the ceremony was not only the United States' doing: from the 1833 incident it can be seen that some Pawnee, even Skiri themselves, opposed it, and the visionary and priest who performed the sacrifice were always filled with remorse for the deed they were obliged to do.[93]

Other ceremonies and societies fell more quietly into disuse. The Skiri's Corn Planting Ceremony was last performed in 1856.[94] Why this important ceremony, whereby the evening star vivified the ground in preparation for spring planting, was dropped at such an early date (and when farming systems were still traditional) is not clear. Nor is it clear why the Omaha's *wathiⁿ'ethe*, the process of gaining entrance into the circle of chiefs by acts of generosity, lapsed soon after mid-century. Other early deductions from the Omaha's ceremonial life by about 1850 include the T'ega'xe society, whose function had been to perform songs that simulate death, and the Moⁿchú'ithaethe society, whose members drew mystical powers from animals.[95]

Yet, if the experiences of other Plains Indians are any guide, ceremonial life may actually have intensified as living conditions deteriorated. The Mandan, for example, reduced from sixteen hundred to fewer than fifty people by the 1837–38 smallpox epidemic, rebounded and survived as a people by clinging to their ceremonial life like a mooring in a storm. And the Indians of Texas turned to their healing ceremonies to try, in vain, to combat imported diseases.[96] No doubt the Nebraska Indians would also have looked to the sacred powers of their world to deliver them from the disasters which were being visited upon them, but while this may have brought them solace, it did not bring them salvation.

One small incision right into the core of Indian cultures had been made by 1850. American authorities had long since realized that the way to change the Indians was to shape their children through education. It is true that at mid-century, attendance in mission schools like McKinney's was sparse and irregular, but lasting effects on Indian cultures were being set in motion. At McKinney's school at Bellevue in 1851, the forty-seven students included boys and girls from all four Nebraska societies. Seventeen of the students were mixed-bloods, probably from families living at the trading post and agency. As a general rule, mixed-bloods learned English and accepted American tenets more readily than the other students did, so they became models of transformed Indians. Many of the students were the sons of chiefs, suggesting strongly that some Indian leaders knew very well which way the winds of change were blowing and where the advantage would lie in the future.

At the school the Indian children were taught to reject all they had known, and were prepared for entry into American society in ways that reveal much about the United States at that time. The twenty-six boys and twenty-one girls were all taught English, but only the boys were deemed worthy of arithmetic and geography. The boys were instructed in farming and blacksmithing; the girls were taught to be housewives. And so there was created the first in a series of generations of Indians who stood astride two worlds, but belonged fully to neither: they were increasingly cut off from their own traditions, but they would never be accepted into American society, except at its margins.[97]

Indian adults were equally confused over how to face the future. Agent Miller, referring to the Otoe-Missouria in 1842, thought that the "more reflecting of them" were resigned to change. Superintendent Mitchell noticed a similar resignation on the part of the Nebraska Indians a decade later.[98] Others were determined to resist any change. By midcentury, however, most of the Indians must have understood the immensity of American power. Many had been to St.

Louis, in 1850 a fast-growing city of almost thirty thousand people. Influential chiefs like Big Elk and Charachaush had been to Washington, D.C., passing through more than one thousand miles of settled country on the way. Charachaush told how he had seen ships there, and how he "rode in houses drawn by an iron horse."[99] But even for skeptics who refused to accept the reports of American power, the evidence of Big Elk's "coming flood" was as clear as the cabins on the bluffs across the Missouri.

CHAPTER FOUR

Restriction to Reservations

1854–1861

On May 30, 1854, after a decade of political maneuvering over issues of slavery and western railroad routes, the Kansas-Nebraska Act became law, thereby creating the territories of Kansas and Nebraska. Settlers had difficulty restraining themselves from crossing the Missouri River while politicians worked out the details of the bill. Families had traveled great distances in anticipation of the opening of the new lands. In swollen communities up and down the western borders of Iowa and Missouri, petitions were drawn up urging the immediate cancellation of the Indians' title to the land and its opening to American settlement. Nebraska balls were held nearly every Saturday night in the bustling frontier towns, Nebraska newspapers were being printed as early as 1853, and precocious settlers even set up a provisional government for the new territory and elected a governor.[1]

A new image of Nebraska, and a new conception of the Indians' legal status, were forged in this frenzied frontier atmosphere. An area that had once been branded on maps as the Great American Desert was now heralded in the frontier press as "beautiful country . . . destined to belong to the white man and be made to blossom like a rose."[2] Readers were told that Nebraska was well-timbered (which was certainly an exaggeration), well-watered (an expectation soon dispelled by a protracted drought), and fertile (which no one could deny). They were also falsely told that coal, lead, and other minerals were there for the taking. In addition, there was the prospect of cheap land, quite an attraction considering that choice plots in western Iowa were already selling for ten dollars an acre.

Moreover, the Nebraska Indians, apparently, had no legal claim to the land: "We can see no good or valid objection to the whites moving upon the government lands," the *St. Joseph Gazette* proclaimed in 1853.[3] The argument, proposed also by that tireless expansionist, Senator Thomas Hart Benton of Missouri, was that the Pawnee had given up their right to southern Nebraska when they agreed to the 1833 treaty. These lands had never been settled by emigrant Indians, Benton reasoned; therefore, they should now be made available to

Americans. This ignored, of course, the clause in the 1833 treaty which permitted the Pawnee, Otoe-Missouria, Kansa, and emigrant Indians to use the area as a common hunting ground, which they continued to do.

The newly appointed commissioner of Indian affairs, George W. Manypenny, understood that these hunting rights had never been canceled and that the land was not yet public domain. The original sales, he maintained, had been made to accommodate displaced Indians, not Americans. As one of his first acts in office, Manypenny visited the western borders, holding councils with the various Indians (including the Omaha and Otoe-Missouria, but not the Ponca and Pawnee) in the fall of 1853. He found them in desperate straits and in a state of alarm over the impending invasion. Some settlers had even crossed the Missouri to stake out the best land. While Manypenny had no desire to slow the American settlement of Nebraska, and indeed advocated that the country be "speedily opened" and sold on "the most liberal terms," he insisted on the proper extinguishment of Indian title.[4] The Indians at first balked at selling their homelands, but Manypenny persuaded them that there was no stopping the American tide, and that they must necessarily change. To his credit, Manypenny agreed to the Indians' request for time to discuss and reflect upon the terms of the proposed treaties. Delegations from the Omaha, Otoe-Missouria, and, later, the Ponca, were to travel to Washington, D.C., for further talks, and after the treaties were signed, all four Nebraska Indian nations were given a year to relocate on their reservations. So the expansionists were temporarily held at bay, and Manypenny was lambasted along the western borders.

While this build-up of settlement was taking place in 1853 and in the early months of 1854, the Nebraska Indians continued to starve and to die at the hands of the Brulé and Oglala Dakota. They had no annuities or any other means of consistent support. Their only asset was their remaining territory. Having been brought to the brink by American expansion, they were now obliged to sell their territories just to relieve their poverty. Consequently, in a series of treaties, beginning with the Otoe-Missouria and Omaha in March of 1854 and ending with the Pawnee and Ponca in 1857 and 1858, respectively, the Nebraska Indians parted with the bulk of their remaining lands in exchange for annuities and Manypenny's promise of a brighter future on reservations. Specifically, the Otoe-Missouria sold what remained of their southeastern Nebraska lands and took up residence on a 162,000-acre reservation on the Big Blue River, straddling the Kansas line; the Omaha sold northeastern Nebraska and settled on a 302,800-acre reservation in the Blackbird Hills; the Pawnee sold all their remaining territory north of the Platte, retaining only a 288,000-acre reservation on the Loup; and the Ponca sold a wedge of country stretching from the mouth of the Niobrara north into what is now South Dakota, and were assigned a reservation of about 58,000 acres between the Niobrara and Ponca Creek (fig. 13).

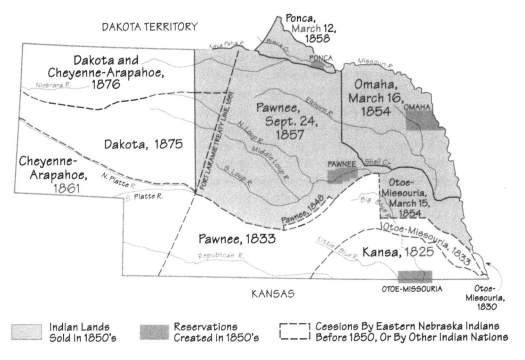

DAKOTA TERRITORY

Ponca,
March 12,
1858

Dakota and
Cheyenne-Arapahoe,
1876

Niobrara R.

PONCA

Omaha,
March 16,
1854

OMAHA

Dakota, 1875

Pawnee,
Sept. 24,
1857

Cheyenne-
Arapahoe,
1861

N. Platte R.

S. Platte R.

PAWNEE

Shell C.

Otoe-
Missouria,
March 15,
1854

Pawnee, 1840

Otoe-Missouria, 1833

Pawnee, 1833

Republican R.

Little Blue R.

Kansa, 1825

KANSAS

OTOE-MISSOURIA

Otoe-
Missouria,
1830

Indian Lands
Sold in 1850's

Reservations
Created in 1850's

Cessions By Eastern Nebraska Indians
Before 1850, Or By Other Indian Nations

Fig. 13   Land Cessions in the 1850s

Reservation Policy and the Frontier: Images and Realities

It was clear from the onset in the early 1850s that reservations were intended only as a means to an end, the end being assimilated Indians living on allotments and the remaining lands settled by Americans. Commissioners of Indian affairs from Manypenny on looked back over the policies of the previous twenty years with a critical eye: they concluded that the Indians had been left with too much land, that they had been given (incredibly) too much money for their cessions (leading, it was claimed, to indolence), and that they had been permitted too long to live in traditional, communal ways. Besides, as Manypenny explained in his 1854 report, there was nowhere left to remove them to; their destinies would have to be worked out in place.[5]

The revised policy of the 1850s, therefore, did not deviate from the long-established objective of assimilation, but carried it out with more intensity, and in a more concentrated geographical context, than ever before. Commissioner Albert Greenwood summarized the emerging reservation policy well in 1859: "At present the policy of the government is to gather the Indians upon small tribal reservations, within the well-defined exterior boundaries of which small tracts of land are assigned, in severalty, to the individual members of the tribe, with all the rights incident to an estate in fee-simple, except the power of alienation."[6]

The same understanding—that the size of the reservations created in the 1850s would necessarily be diminished when the Indians took out allotments—ran through superintendents' and agents' reports, as well as the frontier press. Superintendent Mitchell, for example, reporting in 1851, asked the question, "What shall be done with the Indians" living in the proposed Nebraska Territory? His own answer was to give one section of land to each head of family, thus freeing up a "large surplus" of "fine agricultural lands" for settlers. His successor, Alfred Cuming, in his 1857 report, argued that the newly created Nebraska reservations were "unnecessarily large." His recommendation was to combine the Ponca with the Omaha and the Pawnee with the Otoe-Missouria, get the Indians on their own pieces of private property, and open up the remaining lands to American farmers. The editors of the St. Joseph Gazette were trumpeting the cause of allotments as early as 1853, though clearly they were more interested in the benefits that would accrue to Americans than to Indians: "Let the Government guarantee a good farm," they wrote, "and utensils of husbandry to those who wish to stay and become citizens, and give all their children and youth a good industrial education in perpetuity." Those who did not wish to stay on these terms would be deported further west until they changed their ways or perished.[7]

The emerging reservation policy was clearly enunciated in the terms of the treaties negotiated with the Nebraska Indians.[8] The four treaties had significant differences, because each nation was a specific case, but these differences were far fewer than the similarities. The clauses on allotments were most specific in the Otoe-Missouria and Omaha treaties, where it was stipulated that the president, "at his discretion," was empowered to order the survey of the reservations into "lots" that would be assigned to those Indians who were interested in establishing a "permanent home." The size of the allotments would be proportionate to the size of each family: one-eighth of a section (eighty acres) for a single person over twenty-one; one-quarter of a section for each family of two, and so on, up to and beyond a full section for each family of six to ten. The details were not as explicitly stated in the Pawnee and Ponca treaties, but the desirability of dividing up the land into allotments was reiterated.

The treaties also specified the means by which the Indians would be "domesticated, improved, and elevated" (again using Manypenny's words).[9] Nothing in the terms of the treaties would have seemed strange to John Dougherty, who had advocated a similar strategy for Indian assimilation thirty years earlier. Each group was given a graduated annuity as payment for their lands, annual payments that would decline over the years as the Indians, theoretically, made the transition to American-style self-sufficiency. The size of each annuity seems to have been loosely fixed according to the amount of acres ceded, but it bore little relationship to the actual size of the population that needed to be supported (table 6).

The annuities would be used as a lever to pry the Indians from their past and to control their behavior. Superintendent Alexander Robinson was quite explicit on this in 1860 when he argued that the value of annuities was that they made the Indians' "dependence on the government a matter of more importance to them." It was left up to the president to decide what portion, "if any," of the payments would be made in cash, and what portion would be applied to the Indians' "moral improvement" through education, agricultural training, and other means "calculated to advance them in civilization." Annuities could be withheld to pay depredations, as a punishment for not keeping their children in school, and as a penalty for importing or using alcohol. Every treaty included, either in the annuities or in separate clauses, money for schools, farming equipment, other tools, mills, and salaries for teachers, farmers, and blacksmiths. Each nation formally acknowledged their dependence on the United States, who agreed to protect them. Finally, in candid recognition that the Indians would not be allowed to block the frontier, the United States was given the right to build forts and roads on the reservations.

While the main goal of federal Indian policy remained remarkably consistent, the spirit with which it was carried out varied greatly according to who was in charge. Some commissioners—as well as some superintendents, agents, and agency employees—approached their job with a higher sense of moral obligation than others. George Manypenny was a humanitarian along the lines of Thomas McKenney. His main concern was to protect his "wards" while they made the mandatory cultural changes by securing them in the possession of their lands and shielding them from traders and other settlers who sought to exploit them. He was also willing to give the civilization program time to work before imposing allotments. On the other hand, John Denver, who served as commissioner in 1857 and 1858–59, had no such patience. His main objective was to acquire Indian lands for frontier expansion. The allotment program was to be expedited, and those Indians who did not want to work the land—"the worthless idlers and vagrants"—would be shipped off to colonies on the western Great Plains. Denver's own involvement in amassing western property, including lands in the Nemaha Half-Breed Tract, was probably not unrelated to the way he prosecuted his duties.[10]

None of the intrinsic problems that had plagued federal Indian policy in the 1830s had been solved by the 1850s. The 1850s treaties did give the Nebraska Indians higher payments for their lands than had previously been the case. There are at least four reasons for this: first, with the frontier right at hand, and with land selling under the 1841 Preemption Act for $1.25 an acre, the government could quickly recoup any outlays for Indian cessions; second, the Nebraska Indians could no longer sustain themselves by hunting, so higher pay-

Table 6 The 1850s' Treaties

Indian Group	Treaty	Acreage	Annuity Payments	Other Payments	Total Payments	Payment Per Acre	Payment Per Capita
Otoe-Missouria	Mar. 15, 1854	1,087,893	$20,000 for 3 years $13,000 for 10 years $9,000 for 15 years $5,000 for 12 years	$20,000 for resettlement Payment for a saw and grist mill and blacksmith's shop, and the services of a miller, blacksmith and farmer for 10 years	$463,424	42.6 cents	$777
Omaha	Mar. 16, 1854	4,983,365	$40,000 for 3 years $30,000 for 10 years $20,000 for 15 years $10,000 for 12 years	$41,000 for resettlement Payment for a saw and grist mill and blacksmith's shop and the services of a miller, blacksmith, and farmer for 10 years	$881,000	17.8 cents	$1,125
Pawnee	Sept. 24, 1857	9,878,000	$40,000 for 5 years $30,000 a year in perpetuity	$5,000 for each of two schools, $500 a year for iron, steel, etc., $1200 a year for farming equipment, all the above for as long as the president decrees. $750 for blacksmith tools, $500 for blacksmith shops, $6,000 for steam mill, services of farmer, two blacksmiths, miller, and engineer.	$2,144,610	21.7 cents	$536

Table 6 *Continued*

Indian Group	Treaty	Acreage	Annuity Payments	Other Payments	Total Payments	Payment Per Acre	Paymer Per Capi
Ponca	Mar. 12, 1858	2,334,000	$12,000 for 5 years $10,000 for 10 years $8,000 for 15 years	$20,000 for resettlement $5,000 for 10 years for school $10,500 for mill and workshops $7,500 for 10 years for agricultural aid $20,000 to pay off past depredations	$455,000	19.5 cents	$650

Sources: Kappler, *Indian Treaties*, vol. 2, 608–14, 764; 7, 772–75, and Wishart, "Compensation for Dispossession," Table 1. Acreage figures are estimates derived from primary sources and agreed upon in claims cases in the 1950s 1960s, and 1970s. The Pawnee's perpetual annuity is counted only as the principal ($600,000) that was deposited on their behalf and yielded, at 5 percent interest, a continuous payment of $30,000 a year. Total payments in all cases include annuities and the various funds earmarked for schools, agricultural aid, and other aspects of the civilization program. Payment per capita is total compensation divided by population and should not be confus with individual cash payments which were given to each Indian as part of the annuities

ments were given to prevent total catastrophe and preserve the United States' proclaimed humanitarian agenda; third, the intensification of acculturation efforts required more funds than before, at least (or so the theory went) until the Indians could free themselves from federal support; and finally, with twenty years of experience behind them since the first cessions had been made, the Nebraska Indians were more aware of what their lands were worth to Americans, and they argued strenuously for fairer payments.

Nevertheless, payments per acre and per capita were still woefully low, and the land was acquired for much less than its fair market value. Consequently, programs designed to prepare the Indians for entry into American society, and to support them while they made this radical transition, were inadequately funded. Add to this, problems of mismanagement and outright corruption in the administration of the Indians' monies, and it becomes clear that the lofty ideals of the reservation policy were not backed up by the necessary commitment. Finally, there remained the extraordinary assumption that cultural beliefs nurtured over hundreds of years could be left behind within the space of a

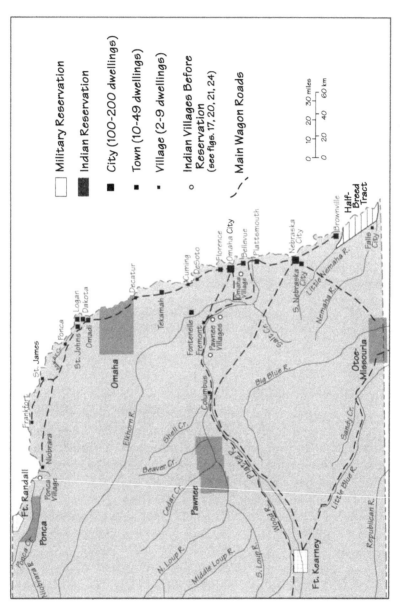

Fig. 14 Eastern Nebraska, circa 1860

Military Reservation

Indian Reservation

City (100-200 dwellings)

Town (10-49 dwellings)

Village (2-9 dwellings)

Indian Villages Before
Reservation
(see figs. 17, 20, 21, 24)

Main Wagon Roads

0 10 20 30 miles
0 20 40 60 km

generation or two. Most Nebraska Indians let go of traditional beliefs and behavior reluctantly and slowly. In the meantime, their reservations were enveloped by settlers, most of whom resented the Indians' continued presence in their new world.

It is no small irony that the settlers who poured into Nebraska in 1854 were not, in the main, the yeoman farmers that the Indians were supposed to emulate. There were genuine farmer-settlers, of course, but there were even more small- and large-scale speculators bent on exploiting the fluid frontier economies. The rush to create "paper towns," the rapid turnover of rural and city populations (including a massive exodus to the Colorado gold fields in 1859), the small amount of land that was improved by 1860, and the chiseling of land laws at every opportunity, point to the conclusion that most early Nebraskans were attached not to a place, but to the process of making money, especially on real estate. Addison Sheldon, the preeminent Nebraska historian in the late nineteenth and early twentieth centuries, concluded that much of the land sold under the Preemption Act, and most of the land sold via military bounty land warrants (which together accounted for almost all of the land alienated in Nebraska Territory before the Homestead Act of 1862) went to speculators first, and to genuine settlers only at a later date.[11] The scale of this speculation on land would only increase in the next decade.

The 28,826 settlers who had crossed the Missouri on ferries to Nebraska Territory by 1860, or else disembarked from one of the frequent steamboats from St. Louis, were drawn, in descending order, from Ohio, New York, Pennsylvania, Indiana, Illinois, and Iowa.[12] Missouri contributed some, but most southerners went to Kansas. Almost a quarter of the newcomers were foreign-born, mainly Germans, English, and Irish. So rapid was the settlement that it ran ahead of the government surveyors. Special permission was granted to make settlements on unsurveyed land and to later fit the claim to the closest survey lines.

Fully two-thirds of the settlers chose to locate in the booming, competing towns that lined the west bank of the Missouri from Omaha City on down (fig. 14). They found work there in construction and outfitting, or, if they had cash, they speculated on the rising values of town lots. The largest of the towns— Omaha City, Nebraska City, and Bellevue—each had more than one thousand inhabitants by 1860, along with banks, hotels, warehouses, ferry services, and a wide variety of stores that served local farmers and far-flung emigrants. Farmhouses were spread along the small timbered creeks that ran into the Missouri, but poor transportation tied settlers tightly to within fifteen or twenty miles of that navigable river. Many rural settlers simply registered their preemption claim and then, defying the law's residency rule, took off to work in the towns. The value of such idle lands rapidly appreciated: by 1860, good farming land near Nebraska City was selling for $8.25 an acre.[13]

Northward from Omaha City, past Florence, Tekama, and the hamlet of Decatur, settlement thinned. The thriving town of Dakota had the northernmost ferry crossing, and from there stagecoaches followed the wagon road to Ponca, St. James, the German settlement of Frankfort, and finally, at the edge of the frontier, the village of Niobrara. In 1858, Niobrara had twenty houses, a hotel, and a sawmill which drew from large stands of timber growing on islands in the river of the same name.

The only significant extension of settlement westward from the Missouri was along the north bank of the Platte. Stage stations and road ranches (whose owners made a good living overcharging emigrants for hay and food) were strung like beads along the well-traveled route to Fort Kearney and beyond. Fremont and Columbus were frontier villages, each with about twenty houses and a lot of ongoing construction. Columbus, benefiting from its control of the Loup ferry, also boasted a store and a tavern. South of the Platte, settlement was held back by poor transportation, deeply incised streams, lack of timber, and fear of the combination of isolation and Indians.

Settlers' attitudes toward the Nebraska Indians varied, because of diversity in both groups, but generally they viewed the Indians with disdain. They saw the Indians as impediments in the way of progress, as anachronisms in a modernizing world, and (without analyzing the causes) as sorry remnants of nations once proud and independent. They particularly resented government annuities, seeing them as a form of welfare when, of course, they were due compensation for land cessions. This particular feeling was exacerbated by the financial panic of 1857 (brought on by rampant speculation), which left many settlers destitute. Settlers were also afraid of the Indians, and any minor clash put the frontier in a panic, and produced editorials like this one on the Pawnee, from *The Nebraskian* of Omaha City: "If the Government will not protect the inhabitants of Nebraska against these red rascals, then we are in favor of calling out the militia and scalping the tribe."[14] Territorial authorities were antagonistic toward the Indians because they believed that their presence diverted immigration from Nebraska.

Similar sentiments were expressed by government surveyors, who frequently ran into Indians while squaring off the land. Augustus Ford Harvey, for example, was bothered by Pawnee as he surveyed the Republican valley in the fall of 1858. His preconceived bias against Indians was confirmed by this experience: "I've always thought that there was too much lackadaisical sympathy for the redskins and this trip has taken away the last of my sympathy of any sort." Harvey's recommendation was "to exterminate the last mother's son of them from the face of the earth."[15]

Most Nebraskans were probably less vehement in their dislike of Indians than Harvey; some were even sympathetic, and this was a feeling that would develop as the Indians became less of a perceived threat. Still, most of the settlers who were crowding around the Pawnee in 1858, according to Agent William Dennison, were "less civilized than the Indians." It was quite a coincidence, he sarcastically remarked, that there was always a flurry of depredations claims against the Indians just before their annuities arrived.[16] The Omaha, Ponca, and Otoe-Missouria experienced the same. Veteran trader Pierre Chouteau, Jr., who knew the Nebraska frontier as well as anyone, informed the Indian Office that it was the local citizens, not the Indians, who were mainly responsible for hostilities.[17] But these were minority voices: when it came to Indians in territorial Nebraska, sympathy and understanding were as scarce as good timber.

Removal to the Reservations

Sanctuary on the Blue

The Otoe-Missouria were the first to be settled on their reservation, but it was not a straightforward process. For a year following the return of their treaty delegation from Washington, D.C., in April 1854, they continued to frequent what Manypenny called "their old haunts on the Missouri."[18] Most likely they lived in tipi and earth-lodge villages on the south bank of the Platte between Salt Creek and the booming emigrant town of Plattsmouth. Government surveyors who measured this area in late 1855 and early 1856 found the remains of a village that had "lately been abandoned," near the junction of Salt Creek and the Platte. They attributed this site to the Pawnee, who were certainly in the vicinity in 1855–56, but from its location the village was just as likely to have belonged to the Otoe-Missouria. Further down, near the mouth of the Platte, surveyors came across "cornstalks and bean poles" and other evidence of recent occupancy. There was also a "great place for Indian encampments [with] many wigwams still standing" just to the west of Nebraska City.[19] These were the remains of the last settlements of the Otoe-Missouria before they were removed to their reservation. They had taken their full allotted year to move, probably because they needed to see the fall harvest and winter hunt through to completion. But there was also considerable confusion on all sides regarding the precise location of the new reservation, which resulted in additional delays.

Article 1 of the 1854 treaty had specified that the Otoe-Missouria were to retain a reservation ten miles wide by twenty-five miles long on the Big Blue.[20] The coordinates of the proposed reservation were nebulous, with reference to a "place called by the Indians the Islands," and to the vaguely defined western boundary of the ceded land. A map prepared for the Indian Office by Captain Seth Eastman in 1854 put the reservation near the headwaters of the Big Blue (fig. 15). Manypenny gave his stamp of approval by noting on the map that the reservations were "correct." But, with reference to the Otoe-Missouria, the map was correct only in the general size of the reservation; the location was a good

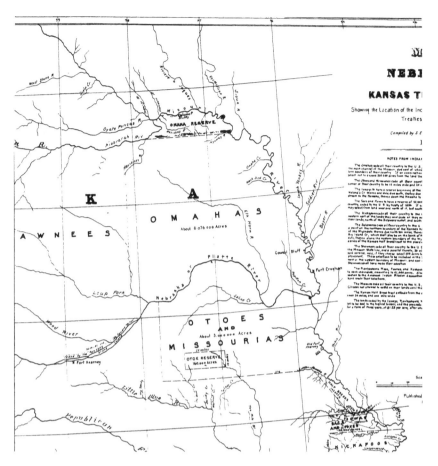

Fig. 15 Eastman's Map of Nebraska and Kansas Territories, 1854 (Portion). General Map Files, National Archives, RG 75, Map 974

forty miles north of where the Indians had intended it to be—on the Big Blue where it cuts across the Kansas-Nebraska line.

Even in October 1854 the matter was not settled. When the Otoe-Missouria visited the proposed site on the Kansas-Nebraska line, they found that the reservation was almost completely west of the Big Blue and virtually devoid of timber. According to their agent, George Hepner, they also felt that they would be much more exposed to enemy attack on the west side of the Big Blue.[21] Hepner proposed that the reservation be moved five miles to the east, to take in the stands of timber and to permit the Indians to build their village in a location "less liable to the intrusions of their enemies." He told Manypenny that the Otoe-Missouria would not move (short of being forced) unless this was done. Manypenny agreed, but he made it clear that the need for the change should be attributed to a mistake on the Indians' part, not the government's. Accordingly, on December 9, 1854, the original treaty was modified. The reservation was moved five miles to the east, giving the Otoe-Missouria extra resources of timber and water and lessening their feelings of vulnerability. The new treaty was specific in explaining that the change was brought about because the Indians had been mistaken in their initial choice of a site for the reservation.[22]

The Otoe-Missouria were settled on the reservation by July 1855. It was good land in almost every respect. In addition to the large reserves of timber, rich, well-drained soils underlay the flowing big bluestem prairie of the uplands, and fertile alluvium lined the valley floors and terraces. When the reservation was eventually surveyed in 1875, prior to its sale and Otoe-Missouria removal to Indian Territory, the land was described as "considerably above the average . . . in this section of the state."[23] And it was a fertile part of the state. There was also local game, such as deer and beaver (the latter now making a comeback after the earlier serious depletion). Most important, the reservation was close to the bison range of central and western Kansas but safely distant from the marauding Brulé, though the Otoe-Missouria continued to have problems with other Indians.

Nor, at first, was the reservation under any great pressure from American settlers (fig. 16). Surveyors who worked through the area in 1856–57 found only Gideon Bennett's trading post and the beginnings of towns at Blue Springs, Nebraska and Oketo, Kansas. By 1861 the valley of the Big Blue River, with its rich soils and abundant timber, had emerged as the main axis of settlement to the north and south of the reservation. Smaller streams, such as Plum Creek and Wolf Creek to the east of the reservation, and Deer Creek and Horseshoe Creek to the south, also attracted genuine settlers who registered preemption claims. Early settlers also took out land along the Little Blue, where they made a living serving emigrants on the trail that led to Fort Kearney and points west. The nearest substantial settlements in 1861 were Beatrice, Nebraska, and Marysville, Kansas, each located about ten miles from the boundary of the reservation. The large block of claimed land in northeastern Marshall County was held by a few speculators who amassed it by purchase with military bounty warrants. This land, which remained unfenced and unbroken, was not actually settled. Land speculation set the pattern for the following decade, when the bulk of the lands surrounding the Otoe-Missouria reservation (especially the upland prairies) passed into the hands of speculators.[24]

The Indians built their village on a slight elevation just east of the junction of Plum Creek and the Big Blue, where a crystal-clear spring issued from a ledge of limestone (fig. 16). There were about forty earth lodges, and a few bark-covered lodges similar to those built by the Sauk and Fox. Bradbury, who had carefully examined the old Otoe village in 1811, would have recognized the indigenous scene. But now, in addition, there was the agent's house, built one hundred feet

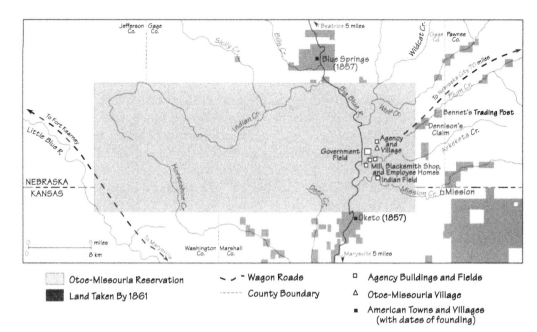

Fig. 16 Otoe-Missouria Reservation and Vicinity, circa 1861

north of the spring in the summer of 1856, when the separate Otoe Agency was established. By that time also, one hundred acres of prairie had been broken by agency farmers, and work had commenced on the blacksmith shop, the steam saw and grist mill, and employees' houses, all located about one mile to the south, on the other side of Plum Creek. Six miles from the village, and one and a quarter miles off the reservation to the east, the Presbyterian Board of Foreign Missions, operating under contract with the Indian Office, started construction on the three-story concrete building that would house the school.[25]

Despite this promising start, progress in implementing treaty obligations was slow. The delays were caused by dereliction in the operation of Indian affairs. The last two agents affiliated with the Council Bluffs Agency (James M. Gatewood and George Hepner) were dismissed for abusing their authority.[26] Even if they had been honest, it is doubtful that they could have handled all the problems associated with the Omaha, Pawnee, and Otoe-Missouria in the turbulent period preceding and immediately following the Kansas-Nebraska Act. The Otoe-Missouria's first designated agent, John Alston, apparently did not make it west of South Carolina, so the Indians were effectively without supervision until William Dennison was appointed in February 1857. Even then, Dennison had to divide his efforts between the Otoe-Missouria and the Pawnee, who were assigned to the Otoe-Missouria Agency until their own agent was appointed in

1859. Dennison turned out to be an unmitigated disaster as an agent, and the quality of the other agency employees was also poor. The blacksmith, for example, had just been released from the Kansas Penitentiary at Leavenworth, and, according to the Indians, he "thought more about the squaws than his business."[27]

During these early reservation years, the annuity system was virtually inoperable. Manypenny had reintroduced the concept of biannual deliveries on the grounds that meting out the money and goods would prevent so much of the resources from being diverted to traders. The goods were delivered by merchants like Chouteau to Brownsville or Nebraska City, then carried overland on rough roads to the reservation. Rarely were they delivered on time. The first installment should have been paid in May 1856, but it reached the Otoe-Missouria in March 1857. Similarly, in 1859 the fall annuities were supposed to arrive by the beginning of September, but they were still not there in December. This, Dennison explained, left the Indians in an "ill humor . . . weighing in their own minds which was of most importance, their payment or their Buffalo Hunt."[28] The Indians' calendar was becoming increasingly orientated to the Americans' timetable, and less attuned to the signs of nature.

But even if the system had functioned well, the funds appropriated to support the Otoe-Missouria were too small to accomplish the vaunted goals of the civilization program. By 1860 the Otoe-Missouria were receiving thirteen thousand dollars a year, in accordance with the 1854 treaty. After expenditures on their behalf by the Indian Office for "useful goods," they were left with nine thousand dollars to be allocated to individuals. This worked out to about eighteen dollars per person. How could they live on this, Dennison asked his superiors, when blankets cost eight dollars each, flour ran at fifteen dollars a bag, and coffee was twenty-five cents a pound?[29] At best, per capita payments paid off a portion of the previous year's debts to the trader.

The steam saw and grist mill was the singular success of these early reservation years. The mill was operating by the fall of 1858, mainly to cut timber for fences and agency buildings. One day a week was set aside for grinding the Indians' corn. From January to June of 1859, for example, 782 bushels of corn were ground and 12,441 feet of timber sawn.[30] There were ambitious plans for expanding into custom grinding and milling, serving the surrounding settlers and earning the Otoe-Missouria profits through private enterprise.

Other than the mill, the government's program floundered. The Otoe-Missouria were not interested in sending their children to the mission school. As a matter of fact, even Dennison was not enthusiastic about the school, and went on record as saying that "one mill is worth all the missions combined."[31] Any attendance was temporary and ended when the Indians left for their hunt. In the summer of 1857, for example, the teacher, D. A. Murdock, reported fourteen boys and two girls in attendance, but school emptied out in mid-July when the bison hunt started. No progress at all was made in persuading Otoe-Missouria men to farm: for men to farm, Dennison explained, would be "to make squaws of themselves."[32]

Problems other than the ineffectiveness of the government's program plagued the Otoe-Missouria during the first reservation years. Despite yet another revision of the Intercourse Laws in 1847, alcohol was even more available than before, legally dispensed outside the boundaries of the reservation. In February 1860, for example, the Otoe-Missouria were returning from their winter hunt when they encountered a party of Americans on the Big Sandy tributary of the Big Blue, about twenty-five miles west of the reservation. Whiskey was traded and consumed, a fight broke out between Otoe and Missouria divisions, and a young Missouria chief was stabbed to death. He was carried back to the reservation and buried along with his horse. Dennison had great difficulty in restraining the dead man's relatives from taking revenge on the killers and their families.[33]

Hostilities with other Indians did not cease with the move to the reservation. The Cheyenne, in particular, were a threat. In the summer of 1858, a Cheyenne war party shadowed the Otoe-Missouria on their hunt, driving the bison ahead of them, trying to entice them out to a distant, dangerous range. As a result, the Otoe-Missouria did not take a single bison and were forced to subsist on green corn until the main harvest came in. That fall, thirty to forty Indians died of starvation, "intermittent fever," and diarrhea. An attempt by Ar-ka-ke-ta (Stay By It), the head chief of the Otoe-Missouria, to make a treaty with the Cheyenne at the Big Timbers on the Arkansas in September came to nothing.[34]

Nor was their village secure. In July 1857, while they were out hunting, about forty Kansa pillaged their lodges, cut up their tent covers, spilled their flour on the ground, and stole all they could carry. This attack deepened the Otoe-Missouria's conviction that it was not safe to leave their children behind at the mission school while they hunted. The mission never got off the ground, the contract with the Presbyterian Board of Foreign Missions was allowed to lapse in 1860, and the Otoe-Missouria were without a school for a decade.[35]

Strangely, given the unsettled situation that surrounded them, the Otoe-Missouria increased their population in the second half of the 1850s. By 1861, according to the best estimate, there were 708 Otoe-Missourias, consisting of 303 males and 405 females (fig. 10).[36] The lack of a major epidemic during these years—thanks in part to a vaccination campaign in 1852—seems to have allowed a population recovery. There had been some good seasons among the bad, which temporarily secured the subsistence base: the summer hunts of 1857 and 1859 were successful, and crop yields were high in 1858 and 1859. The annuity program, no matter how flawed, helped too.

Then a severe drought struck southeastern Nebraska in 1860. In August Dennison reported that for three months there had not been enough rain "to lay the dust." The Otoe-Missouria's harvest was a total failure. Local settlers were also devastated by the drought, and Dennison witnessed the "daily occurrence" of land abandonment and retreat to the east of the Missouri. But the Otoe-Missouria had no such options, and they entered the decade of the 1860s facing starvation. The small population increase had only been a minor reversal of the downward plunge.[37]

Home to the Blackbird Hills

The Omaha's passage to their reservation was complicated and delayed by two factors: federal policy and the Dakota. Initially, the Indian Office wanted to locate the reservation between Ayoway (Aowa) Creek and the Niobrara, in extreme northeastern Nebraska. Eastman's map clearly shows this intention (fig. 15). Manypenny may have felt that this location was preferable because it was more removed from settlers than the country to the south. The settlers themselves liked the idea because they did not want to see the Blackbird Hills, the Omaha's old home territory, tied up in an Indian reservation, and because they were concerned that the Omaha's presence in their vicinity would attract Dakota raiding parties. Throughout 1854 and the first half of 1855 settlers repeatedly petitioned Manypenny and Secretary of the Interior Robert McClelland to remove the Omaha to Ayoway Creek, or else put them south of the Platte.[38]

In August 1854, Agent Hepner accompanied an Omaha party on a survey of the proposed reservation. They were unimpressed: the country was too dissected, there was little timber, and it was dangerously close to the Dakota and Ponca. Led by their mixed-blood chiefs, Joseph La Flesche and Logan Fontenelle, the Omaha adopted what Hepner described as a "savvy and contrary attitude" and steadfastly insisted upon the Blackbird Hills for their future home.[39] Manypenny, again showing a willingness to allow the Indians to make their own decision on where to live (as the 1854 treaty specified) acquiesced, and by May 1855 they were settling in on Blackbird Creek.

As in the past, their plans were thwarted by the Dakota. While they were out on their summer hunt, on Beaver Creek in the southeastern Sand Hills, Logan Fontenelle separated from the main party to pick gooseberries. He was cornered in a ravine by Dakota, killed, and scalped.[40] The Omaha's map added yet another bloody coordinate—Thugina gaxthiitho^n, the place where Thugina (Fontenelle) was slain. The Omaha, described by Hepner as "frantic with fear," once again retreated to their refuge village west of Bellevue.[41] Government surveyors located the village near the forks of Papillion Creek (fig. 17). Manypenny gave them permission to stay there until the following spring. They harvested no crops that fall and were too afraid to go west of the Elkhorn for meat. Government rations of beef, bacon, flour, and sugar helped them survive the winter, and they moved back to the Blackbird Hills for good in May 1856.

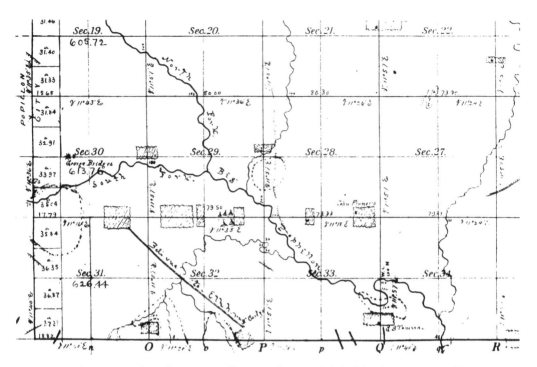

Fig. 17 Omaha Village on Papillion Creek, 1856. Original land survey, township 14 north, range 13 east of the 6th principal meridian. Courtesy of Nebraska State Historical Society

Like the Otoe-Missouria, the Omaha (thanks to their own insistence) acquired very good land for their reservation. Agent Orsamus Irish left a detailed account of the reservation's early geography in the form of a map and accompanying letter that he submitted to Superintendent Harrison Branch in 1862 (fig. 18). The fertile Missouri River flood plain was "heavily timbered" with cottonwood, elm, willow, and ash. Spectacular bluffs, rising in some areas five hundred feet from the river, were covered with oak, hickory, and basswood. Numerous springs issued from the base of the bluffs. West from the crest of the bluffs were expanses of rolling big bluestem prairie. Ribbons of timber followed the creeks out into the grassland. There was some game, including deer, and plenty of fish. There may not have been the anticipated deposits of bituminous coal, but there was no doubt in Irish's mind that the reservation was "as fine a farming country as could be desired."[42]

The settlers thought so too, and even by 1860 they were pressing against the southern and northern boundaries of the reservation (fig. 19). At the southeast end settlers clustered around the hamlet of Decatur, where Peter Sarpy ran his trading store. To the north the Missouri flood plain was thickly settled all the

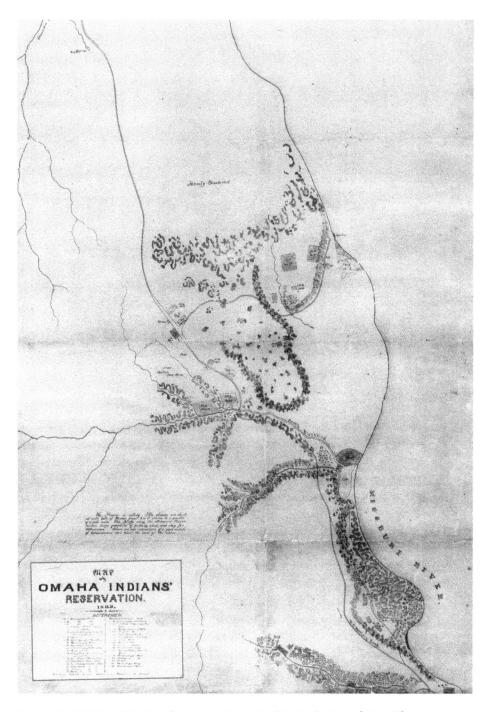

Fig. 18 Irish's Map of the Omaha Reservation, 1862 (Portion). Central Map Files, National Archives, RG 75, No. 342

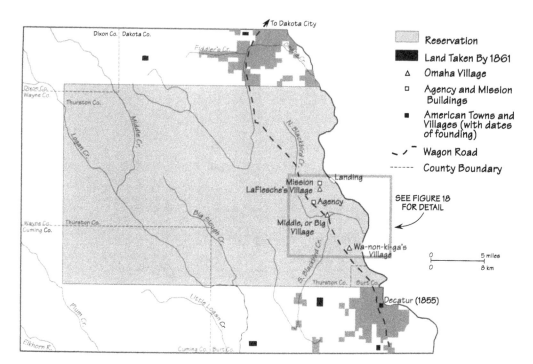

Fig. 19 Omaha Reservation and Vicinity, circa 1861

way to Dakota City—only twelve miles away and already, in 1859, a town of seventy houses, two hotels, and a wide variety of stores. Settlers, most of them coming in 1859 and 1860 and using military land warrants and preemption claims, also took land along Omaha Creek and its small tributaries. The country to the west of the reservation was virtually empty: Cuming County had only sixty residents in 1860.

The close contact between such different peoples brought conflicts, as the barrage of depredation claims attests. There was even an alleged serious incident, never proven, involving the shooting of Chauncy Horr, a settler from near Homer. Though Indian involvement was never proven, the incident incited local Americans. But, if the agents and local newspapers are to be believed, the relations between the Omaha and the surrounding settlers were relatively amicable. The Indians were no threat, and besides, as the newspapers frequently reminded their readers, if they did step out of line, Article 10 of their treaty ensured that they would pay for it through confiscation of their annuities.[43]

In their first year on the reservation the Omaha split into three settlements, all located in the southeastern portion, near the Missouri (figs. 18 and 19). The largest, an earth-lodge settlement known as Big, or Middle, Village, was built at the junction of North and South Blackbird creeks. The wagon road linking

Decatur and Dakota City ran along the bluffs immediately to the west of the village. About three miles to the north, near where Horsehead Creek flows out of the bluffs, Joseph La Flesche and his followers built a village of frame and log houses that would be known derisively in the 1860s as the "Village of Make-Believe White Men." A third settlement, known as Wa-non-ki-ga's village, sat on the bluffs near the wagon road, not far above Decatur. This settlement was also known as Ton'-won-ga-hae's village, or the "wood-eaters'" village, because residents made money by selling timber to the settlers around Decatur. A number of Indians and mixed-bloods, including La Flesche, Henry Fontenelle, and John Pilcher, had their own separate homes and properties, giving the reservation (in Agent Moore's eyes) the "appearance of a settlement of white men." No settlements were built on the venerable location on Omaha Creek, where Lewis and Clark's men had found the abandoned village in 1804, because it was too exposed to Dakota raids.

Indian and agency landscapes intermingled. The agency was located about three miles west of the Missouri on the wagon road. A secondary road, or track, ran from the agency through the bluffs and across the flood plain to the Missouri landing, where annuities and other supplies were delivered. The mission—a three-story limestone structure with seventeen rooms—was built in 1857 on a bluff above the landing. Below stood the saw and grist mill, blacksmith's shop, and employees' housing. Just to the west was La Flesche's village, ideally located to take advantage of the services that the United States was offering.[44]

The success of the Omaha's adaptation to the reservation was remarkable. By the fall of 1856 Agent John Robertson could report "cheering signs of improvement in their condition." They raised six thousand bushels of corn that season on the 125-acre government field and in their own fields. They also made successful winter and summer hunts in 1856–57, bringing in eight hundred robes, many other skins, and large amounts of bison and deer meat. In 1857 Robertson again reported that the Omaha were "abundantly blessed" with high yields of corn and other vegetables. They made another successful hunt in the summer of 1858, but, realizing that game was bound to become scarcer each year as the country filled up, they intensified their farming efforts and reaped the benefits. In 1861 they produced a "bounteous harvest" of twenty thousand bushels of corn. Some fields yielded eighty bushels an acre. There was enough food to be able to give large amounts to "their friends, the Ponca," who were starving, and to contemplate marketing the surplus in the American settlements. With abundant food and no major health problems, the Omaha increased their population each year to reach 950 in 1861 (450 males and 500 females).[45]

Some credit for this recovery from their dreadful pre-reservation condition is due to the Indian Office and its Americanization policy. For some unexplained reason (probably associated with their longstanding favorable reputation), the Omaha received more support from the government than did the other Nebraska Indians. Their total payments per capita from the 1854 treaty were twice as high as the Ponca's and Pawnee's and considerably higher than the Otoe-Missouria's (table 6). Individual cash payments from the annuity were $21.50 per year. By 1861 they were also receiving thirty-five hundred dollars a year in agricultural aid. Agency farmers plowed the various government fields each spring and furnished seeds, teams, and implements where needed. Thanks to their efforts, some Indians were successfully growing wheat and sorghum, as well as their traditional crops. The Omaha mission was also well-endowed, to the sum of twenty-five hundred dollars a year, and the associated school opened energetically and claimed fifty-four pupils in 1861. There were more boys than girls at the school because, as teacher Charles Sturgis explained, the mothers could not do without the services of the girls at home.[46]

But most of the Omaha's success was through their own efforts, and despite American negligence. The steam saw and grist mill was slow in construction, broken-down most of the time, and in a state of "incipient decay" by 1861. The engineer at the mill blamed incompetent workers (they blew up the boiler in 1859). In general, the quality of agency employees was poor. Agents came and left with great rapidity. Hepner was accused of skimming the Omaha's annuities, and the local press and the Indian office believed it to be the case. (Suspicions were later confirmed, in 1918, when the Court of Claims ruled that Hepner had "misappropriated" $15,069 of the Omaha's money). William Wilson lasted only a year, and spent most of it at his home in Decatur. He forced the Indians to travel there for their annuities, handing them out (the Omaha chiefs protested) only two hundred yards from a whiskey house. At least one of the missionaries was no better. In 1857 the Reverend William Hamilton borrowed eighteen hundred dollars from Joseph La Flesche, his total life savings. Hamilton promised a quick return and 10 percent interest, but by 1859, when La Flesche complained to Commissioner Mix, only three hundred dollars and two broken-down mules worth two hundred dollars that were "not able to pull a barrel of water" had been paid back. Moreover, Hamilton disappeared for a while in 1858. The debt must have been paid eventually, because Hamilton continued to preach among the Omaha and had a close association with La Flesche, but the incident caused La Flesche to yearn for "the day the government shall send us to teach our children, some honest men who will attend to the discharge of their duties and not make the poor Indians the object of their speculations."[47]

The government's other major failing was in not protecting the Omaha, an obligation explicitly acknowledged in Article 7 of the 1854 treaty. In January 1860, Omaha leaders met in council at La Flesche's home and demanded that the clause on protection be honored. They listed the recent raids: the Santee

Dakota had raided the reservation three times since 1855, stealing horses and committing violence, and in 1859 a Brulé war party had attacked the Omaha on their way back from the summer hunt, leaving seven Omaha dead. The attacks kept the Omaha in a state of "continual alarm and dread," and at one point in 1860 they abandoned their villages and set their tipis up in the safety of the American settlements south of the reservation.[48]

The fact that the Omaha did prosper, despite adversities, had much to do with the forceful leadership of La Flesche. The son of a French fur trader and an Omaha or Ponca woman, La Flesche was born around 1818 in Large Village on Omaha Creek. He grew up experiencing both Omaha and American worlds, living with relatives among the Dakota when he was a child, and accompanying his father on trading expeditions to St. Louis. By the time he was a young man he could speak Dakota, Pawnee, Iowa, and French. During the 1840s, those desperate years at Bellevue when extinction loomed as a possibility, La Flesche was taken under Big Elk's care, and he adopted his mentor's pragmatic views on the necessity to adapt to American ways. La Flesche became convinced (as later, on the eve of allotments, he rather bitterly explained) that the Indians' only chance to survive was to "become as the white man."[49]

Yet, despite this conviction, La Flesche chose to live in Omaha society. He progressed toward the position of chief in traditional ways, joining the preparatory council for the bison hunt in the late 1840s (at Big Elk's invitation), and making the hundred gifts (*wathiⁿ'ethe*) to the established leaders. When Big Elk's young son and successor died in the early 1850s, La Flesche was virtually adopted in his place, bending kinship rules in the process. When Big Elk himself died in 1853, La Flesche took his position as one of the two principal chiefs of the Omaha.

As a principal chief during the early reservation days, La Flesche was tenacious in pursuing Omaha treaty rights and strict in enforcing order among his people. In 1856 he and Agent Robertson established a police force headed by Ma-hu-nin-ga (No Knife) to eliminate alcohol use on the reservation. Anyone who broke the rules was given, in missionary R. J. Burtt's words, "a beating severe enough to lay them up for a week." The police were also used to enforce attendance at the mission school, to punish thieves, and to reduce corruption. By 1860 the sum of twelve hundred dollars was being taken out of the annuity each year to support this force. In 1858, in response to indications that the Indian Office was considering reducing the size of the Omaha reservation, La Flesche organized a "great council" of his people. They affirmed their commitment to the Americanization program, including allotments, but they strenuously opposed any efforts to tamper with their land. The Omaha were increasing in numbers, La Flesche argued, and they would soon fill out the reservation.

In 1860 La Flesche was again championing Omaha rights, drawing up a code of ethics to regulate the agents' conduct, including making it mandatory for them to live on the reservation. Throughout this time, La Flesche kept up an obsessive (but warranted) surveillance over annuity payments. He used his confidant, the Reverend Burtt of the Presbyterian mission, to go over the accounts with him, because he suspected a "collusion" between the agent and the superintendent. He made sure that the Omaha were paid their per capita payments in coin, not paper money, and he was behind the drive to get the annuity funds spent on agricultural implements, medicine, and other practical items, rather than "gaudy articles." La Flesche had determined that even if the Omaha were obliged to live under American rule, they did not have to live in ignorance of it.[50]

At this stage, at least, his efforts were greatly appreciated by the Indian Office. This was the kind of success story they wanted, and the Omaha were held up as a model for other Indians. Agents praised La Flesche for his "sagacity, integrity, and intelligence," and for his "excellent example" and "untiring efforts" to advance the conditions of his people.[51] And indeed he was a success. By 1861 his village had more occupied frame houses than Decatur, and his fields, cultivated by his band with their own teams, yielded a surplus for sale.[52] The fact that he had eighteen hundred dollars to loan Hamilton speaks for itself.

But La Flesche did not speak for all the Omaha, not even for the majority. Big Village, and Wa-non-ki-ga's village remained conservative. The Reverend Burtt was always welcome at La Flesche's village, where he found an enthusiastic, if uncomprehending, congregation. But when he offered to set up a bower for Sunday preaching in Big Village, he was rebuffed by Indians who accused him of trying to poison their minds.[53] They continued to live in their earth lodges and tipis, to adhere to traditions, and to reject the Americanization program. Fletcher and La Flesche considered that the division of the Omaha into three settlements at this time had "no tribal significance," and it is true that they all still met in council and camped in the *hu'thuga* while on the bison hunt.[54] But clearly, by 1861, this circle, if not broken, contained two divergent sectors, one pointing at the Indian past, the other looking to an American future.

Besieged on the Loup

The Pawnee made the most turbulent transition to the reservation. Despite their protracted decline, they were still a powerful nation that could put four hundred to five hundred warriors in the field, all of them mounted. Their total population—3,414 in 1861—was much larger than that of any single town in Nebraska Territory, and their total number of horses—twelve hundred to fifteen hundred—made them by far the wealthiest Indians in the area. Prior to the summer of 1859, when they were moved to the reservation on the Loup, they continued to occupy the three villages on the south bank of the Platte where they had been driven by the Dakota in the late 1840s (fig. 14). Two of the villages, known at the time as Upper Village and Lower Village, were pinpointed by

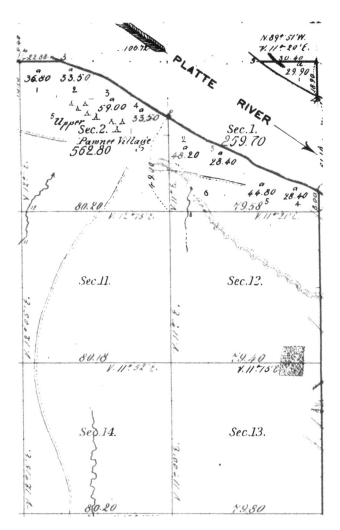

Fig. 20 Upper Pawnee Village, 1858. From the original land survey, township 16 north, range 8 east of the 6th Principal Meridian. Courtesy of Nebraska State Historical Society

government surveyors in 1856 and 1858 (figs. 20 and 21). This, of course, was government land, acquired through the treaty of 1833, and now it was needed for American settlement. To the north of the river, almost in sight from the bluffs near the Upper Village, emigrants trekked westward in increasing numbers each year; some came to stay, founding the towns of Fremont, Columbus, and Fontenelle, or settling in outlying rural communities, like the Irish colony on Shell Creek. The country west of Shell Creek had traditionally been recognized by the Nebraska Indians and by knowledgeable Americans as Pawnee

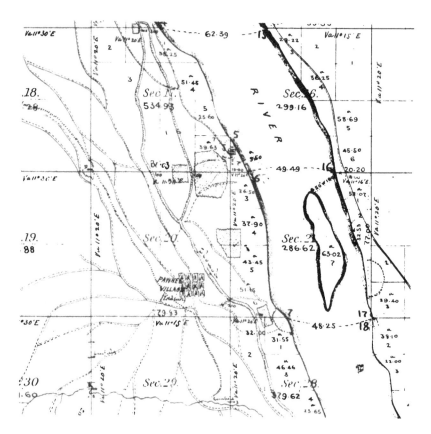

Fig. 21 Lower Pawnee Village, 1858. From the original land survey, township 16 north, range 9 east of the 6th Principal Meridian. Courtesy of Nebraska State Historical Society

land, but it had been sold by the Omaha in 1854 (fig. 13). The Pawnee were incensed over this, and they regarded the Americans who moved into the ceded land as intruders.[55]

Under the circumstances, conflicts were inevitable. Their causes can be variously attributed to Pawnee stealing and intimidation, settlers' encroachment and hostility, and cultural misunderstandings. Fear on both sides transformed minor incidents into major events. This combination of factors was behind the outbursts of violence that began in the fall of 1856 and continued until the following spring. The Pawnee were starving, with only small amounts of corn to eat. Their horses were too weak to undertake the winter hunt, and in any case the Dakota were waiting for them out on the plains. They had no annuities from the United States, and their agent, William Dennison, was shared with the

Otoe-Missouria and gave them little attention. They complained to Samuel Allis (at this time their interpreter) that "white men were settling close around them, and cutting off their timber from their land." The settlers, in turn, complained to the Indian Office that the Pawnee were hanging around their homesteads, burning the prairies, threatening violence, "begging, stealing, and cussing." They should be moved to the Loup, they insisted, because they were "not fit to live among the whites." The Pawnee chiefs admitted that their young men had committed misdemeanors, but more often, they explained to Dennison, their intentions were misconstrued. Why is it, La-Pe-tara-na-sharo (Comanche chief) asked, that they "could not visit a white man's house without being abused?"[56]

Tensions mounted and culminated in the killing of the Chaui chief, Te-ra-eta-its, in the spring of 1857. Unable to go west to hunt, a party of Pawnee had wintered near the Missouri, where settlers stole their horses. On their return, Te-ra-eta-its and a companion, Sh-laa-wa-te-de, a Kitkahahki, approached a settler's cabin to ask for food. Te-ra-eta-its knocked on the door, while his friend nervously kept his distance. The settler, a man named Davis, came out and hit Te-ra-eta-its several times with a stick. He then went back into the house for his gun and shot the Chaui chief. Dennison, after listening to Sh-laa-wa-te-de tell his story in a council at the Pawnee village on April 27, concluded that it had been the Pawnee's desperate condition and Davis's "rashness" that had led to the killing. A wave of terror reverberated through the frontier communities. Droves of settlers, fearing retaliation, withdrew to the Missouri, and militias were formed with the stated intention of shooting every Indian they met "south of Salt Creek." Territorial newspapers fanned the flames of panic and called for "Uncle Sam" to move the Pawnee away from the frontier.[57]

The Pawnee also wanted to be moved to a safer location. They had been asking for a treaty and the associated annuities since 1855, but they wanted a reservation south of the Platte, away from the Dakota. This was unacceptable to the government. Moreover, as Ta-ra-ta-putz (a relative of the murdered chief) complained to Dennison at the April council, this time they wanted a fair payment for their lands: "We received but little when we made our last treaty," he recalled, "and now that lands have become increased in value [we] expect to receive a much higher payment."[58] When the treaty was finally signed, on September 24, 1857, at Table Rock, Nebraska Territory, the Pawnee did receive a higher payment per acre than they had been given in 1833 and 1848, but when apportioned to their population it was still a miserably low compensation (table 6). Even during the first five years, when payments were highest, they were given annually about twenty thousand dollars worth of goods (mainly blankets, cloth of various kinds, knives, axes, and kettles) and twenty thousand dollars in coin, which worked out to about six dollars per person. Moreover, they were obliged to accept a reservation on the Loup, to which they consented only "reluctantly," and with justifiable trepidation, because it put them back at the mercy of the Dakota.

They continued to live in limbo during 1858 and the first half of 1859, squeezed between the American settlers on one side and the Brulé and Oglala Dakota on the other. Dennison reported in 1858 that they had been "very patient," waiting for their treaty to be ratified and for their first annuities (which were delivered, late, in the fall of that year), and enduring the gradual takeover of their traditional lands by settlers. These settlers included, according to Dennison, a "class of desperadoes" who hung around the Pawnee villages, making a living dealing whiskey and buying annuities for a pittance.[59]

Then, in the spring and early summer of 1859, there was another flare-up in hostilities between the Pawnee and the settlers. The Pawnee were again starving, having been cut off from their hunting grounds by the Dakota during the previous winter. In March, then again in July, young Pawnee warriors rampaged along the Elkhorn, stealing horses and sheep, stripping cabins, destroying the post office, and threatening newly arrived families. No settlers were killed, though one was seriously wounded, and many left for the Colorado mines to "repair their drooping fortunes." The Pawnee lost four men in the clashes. Dragoons were dispatched from Fort Kearney to Fontenelle, and volunteer militias converged from all sides. A false rumor spread that the Pawnee had amassed one thousand warriors on Shell Creek, waiting to attack. Further violence was prevented by the removal of the Pawnee to the safe remoteness of their new reservation, but the matter was not finished: ten thousand dollars was deducted from their annuity that year to pay for damages, despite protests from their new agent, James Gillis, that many of the claims had been fabricated.[60]

The reservation, however, was already occupied by a different group of outcasts. In the spring of 1857 a contingent of Mormons had established the town of Genoa on a slight rise just east of Beaver Creek, near its junction with the Loup. They laid the town out in blocks, erected log houses and various other buildings, and plowed up one thousand acres of bottomland. Just to the south, in a cottonwood grove on the banks of Beaver Creek, they built a steam saw and grist mill. By August 1859 there were as many as two hundred inhabitants in this isolated frontier community. Suddenly the Mormons found themselves on an Indian reservation. They petitioned the Indian Office to shift the eastern boundary of the reservation to the west of Beaver Creek, so that they could retain their homes. But the Mormons were disliked even more than the Indians, and after promising them compensation for their buildings, Gillis ordered them to leave. By the spring of 1860 they were gone, heading to a new sanctuary in Utah.[61]

So the Pawnee, to their advantage, inherited a reservation that was already

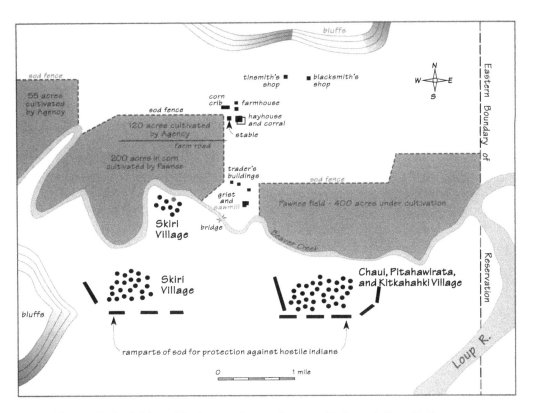

Fig. 22 DePuy's Map of the Pawnee Reservation, 1861 (Redrawn). From DePuy to Branch, July 30, 1861. LR Pawnee Agency, 1859–62. Courtesy of Nebraska State Historical Society, RG 508

substantially improved. Henry DePuy, who replaced Gillis as agent in April 1861, submitted a detailed account and map of its geography to superintendent Branch soon after he took up his post (fig. 22).[62] It was a place of "great beauty and fertility," he wrote without exaggeration. An expanse of fertile bottomland stretched for a mile from the Loup to the bluffs on the north; streams like Beaver Creek, Cedar Creek, and Plum Creek flowed out of the hills, their bottoms lined with timber and covered with rich soil; and to the south gently rolling prairie sloped down toward the Platte.

The Pawnee settled in three villages in the point of land between Beaver Creek and the Loup, each defended by earth ramparts facing south and by the creek on the north. The Skiri, numbering 1,166, occupied the two western villages; the other three bands, thrown closer together by population decline, intermarriage, and security needs, occupied the other. There were 903 Chaui, 561 Pitahawirata, and 784 Kitkahahki. Altogether, there were two hundred lodges, most about fifty to sixty feet in diameter, and some already decaying after only two years' occupancy. DePuy archly described the scene as "not over-tidy on a near view," but "picturesque . . . from a distance."

The various buildings of the agency, most of them purchased cheaply from the Mormons, occupied the old town site of Genoa. They included a frame farmhouse in bad repair, a sixty-foot-square log building that was used as the agent's office, a "substantial" corn crib with a carriage way through the center and a capacity for twenty-five hundred bushels, some "tumble-down" stables that would last only one more winter, a blacksmith's shop that was "quite in ruins" and which had been purchased from the Mormons for seven bushels of corn, and the agent's house, an unplastered frame building which let in rain and snow. About one-half mile to the south of the agent's house stood the steam saw and grist mill, a two-story building set on oak blocks, its pump broken and pipes twisted. All the buildings were made of untreated cottonwood, and all were rotting and "very shabby." DePuy put their collective worth at five thousand dollars.

By 1861, one thousand acres were ready for cultivation, thanks to the Mormons' efforts in breaking the sod. Of these, 825 acres were being cultivated by Pawnee women and the remainder was worked by agency farmers. DePuy estimated that the Pawnee could get twenty bushels of corn an acre from the fields, a yield that could greatly be increased, he suggested, by further plowing. The most urgent need, he concluded, was a school, a planned two-story structure thirty-two feet by seventy-six feet that would house seventy-five children. There was little population pressure on the Pawnee at this time, only isolated settlers' cabins along the Loup toward Columbus, and intermittent road ranches on the overland trail that veered to the southwest of the reservation, following the Platte valley (fig. 23).

The main disadvantage of the reservation, however, became immediately apparent. In the first year the villages were attacked at least eight times, leaving thirteen Pawnee dead, thirty horses stolen, and sixty lodges destroyed. The Pawnee were not defenseless, of course, and on one occasion, in September 1860, they chased a party of Cheyenne out onto the plains, recaptured their horses, took eight others, and killed two of the raiders. But the Brulé and Oglala Dakota were dangerous enemies. Not only were they, in amalgamation, more numerous than the Pawnee, but they were well armed, supplied with guns by a government bent on appeasement and by traders who would do anything for robes. Their tactic was to attack the reservation while the Pawnee were absent on the summer hunt. At that time only the sick and the very old and very young were at home. From April to September of 1860 they stayed close to the reservation. They struck twice in late June, killing and scalping Pawnee women who had stayed behind, burning lodges, and stealing horses. They came again on July 5 and burned more lodges in the course of a three-hour-long occupation. Agent Gillis saved the women and children this time by hiding them in a cellar

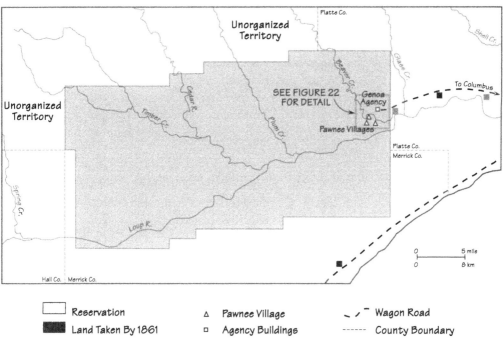

Fig. 23 Pawnee Reservation and Vicinity, circa 1861

under his house. Each time, Gillis (who had immunity as an American) persuaded the Dakota to leave; each time, as they withdrew across the Loup, they vowed to return. In early September, a war party of four hundred to five hundred warriors gathered to the west of the reservation, determined to attack. Troops from Fort Kearney led by Captain Alfred Sully moved in to protect the Pawnee, and the Dakota withdrew to their own territory. But, to Gillis's dismay, the troops stayed only until late October.[63] This was the extent of the government's protection.

The constant fear of attack and sense of encirclement left the Pawnee demoralized and destitute. The women were afraid to work in the fields or to venture out in search of roots, and the Dakota sabotaged the hunts by burning the prairie and driving the bison away. Even nature seemed to conspire against the Pawnee. A parching drought destroyed what few crops were sown in 1860, and the severity of the following winter took a heavy toll on the horses. When DePuy arrived at the reservation in the spring of 1861, the Pawnee had been reduced to a state of "absolute starvation" and were considering abandoning the reservation and retreating east to the Missouri.[64] This, of course, would not have been allowed, and in any case it would not have brought the beleaguered Pawnee any peace.

The unsettled conditions also nullified the agents' efforts to "improve" the Pawnee. The saw and grist mill was repaired, though work was slowed by the Dakota raids, and Beaver Creek was bridged, linking the agency to the Indian villages and to the stands of cottonwoods that bordered the Loup. But no progress at all was made in agricultural instruction, partly because of the dangers involved, but also because the Pawnee men "manifested but little disposition towards tilling the soil."[65] The manual-labor school remained only an empty promise in the 1857 treaty. The agents repeatedly asked for military protection or, failing that, for guns and ammunition so that the Pawnee could defend themselves. Some powder and ammunition were furnished in the 1861 annuities, and Gillis organized a police force made up of "six of the most reliable braves from each of the four bands."[66] But these measures were not enough to provide the security that the Pawnee needed in order to obtain their clothes and food, and which the agents needed in order to pursue their acculturation program.

In a sense, the Dakota were a convenient scapegoat to divert attention from the agency's own failings. Gillis spent five months of his brief period in office visiting Pittsburgh, and in 1861 he was investigated by the United States attorney for Nebraska Territory for diverting money from the Pawnee's funds. DePuy seems to have been more honest, but (probably because of this) he became entangled in disputes at the agency, which consumed much of his time. His main opponents were the traders, James Hollis (in DePuy's opinion a "noisy, quarrelsome, and extremely disgusting man") and Lester Platt, who, together with a number of disgruntled former agency employees, hovered around the reservation "like obscene birds of prey."[67] They were angry with DePuy, he claimed, because he had prevented the Pawnee from pawning their blankets and annuities. DePuy made a convincing case, but complaints against him led to an official investigation, and eventually to his dismissal in the spring of 1862.

The pattern for the Pawnee's remaining, tragic life in Nebraska was set in these harrowing early years: the government's perverse refusal to adequately provide them with guns or other protection, increasing control by corrupt or ineffectual agents, unremitting attacks by the Brulé and Oglala Dakota, manipulation by traders and other settlers who wanted their resources and eventually their lands, and season after season of grinding poverty and steadily declining population. This was a far cry from the nurturing environment that Manypenny had hoped the reservation would provide.

Expulsion to the West

The Ponca were the last of the eastern Nebraska Indians to be settled on their reservation, although, given their living conditions on that inadequate and dangerous strip of land, it could hardly be called "settled." Their problems began in 1854 when the Omaha sold territory in northeastern Nebraska that the

Ponca claimed as their historic homeland (fig. 13). Specifically, the Ponca insisted that the land between Aoyway Creek and the Niobrara was not the Omaha's to sell, and they threatened to "come down" on their relatives and "exterminate them."[68] By 1857 settlers were moving into this ceded land, following the wagon road along the bluffs to the terminal at Niobrara, right into the Ponca's cornfields.

At the same time, the Brulé, numbering at least thirty-eight hundred people, including eight hundred warriors, were pressing down from the White River and maintaining a cordon around the Ponca that cut them off from their hunting grounds.[69] Because of this pressure, the Ponca abandoned Húbdon (Fish-Smell) Village and amassed at their other customary location near the mouth of the Niobrara. Some even settled adjacent to the town site of Niobrara. Tensions flared as starving Indians stole crops and cattle from settlers whom they regarded as intruders. The settlers showed some understanding of the Ponca's predicament, but they were afraid because their own situation was precarious, following the collapse of the economy in 1857. They launched batteries of complaints to the Indian Office, warning of an impending "major collision" unless steps were taken to remove the Ponca from their town.[70]

The Ponca also wanted the Indian Office to act. From 1855 on they repeatedly expressed their willingness to sell their lands in return for a reservation and annuities. On June 16, 1857, for example, Alexander Redfield, on his way to his agency on the upper Missouri, encountered a large group of Ponca near the mouth of the Niobrara. The Ponca, led by The Drum ("a fine looking fellow"), complained bitterly about the Omaha's sale of their land and its subsequent settlement by Americans. All the other Nebraska Indians had annuities, they pointed out, and they wanted the same treatment. In the following fall, John Robertson, the Omaha's agent (and by proxy, the man responsible for the Ponca) was dispatched to the Niobrara to invite the Ponca to send a treaty delegation to Washington, D.C. Robertson selected six of their "leading men" to make the journey: The Whip, Strong Walker, Lone Chief, Threatening Clouds, Standing Buffalo, and the mixed-blood, Michael Cerré. The second principal chief, The Drum, may have stayed home to look after his people. The delegation reached the capital in late December 1857.[71]

The ensuing meetings with Commissioner Charles Mix on December 29 and January 5 demonstrate that while the commissioner was quite willing to discuss issues (in language comically catered to the Indians) he left no room for compromise.[72] Although the first meeting was not meant to be a negotiation session, but rather a formal greeting, Mix did not hesitate to lay out the American terms. It was time, he told the Ponca leaders, to "effect a radical change" in their situation. They were told that they must gather in one village, give up the hunt, and devote all their time to farming. Mix assured them that the reason he referred to them as "children" was that they required a father to "protect, guide, and direct" them. After this lecture they all shook hands, and the Indians left for their lodgings.

In the course of the next five days, the Ponca delegation drew up a proposal detailing what they wanted in exchange for their lands. They first defined their territory as extending from the Missouri at Aoyway Creek to the White River and west to the Black Hills, an extensive claim that both they and the commissioner knew was challenged by the Omaha and Dakota. In return for the sale of this land, they requested payments of forty thousand dollars for each of the first ten years, half of this to be paid in cash, then a perpetual annuity of thirty thousand dollars a year, again with half in cash. They also wanted thirty thousand dollars for removal expenses, a sawmill, blacksmith shop, manual labor school, and a "liberal provision" for their mixed-bloods. Clearly, the Ponca chiefs had done their homework, because these provisions were modeled on the Pawnee treaty that had recently been signed.

The Whip handed Mix the petition at the January meeting. The commissioner praised them for a businesslike proposal, but queried the legitimacy of their vast territorial claim. The Whip angrily replied that this land had been given to the Ponca by the "Great Spirit" long before their "pale-faced brethren" had crossed the "Great Water." But, he conceded, the "Great Spirit" had seen fit to give the Americans more power: he had visited their great museums, filled with the Indians' "utensils," and it left him saddened and "lost in reflection." The Ponca, he continued, had never been given anything by the United States, and his people had never "wasted a gunful of gunpowder" on Americans. But now they had a "large scope" of land to sell, and they had come to "do business." Strong Walker and Cerré then spoke, reiterating The Whip's message with much the same mixture of anger and pride.

Mix's reply was terse and categorical. Yes, whites had come across the sea, but that was two hundred years before. Moreover, Americans, he claimed, had done nothing worse to Indians than they, the Indians, had done to each other. He would not recognize their extensive territorial claim. How could he, he asked, when the land between Aoyway Creek and the Niobrara was already government property, and when the Brulé also claimed the country between the Niobrara and White rivers? Mix also insisted that the Ponca could not have a reservation near the Missouri, because it was too near settlers and infectious disease. Finally, with a display of petulance, he pointed to the medal The Whip wore around his neck and ridiculed the assertion that the Ponca had never received anything from the United States.

The Whip, now humiliated and distressed, pleaded with the commissioner not to move them from their ancestral homeland bordering the Missouri, between Ponca Creek and the Niobrara. As for his medal, he explained, it had been given to his brother many years before by Benjamin O'Fallon. But the Indians' pleas and arguments were to no avail. When the treaty was signed on

March 12, 1858, the Ponca received only a fraction of the payments they had requested (table 6). They were given a year to move twenty-five miles up Ponca Creek to the rugged tract of land that was reserved for their future home.

While the delegation was in Washington, the situation at Niobrara deteriorated rapidly.[73] The Ponca, or a large portion of them, spent the winter camped at the town. They were largely without food. The land on the valley floor that they had customarily farmed was occupied by settlers. This was good land, because the soil was easily tilled and yielded abundantly after so many years of attention. The Ponca did not have the implements to break new prairie sod and plant elsewhere. The chiefs were unable to prevent the young men from lashing out. Tensions reached a peak on January 11, when a group of warriors stormed the town's saw and grist mill, destroying machinery and stealing food. Troops were brought down from Fort Randall to restore order. Meanwhile, the Brulé had learned that the Ponca were making a treaty with the United States, and they sent word promising to wipe them out, along with those other turncoat treaty Indians, the Omaha and Pawnee.

In April 1858, Special Agent J. Shaw Gregory arrived at Niobrara to take charge. His first act was to move the Ponca away from Niobrara to Ponca Creek. This was the vicinity, he explained to William Wilson, his counterpart at the Omaha Agency, where fifty lodges of the Ponca had lived for a good many years (that is, at or near the Húbdon village). When the surveyors worked through in August of 1858, they located the village between a bluff and a slough just south of the mouth of Ponca Creek (fig. 24). Gregory claimed that since the move, there had been no depredations, no squatters, and no whiskey. Much of his success, he claimed, was due to the police force of twenty braves that he had appointed "immediately upon assuming charge of the tribe."[74]

The Ponca went out on their summer hunt under the protection of the Pawnee, but there was little meat to be found, and they also returned to failed crops. They were kept alive that fall and through the winter of 1858–59 with five hundred sacks of flour, one hundred eighty pounds of beef, one hundred sacks of sugar, sixty-two sacks of coffee, and one thousand bushels of corn that Gregory obtained with great difficulty from St. Johns and Sioux City.[75] For much of this time the Brulé—one hundred lodges under the command of Medicine Cup and White Black Bird—were poised, like a threatening storm, forty miles up Ponca Creek, waiting for an opportunity to attack.

The crisis deepened for the Ponca in the summer of 1859. They planted "every available spot" to corn before leaving to hunt on the Elkhorn. Gregory had warned them not to hunt north of the Niobrara because of the Brulé. But the Brulé (and possibly some Cheyenne) came to them, a "vastly superior force" that swept down on their camp on July 28, killing Shu-kah-bi (Heavy Chief), the third chief of the nation, and thirteen others, and carrying children off into captivity. Nearly all the Ponca's tipis were destroyed, their horses taken,

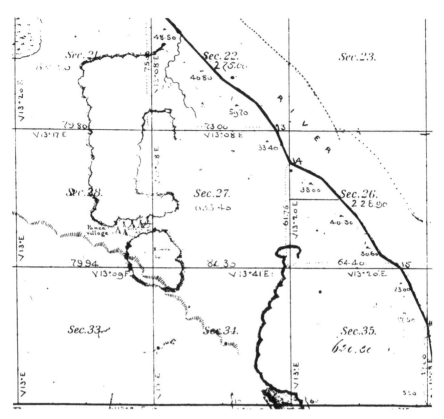

Fig. 24 Ponca Village, 1858. Original land survey, township 33 north, range 7 west of the 6th principal meridian. Courtesy of Nebraska State Historical Society

their meat burned. The Brulé even cut their moccasins into pieces. The Ponca were left with few horses, four guns, and no ammunition. Gregory asked for two companies of troops to protect the Ponca and one thousand dollars worth of food, guns, and ammunition, but his request fell upon deaf ears.[76]

The Ponca staggered back into their village near Ponca Creek and immediately went into council. The Whip handed Gregory the blood-stained arrows that had killed his kinsmen. He lamented over Shu-kah-bi's death, saying that he was a man who had supported the treaty, even though the young men had mocked him for his compliancy. The Brulé were also mocking them and calling them women for listening to the "Great Father." Why, he demanded to know, were the Dakota given weapons when they, the Ponca, received none? In disgust, he swore never again to wear the medal that Mix had given him on the visit to Washington, D.C. In the future, he vowed, he would be a warrior and die with some honor.[77]

On September 1, 1859, the Brulé struck again, this time attacking the village, and the Ponca fled back to Niobrara. They camped on the point of land between the Missouri and Niobrara rivers, immediately to the west of the town. Settlers from outlying homesteads also withdrew into Niobrara. Gregory warned Mix that the Ponca had only five weeks of provisions left, and that they were living in fear of annihilation. Their annuity funds had still not been appropriated by Congress (a full eighteen months after the signing of the treaty), so once again the Indians survived on rations—four thousand pounds of pork, four thousand pounds of flour, and four thousand pounds of hard bread—from Fort Randall. Despite the imminent danger, Gregory felt obliged to advise the Ponca to go out on their winter hunt, because the situation at Niobrara had deteriorated to the point that Indians were being shot on the street.[78]

While the Ponca fretted and starved, plans went ahead for the survey of the new reservation, as stipulated in the 1858 treaty. In May 1859 the appointed surveyor, Thomas J. Stone, ran his line twenty-five miles up the winding course of Ponca Creek to a western boundary demarcated only by an oak tree six inches in diameter. He then measured south to the Niobrara, and ten miles down that river to the dividing line between ranges 8 and 9 west of the 6th principal meridian (fig. 25). Upon receiving Stone's report, Gregory concluded that the proposed reservation was "totally unfit for occupation of the Indians, not having sufficient timber or good soil to afford them a home to sustain themselves." Moreover, he added, the location was twelve miles further up the river than the Ponca wished. But, because the land to the east of range 9 had already been surveyed in preparation for American settlement, he felt that he had no choice but to proceed with the removal of the Indians to their new home. Perhaps, he hopefully suggested to Robinson, a future supplemental treaty would change the location and give the Ponca the reservation they wanted nearer the Missouri.[79]

The Ponca continued to resist efforts to move them west. "We do not want to go up there," Hard Walker informed Gregory in council on February 3, 1860. "Let us die by our old place on the river," pleaded The Whip.[80] Young Ponca warriors even tried to stop the survey team from leaving in May, and troops from Fort Randall were called in to enforce law and order. As a punishment, four of the warriors were dismissed from the police force.[81] The Indian Office would condone no deviation from the original plan, and in the fall of 1860 Gregory moved the reluctant Ponca to their new home. It is a measure of their fear that they established the village at the extreme eastern end of the tract (fig. 25).

Unlike the other Nebraska Indians, the Ponca received a poor reservation. Much of the land was rugged, there was no local hay for their horses, and good soils were restricted to the narrow river terraces. There was little timber even in the river valleys, and the Indians had to stock fuel by hauling logs from islands

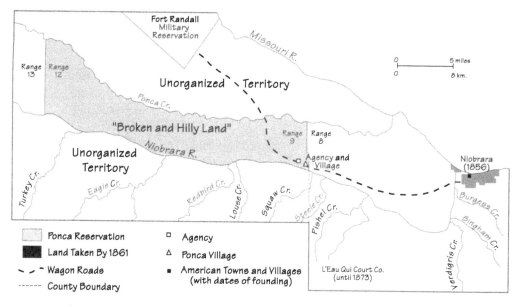

Fig. 25 Ponca Reservation and Vicinity, circa 1861

in the Niobrara when the water was iced over. The reservation was also remote. It was twenty miles to the town of Niobrara, and this involved crossing the river (figs. 25 and 26). It was thirty-two difficult miles by trail to Fort Randall, including a treacherous crossing of Ponca Creek. Annuities were either hauled by oxen from Fort Randall, or else delivered at a dock to the north of the mouth of the Niobrara, where there were no buildings, and the goods lay exposed to the elements.[82] The reservation's only proximity was to the Dakota.

Yet, in November 1860, Gregory optimistically reported that the future was looking brighter for the Ponca. A delegation from the Brulé had come into the agency to tell the Ponca magnanimously that they would be too busy raiding the Omaha and Pawnee to bother with them.[83] But peace was a false hope. On November 29 a small party of Dakota, mostly Santee, quietly raided the reservation and drove away nearly all the Ponca and agency horses. The Ponca assembled in yet another depressing council. Where was the promised protection, Lone Chief demanded to know? How could they hunt with only twenty horses between them? Despite this, he continued, they would indeed hunt, because "it was better to die on the prairie as a warrior" than to starve on the reservation.[84] They did go out on their winter hunt, but they found little except misery, and by January they were back in their refuge at the town of Niobrara.

Because of the disruptions of war and the poor environment of the reservation, the agency was slow in getting established. Gregory had stationed himself at Niobrara and had made few improvements at the agency by June 1, 1861, when he was replaced by Joshua Hoffman. When Hoffman arrived, bringing his family, he found a dilapidated saw and grist mill and two cottonwood plank buildings that were being used mainly as storehouses (fig. 26). The garret of one of the buildings was used as sleeping quarters for the unfortunate agency employees. Hoffman complained to Branch that there was nowhere to live in this "community of bachelors," and he sent his wife and children back to Fort Randall. Sixty acres of land had been broken in 1860, but it had not been cross plowed because of a shortage of plows, and it was not ready for cultivation.[85]

Hoffman ordered the Ponca back to the reservation in July, just after they had received their first delivery of annuities. After the usual expenditures on "useful goods," the Ponca were left with $6,999 to be distributed in cash, which came to $7 for each individual. They moved back to the reservation "with great reluctance" because of their fear of the Dakota. When they arrived there, they refused to go even a half-mile from the agency to plant their fields, and they would go nowhere near the bluffs in case the Dakota were lying in wait. Hoffman increased the size of the Ponca police force, and dressed them in fine regalia, but this was less an effective protection than a means of putting the Ponca "more directly under his control."[86]

A few patches of corn had been planted in the spring of 1861 and twenty acres were cultivated in the agency field, but there was no rain and the crops withered in the ground. The Indians could not survive on this impoverished land, yet they were afraid to leave on the summer hunt. They had only one horse for every three warriors; even if they managed to find the herds without being

Fig. 26 Hoffman's Map of the Ponca Agency, 1861. Central Map Files, National Archives, RG 75, No. CA 380–81

attacked, they would not be able to carry much meat back to the reservation. Hoffman (rather casually) allayed their fears and sent them off to the southwest toward the Elkhorn. But they traveled no more than fifty miles from the reservation before turning back, starving and exhausted. The Ponca scattered that fall, some going to live with the Omaha, others to the Pawnee. Those who stayed at the agency roasted the few ears of corn that had survived the drought, then lived on wild plums and turnips. They also traded their blankets and other annuity goods for food, sacrificing future security to immediate need.

It is difficult to reconcile these terrible living conditions with statistics that show that the Ponca's population was increasing, but that seems to have been the case (fig. 8). Gregory and Hoffman both made definitive population counts when they drew up the annuity rolls.[87] In 1861, for example, there were 973 names on the roster, 428 male and 545 female. The roster was organized into six traditional clans, each headed by a chief. The Whip was recognized as the principal chief, and the former leader, The Drum, appeared nowhere on the list, indicating that he had died since his meeting with Redfield in 1857. It is possible that many of the names on the rolls were mixed-bloods, and that the Ponca's population had been swelled by an influx of relatives eager to get in on the payments. Whatever the cause, the Ponca had a new, higher, official population, a new total from which to continue declining.

CHAPTER FIVE

Life on the Reservations in the 1860s

The Nebraska Indians' options continued to foreclose in the 1860s. Increasingly their fates were decreed in Washington, D.C. Their ability to chart their own course, following the traditional cycle, was severely compromised as the bison hunts became progressively more perilous and less productive, and as their agents intruded ever more deeply into their lives. Americans, whether hostile or sympathetic, took for granted that the Indians could no longer live as Indians, hunting over extensive areas, raiding for horses and glory, and living communally. They were being crowded out, their traditions maligned, their very right to exist called into question. Charles Mix, the leading architect of the reservation policy, explained the situation rather more sympathetically than most in his 1867 report: "The plea of 'manifest destiny' is paramount and the Indian must give way though it may be at the sacrifice of what may be as dear as life."[1]

The question was: would the Nebraska Indians "give way" by taking out allotments and merging with Americans, or would they be forced to move to Indian Territory to make room for settlers? Indeed, would they persist in clinging to their time-honored ways in a world that rejected them and "give way" by dying out altogether? Samuel Allis, who still lived in frontier Nebraska thirty years after first coming as a missionary in 1834, thought that the last course was most likely for the Pawnee, who were "running out as a race."[2]

Allotments, and associated values like individualism and the work ethic, remained the primary goal of the reservation policy. Large portions of the annuities, including the agricultural and education funds, were applied to this end. Once on allotments, the argument went, the Indians would become self-sufficient, and the United States would no longer have to support them. The Indians would gain a sense of private property, and Americans would in turn gain their "surplus" lands. These ideas were repeated like a litany in every commissioner's report of the decade.

This enduring program of allotments was energized in 1869 when, as part of President Grant's "Peace Policy," Commissioner Ely Samuel Parker (himself a full-blood Seneca) appointed Quakers—a "different class of men"—to operate sixteen separate agencies.[3] In Nebraska, Hicksite Quakers were put in charge of the Omaha, Otoe-Missouria, and Pawnee agencies, and later, in 1871, a Protestant Episcopal agent was appointed to the Ponca. The Quakers and other religious leaders strenuously advocated allotments and industrial education as the route to civilization. This was the only way, the Quakers wrote in a manifesto in 1869, that the Indians could at least "tread closely on the heels, if not entirely pass, *the hindmost of the white race.*"[4] Beyond the assumed spiritual benefits of land ownership, they saw allotments as the Indians' only remaining opportunity to hold onto any land at all.

Yet in 1870 no Nebraska Indians were living on allotments, and almost all continued to go on the semiannual bison hunts. Meanwhile, settlers engulfed the Omaha and Otoe-Missouria reservations and pushed up against the others. After a cessation of immigration during the Civil War, settlers had once again poured into Nebraska. Taking advantage of virtually free land offered under the Homestead Act of 1862, they channeled along the river valleys where wood and water were available. The extension of railroads into the state allowed the settlers to break free from the Missouri valley, and by 1870 the even-numbered sections in the Union Pacific land grant, which were open to homesteading, were rapidly being taken. Also by 1870 the grid of the land surveyors had been laid across all of eastern Nebraska in anticipation of future settlement (fig. 27).

Beyond the river valleys and the railroad land grants, on the upland prairies, almost all the land was taken by speculators who rightly anticipated that the value of their holdings would greatly increase as the railroads penetrated the open spaces and the country filled up with settlers. Soldiers' bounty land warrants remained a favorite speculative device, but after the Morrill Act of 1863, the most effective method of acquiring large amounts of land was agricultural college script. The Morrill Act gave each state thirty thousand acres of land for every senator and representative it had in Congress. The objective was to create an endowment for agricultural and mechanical colleges. States could either locate the acreages on the public domain, later selling them as needed, or receive the equivalency in script which could be sold to potential purchasers of land. From 1863 to 1872 more than one million two hundred thousand acres in Nebraska were taken off the market and held for future profit through this means. Most of the purchasers were from the eastern states. This was almost as much land as passed to genuine settlers through homesteads and preemptions combined over the same period. Add to this the four million acres of odd-numbered sections that were wrapped up in railroad land grants and later sold for the benefit of the railroads at $2.50 an acre (a price beyond the means of most settlers in 1870) and the withholding of sections 16 and 36 in each township for the support of schools, and it can be understood why the Indian

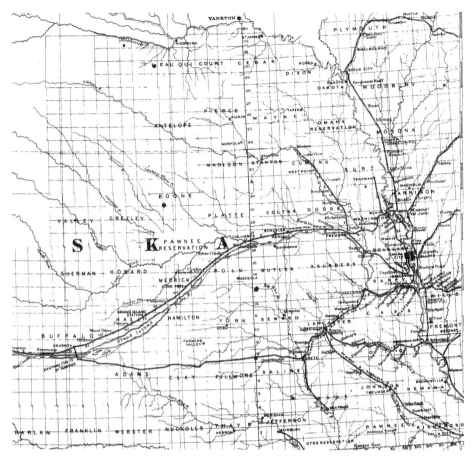

Fig. 27 Eastern Nebraska and Adjacent Areas, 1871. Portion of Asher and Adams' "Nebraska." Courtesy of Nebraska State Historical Society, M782, AS3

reservations came to be viewed by settlers and speculators alike as the best bet for future land acquisition.[5]

Most Nebraskans had no intention of giving the reservation policy time to work, and as the decade wore on the demand to remove the Nebraska Indians to Indian Territory became ever more clamorous. This idea of concentrating the Nebraska and Kansas Indians in Indian Territory (or on a giant reservation on the northern Great Plains) had remained an important subtheme in the Indian Office since its inception in the late 1840s: humanitarians like Commissioner Nathaniel Taylor (1867–69) saw it as an opportunity to save the Indians from extinction, while less idealistic supporters saw it as a way to get control of the remaining Indian lands.[6] Senator Thomas W. Tipton of Nebraska fell into the latter category, reflecting the views of most of his constituents: "They are still living in their wigwams," he proclaimed to the Senate in 1870, "making no advance whatever in agriculture, while our poor homestead settlers all around with their hands are making livings." Tipton ended by referring to the reservations as "cankers in the body politic of Nebraska," and he called for the Indians' removal and the opening of their lands to settlers.[7] Similar sentiments were frequently expressed in the press, in the state legislature, and in governors' annual messages.

Occasionally, humane voices could be heard above the crowd. Moses K. Turner, for example, the enlightened editor of *The Platte Journal* (Columbus), considered the Pawnee and other Nebraska Indians to be "more sinned against than sinning."[8] But such reformist views were more typical of New England than Nebraska, and even well-meaning people like Turner thought that it would be best for the Indians if they were removed to Indian Territory, away from the polluting influence of the frontier. And so, as the 1860s ended, a race had developed between allotments and removal; no one, it seems, believed that the reservations would survive intact.

In the midst of all these pressures and changes, the Nebraska Indians tried to eke out an existence on the reservations. Their situations were similar in many ways: they all suffered (as settlers did) from drought and grasshoppers, endured violent conflicts with Americans and hostile Indians, faced the passing of a way of life as the bison herds were slaughtered, and were obliged to rely on inadequate support from the government. But there were differences too, differences that can only be understood in the context of a specific society and a specific reservation. The Ponca survived poorly on rations for much of the decade and ended up with no legal title to their lands; the Omaha experienced a measure of success, increased their population, and moved toward securing at least some of their lands through allotments; the Otoe-Missouria were shackled with corrupt agents who squandered their annuities, and their population dropped to a dangerous low; and the Pawnee, left virtually unprotected on the front line by the United States, bore the brunt of the wrath of the Dakota.

Life on Rations

For the Ponca, the 1860s was a decade of misery, a time of fear, insecurity, and hunger. They witnessed the collapse of their subsistence base, and in their weakened condition they were virtually powerless against their enemies. They were victims of grave injustices at the hands of Americans, both on the frontier and in Washington, D.C., injustices that were never redressed. They stuck by their end of the 1858 treaty bargain, while at the same time the United States failed to live up to its obligations. By 1870 they were living a submarginal existence on rations, and their population had dropped to 750 (fig. 8).

During the entire decade the Ponca reaped only two good harvests and completed only three worthwhile bison hunts. This poor record was no fault of their own. Agents repeatedly praised them for their willingness to work in the fields, for their interest in American methods of cultivation, and for their acknowledgment that they could no longer live by the hunt. They were characterized as "friendly," "loyal," "peaceable," and "well-behaved." As early as 1862, for example, The Whip, (the most "progressive" of the chiefs, according to Agent Hoffman) requested that his indemnity money for loss of horses to the Dakota should be paid to him in the form of cattle, wagons, and plows.[9] As it turned out, the payment was long delayed, and neither The Whip, nor any other Ponca, would have any say in how it was spent.

The Ponca's efforts to sustain themselves were damned by adverse environmental conditions, by the upheavals associated with the removal of the agency from the Niobrara to the Missouri in 1866–67, by the failures of the reservation policy, and by the Brulé, who stalked them on their hunts and killed them in their fields.

Despite substantial improvements at the agency on the Niobrara in the early 1860s, including Hoffman's construction of a two-story schoolhouse, a large barn, and twenty-five log houses for the Indians, the locale could in no way support the roughly one thousand Ponca. Hay still had to be hauled from the Missouri bottoms, and by 1863 the nearest fuel (apart from worthless green cottonwood) was six miles away on the other side of the river. According to The Whip, the burden of carrying this fuel across the ice was killing the Ponca women.[10] Hoffman and agency workers built a sixty-foot bridge across Ponca Creek in the spring of 1862, which eased the problems of haulage from Fort Randall. But remoteness from the Missouri continued to cause delays in the delivery of annuities and agricultural equipment. Ironically, even remoteness from Americans was a problem. Little of the surrounding country was settled (fig. 28), so there was no cordon of farmers around the reservation to discourage Brulé raids. Moreover, the agents were unable to find anyone within a sixty-mile radius who was equipped to custom plow the government fields.

Two fields, one three hundred acres, the other sixty acres, were plowed and fenced, but very little was grown in them. The Ponca and the agency employees were too afraid to go out to farm. The Brulé were never far away, and the Ponca were convinced that these inveterate enemies were being reinforced by other hostile Dakota who had fled west following the Minnesota uprising of 1862. The atmosphere at the agency in the first half of the 1860s was filled with foreboding. It was like the "lull before the storm," Hoffman wrote in 1862, and he seriously considered abandoning his post.[11] He and the Ponca stayed, but their fears were partly realized in the spring of 1865 when two women were killed and scalped while planting seeds.

Even crops that were sown came to nothing. Every year from 1861 through

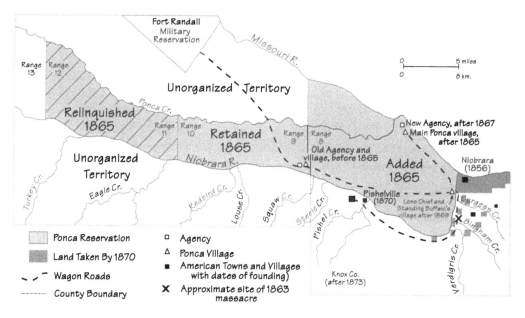

Fig. 28　Ponca Reservation and Vicinity, circa 1870

1864 the corn and vegetables were destroyed by drought or grasshoppers, or both. From August 1862 to August 1864 there was not a single heavy rain; even the wild plums withered and dried on the bushes. The women boiled the dry corn stalks into a thin soup, the government sent emergency rations from Fort Randall, the Omaha and Pawnee donated surplus corn and seed for the next year, and total starvation was held at bay.[12]

Good summer hunts in 1862 and 1864 helped too. In those years there were enough clothes and meat to see the Ponca through to the winter (shelter was no longer so dependent on the bison hunt because most of the tipis at the agency— 110 from 130 in 1861–62—were covered with canvas sheeting). But hunting had become an unreliable source of food and an increasingly dangerous occupation. The range was overcrowded and bitterly contested. In the summer of 1863, for example, the Yankton took all the accessible bison, and in 1861 and 1865 the plains were overrun by Brulé hunting parties and the Ponca were too afraid to venture out. They were not cowards, Hoffman explained to his superiors; they were just outnumbered and had few horses or guns. The small number of horses (Agent Potter estimated that there were eighty in 1865) made it very difficult to move all the people hundreds of miles on a bison hunt (table 7). Typically, a mounted party would leave first, with the others following on foot to a prearranged rendezvous, generally on the Elkhorn. The sick, the old, and the very young would stay at the agency and survive as best they could. Hoffman used to send the hunting party out with a pass, in case they were mistaken for hostile Indians. He would also tell them to stay out on the range for as long as possible because there was little to live on at the agency.[13]

There was talk in 1864 of moving the Ponca from their beleaguered reservation to live with their friends, the Omaha. The hapless Winnebago, who had been driven from successive homes in Wisconsin, Iowa, and Minnesota and located on the barren Crow Creek reservation in Dakota Territory in 1863, were already in the process of finding refuge there. Commissioner Dole liked the idea for its economy—three agencies would be run by one agent. The Ponca did not like the plan at all. They were worried about practical matters: would they be reimbursed for improvements at the old agency? Would they be able to maintain an independent government and village on the Omaha reservation? Would they be allowed to visit their old hunting grounds?[14] Besides, no matter how difficult their lives, they were still deeply attached to the Niobrara country, especially the old homeland near the Missouri.

Finally, the Indian Office decided to reward the Ponca for their "constant fidelity" by returning to them their "old burial grounds and cornfields" near the mouth of Ponca Creek. In a "supplemental treaty" signed by the chiefs in Washington, D.C., on March 19, 1865, the Ponca were given back the country lying to the east of their reservation and bounded by Ponca Creek and the Niobrara and Missouri rivers (fig. 28). In return they relinquished thirty thousand acres from the west of the old reservation. The resulting, enlarged, reservation was ninety-six thousand acres. The Ponca were obliged to pay a total of five thousand dollars in compensation from their 1858 treaty annuities to five settlers (including their former agent, J. Shaw Gregory) who had previously taken out claims in the area that was added to the reservation. However, they were

Table 7   Estimates of the Indians' Wealth in the 1860s

	Omaha	Pawnee	Ponca	Otoe-Missouria
Total Wealth	$70,000– $108,000	$100,000	$5,000– $10,000	$10,000– $20,000
Horses	500–1,225	1,500	80	300
Average Corn Production (bushels)	20,000– 25,000	20,000	less than 5,000	5,000

Sources: Letters Received from each agency, 1860–70, and ARCIA, 1860–70. These are only general figures, useful for the purposes of comparison, and numbers in all three categories tended to vary widely from year to year, reflecting the general instability of life

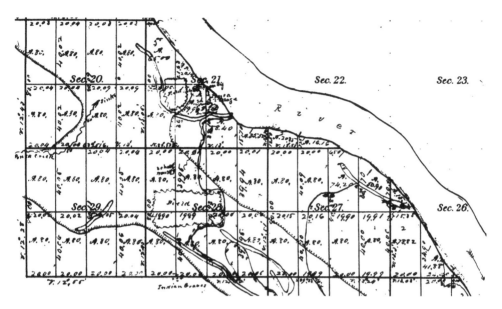

Fig. 29 Ponca Village and Agency, 1871. Original land survey, township 33 north, range 7 west of the 6th principal meridian. Courtesy of Nebraska State Historical Society

belatedly granted $15,080 to pay for "spoilations" committed by the Dakota over the previous seven years, most specifically for the theft of more than one hundred horses in November 1860.[15]

The Ponca abandoned the old agency in January 1866. Agent Potter waited until the treaty was ratified before officially moving the agency in August 1867. The buildings were hauled from the old to the new site over the following two years. The agency and main Ponca village were built on the low-lying flood plain close to the Missouri, a short distance below the mouth of Ponca Creek (figs. 28 and 29). The Missouri on one side and a natural drainage ditch on the other afforded some protection against attack. The reassembled schoolhouse stood one-half mile to the south. Indian graves perched on the nearby high bluffs. A track ran from the agency parallel with the bluffs past the schoolhouse and fields to the Niobrara. By 1869 there was a second, smaller Ponca village, home to the bands led by Lone Chief and Standing Buffalo, located nine miles below the agency near the Niobrara River.[16] These were the more independent Ponca, full-bloods who wished to stay disassociated from the agency and the government's program. Just to the east of Niobrara lay the Santee Reservation, newly created for refugees from the Minnesota uprising.

Compared to the old agency site, this was very good land, and at first the move boded well. There was abundant cottonwood, oak, and ash, and a "luxuriant" cover of grass on the flood plain. The soil was fertile alluvium, watered by numerous springs that ran out of the bluffs. Proximity to the Missouri meant that the Ponca could oversee the delivery of their annuities (they suspected that they were not getting the full amount), and they had ambitious plans to make money by selling firewood to the steamboats. Even before the move was completed in the fall of 1865, Ponca women raised a good crop of corn in their freshly cleared fields. The following spring they planted five hundred acres to corn, and in the fall they harvested enough to give large amounts to the Yankton. The men killed thousands of waterfowl in the spring and brought in plenty of meat from the summer hunt. The only reversal was an outbreak of "miasmatic fever" caused by Missouri River flooding.[17]

But the years 1865 and 1866 were only a brief respite, after which living conditions declined even more precipitously than before. Progress at the agency stalled. When William Hugo took over for his brief stint as agent in July 1869, he found 540 acres under cultivation, but 528 of them were Indian plots. The agency's twelve acres held a meager stand of wheat and barley that was "choked with grass." The saw mill was in disrepair, so none of the fields were fenced, and horses and cattle ate the crops at will. The government school, a provision of the 1858 treaty, opened in January 1868, then closed for want of funds in June 1869. In fact, all the funds for agriculture, education, and the "mechanical arts" lapsed in 1869 because they had only been appropriated for ten years. So almost as soon as they had settled in, the Ponca chiefs were forced to consider selling most of their reservation to fund new assistance from the United States.[18]

In 1867 the grasshoppers returned and ate everything that grew. They destroyed the crops again in 1868 and 1869, and drought added its toll in 1870. The Brulé stepped up their attacks on the reservation. From August to November of 1869 they raided four times, stealing more than fifty horses and killing and scalping a young Ponca warrior, White Bird (Wah-zhing-gah-skah), who was caught hunting near the boundary of the reservation. The Ponca combined with the Pawnee to hunt in 1868 and 1870, but the Brulé were everywhere on the range, and the Ponca brought home no meat. By 1870, according to Agent Hugo, they "rarely hunted" at all unless in association with the Omaha or Pawnee.[19]

Agents' reports during these years describe the Ponca as "destitute," "starving," and "broken." They lived on wild potatoes and rations that were hauled from Fort Randall or the Yankton Agency. The women and children, as portrayed in a plaintive speech by Standing Buffalo in 1870, were "half naked and ashamed to see strangers."[20] Death rates soured as bronchitis, pneumonia, and tuberculosis ran rampant. John Burbank, governor of Dakota Territory and head of the Dakota Superintendency, visited the stricken reservation in June 1870. Most of the Ponca were on a distant hunt along the Platte with the Pawnee and the village was left to the old, the lame, and the blind. These starving, ragged people crowded around Burbank, begging for food. He had none to give. As he left he saw them all gathered together on the prairie, cooking a communal meal of roots and plants. One old woman was singing to the Great Spirit to take pity on them.[21]

Government assistance was a poor substitute for the Ponca's once reliable subsistence base. Rations were no more than a stopgap, and individual allocations were incrementally reduced from 1867 to 1870. Burbank suggested building a soup kitchen and feeding the Ponca from three large kettles so that the rations would go further. During the early 1860s the rations were paid for from the Ponca's education fund, and later, as the Ponca discovered to their amazement and anger in 1869, they were financed from the 1865 treaty's "spoilation fund." Why had they not been told this? Lone Chief demanded to know at a council held at the agency on January 13, 1870. The spoilation fund had been their money to pay sufferers for loss of life and property, and they knew how to use it better than anyone else. The Ponca could not get an accounting of what had been spent and what was left of their fund.[22]

The inadequate rations were only one example of the failure of the reservation policy to secure the lives of the Ponca. Their annuity from the 1858 treaty was, as Hoffman had pointed out in 1862, inadequate, being about "one-third to one-half as much per capita as [that of] the other Tribes which they visit." Their annual cash payment in the second half of the 1860s was less than five dollars per person. After payment of the previous year's debts they often had nothing left. The remainder of the annuity—the "useful goods"—also left much to be desired. The delivery in 1862, for example, included a large amount of useless axes, a supply of fish hooks and lines which did not work for catching fish, thirty-six dozen pairs of mirrors which were simply left on the ground, and spoons, butcher knives, and scissors which were already in abundance at the village.[23]

There were more blatant breaches of faith on the United States' part. The protection that was promised in Article 2 of the 1858 treaty was never available. Troop strength on the Nebraska frontier was depleted by the Civil War and by General Alfred Sully's campaigns against the Dakota on the upper Missouri. By 1864 there were only fifty-nine foot soldiers at Fort Randall, and most of them were not fit, physically or mentally, for duty. The only protection the Niobrara Agency received was a small troop of "invalids" who accompanied Hoffman back from Fort Randall on May 14, 1864, and who stayed a month. According to Hoffman, the Ponca knew very well that Fort Randall offered no protection. They had told him that the fort "would require more soldiers to defend it than it would Indians to destroy it." Left to his own devices, Hoffman built a sturdy blockhouse and stockade at the agency and obtained, "by repeated applications," one hundred muskets and ammunition. But his requests for two small cannon were ignored, as was his innovative plan to employ Ponca warriors as soldiers who would be outfitted and paid by the army to guard the agency year-round.[24]

Not only was the army no help to the Ponca, but it was actually a serious threat. Especially near the end of the Civil War, when regular troops were engaged elsewhere, soldiers on the Nebraska frontier were badly paid volunteers, and they were often dubious characters. Most of them were drawn from the western states and territories, and their attitudes toward Indians were typically vindictive. Moreover, following the Minnesota uprising the entire frontier was swept up in what Newton Edmunds, the governor of Dakota Territory, described as a "state of nervous insecurity."[25] Wild rumors of a coordinated Indian and Confederacy uprising reverberated along the border. Both the Ponca and the Omaha would find out to their expense that any Indian was fair game in this paranoid and belligerent atmosphere.

On December 3 and 4, 1863, the Ponca were victims of what Hoffman euphemistically described as "a very unfortunate occurrence."[26] On the morning of December 3, a small party of Ponca (four men, a youth, five women, and five children) set up camp at the farm of a friendly settler, William Huddleston, just south of the town of Niobrara (fig. 28). They were returning with a store of corn from a visit to the Omaha. At sunset two soldiers who had been hunting nearby rode into the camp. They demanded to know if the Ponca had a pass allowing them to be off the reservation. They did not. The soldiers departed, and the Indians thought that the matter was over.

A few hours later, as the Ponca were preparing to sleep, fifteen mounted soldiers returned to the camp. One Is There (A-de-tah), the warrior in charge who later testified in court, came out of the tipi and shook hands with the soldiers. They went inside and the soldiers immediately demanded access to the women. A soldier with a black moustache and beard, and dressed in a wolfskin coat, offered One Is There money for the use of his wife. Another, who had a short nose and large eyes and wore a cavalry jacket with lace on the collar and emblems on the sleeves, also offered money for a woman while gesturing with a knife that he would cut throats if he was refused. A third soldier, who wore a wolf tail on his hat, drew his revolver and approached what he thought was a woman wrapped in a blanket. When he pulled the blanket off to find a youth instead, the Indians panicked, threw up the side of the tipi, and escaped into a copse of willows. The soldiers fired on them without hitting anyone, then proceeded to destroy the camp, cutting the tipi into pieces, burning the blankets and saddles, shooting the kettles full of holes, and scattering the corn over the ground. They left, taking with them seventeen beaver skins, two buffalo robes, three guns, and other items, while an old Indian, Dirty Face (In-da-ma-sha-da), looked on from a nearby hiding place.

The Indians waited until it seemed safe, then returned to the camp to salvage their possessions. But two hours later the soldiers came back with a wagon, and the Indians once again ran into hiding. The soldiers filled the wagon with traps and a tipi cover before leaving, heading north toward Niobrara. Just before dawn the Ponca quickly gathered up the corn, packed their horses (which had been safely tethered for the night in the willows), and left for the agency. At sunrise, near the Niobrara, they stopped to eat and build a fire. Some of the women and children went out to look for wild beans. The soldiers returned once more. The men and three women at the camp ran off under fire. One woman was shot in her thigh, another was hit by a bullet that passed through her side and into the thigh of the child she was carrying. She was shot again as she tried to get across the ice to the other side of the river. The soldier in the wolf-tail hat, and another who had "swelled lips," gathered the Indians' horses and packed their wagon with the Indians' remaining possessions.

The women and children who had gone out for the beans had heard the gunfire and were hiding half a mile below the camp. As the soldiers passed by, the Indians' dog barked and they were exposed. One of the children, a small boy, survived to describe the ensuing atrocities. Two soldiers dismounted and approached the women with drawn revolvers. They shot three women in their foreheads, and riddled a twelve-year-old girl's breast with bullets. They stripped the clothes off one of the dead women and almost decapitated another with a saber. The youth managed to escape across the ice and brought the news of the massacre to the agency. Dirty Face gathered the bodies together, and they and the wounded were taken up to the agency during the course of the day.

Hoffman, who was respected by the Ponca as an honest agent, was outraged and demanded an official investigation. He also demanded compensation for the victims and their families: six hundred dollars for each life lost (a total of twenty-four hundred dollars), two hundred dollars for each person wounded (a six hundred dollar total), and one thousand dollars for stolen property. Brigadier General Thomas McKean, commander of the military for the district of Nebraska, put a Major Armstrong in charge of the investigation. Governor Edmunds cautiously added his weight, saying that the Indians' account had at least a "semblance of truthfulness."[27]

Armstrong spent only one day in Niobrara on the investigation. Hoffman spoke with him briefly and came away convinced that the major had already concluded that the Ponca were as much to blame for the incident as the soldiers. Edmunds showed which side he was on by writing to Dole that the Indians should not have been off the reservation without a pass. So, despite the detailed eyewitness accounts, and despite the fact that it was common knowledge in the town of Niobrara that the men involved belonged to a Captain Wilcox's company and that on the night before the massacre they had been paid and were drunk, no one was charged with the murders. In his report for the year 1865, commissioner of Indian affairs, Dennis Cooley, closed the investigation, saying that there was "no probability" that the murderers would be found.

Cooley recommended that the compensation be paid to the Ponca, but there is no evidence that it ever was, unless it was part of the $15,080 "spoilation fund." Hoffman, disgusted with this "farce" of an investigation, and weary from trying to manage a neglected agency, resigned in the summer of 1864.[28]

The Ponca's greatest tragedy, however, and the United States' greatest injustice during these years, took place less dramatically and without any apparent notice. On April 29, 1868, at Fort Laramie, the Dakota ceded their vast hunting grounds and agreed to settle on the Great Sioux Reservation west of the Missouri River in Dakota Territory.[29] The boundaries of this reservation were spelled out in Article 2 of the treaty. In the southeast the reservation was delineated by the Missouri River and the northern line of the state of Nebraska, which ran along the Niobrara. Through this incredible oversight, the Ponca's reservation was included in the Great Sioux Reserve, their right of title to their lands was compromised, and the Dakota had one more reason for raiding this unfortunate people.

A Measure of Success

The Omaha were the only Nebraska Indians to prosper to any degree at all during the 1860s. They consistently produced good crops, and in most years there was a surplus to sell to settlers or to give away to the Ponca and, initially, the Winnebago. They never had to draw on the United States for rations. They continued to be held up by the Indian Office as proof of the feasibility of the reservation policy: "No other Indians," agent William Callon reported in 1868, "had a better reputation or prided themselves more on their progressive image."[30]

But this prosperity was only relative—relative, that is, to the disastrous conditions on the other three reservations. The Omaha's population, the best gauge of trends in standards of living, did increase over the decade, but only marginally and to a new plateau. High death rates from scrofula and other forms of tuberculosis, measles, pneumonia, and influenza, kept growth in check. The bison hunts brought in less meat and hides, and by the end of the decade the Omaha seemed to be reconciled to the hard reality that this pillar of their traditional life was being cut out from under them. Their traditions were also under attack from agents like Robert W. Furnas (1864–66) who worked to usurp the powers of the chiefs and widened the internal divisions in their society. Settlers clamored for the remaining Omaha lands, forcing the Indians to push hard for allotments and American titles of ownership. But the Indian Office failed to come up with the money to enable this transition to be made, even though it was the main goal of their assimilation policy. By 1870 the Omaha were in the paradoxical position of trying to sell yet another part of their diminishing reservation to finance the move to allotments.

During the first half of the decade, the Omaha continued to inhabit the three settlements (Big Village, La Flesche's village, and Wa-non-ki-ga's village) that Irish had recognized on his 1862 map (fig. 18). Sometime between the end of 1865, when Furnas made specific reference to the three villages, and May 1867, when government surveyors recorded only two, Wa-non-ki-ga's village was disbanded. Wa-non-ki-ga, or Noise, was already a very old man in 1863 when Reverend Burtt referred to him as the "best of the chiefs," so, his death may well have precipitated the dissolution of his village. His followers may have moved to Big Village, which remained the main settlement on the reservation. Most of the Omaha chiefs, including Standing Hawk, Fire Chief, No Knife, Little Chief, and Hard Walker, lived there with their families in earth lodges and tipis. Irish had commented in 1861 that as the Indians became "partly civilized" they abandoned the earth lodges of Big Village for the frame houses of La Flesche's settlement. By one estimate, there were forty-four frame houses on the reservation by 1865, most of them in La Flesche's village.[31]

The Omaha's population inched up to 1,020 by 1870, an increase of about fifty people over the course of the decade (fig. 9). Almost four hundred from this total were children, and among the adults there were about forty more women than men, a narrowing gender gap that probably reflected the decreasing frequency of raiding. When a definitive census was taken in 1869, in preparation for the allocation of allotments, there were found to be 278 heads of families, together with forty-six single men and ten single women over the age of eighteen. Women were too much in demand for their labor and skills to remain unmarried for long: when Callon called the chiefs together in 1867 to discuss extending allotment rights to single adult women, he watched smiles spread over their "usually solemn countenances" because they doubted that there were any women in that category in the entire society. Polygyny was still common—the same census revealed that eighteen men had two wives, three (including Joseph La Flesche) had three, and one had four.[32]

There were, at any one time, about twenty American adults on the reservation, including the agent, his employees (farmer, blacksmith, carpenter, miller, and their assistants), missionaries, and teachers. The agency landscape changed little during the 1860s, except to become more dilapidated. The main addition was the large, octagonal log blockhouse that Furnas built between the agent's house and the farm building in the nervous year of 1864 (fig. 30). Furnas wanted to add an elaborate earthwork defensive system, complete with rifle pits on the high ground, but his superiors did not produce the money.[33] The mission boarding school and the nearby (and generally silent) saw and grist mill still stood near the Missouri landing. So did the blacksmith's shop, until it burned down in 1864. An adjacent field, shown on Irish's map of 1862, was eroding into the river by 1868, and the once well-wooded flood plain around the mission was rapidly becoming stripped of its useful timber.

By 1870 almost all the land around the reservation had been taken by Ameri-

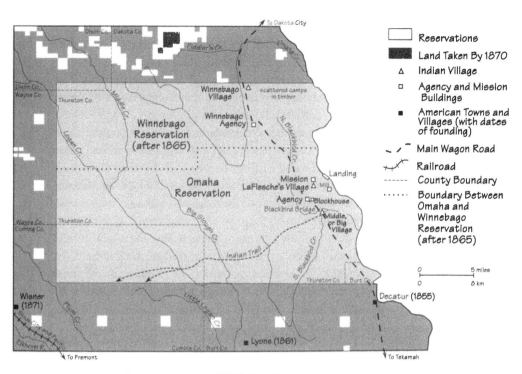

Fig. 30 Omaha Reservation and Vicinity, circa 1870

cans (fig. 30). This does not mean, however, that it was all actually settled. Genuine settlers, registering for homesteads or preemptions, filled the valleys of Omaha Creek and its tributaries to the north, and to the south farmers spread out from the ramshackle town of Decatur. Settlers also moved up Logan Creek in the early 1860s, and the outlying hamlet of Lyons had a store, a church, and a grist mill by 1870. Further west again, settlers pushed up the Elkhorn Valley, keeping pace with the construction of the Fremont, Elkhorn, and Missouri Valley Railroad, which reached the nascent town of Wisner in 1871. But beyond the valleys, on the rolling upland prairies, the land was taken, but not settled. In 1867–68 especially, speculators used transferred agricultural college script to gain control of vast acreages. Extensive areas were also taken out of settlement and reserved for future sales as state lands. Consequently, much of the country between the reservation and the Elkhorn remained unfenced and uncultivated. Here, at least, was an outlet to the bison range.

The presence of increasing numbers of Americans in the vicinity of the reservation had both advantages and disadvantages for the Omaha. One advantage was that it deterred the Brulé from raiding. There was, as Furnas had feared, a spate of attacks in 1864 and 1865 which left two Omaha women dead and about twenty horses stolen. But after 1865 the raids became less frequent, and compared to the Ponca and Pawnee situations, the Omaha had a relatively safe reservation. Settlers also provided an enlarged market for the Omaha's crops and furs, and especially during and immediately after the Civil War, when there was a shortage of labor in eastern Nebraska and western Iowa, Omaha men were engaged as temporary farm hands for about one dollar a day. This may seem to be a drastic reversal of roles, but by the late 1860s some Omaha men were also working the fields on the reservation.[34]

The increased contact between the Omaha and frontier Americans also brought its share of conflict. Two incidents in particular illustrate the uneasy state of coexistence that prevailed during the 1860s. In September 1863, an Omaha man named Cha-gras-ka-mo-ni was accused of raping a "respectable white woman" (a Mrs. Kidner) who lived near the reservation. Cha-gras-ka-mo-ni was a close relative of Little Chief, the most recalcitrant of the Omaha leaders, and Agent Irish saw an opportunity to strike at what he called the "wild Indians." Cha-gras-ka-mo-ni, who had a reputation for violence and may well have been guilty of the offense, sought refuge with Little Chief and was arrested only after a dangerous confrontation between the Omaha police (headed by No Knife) and Little Chief's followers. Little Chief protested that Cha-gras-ka-mo-ni's guilt or innocence should have been decided in an Indian council, and he complained bitterly that Irish treated the Omaha "like babies." Irish, concerned that incensed settlers would take matters into their own hands, handed Cha-gras-ka-mo-ni over to the military, and he was taken in chains to Omaha for trial. On November 8, only a day after his arrival, he escaped (with the help of his wife) and though the authorities suspected that he had been hidden by Little Chief they were unable to recapture him.[35]

The second incident is remarkably reminiscent of the savage attack on the Ponca in 1863. In early June 1864, two Omaha women (the wife and mother-in-law of Louis Sansouci, the Omaha interpreter) were attacked by four soldiers who were stationed at Dakota City. The older woman was shot dead from her horse and the other was "inhumanly cut up with a sabre." She managed to survive, much to the amazement of Reverend Burtt, who saw the "mangled" body when it was brought to the agency. The military commander for the district of Nebraska promised prompt action, and a court-martial was held. The soldiers were quickly acquitted on grounds of insufficient evidence. There was no doubt that soldiers had committed the murder, Furnas reported, but *which* soldiers, he lamely added, was more in doubt. Furnas suggested that Louis Sansouci should be compensated to the amount of $160 for his losses, and that his angry compatriots could be "pacified" with $150 worth of gifts. Commissioner Dole requisitioned the payments in July and, as far as the Indian Office was concerned, the matter was finished.[36]

Amid all these conflicts and changes, the Omaha—or at least the vast majority of them—endeavored to follow their traditional cycle of activities. By the late

1860s, however, the cycle was becoming abridged with the curtailment of the bison hunts. This was not initially caused so much by bison depletion as by restrictions imposed by the agents. The Nebraska Sand Hills, remote from American inroads, seemed to have remained a sanctuary for the herds, and the Omaha had an unimpeded corridor of access from their reservation right into the range. The Sand Hills also still teemed with elk, deer, and small game. Until 1869 the Omaha hunted in mass twice a year, and usually with success. The entire nation went out, except for a small number of "stay-at-homes" from La Flesche's village. Unlike the Ponca, the Omaha had plenty of horses, so transportation was not a problem, and they stayed to the southeast of the bloody path of the Brulé. The only poor season was the summer of 1864 when the Brulé did attack, leaving several Omaha dead, but even then the Omaha were able to get meat by trading corn to the Ponca, who had made a rare good hunt. The continued viability of the hunts is attested to by the value of the Omaha's trade in furs, which amounted to five thousand to six thousand dollars a year in the mid-1860s.[37]

After Furnas took over as agent in 1864, however, the pressure to give up the bison hunts and remain on the reservation year-round intensified. In his first annual report to Commissioner Dole he spelled out his agenda in no uncertain terms: he intended to stop the bison hunts and promote cattle as a source of meat; he wanted to settle the Omaha down on farms—to "individualize their interest"—and he would allow no Indian to leave the reservation without a pass.[38] The Omaha did not submit readily to this spatial restriction. Furnas was left to complain each year that they went on their hunts despite his efforts to contain them.

The situation changed for the worse in 1868. That summer the Brulé were out in force, and the Omaha garnered little meat and skins. The winter hunt of 1868–69 was also unsuccessful. The following year the newly appointed Quaker agent, Edward Painter, persuaded the Omaha to forgo their summer hunt. They did this reluctantly, but (according to him) "without a murmur" of protest.[39] Their compliance in this case had much to do with their determination to secure their homes by getting titles for allotments. The chiefs felt obliged to show the authorities that they were willing to settle down. They wanted to hunt, one chief told Painter, but they wanted titles even more. Many Omaha walked on thin moccasins that year, they ate little meat, and the cold wind blew through the muslin that they used to cover their tipis in the absence of skins (fig. 31).

When Painter gave them permission to go out on the summer hunt in 1870, they were "overjoyed." They hunted with the four bands of the Pawnee, and despite squabbles with the Kitkahahki they came back with their horses laden with skins and meat. Painter tried to stop them from leaving for their winter hunt, but they defied him, saying that they needed the robes to trade so they

Fig. 31 Ga-hi-ge's Tipi, by William H. Jackson, 1868–69. Courtesy of Smithsonian Institution Anthropological Archives, No. 4044

could improve their allotments. Besides, they added, there was nothing to do on the reservation in winter.

If it had just been a matter of food, as opposed to clothes, shelter, and traditions, the Omaha could have dispensed with the bison hunts. Their agricultural system was remarkably productive. Each year they planted about one thousand acres of corn in the large communal fields, and smaller areas of wheat, sorghum, potatoes, and other vegetables. Every year they harvested more than twenty thousand bushels of corn; in some years they actually restricted their corn acreage because their stores were still full from the previous season. In 1866 alone they sold ten thousand bushels to settlers, carting the surplus as far as Sioux City. They were also self-sufficient in flour, sugar (from sorghum), and hay. Even in the drought year of 1864 they had a surplus. This was "very gratifying," Callon smugly wrote in 1869, "for those who had always believed that reservation Indians could be self-supporting."[40]

The Omaha's other source of income was their annuities. Until 1868 they received thirty thousand dollars a year. Per capita payments of about twenty dollars each accounted for twenty thousand dollars from this total; the remainder went into agricultural and mechanical aid, to support the mission school ($3,750), to buy medicine (one hundred to one hundred fifty dollars), and to pay the police (five hundred dollars). The chiefs kept a close check on these payments and resisted attempts by the Indian Office to spend their money for them. As Callon wrote in 1867, "There are intelligent men among them who know just how much they ought to have."[41] This vigilance obviously did not deter Callon, who was later suspended for "irregularities" in his accounts.

Because of their agricultural success, their fur trade, and their relatively high annuity, the Omaha were the wealthiest of the Nebraska Indians. Even the more numerous Pawnee owned no more in "individual property," though they did possess more horses (table 7). This wealth, however, was not evenly distributed through the society. While some poor Omaha went without moccasins and contracted scrofula and dysentery from living poorly in dark, crowded lodges, others accumulated considerable riches. Wealth still percolated to the top: Joseph La Flesche, for example, made a great deal of money in the first half of the 1860s by operating as the reservation's trader and moneylender, and he owned fifty head of cattle and could harvest two thousand bushels of corn from his land. This conspicuous wealth may be one reason why seven-eighths of the Omaha opposed La Flesche by 1868. Other reasons include his mixed heritage and his championed adoption of American ways.[42]

In 1865, in accordance with the terms of the 1854 treaty (table 6), the amount of government support was to be reduced. The funds to keep the mill and blacksmith's shop in repair, and to pay the miller, blacksmith, and farmer, expired that year (the fact that the mill had actually run for only five and a half years of its allotted ten was naturally a sore point with the Omaha). The Omaha also realized that by 1868 their annuity would be reduced to twenty thousand dollars a year and their per capita payments to about fourteen dollars. It was fortunate, therefore, at least in the short run, that in 1865 the Winnebago needed a home and the Omaha had land they felt they could afford to sell.

In the fall of 1863, five distressed Winnebago had come down from that growing graveyard at Crow Creek to ask if one hundred fifty of their people could be subsisted on the Omaha reservation. The offer was extended and by the following spring there were twelve hundred starving Winnebago camped on the bottomland where Blackbird Creek flows into the Missouri. They had come down the Missouri in crowded fifteen-person canoes, and they had brought little with them. They had no horses, so they could not go out on bison hunts. The Omaha gave them corn and the government gave them rations, but their condition remained "pitiful."[43] On May 3 the Omaha chiefs met in council and agreed to let the Winnebago stay, providing that they observe "stringent by-laws" prohibiting drinking, gambling, war dances, setting fire to the prairies, and leaving the reservation without a permit. The arrival of the entire Ponca nation on September 10, seeking corn, added to the strain on the Omaha's resources.

On January 28, 1865, Commissioner Dole ordered Furnas to bring a delegation of chiefs to Washington, D.C., to negotiate the sale of part of the reservation to the Winnebago and, perhaps, the Ponca. The delegation (consisting of nine Omaha chiefs, including the principal chiefs, La Flesche and Standing Hawk) went by stagecoach to Sioux City and then on to Nevada, Iowa, where they caught the train to Chicago. After two days of sightseeing in Chicago they went on by rail to the capital. Furnas wrote that the chiefs were amazed by the wealth they saw. On March 7 Dole summoned the delegation to appear before him "in full Indian costume" (figs. 32 and 33). That day the Omaha sold one hundred thousand acres off the north end of their reservation to provide a home for the Winnebago. In return, they were paid fifty thousand dollars, or fifty cents an acre, plus seven thousand dollars in reparations for subsisting the Winnebago over the previous year. They were also granted an extension of aid for the mill, blacksmith shop, and agriculture for another ten years. On March 8 the Winnebago concluded their treaty, exchanging Crow Creek reservation for their new home. The Ponca made their separate agreement on March 10 and stayed on the Niobrara. When the treaties were finally ratified in February 1866, the Winnebago moved up to their new agency on Omaha Creek, where they continued to die in large numbers. Subsequent thefts of horses by Winnebago quickly engendered bad relations with the Omaha, animosities that endured.[44]

On February 1, 1867, the Omaha met in council to decide how to spend their $57,000. It was agreed to spend almost $28,000 immediately, mainly on agricultural aid: the large items included $6,781 for fifty wagons, $8,400 for sixty yoke of oxen, $2,531 for fifty sets of harnesses, and lesser amounts for plows, stoves (for the new frame houses), rifles, and revolvers. There was also a strange payment of $2,500 to Joseph La Flesche for his consenting to sign the treaty. The remaining $29,000 was to be held until their lands were allotted and then spent on stock, fences, and houses.[45]

The Omaha leaders had let it be known in various petitions to the commissioner of Indian affairs that they were "exceedingly anxious" to settle on allotments. They were justifiably concerned that, given the prevailing hostile atmosphere toward Indians in Nebraska, they would soon be moved to Indian Territory. Certainly rumors were in the air: in the fall of 1867, for example,

Frank Ellick, president of the Bohemian Settlement Association, wrote letters to the secretary of the interior and commissioner of Indian affairs asking when the Omaha would be removed, because he had nine thousand colonists who were looking for a home. They would pay cash for the land, he added, and he urged that every possible step should be taken to persuade the Omaha to leave. Agent Callon replied that the Omaha would never leave Nebraska, because "a thousand recollections, tender and warlike" attached them to these "scenes of childhood."[46]

The initial fieldwork for the survey of the reservation into 40-, 80-, and 160-acre portions was completed on June 27, 1867.[47] That was all that was accomplished, however, and thereafter the allotment process stalled. The Omaha realized too late that the conditions for allotments stipulated in Article 4 of the 1865 treaty were much inferior to the original guidelines outlined in Article 6 of the 1854 treaty. Gone was the idea of graduating the amount of land allotted according to the size of each family. The new rules were that each head of family (no matter how large) would receive 160 acres, and each single man and woman over the age of eighteen would get forty acres. It was specifically noted elsewhere that extra acreage would not be given to men who had more than one wife. On February 8, 1868, the chiefs issued a petition protesting the change. Many families, they argued, had six to ten members, and a 160-acre holding would not suffice for them. Moreover, they maintained that they had signed the 1865 treaty without being told that this significant alteration had been made.[48]

The Indian Office gave no ground on this matter. The Omaha held out until June 1869 when Agent Painter persuaded them to accept the conditions of the 1865 treaty. He wanted the allotments to be assigned and the ground broken for farming in time for spring planting in 1870. Some progress was made that summer: 130 farms of 160 acres each were assigned to heads of families, the corners were marked with stones or stakes, and it was agreed to keep some woodland in common for the benefit of all because there could not be timber on every allotment.

This progress came to a halt in 1870, when the available funds dried up. The Omaha (even the chiefs, who normally avoided manual labor) had worked hard cutting timber and hauling it to the mill for planing; but the planks just sat in piles because they could not afford nails. On May 17 the chiefs reiterated their support for the official policy and promised to live in frame houses and give up the hunt. They also promised to encourage their young men to work in the fields. Still no money was forthcoming. Finally, on November 8 Painter and the chiefs proposed a plan to sell fifty thousand acres from the west end of the reservation to pay for the agricultural improvements and buildings that would permit the Omaha to decentralize.[49] Again there was no response from the Indian Office, and the Omaha were left hanging, their future clouded by uncertainty.

Fig. 32 "Educated" Omaha Chiefs, 1865. Courtesy of Nebraska State Historical Society, 1394–90

Fig. 33 "Uneducated" Omaha Chiefs, 1865. Note: the designation of the chiefs in this photograph and in figure 32 as "educated" or "uneducated" has everything to do with Americans' perception of "civilization" and nothing to do with the Indians' accomplishments. Note also that the date on the photographs seems to be incorrect. Courtesy of Nebraska State Historical Society, 1394–97

The fact that all the Omaha chiefs consented to allotments (they all signed the treaties and petitions) is indicative of their realism, their understanding that the old ways were dying. It is also indicative of the degree to which the agents had usurped their authority. By 1869, according to Dorsey, three of the seven chiefs were agent appointees. As early as 1863, Irish had used the Cha-gras-ka-mo-ni rape incident to undermine the influence of Little Chief, and in his report that year he advocated that the chiefs should be "done away with" altogether.[50] Furnas also went after Little Chief (that "very troublesome" man) and tried to depose him, and he suspended Fire Chief for six months (with reinstatement dependent on "good behavior") for allegedly stealing twenty dollars from the annuity pay table. Furnas made it abundantly clear who was in charge on the reservation in a letter to Superintendent Albin: "I am not aware of the precise authority or power conferred upon agents," he wrote, "but long experience with Indians convinces me that it should be sufficient to make the chiefs feel and acknowledge at all times the authority of the agent over them."[51]

Furnas saved his particular ire for Joseph La Flesche. His campaign to depose La Flesche is best explained as a power play against one who would not be dominated. Furnas was later to admit that La Flesche's sin was that he was "never willing to be subordinate to agents." In particular he had opposed Furnas's attempts to make school attendance mandatory for Omaha children between the ages of five and sixteen, with breaches of the rule to be punishable by deductions from the parents' annuities. Beginning with a curt letter of warning on June 3, 1864, and continuing with a long series of invectives to his superiors in the Indian Office, Furnas waged a war of bitter words against La Flesche. The chief was lambasted as a "grand rascal," a "half-breed Ponca" who drained the people of their wealth. Furnas criticized La Flesche for holding onto his power by giving lavish feasts and presents, even though this was entirely compatible with Indian procedures, and he removed him from his position as trader on the (legally valid) grounds that only American citizens could be licensed in that capacity. By the spring of 1866 he had persuaded Commissioner Taylor that he had a case against La Flesche, a case made stronger by the fact that most Omaha also opposed him. La Flesche understood this and on April 17 he took his children out of the mission school and left the reservation for the Pawnee villages. He took the tribal archives with him, but Furnas sent the police to retrieve them and then personally, like a kingmaker, placed them in the hands of No Knife, the designated new principal chief.[52]

This campaign against the authority of the chiefs, the efforts to prevent the bison hunts, the proposals for mandatory education, and the requirement that Indians obtain a pass before leaving the reservation are indicative of the deepening intrusion of Americans into Omaha lives. Traditional societies and ceremonies began to fall more rapidly by the wayside during these years: the "old customs," wrote Fletcher and La Flesche, "could not be made to bend to the new ways forced on the people."[53] In September 1870, for example, Edward Painter canceled the Omaha's planned calumet ceremony with the Iowa, Sauk and Fox, Otoe, Pawnee, and Ponca on the grounds that it "gave rise to jealousies and thefts."[54] The Pu'gtho^n society, with its songs that celebrated past deeds of valor, ceased to exist by 1870, as did the Ki'kunethe society, the ritual gathering of the leading men around a fire to discuss important events. But the agents never succeeded in erasing the Omaha's cultural distinctiveness, even when the Indians were scattered on allotments and their sacred icons lay dormant in east coast museums.

Corruption and Decline

Americans' impressions of the Otoe-Missouria in the 1860s, like their earlier impressions of those Indians, were unfavorable, the complete opposite of the way they felt about the Omaha. After all their treaties, Commissioner Cooley wrote in 1866, they were still "nearly as wild as before." Commissioner Mix was even more critical in 1867, describing them as "retrograding." Unlike the Omaha, the Otoe-Missouria showed little interest in the Americanization program, remaining uniformly opposed to new farming systems and allotments until the end of the decade. This was enough evidence for Superintendent Janney to dismiss them as an "ignorant and superstitious people."[55]

These ethnocentric judgments aside, there is no doubt that life on the Otoe-Missouria reservation was mired in poverty, suffering, and strife. Their own agricultural system stagnated: in 1862 they had 137 acres in crops, mainly corn; by 1869, after fifteen years of supposed agricultural aid, this figure had increased by only three acres. Annual corn production was less than five thousand bushels, one-quarter that of the Omaha (table 7). Most of the time they had no cattle. Their total wealth, consisting almost entirely of horses (of which they had about three hundred), was between ten thousand dollars and twenty thousand dollars.[56] The bison hunts were quickly becoming an exercise in futility. They continued to go out twice a year, with the exception of the summer of 1869 when, in the aftermath of a bloody raid by Cheyenne on settlers along the Little Blue, they were ordered to stay on the reservation in case they were mistaken for "wild Indians" and shot. The old hunting grounds were now settled, and they were forced to go further afield to the Republican to find bison. There they risked encountering the Dakota and Cheyenne, and in many years fear drove them back home before they had sufficient meat and hides.

In April 1867, for example, following a frigid winter and heavy spring flooding, they ran out of supplies and were reduced to scouring the countryside around the reservation for dead cattle and hogs. Twenty-one Indians died that spring from eating tainted meat. In 1868 their crops were completely destroyed by drought and grasshoppers, and they came home with only six weeks' worth of meat from their summer hunt. The spring of 1869 found them trading robes, horses, and other meager possessions for food. Only emergency deliveries of flour, bacon, and beef (paid for by an advance on their annuity) kept total starvation at bay.[57] Their population fluctuated with the short-term changes in the standard of living, but the long-term trend was toward decline (fig. 10). Their numbers plummeted to 470 in the disruptive years of the early 1860s, recovered slightly to 511 in 1866, then continued to decline to an all-time low of 434 in 1870.[58] About 40 percent of the total were children, indicating a continued high birth rate and a low life expectancy. However, the death rate of children was also high, starvation and tuberculosis being the two main killers. Children born to malnourished and sick women had a poor chance of surviving. In the spring of 1869 alone, forty-eight children—one-quarter of all the children—perished.

Yet all this misery was taking place on a reservation that was widely regarded as having some of the best land in Nebraska.[59] The bottomlands along the Big Blue were fertile and still well timbered, and the upland prairies were fine country for hay and grazing. By the 1860s the reservation was also relatively safe. There were raids, as in the fall of 1868 when their longtime enemies, the Osage, killed several women who were working in the fields, and in 1869 when the Omaha stole some horses. But the horses were recovered (along with Omaha prisoners, who were returned in disgrace to their agent), and peace was made with the Osage in 1870.[60] These incidents did prompt the Otoe-Missouria to cut down the stands of hemp and sunflowers around the main village to rid prospective raiders of any cover, but clearly fear of hostile Indians did not have the paralyzing effect here that it had on the Ponca and Pawnee reservations.

The main reason for the inertia of the Otoe-Missouria was their agents, who were singularly inefficient and corrupt. When John Baker took over from William Dennison in 1861, he found a "truly deplorable" situation at the agency. Dennison, feigning illness, had absconded to Nebraska City with the Indians' money. Neither the Indians nor the agency employees had been paid in more than a year. Agency property—horses, wagons, implements—were in the hands of settlers as far away as Iowa and Missouri. Needless to say, there was "much dissatisfaction" among the Indians over this deception. In February 1861 a large contingent of Otoe-Missouria traveled the seventy miles to Nebraska City to get their money. There was widespread panic in the town as rumors circulated that the Indians were there to reclaim their ancestral lands. The Indian Office appointed J. Shaw Gregory, former agent to the Ponca, as a special investigator. Dennison left Nebraska City the same day that Gregory arrived, having deposited four thousand dollars belonging to the Otoe-Missouria in the banking house of J. A. Ware. It would take years of legal wrangling before the Indians regained their money. Meanwhile, they were mollified by an advance of one thousand dollars from their unpaid annuities to keep them in food.[61]

Baker was no better, and his high-handed manner quickly earned the disrespect of the chiefs. "He came down so low," the chiefs complained to Commissioner Dole, "as to quarrel with our children and poison our dogs." Realizing no gain from their annuities, they questioned Baker's honesty: "We would like to know why our farming operations cost so much when the benefits we derive from them are so small?" they asked Dole. They pointed out that a total of twenty-eight hundred dollars had been taken out of their annuities for agriculture in 1861–62, yet the value of their crops had increased by only five hundred dollars. "We should be getting rich now," they complained, when in reality they were "getting poorer each day." The chiefs demanded the appointment of a new agent, an "honest man," and they vowed that if the situation did not improve they would leave the agency and join the Indians on the western plains who were resisting American inroads. Baker defended himself by claiming that settlers around the reservation were sabotaging his efforts by turning the chiefs against him, and he tried to regain control over the agency by threatening to depose Ar-ka-ke-ta, the principal chief. Ar-ka-ke-ta bluntly told Baker that the agent had no authority to do that. Relations did not improve, and by the fall of 1863 Baker was gone.[62]

The parade of incompetents continued. Baker's successor, William Daily, spent most of his time in office away from the reservation. The chiefs again petitioned for their agent's removal, this time bypassing the commissioner of Indian affairs and the secretary of the interior by writing directly to President Lincoln.[63] They accused Daily of being in partnership with the licensed trader, and of forcing them to buy from him, even though his prices were twice as high as the general market value. The implication was that Daily was receiving a share of the profits. Daily retaliated by recommending that Ar-ka-ke-ta and another leading chief, Medicine Horse (Shun-geeh-hoy) be imprisoned for a "short time" to learn some respect. The Indian Office sided with the chiefs and removed Daily from his post in 1866.

John Smith, the last in this succession of charlatans, put most of his energy into trying to secure the sale of a large portion of the reservation, making sure that there would be ample provision for his own welfare. He also sought to get his salary increased, arguing that an "honest man" could not live on it. Nor could *he*, and the Indian Office was still trying to sort out his tangled accounts years after his removal.[64] Finally, in 1869, the Otoe-Missouria got the agent they deserved, the Quaker, Albert Green, who was trustworthy and caring and proved to be a staunch defender of the Indians' rights (though not, of course, of their customs).

Even Green could not accomplish much with the Otoe-Missouria's puny annuity. In keeping with the terms of the 1854 treaty, they were due annual payments of thirteen thousand dollars until 1867 and nine thousand dollars a year thereafter. Between two thousand dollars and three thousand dollars were

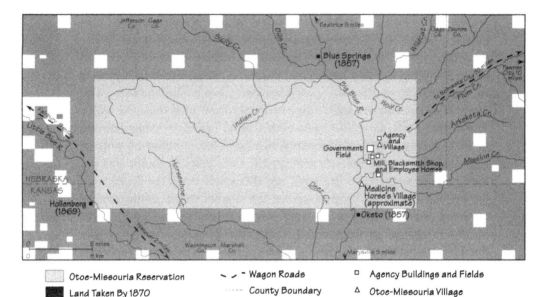

Fig. 34   Otoe-Missouria Reservation and Vicinity, circa 1870

taken out each year for agricultural aid, and there were often other deductions for repairs or innovations at the agency. The additional payments for the mill and blacksmith shop and for salaries for the miller, blacksmith, and farmer expired in 1867, and any subsequent expenses for these services also came out of the reduced annuity. Even the thirteen thousand dollars did not go far during the Civil War years, when prices for all goods were inflated. The Indians lived in perennial debt to the trader, always a year behind on their payments. By the end of the decade their total per capita allocation was less than three thousand dollars, or about seven dollars a person. Moreover, they were paid most of their money in treasury notes, not the more tangible coin, and this was a source of great dissatisfaction among them. Throughout the decade they complained that "they were not as well treated as their neighboring tribes."[65] This was not strictly true in financial terms (table 6), but when the nefariousness of their agents is taken into account, they had a good case. In council after council they expressed their distrust of the United States, their complaints working "like serpents of discord in their hearts" (to use Green's words).[66]

The Indians' discontent was also fueled by their dealings with local settlers, who more often than not were antagonistic. By 1870 virtually all the land around the Otoe-Missouria reservation had been taken (fig. 34). Most of the genuine settlers came in the burst of migration that followed the ending of the

Civil War. They took out homesteads and preemption claims along the creeks, filling in the gaps that remained. New towns, like Hanover and Hollenberg, Kansas, and Fairbury, Nebraska, emerged to serve the surrounding settlers. The vast majority of the land, however, mainly upland prairies, passed into the hands of speculators who used agricultural college script as a holding device until, decades later when land values had risen, it was profitable to sell. Indeed, it would be difficult to find any other part of the American frontier that was more dominated by speculators than the counties surrounding the Otoe-Missouria reservation.[67] Large areas were also taken off the market, especially in 1868, for the future benefit of the states of Nebraska and Kansas. The effect, of course, was to reduce the amount of land available to settlers, so it is no wonder that the choice Otoe-Missouria reservation became "much coveted by surrounding whites."[68]

Timber thefts were a particularly sore point. The reservation remained well wooded long after the surrounding settlers had used all the available wood on their own lands. Timber could not be brought in from the Missouri River because there was no railroad in the vicinity until 1871. Nebraska City was three hard days away over a rutted wagon road. In the harsh winters, settlers had the choice of freezing to death or stealing the Indians' timber. The situation was further complicated by the fact that the reservation's boundaries were not demarcated on the ground, and no one locally knew their exact extent. On a number of occasions settlers were caught cutting wood on the reservation and remanded in district court. No one was ever convicted.

There was also a particularly brazen theft of ten horses by settlers from Marysville on February 5, 1870. The thieves were eventually caught and convicted. According to Agent Green, the regulations of the Indian Bureau stipulated that thefts from "friendly Indians" had to be compensated with payments by the guilty parties of twice the value or amount of the stolen goods. But these particular Kansans had nothing, and the ponies were already scattered through Iowa and Missouri.[69] It seems that the matter was just dropped.

Demands from settlers and speculators, an unscrupulous agent, and the Indians' biting poverty combined after 1867 in a building pressure to sell part, or all, of the reservation. The first official mention of such a sale came at a council convened by Agent Smith on February 1, 1867. Smith was able to get all eight chiefs to agree to sell part of their land, and he proposed that a delegation should be sent to Washington, D.C., to make a new treaty to that end. Superintendent Denman approvingly forwarded Smith's proposal to Commissioner Taylor, adding that the Otoe-Missouria had enough land for fifteen thousand Indians and that the extra money from the sale might reduce their current state of discontent. Discussions continued back and forth over the course of the following year with nothing resolved. By June 12, 1868, extra details had been attached to the plan: the Indian Office wanted the Indians to sell 100,000 to

125,000 acres (from the total 160,000) and use the revenues for horses, stock, and schools; and the Otoe-Missouria were insisting that the sale come from the western part of the reservation, not the east, where they had their villages, fields, and graves.[70]

Finally, in February 1869 Smith, interpreter Batiste Barneby, mixed-blood Batiste Deroin, and four Otoe-Missouria chiefs—Medicine Horse, Buffalo Chief (Tcha-wan-na-ga-he), Little Pipe (La-no-wa-ing-ha), and Raw Eater (Wa-tha-ka-ro-cha)—traveled to the nation's capital at the Indians' own expense. There they concluded a treaty with the United States that is remarkable mainly for the blatant self-interest on the parts of Agent Smith and the heads of two railroad companies, the St. Louis and Nebraska Trunk and the Atchison and Nebraska. The agreement was this: the Otoe-Missouria would sell ninety-two thousand acres from the western part of the reservation, a fifteen-mile-long by ten-mile-wide swath that was essentially a land grant to the railroads; the Indians would be paid $1.25 an acre for the cession by the railroad companies, via the secretary of the interior; the money would be used to resettle the Otoe-Missouria on a new, smaller reservation in Indian Territory, or, if that was not satisfactory to them, to improve their condition on the eastern remnant of their current reservation. The four chiefs signed the treaty and were given one hundred dollars each "to enable them to purchase presents for their people."[71]

The treaty was moving toward ratification in the Senate in the fall of 1869 when Agent Green and Superintendent Janney intervened. On February 3, 1870, Green met the chiefs (along with the Indian police and braves—more than one hundred men in all) in council and they agreed to repudiate the treaty, which, it was stated, had been foisted on them by Smith, a "corrupt and designing man" who sought "to rob them of their scanty possessions." Janney added his weight to the appeal, telling Commissioner Parker that the proposed selling price was not even half of what the land was worth, and that the main beneficiaries would be the railroads and Smith, who had a special section reserved for himself.[72] These efforts were successful, and the treaty was withdrawn in February 1870.

The predatory forces were beaten back this time, but the issue of selling the reservation would not go away. In fact, Green and Janney actually supported a partial sale, at a good price, so that the Indians could be lifted out of poverty. But Green remained "resolutely opposed" to any removal to Indian Territory. He wanted to secure the Indians in possession of what remained of their lands through allotments, not uproot them.[73]

Despite their rapid envelopment by Americans and the concerted efforts to change them, the Otoe-Missouria remained defiantly traditional throughout the decade of the 1860s. Any Indians who were even thought to aspire to American ways were treated with contempt. Green, a perceptive and compassionate observer, described them as "wholly aboriginal."[74] The bison hunts retained their conventional order. In these final years they were led by Eagle, an

Fig. 35 Green's Sketch of the Otoe-Missouria Village, circa 1870 (Portion). From *Green Papers.* Courtesy of Nebraska State Historical Society, G798–146

old (seventy-five in 1869) hereditary Missouria chief. Eagle, in keeping with tradition, was not one of the main chiefs of the Otoe-Missouria, and his name is notably absent from treaties and most petitions, but on the bison hunt he had "autocratic power." When the young Otoe chief, Pipe Stem, broke the rules on the summer hunt in 1870 by attacking on his own initiative, Eagle sentenced him to a hard whipping.

Village life was also much the same as the old people remembered it from their youth. In 1869 there were two villages on the reservation, the main one at the agency and a splinter settlement near the mouth of Mission Creek, where Medicine Horse and his people lived (figs. 34 and 35). Both consisted mainly of earth lodges, but there were also some bark-covered structures. The doors of all the homes faced east. The only frame buildings belonged to the agency. In winter, if families were not out on the hunt, they decentralized on the reservation, living in cotton- or canvas-covered tipis on the wooded creek bottoms, trapping mink and beaver and hunting deer. The women still did most of the manual labor; men hunted, fished, and took care of the horses. Fishing, it might be noted, was deteriorating by 1870 as the clear water of the Big Blue became clouded with silt from the settlers' fields, making it difficult to shoot the

Fig. 36 Ar-ka-ke-ta, or Stay By It, by William H. Jackson, circa 1870. Courtesy of Nebraska State Historical Society, 1396:4–4

fish with the bow and arrow. No men were farming in 1870; they retained what Green accurately described as a "hereditary opposition" to it and prided themselves on being exempt from all onerous work. Polygyny was still practiced by the prominent men, and the wives were generally sisters. Only three men on the reservation, all mixed-bloods (Jim Whitewater, Batiste Deroin, and Batiste Barneby), could read and write English. Also, only three men, most likely the same three, wore "citizen's clothes." Everyone else wore moccasins, blankets, robes, breech cloths, and leggings (fig. 36). Clothes donated by the Philadelphia Society of Friends were cut up and remade in Indian styles. Hats were generally not worn because they interfered with the scalp lock and eagle feathers. The men still painted their faces with vermillion and indigo.

Medical practices also remained traditional. The reservation did not have an American doctor until Phoebe Oliver arrived from Philadelphia with a load of soap in 1871. Nearly all the doctors were old women; the exception was the "Snake doctor," an old man who draped himself in snakeskins and reputedly never failed to cure a bite.[75] The Otoe-Missouria, like the Omaha, believed in the healing power of saliva, and herbs were often prepared in the mouth and the mixture blown into the wound. Cupping blood, by drawing it out through a bison horn, and blistering, or burning, tiny torches of pith on the skin, were also common practices. Many of the Indians had "scarified" appearances because of these treatments. The main healing efforts, however, were ceremonial, and frequently the sound of singing and drum beats rang out over the village for days on end as women doctors, dressed in bison robes, evoked powerful "buffalo medicine" to dispel the evil spirits of sickness. The Otoe word for medicine (*monco*), Green explained, meant much more than a cure and implied the mystery of the unknown.

The dead were buried in sitting positions in jug-shaped graves, along with their possessions. In 1870 Green was attempting to curtail the practice of killing a man's horse at the time of his death. The Otoe-Missouria regarded the horse as a spirit companion for the deceased; Green viewed it as a waste of capital. In the winter, when the ground was frozen, bodies were wrapped in bark and tied in trees. In 1870 the gnarled oaks on the bluffs overlooking the village were hung with these mummified bodies. Like the other Nebraska Indians, the Otoe-Missouria had complete faith in an afterlife, and they thoroughly believed that death brought only the relatively insignificant loss of an earthly body.

Many of the time-honored ceremonies and practices continued in 1870. "Pipe dancing" (the calumet ceremony), for example, was still active. In 1869 Green witnessed such a gathering. A party of Omaha had traveled down from their reservation and camped outside the Otoe-Missouria village. Five men advanced into the village carrying their pipes, eagle feathers, and gourd rattles. They placed the pipes against forked sticks and proceeded to sing. In return for giving the pipe dance the Omaha received a gift of thirty horses. This ceremony confirmed the Otoe-Missouria's generosity and strengthened ties with the Omaha, at least temporarily. But to Green and the other Quaker agents it was an idle means of dissipating time and wealth, and they attempted to quash the practice.

Green also put a stop to raiding, causing great embarrassment to a raiding party that had made all the preparations yet could not get the horses. The chiefs finally saved them from the "shame of failure" by giving them some horses. By 1870 Green had also opened a schoolhouse on the reservation, hired a teacher, Sallie Ely, and was in the process of making attendance mandatory. He had reorganized the police force, the internal arm of his power, and bedecked them in surplus Civil War uniforms. He had deposed Ar-ka-ke-ta because of his resistance to Americanization and appointed Medicine Horse in his place. As part of the bargain, Medicine Horse promised to be living in a frame house by 1871 and pointing the way to allotments, a promise he was never to keep. There is no doubt that Green felt deeply about his "charges": he admired their honesty and genuine, "experiential" religiousness. But this only meant that he was more determined to save them, and he applied the civilization program with much more energy (and of course, much more honesty) than his predecessors. One result of these unrelenting good intentions would be the development of a deep, almost irreparable rift in Otoe-Missouria society in the 1870s, the one side acknowledging the need to change, the other resolutely opposing it.

On the Front Line

When Benjamin Lushbaugh took up his post at the Pawnee Agency on June 30, 1862, following the removal from office of Henry DePuy, he inherited a situation which he described in his usual understated way as "anything but favorable."[76] The Pawnee were in a "half starved and nude state," the result of two years of failed crops and unproductive hunts. Their 1862 harvest would also prove to be "very indifferent" because of grasshoppers, and in any case the farming plots were allocated so unequally—according to status—as to condemn the majority of the populace to a condition of "penury and want." The Brulé and Yankton Dakota had launched a combined raid on the Pawnee villages just before Lushbaugh arrived, killing or wounding sixteen men and women, and they struck again on August 27 with similarly bloody results. Relations with surrounding settlers were bad, and scores of legitimate and trumped-up depredation charges (it is impossible to decipher which was which) were pending against the Indians. No wonder Superintendent Branch considered the Pawnee to be the "most unfortunate Indians" within his jurisdiction.[77]

This appalling situation only got worse over the course of the 1860s. The combined population of the four bands dropped from 3,414 in 1861 to 2,325 in 1870, which was, both numerically and proportionately, the steepest decline of all the Nebraska Indians during these years (fig. 11).[78] This was not a straight decline, however. Like a barometer, the population total responded to rapid changes from time to time in the prevailing conditions on the reservation. Population loss was rapid from 1861 to 1863, with many deaths from starvation. But an "immense crop" of corn harvested that year and a "very good" summer hunt replenished food supplies and allowed a small population increase. In 1864 there was another reversal of fortune: the Brulé drove the Pawnee back from the summer hunt with no meat, and the harvest was an "entire failure" because of drought. About five hundred Pawnee died that year from starvation, or from measles, diphtheria, and dysentery, which were also endemic at the villages. To the Pawnee there would have been no question that the two calamities were linked, because crops could not prosper without the donation of dried bison meat to the bundles; and indeed the only good farming seasons during the 1860s came on the heels of successful bison hunts.

Conditions improved temporarily in 1865–67. The summer hunt in 1865 was "unusually successful," with sixteen hundred bison taken, and the harvest was considered to be "the best ever." Good hunts and crops also occurred in tandem in 1866 and 1867. Death rates fell, and there was a small surge in population growth. But any optimism was dispelled in 1868 when the Brulé sabotaged the summer hunt by stalking the Pawnee all the way to the Republican, picking off small groups of hunters as they scattered to attack the herds. The Pawnee killed plenty of bison, but they could not safely do the butchering, and rotting carcasses littered the plains. They returned to the reservation to promising crops, but in a single, traumatic day grasshoppers descended and stripped the land as bare as winter. Again more than five hundred Pawnee died in a single year. Abundant crops and high-yielding hunts in 1869 and 1870 (fifteen thousand dollars worth of furs were brought home from the winter hunt of 1869–70) checked the steep population decline, but did not reverse it. There was no security left in their lives, no confidence that the next year would not bring yet another crushing famine or another terrifying attack.

Annuity payments alone could not hold famine at bay. Lushbaugh acknowledged this in 1864 when, following the failure of the crops and the hunts, he ominously told superintendent Albin that the annuities would go "but a short way" to supporting the Pawnee in the coming year.[79] The Pawnee were fortunate to have a perpetual annuity of thirty thousand dollars a year (table 6) so, unlike the other Nebraska Indians, their payments did not decline in drastic steps. But thirty thousand dollars did not go far among approximately three thousand people. By stipulation (Article 2 of the 1857 treaty) half of the amount was spent on "useful goods"—large amounts of cotton drilling for clothes, canvas for tipi covers, calico cloth and calico shirts, scarlet cloth, blankets, beads, short-handled hoes, axes, tobacco, and provisions. Some of the goods were not so useful; in fact in 1865 both the agent and the Indians claimed that the bulk of the goods were "entirely useless."[80] Sometimes only empty crates arrived, their contents having been stolen on the way from St. Louis or other supply points. Often the goods found their way into local trading houses, sold for a pittance to provide emergency money for food. The other fifteen thousand dollars of the annuity was divided on a per capita basis, each person receiving about five dollars a year in treasury notes or, occasionally, in coin.

Other funds and services provided through the 1857 treaty were intended to build bridges into American society (table 6). Each year at least five thousand dollars was allocated to pay the farmer, miller, engineer, blacksmiths, and various assistants who were supposed to teach the Pawnee agricultural and mechanical skills and keep their implements in good repair. Another ten thousand

Fig. 37 Genoa Manual-Labor School, by William H. Jackson, circa 1870. Courtesy of Nebraska State Historical Society, 1396:2–2

dollars was provided each year to pay for the construction and maintenance of a manual labor school (the treaty actually specified two schools, but that provision was ignored). Some benefits did accrue from these expenditures. Agency farmers plowed up a large field in which the Pawnee women cultivated their gardens, and on August 18, 1866, the substantial brick schoolhouse opened its doors to students, replacing the previous makeshift school (fig. 37). But even in 1870 no Pawnee men were seriously farming, and American methods of plow cultivation had not taken hold. The change in roles was resisted by Pawnee men and women alike, and in any case it was obvious to the Indians that their own crops, interplanted to conserve moisture, withstood drought much better than the agency's open rows of wheat and corn.[81] Despite the expenditures, the steam-driven saw and grist mill was out of commission much of the time: the cogs were worn out, the boiler cracked and dangerous, and the carriage bed broken. Besides, all the accessible timber had been used. Agents' requests for funds to convert to a water-driven mill were ignored until 1870.[82]

Why, after expenditures of more than one hundred fifty thousand dollars on the civilization program in the 1860s, was so little accomplished? Part of the blame lies with the agents, who, while not as pernicious as the Otoe-Missouria's, were none the less ineffective. It was not easy to get good men to live as agents on this exposed, dangerous reservation for fifteen hundred dollars a year. Lushbaugh thought he was doing a good job, declaring that he "deserved some degree of credit" for the Pawnee's "decided . . . change for the better" in 1863.[83] His superiors did not agree and removed him from office in 1865. His successor, Daniel Wheeler, made the mistake of allowing nine Kitkahahki to accompany Captain R. Moreland on a traveling exhibition. Moreland, the prosecuting attorney for Platte County, was drunk most of the time and mistreated the Pawnee, finally leaving them stranded and destitute in Washington, D.C. Despite Wheeler's protests that he had the chiefs' permission to let the Indians go with Moreland, he was fired by Commissioner Mix in 1866.[84] The next agent, John Becker, did so little in his one year on the job that he hardly entered the historical record, not even making an annual report. He was followed in 1867 by Charles Whaley, who had previously been the agency farmer. Whaley was liked by the Indians, but he was replaced in the wave of reforms that put the Quakers in control of agencies. Jacob Troth, like his Quaker colleagues on the Omaha and Otoe-Missouria reservations, applied the civilization program with single-minded zeal, and more was done to effect change in his first year on the job than in all of the preceding decade. But by that time the Pawnee themselves were beginning to accept the inevitability of drastic change.

In 1870 this was still very much a traditional society (figs. 38 and 39). The Pawnee had all kinds of vested interests, both spiritual and practical, in keeping the old ways going, and as long as there were bison to hunt the new ideas could be largely ignored. The annual cycle, with its interlocking ceremonies and subsistence activities, was still intact. The three villages shown on DePuy's map of 1861 (fig. 22) had been consolidated into two tightly packed settlements, one occupied by the Skiri under Big Eagle, the other containing the three south bands led by Pe-ta-na-sharo, or Man Chief, of the Chaui. Big Eagle followed the conventional practice of important men by having four wives, all sisters. Each band had its own separate burial ground, the Chaui to the south across the Loup, the Skiri on the bluffs to the northwest of their village, the Pitahawirata on a hill north of Beaver Creek, with the Kitkahahki nearby to the east. No one had left the earth-lodge villages to live in a frame house, no one wore "citizens's dress," and while a few of the Pawnee claimed to embrace Christianity, this did not, according to one agency employee, "appear to make any difference to their mode of living."[85] Their possessions were increasingly American-made (few items of Indian manufacture have been found at the villages), but their ideas were still distinctly Pawnee.

In the face of such resistance from the adults, the agents focused their efforts on transforming the Pawnee children before their habits were set. The policy was explicit. On the occasion of the opening of the manual-labor school,

Fig. 38 Group of Pawnee Women, by William H. Jackson, circa 1870. Courtesy of Nebraska State Historical Society, 1396:1–11

Wheeler wrote to Commissioner Taylor that the objective was to educate the children in the hope they would become chiefs and lead the people in the new direction. By the time the Indians reached eighteen, he added, there was no hope of changing them.[86] This strategy of acculturation through education had changed little since Commissioner McKenney had first promoted Indian schools in the 1820s. There was still the intrinsic connection between Christianity and education: as the Pawnee's teacher Elvira Platt wrote in 1869, the "principles of the gospel [are] the foundation upon which we build." Academic subjects included English, arithmetic, and geography, but the emphasis was on work, training the girls to be housewives (cooking, sewing, cleaning) and the boys to be farmers or blacksmiths. This may well have been the best practical plan to prepare Indians for incorporation into American life, but it also had the immediate advantage of providing free labor for the agency farm. A final principle of education at Genoa and other manual-labor schools was separation. It should be "distinctly impressed" on the Indians, teacher J. B. Maxfield reported in 1864, that once the children entered school all control by the parents should cease. Elvira Platt even wanted to build a high fence around the school so that the parents could not visit their segregated children.

The 1857 treaty (Article 3) made it mandatory for every Pawnee child between the ages of seven and eighteen to attend school. Failure to do so could be punished by deductions from the parents' annuities (though there is no evidence that this was done in the 1860s). Yet in 1870 there were only seventy-nine pupils at the Genoa school, fewer than one-tenth of the Pawnee children. There are two reasons for this low attendance. First, the school could not accommodate more. The children, according to Wheeler, were delivered at the school virtually naked, and they had to be clothed and fed and provided with desks and beds. The ten thousand dollars annual payment could only be stretched so far, and in 1870 the problem was exacerbated when Congress cut the fund (a fund, it should be remembered, solemnly promised through treaty) by one-half.

The other reason for the low attendance had to do with the Indians' attitude to the school and the Americanization program. There were real incentives for

Fig. 39 Pawnee Village, by William H. Jackson, 1871. Courtesy of Nebraska State Historical Society, 1396:1–1

the Pawnee to enroll their children in the school. Some Pawnee parents, according to Elvira Platt, saw education as an escape route from poverty, and the number of pupils always increased when times were hard and food was scarce. Also, mixed-blood children were disproportionately represented at the school, perhaps because they were not fully accepted in Pawnee society. But there were many more reasons why the Pawnee resisted the program. Pawnee girls still married at a very early age, so there were few girls at the school and they were all very young. The boys greatly resented missing the bison hunts, and on at least one occasion (1868) they rebelled and joined the adults on the journey to the range. There was also a very high illness rate in the crowded classrooms and dormitories, which was of course a major reason for the Pawnee's reluctance to enroll their children. Measles, diphtheria, respiratory and digestive ailments killed a large number of the students in 1864, and whooping cough was rampant at the school in 1868. Parents and children alike resented the draconian measures that were taken to destroy their traditions, such as the cutting off of the boys' scalp locks, their "badge of courage." The boys resorted to wearing hats to conceal their shame. Finally, and most emphatically, the Pawnee did not want to be separated from their children; this was simply too high a price to pay for some vague promise of a brighter future.

The main problem for the Pawnee in these troubled years, however, and the main failing of the government's reservation policy, was the lack of protection provided against both Indian and American enemies. Their nemesis, the Brulé, raided the reservation every summer, and their war parties were never far away on the bison hunts. On June 22, 1863, for example, a massive force of about five hundred warriors attacked and killed several women and one man within sight of the agent's house; on September 26, 1864, a small raiding party killed three Pawnee and wounded three others while they were cutting hay four miles from the agency; on July 26, 1865, the Brulé killed an "old, quiet, and inoffensive" Pawnee man on the Loup fifteen miles from the agency; in the summer of 1868 they struck at the combined Ponca-Omaha-Pawnee hunt, killing six Pawnee and two Ponca; and in September 1869, 150 Brulé warriors swept down on the reservation, killing and scalping a woman who was herding horses.[87] Many other incidents could be added to this list, but the point is made: in the 1860s the Pawnee reservation was under siege.

Why were the Brulé so intent on eliminating the Pawnee, and why were the Pawnee relatively defenseless against them? First, although the numbers fluctuated with the severity of the winters, the Pawnee were rich in horses, a major attraction for the Dakota (table 7). Moreover, the Pawnee continued to replenish their losses by raiding on the southern plains, so the attraction did not diminish over time.[88] Second, from 1864 to 1866, and then again in the summers of 1868 and 1869, the Pawnee provided more than one hundred warriors to the army to aid in the fight against the Dakota and Cheyenne. These were the celebrated Pawnee scouts who, according to Commissioner Taylor, "did more real service . . . than all the balance of the troops." O. G. Hammond, superintendent of the Union Pacific, had a similarly high opinion of the Pawnee troops, writing in 1870 that "they will go further in the same time than white soldiers, will go where white soldiers cannot, and have so much experience that they can trace the most intricate movements of the enemy."[89] But the removal of these warriors from the reservation left the Pawnee depleted of their strength, and this alliance with the U.S. Army was a blatant affront to the Dakota. It was one reason given by the Oglala chief, Red Cloud, in 1870 for rejecting a peace offer from the Pawnee.[90] Third, especially after the completion of the Union Pacific, the bison herds withdrew into two diminishing ranges on the central plains, one to the north of the North Platte, the other between the Republican and Arkansas rivers. The ranges became heavily contested, not only between the Pawnee and Dakota, but also among the Cheyenne, Arapahoe, Otoe-Missouria, Omaha, Ponca, and American settlers. For all the Indians this was a struggle to survive, materially and spiritually.[91] Finally, after generations of strife, hatred between the Brulé and Pawnee was deeply ingrained, and every raid or murder demanded a reprisal so that honor could be upheld and the spirits of the dead could rest in peace.

Particularly when the Pawnee's best warriors were serving in the army, they were outnumbered by Brulé forces. The Brulé, sometimes with Oglala and Yankton allies, could put five hundred warriors in the field, whereas the Pawnee barely had that many men in total.[92] This is where the United States should have honored its commitment to the 1857 treaty and provided protection for the Pawnee on their reservation and on their bison hunts. But only half-hearted efforts were made. A small detachment of the Second Nebraska Cavalry was stationed on the reservation in 1863, but they were there only briefly, and when the Brulé attacked in June, the soldiers were reluctant to engage them in battle. During 1864 and 1865 Lushbaugh and Superintendent Albin repeatedly asked for a "small force of troops" to defend the reservation until the Pawnee scouts returned from the army, but all they were given was a temporary deployment of Company E of the First Nebraska Veterans Volunteers.[93] Nor would the government furnish the Pawnee with guns; it seems that officials were concerned about arming any Indians in those unsettled times. The Pawnee chiefs met in council in February 1865 and requested that their annuity be spent on two hundred rifles and ammunition. The guns were eventually sent, but two years later they were still being withheld from the Indians. Their supply of guns remained "meager" throughout the decade. The Pawnee were forced to come up with their own protection, building ramparts around their villages and combining with the Ponca and Omaha on their summer hunts in 1867, 1868, and 1870.

The impact of this enveloping threat was to disrupt the Indians' traditional means of subsistence and vitiate the government's civilization program. Pawnee women were afraid to work in the fields or collect wild foods, and the men could not herd their horses or hunt in safety. The wide gender gap in 1870—a census taken that year identified 539 men and 927 women—attests to the constancy of the state of war and the heavy toll it was taking on the warriors.[94] These numbers are all the more remarkable when the high mortality rate of the Pawnee women at the hands of the Brulé is taken into account. Agency employees also suffered, and throughout the 1860s it was very difficult to get Americans to live in this atmosphere of dread for any length of time. By the end of the decade some of the chiefs, sadly anticipating the end of the bison hunts, had begun to express an interest in allotments. But there was no possibility of leaving the defensible villages for exposed farmsteads with the Brulé so close at hand. The decade ended as it had begun: on May 19, 1870, at noon, Brulé warriors struck, killing a number of women, wounding one man in the leg, and stealing horses; on October 6, they attacked again, killing two Pawnee and wounding another.[95] There would be no peace or effective protection for the Pawnee as long as they remained in Nebraska.

Nor would there be peace or justice from their American neighbors. There was not much immediate population pressure on the reservation by 1870, only a discontinuous line of settlers along the Loup thickening toward Columbus and intermittent homesteads along the old Oregon Trail on the north side of the Platte (fig. 40). The area was still isolated from the main centers of settlement in the Missouri valley, and there was still good land to be had to the east. But whenever the Pawnee left the reservation they faced the probability of conflicts with settlers. Superintendent Denman blamed the Pawnee for the troubles, claiming that they were "numerous and bold" and that they did not "hesitate to do what they want." He also claimed, more accurately, that hardly a week passed without settlers complaining about them.[96] But Denman was pushing hard for removal to Indian Territory and his assessment of who was to blame for depredations was biased by his motivations. Most of the conflicts were petty, involving accusations that the Pawnee had stolen timber or cattle or were grazing their horses on settlers' lands. Settlers also regularly stole timber from the reservation. But there were two serious incidents in 1869 that exposed both the prevailing hostility toward the Pawnee and the inadequacies of the justice system on the western frontier.

On March 22, 1869, Whaley reported to Denman that army troops had attacked a party of fourteen Pawnee braves in Ellsworth county in southern Kansas. The Indians had only recently been honorably discharged from military service and were returning home. They were camped near the house of a friendly settler who had furnished them with flour and potatoes when two American soldiers approached and demanded to see their papers. The soldiers left after being shown the discharge papers, but they soon returned with rein-

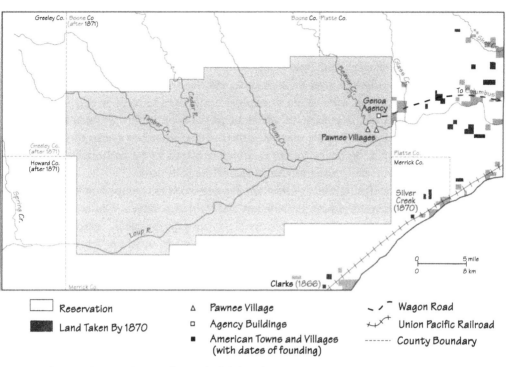

Fig. 40 Pawnee Reservation and Vicinity, circa 1870

forcements and commenced firing on the Indians. Nine Pawnee were killed on the spot; the other five escaped without their possessions, and when they finally found their way to safety they were starving, badly frostbitten, and near death. Six of the dead Pawnee were decapitated and their heads dispatched to Washington, D.C., for what passed as scientific study. The evidence against the soldiers was irrefutable; the Indians' guns had not even been fired. No one was ever charged, much less convicted. All the chiefs could do by way of retaliation was to prevent their young men from enlisting with the army that summer.[97]

Just over a month later, at 8:00 A.M. on Saturday, May 8, Edward McMurty left his home on the south bank of the Platte in northeastern Polk County to cross the river to buy a file in Columbus.[98] When his wife last saw him he had been taking off his boots to wade across. His footprints were later found leading onto an island in the middle of the river, but no footprints were found going off the other side. That same day, according to subsequent court testimony, a Mrs. Philips, who lived on the north side of the Platte, had heard cries from the island and saw Indians on horseback and on foot chasing a white man. She heard shots, then silence. Search parties combed the island during the following two days, but they found only two lodges of Pawnee, twenty men, women, and children in all. One of them, Yellow Sun, a sixty-year-old Chaui, had a wound on his face and blood on his collar.

McMurty was finally found on June 20 partly submerged in a pond on the island. His blanched body was weighted down by a twelve-foot pole. He had been shot in the side three or four times and the bullets had penetrated the lungs; there was an arrow in his mouth that had broken his teeth on entry, and his nose and ears had been cut off. None of the local settlers doubted for a moment that it was Pawnee who had done it. They dispatched a letter to Troth warning that if the guilty parties were not delivered to the authorities they would "wage a war" on any Pawnee found off the reservation.

Janney, Troth, and Whaley called the Pawnee chiefs into council on June 30 and asked them to produce Yellow Sun and the other Indians who had been camped near the scene of the murder. Pe-ta-na-sharo pointedly asked if the killers of the nine Pawnee in Kansas were also to be delivered up. Ter-re-kaw-wah (Pawnee Chief), a Pitahawirata headman, offered a concession, saying "we are willing to say nothing about the men we have lost by the whites, if you will say no more about the white man that has been killed." Janney's response was to threaten to withhold the annuities if the suspected murderers were not handed over. In early July eight men were taken into custody in Omaha by the U.S. marshal. Four of them—Yellow Sun and his fellow Chaui, Blue Hawk, along with Horse Driver, a Kitkahahki, and Little Wolf, a Pitahawirata—were accused of the murder and the others were temporarily held as witnesses.

The accused Pawnee were imprisoned for more than two years, first in Omaha, then in the newly constructed state penitentiary in Lincoln. Yellow Sun twice attempted suicide by cutting his wrists with glass, and Blue Hawk and Horse Driver escaped and were later recaptured. The Pawnee, Janney and Troth, and the Omaha newspapers protested that there was no possibility of a fair trial for an Indian in Nebraska. Based entirely on circumstantial evidence, all four were found guilty in the U.S. district court in November 1869, but the verdict was overturned on a jurisdictional issue, and the case was referred to a grand jury in Butler County, where the crime had taken place.[99] Tensions were running so high in Butler County that Troth feared that the Indians would be lynched, so they were held in prison in Lincoln while the jury once again convicted them. Again the verdict was appealed back to the district court and finally, in October 1871, the four men were released and returned to the reservation.

It was widely believed by the Pawnee, the Quakers, and indeed by Blue Hawk, Horse Driver, and Little Wolf that Yellow Sun had murdered McMurty in a dispute over horses, but the case had become so entangled in jurisdictional disputes and so distorted by the animosity toward Indians that no just outcome was possible. According to Luther North, who recruited and led the Pawnee scouts, all four of the men, worn down by their ordeal, died soon after their release from prison. Nor did the murkiness surrounding the case clear with the passage of time, because, again according to North, another Pawnee, Shooting Star, later confessed to having murdered McMurty.[100]

The Pawnee faithfully continued in their old ways, but increasingly they were made to feel like strangers in their own land. They would ride the Union Pacific freight cars to Omaha, in 1870 a city of sixteen thousand people. But there they were shunned because of their appearance and persecuted because of their begging.[101] When they went on their bison hunts they were obliged to avoid settlers by detouring west along the Loup before dropping down to their Republican hunting grounds, and on the way they crossed the iron tracks of the Union Pacific, the symbol and realization of the indomitable American drive west. Their sacred sites were now in the hands of Americans: Pa:haku, for example, was homesteaded in 1868.[102] Nebraskans loudly agitated for their removal to Indian Territory, and the Dakota vowed to exterminate them. A noose was being drawn tightly around the Pawnee, leaving them no room to breathe in Nebraska.

CHAPTER SIX

Hemmed In
and Forced
Out

1870–1885

The years between 1870 and 1885 were a time of precipitant change for the Nebraska Indians. The shadow that had spread across their country since the early nineteenth century, darkening their lives with disease, famine, and death, finally eclipsed their traditional way of existence. Nebraska filled up with strangers, leaving the Indians surrounded and immured within the boundaries of their reservations. The only choice presented to them was to take out allotments or to move to Indian Territory. There was never any option to retain their reservations intact. The last bison hunts were made in the early 1870s. Commissioner Hayt maintained that this "loss of the bison" was actually a "blessing in disguise" for the Indians, forcing them to accept the new conditions of life in the United States; but in reality it was a disastrous departure which eliminated their subsistence base and rendered a major part of their belief systems obsolete.[1] Their societies became even more divided over which path to follow into the future. Yet, remarkably, they survived through these dimmed days and emerged, in the twentieth century, dispossessed and impoverished, but not beaten.

Despite economic hard times on the frontier (and in the nation as a whole) from 1873 to 1878, Nebraska's white population continued to grow, reaching almost one-half million by 1880. This growth accelerated in the boom years of the 1880s, which saw the state settled to its western borders. Railroads spanned the open spaces, drawing settlers in their wake. By 1880 few places in eastern Nebraska were more than twenty miles—one day's haul—from a railroad. Only the remote Ponca reservation remained outside of this iron grid (fig. 41).

Settlers continued to use and abuse the homestead and preemption laws to acquire land. Petty speculation was given another boost in 1873 with the passage of the easily manipulated Timber Culture Act, which, in effect, presented the opportunity to hold onto 160 acres without payment and tax-free for up to ten years.[2] So intense was the pressure for land that the large tracts taken by major speculators through the Morrill Act of 1863 were bought up by farmers, even though the selling price often exceeded ten dollars an acre. Only the badly drained, rugged, or remote lands remained in the public domain.

More than ever, then, the fertile reservations were looked upon as prime pioneering country that was being underutilized by the Indians and artificially withheld from deserving settlers. Governor David Butler expressed this sentiment in his 1871 message to the Nebraska people, describing the reservations as "some of the choicest agricultural lands in the state" and urging that their titles "be extinguished, and the Indians removed, either to Indian Territory or some other place designated by the general government." His successor, Robert Furnas, who had come a long way in his career (if not in his thinking) since his stint as an Omaha agent, was even blunter in his demands for removal. In speech after speech in 1873 and 1874 Furnas demanded that Nebraskans should be freed from what he called the "retarding influence" of the "nomadic race." All this invective was just a prelude to the real issue: that the "valuable land now held by these aboriginees should be permitted to pass into the hands of intelligent, enterprising citizens, who would render them productive."[3] To Furnas and many other Nebraskans this transition was a right and a necessity.

They would get no argument on this from the Indian Office. Commissioner Francis Walker, an advocate of the "Peace Policy," (which continued to be the guiding idea of Indian policy through the 1870s), expressed the prevailing philosophy in his annual report in 1872: "The Westward course of population is neither to be denied or delayed for the sake of all the Indians that ever called this country home. They must yield or perish."[4] This, of course, could have been written by any of the commissioners from the 1840s on. The difference in the 1870s was that the civilization program was running out of time. The Nebraska reservations were surrounded by settlers, yet most of the Indians were still not on allotments or in any other way ready, or willing, to merge with Americans. Consequently, though federal Indian policy remained essentially the same as before, there were two new developments. First, the civilization program become increasingly mandatory as Indians were forced to labor for their annuities, put their children in schools, and follow the dictates of their agents. Second, the concept of consolidating Indians in Indian Territory was moved from the wings to center stage. For the Nebraska Indians the question now became: would they manage to preserve any of their homelands at all?

By 1880 the question was answered. The Pawnee had been squeezed out and relocated in Indian Territory by 1873–75; the Ponca had made the same move under severe duress in 1877; and the last Otoe-Missouria followed south in 1881. Only the Omaha and a splinter group of the Ponca who refused to live in exile survived the storm and held onto some of their reservations. The abandoned lands were taken by settlers and speculators in a rush, like a tide that had finally broken through a battered retaining wall.

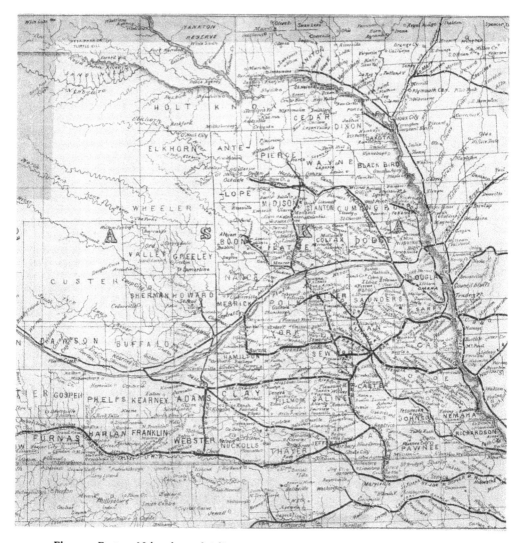

Fig. 41 Eastern Nebraska and Adjacent Areas, 1880. Portion of "Map of the Great State of Nebraska." Courtesy of Nebraska State Historical Society, M782, B92e

Driven South

In October 1873 twenty-seven lodges of Pawnee, 485 people drawn mainly from the Chaui and Pitahawirata bands and under the instigation of the Chaui soldier Big Spotted Horse, left Nebraska for the Wichita Agency in Indian Territory. A year later, at a fateful council on the reservation, the chiefs and other leading men from each band agreed to sell their land and follow them to a

Table 8 Pawnee Demography, 1872 (and Comparisons with 1840)

Band	Men	Women	Children	Band Total	1872 as Percentage of 1840 (see Table 5)
Skiri	154	232	244	630	33.0%
Kitkahahki	124	208	218	550	30.1%
Chaui	140	254	365	759	45.1%
Pitahawirata	91	182	235	508	54.7%
Pawnee Total	509	876	1,062	2,447	38.4%

Source: Troth, "Report," ARCIA, 1872, 224 (from census count taken Sept. 20 and 21, 1872)

new home in Indian Territory. It was a bitter move, each step away a tug against their roots; but it was also a necessary move because life in Nebraska had become so intolerable that their very survival as a people was at stake.

The continued steep decline of their population is evidence of these intolerable living conditions (fig. 11). There were 247 fewer Pawnee in 1875 than in 1872. Viewed over the longer run, by 1875 the Pawnee had barely one-third of the population they had sustained when the Reverend Dunbar took his census in 1840. All the bands had dwindled, but the Skiri and Kitkahahki had fared the worst (table 8). It is a measure of the danger of the times that in 1872 only 36.7 percent of the adults were men. This gender gap, which had closed or substantially narrowed for the other Nebraska Indians by 1870, was actually wider for the Pawnee than it had been in 1840. It was dangerous to go out hunting, and continued raiding on the southern Great Plains also took a heavy toll on the men. In one expedition in early October 1871, 205 Pawnee warriors traveled south to visit, trade, and raid in Indian Territory. Two died at the hands of the Cheyenne, others died of a "brain fever," and altogether, thirty-six men perished. In 1872, 43.4 percent of the Pawnee were children. This was not significantly different from the situation around 1840, when Dunbar and others had been astonished at the multitudes of children at the Pawnee villages, and it suggests that despite malnutrition and general ill health, the women still had a high birth rate. In most years, however, there were far more deaths than births.[5]

Directly and indirectly the Dakota were responsible for most of these deaths, directly because they killed Pawnee at every opportunity, indirectly because they so thoroughly disrupted the Pawnee's subsistence cycle that starvation became the normal condition of life. The Dakota killed at least one hundred Pawnee from 1870 to 1875. Most of these deaths—more than seventy—came on

August 5, 1873, when six hundred to one thousand Oglala and Brulé warriors trapped the Pawnee bison hunters in a ravine off of Frenchman's Fork in southwestern Nebraska, a place known ever since as Massacre Canyon. The Pawnee, consisting of two hundred fifty men, one hundred women, and fifty children, were encumbered by the meat and skins of eight hundred bison, and they were unable to escape. One of the leading chiefs, Sky Chief of the Kitka-hahki, was killed and scalped, cut down while skinning a bison. Women and children died in disproportionate numbers. The dead and the wounded were thrown in a heap and burned. The Dakota lost only two men. The raiders also took more than one hundred Pawnee horses, nearly all their saddles and weap-ons, and all their meat and skins. Altogether, more than two hundred fifty Pawnee horses were stolen by the Dakota from 1871 to 1875, a serious blow to the society's, and to individuals', wealth and power.[6]

The Pawnee were the match of the Dakota in courage and ferocity and, unless the Dakota bands amalgamated, they were still their match in numbers (the Lower Brulé, the Pawnee's most inveterate enemy, had a population of 1,188 in 1876). But the Dakota, being the aggressors, had the advantage of surprise, and they were much better armed than the Pawnee. Garland Blaine, a hereditary Pawnee chief, would later claim that the United States deliberately supplied the Dakota with guns so that the Pawnee would be expelled from Nebraska. If true, this was unnecessary, because the Dakota could still acquire guns through the robe trade (they dominated the bison range from beyond the Black Hills to the Republican) or through raiding. Meanwhile, Pawnee requests for weapons (to be paid for out of their own funds) were repeatedly denied. At the February 2, 1874, council meeting, for example, Agent William Burgess dismissed the Paw-nee's pleas for guns and ammunition, saying that the government was not in the business of supplying weapons to Indians. Burgess told the chiefs that they were free to buy their own guns. This was a hollow statement, because by that time their annuity was almost completely allocated by the agent and the Indian Office, and the Pawnee had no expendable funds themselves.[7]

Nor did they benefit from any worthwhile government protection. Superin-tendent Barclay White, visiting the reservation in October 1871 to dispense annuities and complain about the raid on the Cheyenne, provoked a "derisive laugh" in the council house when he told the assembled chiefs that they had nothing to fear because the United States would protect them.[8] They had heard these grand words many times before, yet still the women died in the fields, the boys in the pastures, and the men on their hunts. Indeed, the military had given such assurances only the day before the hunting party was slaughtered in Massacre Canyon. The lack of protection was all the more criminal because the Pawnee were adhering to the government's policy of not retaliating against Dakota raids, much to the regret of the young warriors and to those whose relatives had been killed. Their only satisfaction was the nine thousand dollars

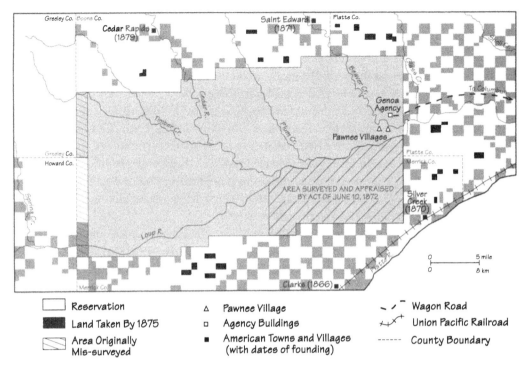

Fig. 42 Pawnee Reservation and Vicinity, circa 1875

that was withheld from the Dakota's annuity as compensation for possessions lost in the August 5, 1873, massacre.[9]

By the early 1870s the Pawnee were seeking peace with the Dakota. They fully realized that they could not continue living in this state of siege. Some of the chiefs, including Eagle Chief and Lone Chief of the Skiri, wanted to go along with Quaker policy and secure land and timber by taking out allotments. Accordingly, Agent Jacob Troth made a start on dividing the land at the eastern end of the reservation, and north of the Loup, into six hundred ten-acre plots in the spring of 1871. By the act of June 10, 1872, a commission was appointed to survey and appraise fifty thousand acres on the south side of the Loup which would be sold to finance the move to individual allotments (fig. 42). But nothing came of the plan because such a dispersal was impossible while the war with the Dakota raged.[10]

A peace treaty was almost arranged in 1871. Over the opposition of a Kitkahahki chief whose wife had recently been killed in a raid and who had no faith that the Dakota would listen because they had "sticks in their ears as big as [his] fist," the Pawnee leaders agreed to meet with Spotted Tail and the Lower Brulé at the Santee Agency in northeastern Nebraska. But Spotted Tail changed his mind, explaining that if he made peace with the Pawnee he would likely provoke the enmity of the other Dakota bands. The Pawnee were angry and humiliated that their overtures had been rejected, and the Dakota continued to attack until the Pawnee's final days in Nebraska.[11]

Pressure from surrounding settlers was less bloody, but no less intense. After 1870, with the Union Pacific bringing better connections to supplies and markets, settlers rapidly moved west and north from the Platte to encircle the once-remote Pawnee reservation (fig. 42). Except for the expensive odd-numbered railroad sections in the Union Pacific land grant, and areas of open prairie and marsh, all the country to the east and south of the reservation was taken by 1875. Settlement was more intermittent to the north and west of the reservation. The first claims to the north, in Boone County, were made in the spring of 1871 by poor homesteaders from the eastern United States who, not unlike the Indians, lived in a communal sod house before moving out into individual frame structures.[12] By 1875 settlers lined the creeks that jutted out from the northern boundary of the reservation. To the west they located along the Loup and its north-bank tributary, Spring Creek. Some took out homesteads immediately adjacent to the western boundary of the reservation only to learn, in the fall on 1872, that the line had been drawn one-half mile too far to the east and that they were actually on the Indians' land (fig. 42). Superintendent White saw no reason to evict the settlers, arguing that the Pawnee already had a surplus of land, but the Indians were paid $1.25 per acre, or six thousand dollars, for the government's mistake.[13]

As early as 1872 all the land with timber, water, and easily worked soils in the vicinity of the reservation was spoken for. The upland prairies and railroad sections were not filled in until the second half of the 1870s, or much later. The reservation was looked upon as an obstacle, "a wall turning back the wave of immigration or hindering its flow by tremendous friction." It was also widely recognized as "four hundred square miles of as good a land, perhaps, as there [is] in Nebraska."[14] It was close to the life line of the Union Pacific, and it contained good soils, abundant water, and some thick stands of timber. There were also rumors of coal deposits, a major attraction in an area that was chronically short of fuel.[15] Consequently, after 1870, as population pressure mounted, the drive to evict the Pawnee began in earnest.

The settlers used the standard arguments in their campaign to excise the Pawnee from Nebraska: they were indolent, they possessed too much land and made little use of it, and they were living on government largesse. This last complaint, which confused welfare with legitimate payments for land, was particularly widespread among poor settlers who were struggling to make a living in a depressed economy.[16] The Quaker program came in for criticism too, ultimately because of their campaign to settle the Pawnee on allotments. Local settlers did not want the Pawnee to retain any land, particularly the well-watered and wooded lands they would obviously select for their allotments. In March 1873, twenty-seven citizens of Platte County lodged a complaint against the Quaker administration on the reservation, a complaint that was a thinly veiled attempt to gain control of agency affairs and precipitate the exodus of the Pawnee. Agent Burgess and the Quakers were exonerated after a lengthy investigation.[17] But the opposition persisted, with local traders Lester Platt and Delane Willard particularly diligent in scheming for Pawnee removal and access to their lands.[18] Needless to say, the Quaker agents had a low opinion of the surrounding settlers: they referred to the traders as "parasites" and they suspected that the "degraded white men" who lived to the north of the reservation were doing as much horse stealing as the Dakota.[19]

A few of the local settlers agreed with the Quakers and objected to the way the Pawnee were being mistreated by the majority. Charles Wooster, for example, who settled in Merrick County in 1872, just to the east of the reservation, considered the Pawnee to be "very peaceable and more afraid of the whites than the whites are of them." Wilhelm Dinesen, a sophisticated Dane who lived in Platte County from 1872 to 1873, saw that the problem lay not with the Pawnee but with rapacious whites and with a totally impractical government policy that required the Indians to acquire "in a few days . . . that which took us thousands of years." And Moses Turner, in frequent editorials in *The Platte Journal*, continued to champion the Indians' rights with a humaneness that was rare on the Nebraska frontier. None of these supporters, however, argued that the Pawnee should be allowed to keep their reservation; none even thought that there was time for them to make the transition to allotments.[20]

Conflicts with the local settlers centered around thefts of the Pawnee's timber. Such thefts had been common enough in the 1860s, but they greatly increased after 1870 as the land filled up and trees were cut for houses and fuel. Although there was little wood left around the agency, the Loup valley, running across the south of the reservation, remained cloaked with cottonwoods and willows. Settlers did not hesitate to steal the wood, especially when winter approached. By 1872 there was a "well-defined road" running from the Loup to the settlements south of the reservation. The Pawnee chiefs asked Troth to investigate the thefts. In early November he followed the road south and saw Pawnee timber at every house all the way to Clarks. Troth found that "the most prominent and influential settlers"—lawyers, ministers, merchants—as well as poor homesteaders, had been taking their share. They admitted to this, but explained that it was a matter of stealing or freezing. Apparently the plan to sell the fifty thousand acres from the south side of the reservation had also given the settlers an excuse to cut the trees. The settlers agreed to pay for the wood, and most of them did, the Pawnee eventually receiving three hundred dollars for their losses.[21]

But, like the Dakota raids, timber thefts continued right up to the Pawnee's departure from Nebraska. The scale of the cutting greatly increased in 1874 when Judge Elmer Dundy ruled in Omaha District Court that the local courts had no jurisdiction over crimes committed on the reservations.[22] Settlers had rarely been brought to justice for such crimes, but this decision was a virtual license to steal. In January 1874 *The Platte Journal* revealed that not only were needy settlers taking wood, but large scale commercial cutting was also taking place. Hundreds of loads were being carried away each day and stacked at sawmills near the reservation.[23] The Pawnee patrolled the area, but it was a lost cause. Clearly, even before the Pawnee left, the settlers had decided that the reservation's resources were available.

The pressures on the Pawnee were not only generated locally, from settlers and Dakota, but also emanated from Washington, D.C., in the form of an increasingly draconian assimilation policy. The Indian Office, through the Quaker superintendents and agents, tightened control over how the Pawnee's money was spent, restricted the Indians' movements off the reservation, and by-passed the chiefs in the decision-making process.

After 1870 the Pawnee's annuity, both cash and goods, was handed out by the agent or superintendent to the heads of families, rather than to the chiefs. This may indeed have been more equitable, because poor families had complained that they did not get their share, but it was a severe insult to the chiefs and a radical innovation to the way wealth had been controlled and redistributed in Pawnee society. The chiefs complained in council after council, but the policy was set. They were finally mollified with an annual salary of one hundred dollars a year, taken out of the annuity, and the four President Grant medals handed out to the head chiefs in 1872 also bought acquiescence. Not that there was any longer much in the way of individual annuities: a characteristic breakdown of the semiannual fifteen thousand dollar payment shows one thousand dollars put into medicine, three thousand dollars for agency repairs and land surveying, three thousand dollars to salaries for chiefs and soldiers, and eight thousand dollars for per capita distribution, leaving each Pawnee the sum of $3.75.[24]

Other Pawnee revenues were also strictly controlled by the agents. Jacob Troth, for example, insisted that future proceeds from the sale of the fifty thousand acres would be put into a treasury account to draw interest, overruling Pawnee requests for the actual money so that they could buy cattle. Even the three hundred dollars that they were, belatedly, paid for their timber went into their "improvement fund," while throughout the villages Pawnee children were starving for want of provisions.[25]

Many other restrictions were being placed upon the Pawnee's freedom, all ostensibly for their own good. Metal annuity goods were now stamped so that the Indians could not sell them to the traders. Flour rations were withheld from parents who did not send their children to school, and one soldier was appointed from each band to enforce attendance. And, in what must have been a most perplexing command for people who had been preached to about the merits of hard work for decades, Troth told the Pawnee that they must refrain from labor on the Sabbath. A startled Sky Chief responded that he had not known that "God had reserved a day to rest."[26]

The main abridgment of freedom was the attempt to confine the Pawnee to the reservation. On May 2, 1873, Burgess announced that owing to "unsafe conditions" no Pawnee could leave the reservation without a pass. Soldiers were sent out to bring Pawnee back from rail depots all the way to Omaha (the year before, Barclay White had complained about the "idle and vagrant members of the tribe" who assembled at stops along the Union Pacific line and "gave travellers a bad impression").[27] So when Big Spotted Horse left in October 1873 with two passes and 485 Indians, heading to Indian Territory, White was furious. He berated the chiefs for allowing members of their bands to leave, warning that if they could not control their people, then he would appoint others who could. Pe-ta-na-sharo protested that he was old and had not done anything wrong. But White cut him short and let it be known in no uncertain terms that "when Government speaks it will be obeyed."[28]

Each year the Pawnee had to request permission to go on their bison hunts. From 1870 to 1873 the agents begrudgingly gave their consent, because they understood that the Pawnee could not survive on their agriculture and annuities alone. They sent the Pawnee out with passes and two American chaperons who were to protect the hunters and prevent any depredations on settlers. Perhaps the Pawnee would have gone out even without permission, because to them the hunt was still imperative. As Pe-ta-na-sharo tried to explain to Troth in 1871, "We want to go on the Buffalo hunt so long as there are any buffaloes—[we] are afraid when we have no meat to offer the Great Spirit he will be angry and punish us." Troth replied, "We don't give the Great Spirit meat yet he favors us."[29]

As it was, the days of the bison hunt were numbered. Every time Eagle Chief went out, he saw fewer bison, he told the council in 1872.[30] Pe-ta-na-sharo blamed Americans, and in an impassioned speech in council he protested to White that "those Buffalo are mine. Our fathers owned both the land and the animals feeding on it. We sold the land to the whites, but reserved the Buffalo."[31] For the Pawnee, the end came even before the herds ran out. The winter hunt of 1872–73 was sabotaged by the Dakota, who burned the prairie ahead of the Pawnee and drew them out into unsafe territory. Hardly any bison were taken and those that were had to be cached on the Republican because the Dakota stole more than one hundred horses, forcing the Pawnee to return to the reservation on foot.[32] One Pawnee boy was killed. This was only the prelude to the disaster that awaited them in August in Massacre Canyon. After that White immediately revoked Pawnee hunting privileges and proposed a plan to subsist them on beef rations—two pounds per head per week—until they were on allotments.[33] There were no more Pawnee hunts in Nebraska.

The aborted hunts were only two in a series of disasters that struck the Pawnee after 1872 and set them careening toward the brink of destruction. From 1870 to 1872 they held their own: their crops flourished even in the drought that parched the agency fields, the summer hunts were successful, and there was a brief respite in Dakota raids.[34] There was even a small population increase (fig. 11). Then there was the 1872–73 winter hunt, which left the Pawnee barely subsisting on cornmeal and beans. This was followed by a wet spring, which delayed the planting and reduced the harvest because the crops did not have time to mature. A swollen Beaver Creek overflowed its banks and destroyed the dam and race of the newly converted saw and grist mill. Then there was Massacre Canyon. White described the Pawnee that year as being in a "destitute condition" that was "almost without a parallel in their history."[35] A medical survey made by Burgess in July revealed widespread occurrence of scrofula, typhoid, and pneumonia.[36] This was the bleak backdrop to Big Spotted Horse's migration in the fall of 1873.

Big Spotted Horse actually had a pass to go to Indian Territory. He and his family and two friends had been given permission by White to withdraw from the Pawnee nation and join the Wichita. This was not a new plan. According to their own story, told in the 1880s to George Bird Grinnell, the plan had originated in 1871 with Lone Chief, a Kitkahahki, and was soon taken up by Big Spotted Horse and the Chaui soldier Frank White. Big Spotted Horse and White visited the Wichita Agency in the spring of 1873 and formally proposed to join them. The Wichita, whose population had declined to 250, welcomed the idea of reinforcements and regaled the Pawnee with embellished reports of abundant buffalo and the "fatness of the land."[37] The Pawnee's successive disasters in 1873 dispelled any doubts and precipitated the migration.

Burgess and Pe-ta-na-sharo at first prevented the upstart Pawnees from leaving, but they were determined to go. In a heated council on October 18, Pe-ta-na-sharo told White that many Chaui had left; Ter-re-kaw-wah admitted that many of his Pitahawirata had gone too; and La-sharo-tu-ri (Good Chief) added that four lodges of his Kitkahahki were waiting for instructions at the Platte.[38] Only the Skiri, who had been the most responsive to Quaker policy, favoring allotments and faithfully sending their children to school, stayed in mass. All the established chiefs opposed the move. They remained in Nebraska to receive the wrath of Superintendent White and ponder their own sudden loss of power.

The absent Pawnee, one-fifth or one-quarter of the population (depending on the source), wintered at the Wichita Agency. Those remaining in Nebraska were, in Burgess' words, "quiet but troubled."[39] They were told that they could not hunt that year and that the nine thousand dollar compensation from the Dakota would be spent for them on cattle and supplies. In an all-out effort to increase agricultural production, Burgess and White stipulated that all the annuity would go to "useful materials" and none to cash. The crops did well until August, when clouds of grasshoppers descended and devoured everything that grew. According to John Williamson, the doctors interpreted this as an undeniable sign to leave. Even the redoubtable Quakers realized that they could no longer hold the Pawnee in Nebraska: "Under the circumstances," Burgess reported, "with their crops destroyed and no prospect of realizing either food, hides, or sinews from the hunt, they feel that the world around them has changed, and they are much discouraged."[40]

By September 1874 the Pawnee were desperately hungry and the majority wanted to leave: "There is nothing but starvation and death if we do not go south where we can hunt game," the chiefs lamented.[41] Platt and Willard made the most of the situation by encouraging the Chaui and Pitahawirata to tear down their lodges and sell their poles and other property. Burgess tried to stop this dismantlement, but he was ignored. Only the Skiri followed his orders, and even they were torn. As one of their chiefs admitted to Williamson, "We are neither white man or Indian now."[42]

The terms of the exodus were laid out in the form of a "treaty" presented to the Pawnee at a council on October 8, 1874.[43] The chiefs disagreed with some of the details, but they knew that they had to leave, and finally acquiesced. The Indian Office would sell the reservation for the Pawnee at its "full market value"; a new reservation, about three hundred square miles in size, would be selected in a "healthy district" of unoccupied Indian Territory, with the selection to be approved by the Pawnee; the proceeds from the sale of the Nebraska reservation would be applied to improving the new home, especially to settling the Pawnee on allotments; no Pawnee funds would be used to finance the removal (a clause that was subsequently ignored); and the Pawnee promised to give up the "chase" once they were settled in the new location. Supplemental resolutions attached to the agreement provided for immediate removal, before the cold weather set in, for a bison hunt with the Wichita to furnish food and other resources during the adjustment period, for a contingent of old and young Pawnee, including some chiefs, to remain behind in Nebraska under government protection until the new home was ready, and for the exclusion of "parasites"—"evil-disposed persons" and "squaw-men"—who had plagued them in the past and should not be allowed to interfere in their lives in the future. This last clause, particularly, bore the stamp of the Quakers, not the Pawnee, because in these final months the Indians actually wanted one of these "parasites," Lester Platt, to take over from Burgess and lead them to Indian Territory. The chiefs had come to the conclusion that "God did not smile" on Burgess.[44]

The Pawnee wasted no time leaving. The historical record of the sequence of the migrations is nebulous, but it seems that an advance group, consisting of about forty lodges, left on October 10, heading south.[45] They reached the Wichita Agency on November 12 in a starving condition. A second party, accompanied by John Williamson, left about two weeks later. This was supposed to be the hunting party of about two hundred fifty "able-bodied men," but by the time they had crossed the Platte and passed by Hastings, more than one thousand men, women, and children were along. Williamson's heavily encumbered party followed the age-old Pawnee route to the southern Great Plains, covering about ten miles a day through the Kansas counties of Jewell, Mitchell, and Lincoln, heading for the Big Bend of the Arkansas River (fig. 43). From there the route lay directly south from Kansas into Indian Territory, and to a warm welcome at the Wichita Agency.

According to White's 1875 report, eighteen hundred Pawnee, the vast majority of the nation, wintered with the Wichita. Pe-ta-na-sharo was not among them, having died in mysterious circumstances from a gunshot wound before his party had crossed the Loup. He was one of only two apparent fatalities on the journey, but the hardships of famine, bad weather, and gnawing homesickness were with them all the way south and adumbrated the terrible conditions that they would face in the years to come in Indian Territory.

Agent Burgess had also headed south, leaving Nebraska at the end of November with instructions from Commissioner Edward Smith to select the new reservation. He picked what he optimistically described as a "fine tract" between the forks of the Arkansas and Cimmarron rivers, just south of the Osage reservation and north of the Sauk and Fox (fig. 43). The 283,026 acres of land would be bought officially from the Cherokee and Creek nations through the act of April 10, 1876, with purchase money that would come, eventually, from the sale of the Nebraska reservation.[46]

In early June 1875 Williamson led the reluctant Pawnee from the Wichita Agency to their new home. They agreed to this last removal, but living with, or near, their friends the Wichita had been a strong incentive to move south, and suddenly they were 150 miles away. Once again they felt manipulated and betrayed. The bands established separate earth-lodge and tipi villages near the agency on Black Bear Creek. Congress had appropriated no funds for their removal and support, so they eked out a living on emergency rations and dispersed along the Kansas border seeking food as they waited for the last refugees to arrive from Nebraska.

In Nebraska, one of Burgess's last acts before leaving for Indian Territory in November 1874 was to give the faithful Skiri permission to tear down their lodges and move near the agency.[47] There, they and others who had stayed behind, including the pupils in the manual-labor school, waited almost a year for permission to join their relatives on the new reservation. As they waited they watched the settlers strip the timber from their lands and, though they now had a small company of troops from the Omaha Barracks to protect them,

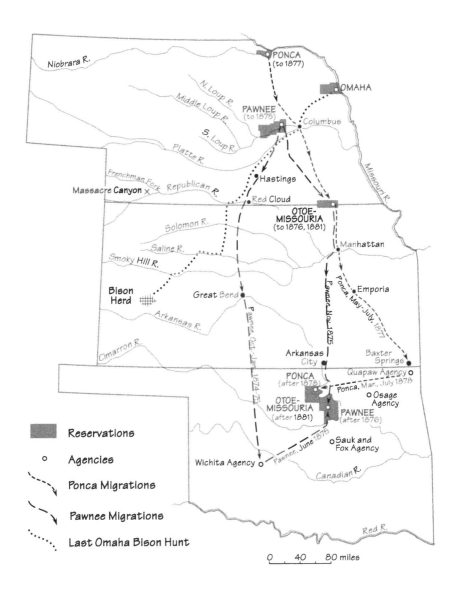

Fig. 43 Migrations to Indian Territory, 1874–1881

fearfully anticipated the inevitable Dakota attacks. These came in August. Despite the soldiers' presence, the Dakota killed Eagle Chief's wife while she was drying corn and shot a boy who was herding horses.[48] The last Pawnee, about 370 in number, left Nebraska in October 1875, traveling in government-supplied wagons on a more easterly route than the one followed by their kinfolk the previous year. They took their hallowed corn seeds with them to plant in their new homeland, but they left behind their sacred sites, their ancestors, and memories of hundreds of years of living in that land.

In Indian Territory, life only got worse. The new reservation was much inferior to their former Nebraska lands, much of it consisting of rough terrain covered by thin soils and scrub timber. Disease, especially malaria and influenza, was rife, and there was a shortage of funds for subsistence and development which left the Pawnee in what Burgess described in his 1875 report as "a bad dilemma." Funds were finally secured in the fall of 1876 by means of a government loan of three hundred thousand dollars to be repaid when the proceeds from the sale of the Nebraska reservation came in. They also had the perpetual annuity of thirty thousand dollars a year from the 1857 treaty and continuing funds for education, agricultural implements, farmers, and blacksmiths. Despite these funds, their population plummeted from 2,036 in 1876 to 1,045 in 1885, at which time their agent declared that they were destined to become extinct (fig. 11).[49]

The Pawnee dwindled in culture as well. The environmental signals which had directed the annual cycle were not the same in Indian Territory, and in any case there was no bison meat available to offer in ceremonies. Many ceremonies—the Four Pole Ceremony symbolizing the formation of the Skiri federation, for example—were "lost beyond recovery."[50] A Chaui chief, speaking to Grinnell in 1889, recalled the recent time when their ceremonial life had been vibrant, when there had been bison meat, and the bundles had been intact, and when the thunder could be depended upon to announce the start of the year; but this had all changed: "Through these sacred things we worshipped and the sacrifices were made to the Ruler above. This seemed to help us, and we used to live, increase, and grow strong. Up north, when we worshipped at the time of the first thunder, we never had cyclones. Down here, now that his worship has been given up, we have them."[51]

Gradually, sometimes forcibly, families were settled on individual farms. The Skiri led the way, while the Pitahawirata remained the most resistant to change, continuing, even in 1889, to live in their earth-lodge village and to eschew "citizen's dress." Allotments were finally imposed in 1893, following the Jerome Agreement of November 23, 1892. The Pawnee reservation was abolished: 111,931.61 acres were allotted in 160- and 80-acre tracts to each family and single adult, leaving 171,088.37 acres of "surplus lands." The Pawnee were initially paid $80,000 in gold coin as compensation. The surplus lands were sold at $1.25 an acre, giving a total of $212,916.71, less the $80,000 advance. The remaining $132,916.71 was not actually paid until 1920, and then only after the Pawnee had taken the case to the U.S. Court of Claims. In 1894 the Pawnee's agent, J. P. Woolsey, triumphantly reported the attainment of the government's ultimate goal, noting that "they have become fully fledged citizens of the United States, and their unallotted lands have become the home of the white man."[52] But allotments brought the Pawnee no relief. Their population dropped to 650 by 1900 and remained below 700 until 1917, before recovering, gradually, in the succeeding years.[53]

Meanwhile, in Nebraska, their reservation was offered for sale in accordance with the act of June 10, 1876. The land was to be sold in 160-acre tracts at public auction to the highest bidder, the terms of the sale being one-third down in cash and the balance to be paid in two annual payments at 6 percent interest. Sales began by auction in 1878 and were continued through private entry at the Grand Island land office. By 1883 the entire reservation had been sold and reorganized as Nance County. There was no limit to the number of tracts that could be bought, no residence requirement, no restrictions on resale, no stipulation that improvements be made; in other words, this was an open invitation to speculators. More than half of the total area went to only fifty-five purchasers. Delane Willard acquired the choice site of Genoa, and he soon owned the elevator, ran the bank, and was mayor of the town. Lester Platt died in 1875, before he could cash in on the bonanza. Most of the land purchased by the major buyers was resold at great profit in the boom years of the 1880s.[54] These were not the yeoman farmers that the Pawnee had been told to emulate.

The total proceeds from the sale of the reservation came to $750,000 ($2.70 per acre), which was close to the appraised value established by the survey commission in 1877. But by the time the Pawnee had reimbursed the government for the three hundred thousand dollars that was used to support them during the first few years in Indian Territory and paid the Creek and Cherokee for their new reservation ($177,010), they were left with only $280,000, or barely $1 an acre, from the sale of their Nebraska lands. They knew the land was worth much more, and at first they held out for a fairer payment.[55] But, as in the past, they were forced by poverty to agree to the government's terms and to sell the last vestige of their homeland just to survive.

Ponca Eviction

The Ponca followed the Pawnee south to Indian Territory in 1877. Even more so than the Pawnee they were forced to leave, not because of Dakota attacks, though they were unremitting, or even because of their own crushing poverty, but because the government decreed it. The injustice of the Ponca removal and the epic return and trial of Standing Bear (leading to the reestablishment of about 170 Ponca in their Niobrara homeland by the early 1880s) became a national cause, a catalyst for a much stronger humanitarian movement to protect the Indians. But for the Ponca the lasting impact of removal was the division of their society and the infliction of a deep wound, carved by tragedy, on their collective memory.

From 1870 to 1877 the eight bands of the Ponca lived in three villages at the

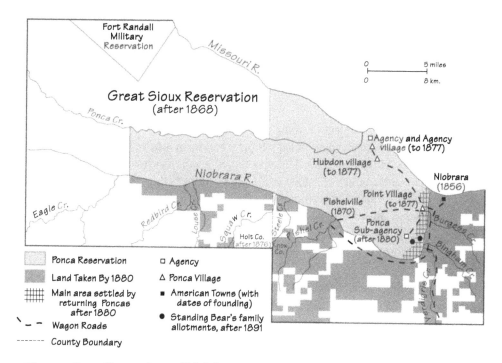

Fig. 44 Ponca Reservation and Vicinity, 1877–1891

eastern end of their reservation (which, in legal terms, had since 1868 been the
southeastern corner of the Great Sioux Reservation). Eighty-nine families, or
377 individuals, occupied earth lodges or log houses at the agency village, next
to the dilapidated warehouses, workshops, and employees' living quarters (figs.
29 and 44). Almost one-third of the Indians at the agency village were mixed-
bloods, drawn mainly from Antoine Primeaux's band. Until 1873 the Missouri
River swept past the agency less than one hundred yards to the east. On July 3 of
that year the river broke its banks and inundated the flood plain, leaving the old
village and fields in the middle of the new channel and forcing Agent Charles
Birkett and the Ponca to rebuild their settlements one-half mile to the west. The
second village was at the venerable Hubdon site, just to the south of the agency.
Twenty-four lodges of full-bloods and a handful of mixed-bloods, about 144
Ponca, lived there. These included a good number from Standing Bear's band.
The third village was on the north bank of the Niobrara, one-half mile from the
river and six miles from the agency. This was Point Village, home to about 250
full-bloods belonging mainly to the bands of White Eagle and Standing Buffalo.
It was an exposed site, vulnerable to Brulé raids from the open country to the
west, and much of the time (especially during the summer) Point village emptied out into a tipi settlement located near the agency.[56]

The misery that had enveloped the Ponca in the 1860s continued unabated. American observers were both horrified and ashamed by the dreadful situation at the villages. The Reverend J. Owen Dorsey, Episcopal missionary to the Ponca from May 1871 to August 1873 and soon to be an acclaimed ethnologist, could hardly bear to witness the suffering. All around he saw starvation, scurvy, scrofula, and death. Most of the Indians went almost naked; the more fortunate wore tattered blankets or robes. Dorsey saw injustice too: a peaceful people who had been virtually abandoned by the government and left at the mercy of the Dakota. While they starved, they watched steamboats heading up the Missouri laden with supplies for the various bands of the Dakota, fulfilling a bargain of rations for peace. The Ponca had no such leverage; they were too weak to be a threat to anyone. Dorsey's impression of the situation was shared by Lieutenant Martin E. Hogan, a member of a small troop that was stationed at the agency in 1872: "In the name of humanity," he appealed to William Welsh (a founding member of the Board of Indian Commissioners), "do something to save the perishing Ponca," or else condemn them to "total annihilation."[57]

This desperate situation was brought about by a succession of calamities, some of which were unavoidable, others the result of government neglect. It must have seemed to the Ponca that nature itself had turned against them. They did not have a single successful growing season in their last seven years on the reservation. Grasshoppers stripped their fields every year, drought added its toll in most years, and hail and Missouri River flooding completed the destruction of the crops. Their herd of horses and stock of oxen was almost wiped out in a devastating April snowstorm in 1873. A family also perished in this storm while they were seeking firewood; they were found frozen in a drift when the weather cleared. Nor was there meat to fill the dietary gap caused by failed crops. The last recorded formal bison hunt had taken place in the summer of 1870. It had simply been too dangerous to leave the reservation and face the prospect of encountering the Brulé on the range. Besides, after 1871 the agent would not allow it.[58]

The government did provide rations—beef, bacon, pork, lard, flour, sugar, and coffee—and these, together with collected roots and beans and the gleanings from the ravaged corn fields, made up the Ponca's starvation diet. After 1872, however, they were forced to work for the rations, answering the summons of the pealing "labor bell" at 8:00 A.M. each morning. This rule, handed down by Commissioner Edward Smith and put into practice by Birkett, was initially resisted by the full-bloods. But eventually even White Eagle fell into line. There was no real alternative: the choice was "no work—no flour."[59]

There were still annuities, dwindling annual payments from the 1858 treaty. The Ponca received ten thousand dollars each year until 1873 and eight thousand dollars a year thereafter until 1888. There were also discretionary monies for agricultural and mechanical aid. But even before 1873, according to Dorsey, annuity payments in goods and money amounted to only about $11.50 per capita each year. Typically these would include one blanket for every two Indians. The small cash payment of about five dollars each could buy little food or clothes in a frontier area where prices were inflated by scarcity and distance. The Ponca made small amounts of money by selling fuel to steamboats and by laboring on settlers' farms at harvest time, but this could not keep families fed. The agricultural aid seemed also to have little effect: in 1876, in the absence of reaping machines, the wheat had to be cut with butcher knives, a process so slow that much of the crop rotted in the fields.[60]

Farming efforts were also thwarted by the Brulé, who boasted, with some accuracy, that the Ponca were "their prisoners." Indian workers did not dare venture more than one-quarter mile from their village; agency workers always kept their guns by their sides. Allotments, of course, were inconceivable, and though the eastern part of the reservation was surveyed into eight-acre lots in 1871 (fig. 29), agents did not even try to encourage dispersal. Every year in spring, as soon as the grass had nutrients to support their horses, Brulé raiders renewed their attacks, stealing ponies, killing stock, and scalping Ponca. The raids were a "weekly occurrence" during the summer months and they continued right up to the Ponca's expulsion to Indian Territory.[61]

Ponca casualties were low (the record shows only four murders from 1870 to 1877), largely because the Indians mounted a courageous defense of their homes. In one incident on June 9, 1873, for example, two hundred Brulé attacked in two prongs, one group moving in from the bluffs, the other following the Missouri down from the north. This time, however, the Ponca were prepared, having been warned by Yankton who signaled from the bluffs across the Missouri. Ponca men and women, aided rather cautiously by the seven resident U.S. soldiers, drove the attackers back out into the prairie. Another major battle, once more involving more than two hundred Brulé, took place on July 6, 1875. Again the raiders were repulsed.

For the most part, the Ponca were left to face the Dakota alone. Small detachments of troops (five to twenty men) were periodically stationed at the agency after July 1872. But they were expressly instructed only to defend the Ponca and the "public buildings" if attacked. They were prohibited from patrolling the fields, from giving pursuit to raiders, or from guarding wagons moving to and from the agency. The government refused to provide the Ponca with means to protect themselves. Dorsey estimated that they had only two good rifles among them, together with old shotguns, a few revolvers, and bows and arrows. Meanwhile the Dakota were mounted and well-armed with breech-loading rifles furnished directly by the government. Agent Birkett repeatedly pleaded with his superiors for guns and ammunition, but none was delivered.[62]

Other conflicts also kept the Ponca impoverished and divided. Their initial agent in the 1870s, Henry Gregory (brother of their first separate agent, J. Shaw

Gregory), was forced to resign in September 1872 after the chiefs lodged complaints against him with the president of the United States. Gregory was accused of pocketing Ponca educational and agricultural funds and of taking Indian women to his house "night after night," including Standing Buffalo's wife (whom the chief subsequently divorced).[63] Thereafter, the agents were appointed by recommendation of the Episcopal Protestant mission, and while they may have been more honest, they were no more effective in relieving the Ponca's woes. Charles Birkett spent much of his time pleading in vain for guns and serving as a makeshift physician. A. J. Carrier, who took over from Birkett in 1875, was a hard man who believed that laziness rather than fear of the Dakota kept the Ponca from working in the fields. Carrier took repressive policy to a new stage by threatening to withhold rations from the children themselves if they did not attend the day school. He also "deposed" the chiefs Standing Buffalo, The Chief, Big Soldier, and Standing Bear for their "pernicious influence," though this action does not seem to have altered their status with the Ponca. Carrier lasted only one year before being deposed himself (for "profaneness") by Episcopal authorities.[64] After Carrier, agents came and went in rapid succession—four in as many years—as they were caught in the maelstrom of Ponca removal.

Considerable conflicts also erupted within Ponca society. These particularly involved differences between the mixed-bloods and full-bloods. The Ponca had a much higher number and percentage of mixed-bloods than did any of the other Nebraska Indians—150 total, or 20 percent, in 1876. The full-bloods considered the mixed-bloods to be "tools" of settlers who lived near the reservation or who had married into Indian families. In one bloody incident in 1873, Antoine Le Revere, a "drunken and brutish man" who had lived on or near the reservation for a number of years, and who had been married to a mixed-blood from the agency village until her death, picked a fight with No Knife, the brother of Standing Buffalo. When it was over, No Knife had four bullets in him, none of them mortal wounds, and Le Revere lay dead on the ground with his brains protruding from his skull.[65] The division between mixed-bloods and full-bloods would only widen as the pressures for removal mounted.

The Ponca, unlike the Pawnee and Otoe-Missouria, did not, however, have serious conflicts with most surrounding settlers. Population pressure on the reservation was not great. Only after 1878 did settlers in any number move south and west from the town of Niobrara toward the outlying hamlet of Pischelville (fig. 44). In 1872 a group of settlers from along Verdigre Creek lodged a rather apologetic petition against the Ponca, complaining that they were stealing crops, grazing ponies on their lands, and begging. The settlers understood that the Ponca were starving, but they too were destitute, victims of the same environmental disasters. There were also a few complaints by the Ponca that settlers were crossing the Niobrara and cutting their timber.[66] Generally, however, relations were good: both groups shared a fear of the Dakota and endured the hardships of isolation. Indeed, local settlers were among the most vocal opponents of Ponca removal.

The first suggestion of removal, resurrecting an idea as old as the Ponca reservation itself, came in 1873. At first the plan was to settle the Ponca on the western part of the Omaha reservation, which had been surveyed and appraised for sale in 1872. Birkett brought up the subject of the move with Commissioner Smith in November 1873, and Smith subsequently gave his endorsement, saying that "both sides want it." In his 1875 report Smith once again advocated the resettlement of the Ponca near the Omaha. The standard rationale was that the Omaha and the Ponca were closely related and considerably intermarried, and that the Ponca would be much safer in a new home on the Omaha reservation. But by 1875 a new purpose had emerged: the vacated Ponca reservation would be a good site for an agency overseeing the "wild bands of the Sioux," particularly the Brulé, headed by Spotted Tail, and the Oglala under Red Cloud. It was thought that it would be easier to supply, and to control, these Indians at a site near the Missouri. In 1876 the Indian Office recommended to Congress that the Ponca should be moved to the Logan Valley on the Omaha reservation, but instead Congress appropriated twenty-five thousand dollars for a more radical removal—to Indian Territory.[67]

This idea had been circulating since at least early 1875 and, of course, it meshed well with the general plan for "consolidating" reservations in Indian Territory. Whereas Birkett had been a proponent of resettlement with the Omaha, Carrier was a staunch advocate of removal to Indian Territory. In his first council with the Ponca, in February 1875, Carrier brought up the subject; in September he requested maps of Indian Territory showing existing reservations and areas available for new ones; and in November he proposed to take a delegation of chiefs to Indian Territory to select a new reservation.[68]

At first the Ponca chiefs, weary from the poverty and strife they had endured, seem to have been interested in the plan. Indeed, in council in September 1875 they all signed a petition which expressed a "strong desire to be removed from [their] present reservation in Dakota Territory to the Indian Territory."[69] This enthusiasm may have been manufactured by Carrier, because it quickly became apparent that the Ponca had serious qualms about leaving their homeland. They supported a preliminary investigation of potential sites in Indian Territory, and as always they were enthusiastic about visiting Washington, D.C., and discussing their future prospects with the president, but they began to balk at removal. But by 1876 it was already too late: the money was appropriated, minds in the Indian Office were made up, and the stage was set for one of the most shameful episodes in the history of federal-Indian relations.

Later, in Indian Territory, their agent, William Whiteman, would purport to give the "true history" of Ponca removal, rationalizing it as an escape from the

Dakota and "the only just and humane thing" the government could do. White-man argued that the Ponca had petitioned to be removed and that they had gone willingly. Subsequent investigations by government commissions proved that Whiteman's interpretation was a distortion of the facts, that the removal was coerced, and that the entire sorry procedure was illegal and unjust.[70]

The 1876 congressional appropriation bill was explicit in stating that the Ponca could not be moved anywhere without their permission. Yet when gov-ernment inspector E. C. Kemble arrived at the Ponca Agency in January 1877, it was immediately apparent that he was determined to move them by any means necessary.

Later, in 1880, the Senate investigation committee would lay much of the blame for the Ponca tragedy on Kemble, characterizing him as a man who had "failed to comprehend his mission."[71] It is true that Kemble was imperious and indifferent to the feelings of the Ponca: Standing Bear would tell the committee that he "showed no pity" for them. But much of the blame should have been directed to Kemble's superiors in the Indian Office, who allowed the removal to proceed because they already had their minds set on relocating Dakota at the Ponca Agency. Commissioner John Q. Smith was explicit on this in a letter to Kemble, writing, "Removal of the Poncas will be insisted upon. Spotted Tail and Red Cloud must move this summer to the Missouri River. Their presence there will render further stay of the Poncas at the old location impossible." Senator Samuel J. Kirkwood of Iowa, in a minority opinion attached to the committee's report, referred to Kemble as a "scapegoat" and asked the apt question: why hadn't the government previously done anything to rectify its 1868 "blunder" of incorporating the Ponca into the Great Sioux Reservation? He might also have asked why the government had failed to fulfill its promise to protect the Ponca on their reservation.

Kemble's first act was to organize a delegation of the ten leading Ponca chiefs, including White Eagle, Standing Buffalo, Standing Bear, and Smoke Maker, to accompany him to Indian Territory and select a site for a new reservation. His plan was then to take the chiefs on to Washington, D.C., to formalize the exchange of lands and clear up any matters that remained. In his haste Kemble made inadequate arrangements for the trip. The Ponca chiefs were given a cold reception by the Osage, who refused to sell any land. By the time they had traveled to the Kaw (Kansa) Reservation they were homesick and worried; they had seen nothing to please them in what White Eagle later described as a land of "rocks and stunted trees." The chiefs asked Kemble to take them home, but he refused, saying that he was only empowered to continue to Washington.

They then took matters into their own hands and eight of them (the other two being too old, which must have been very old indeed, because Smoke Maker, who went, was sixty-seven) set off on foot for the Niobrara. Standing Bear, in subsequent testimony before the Senate committee, told how they sold

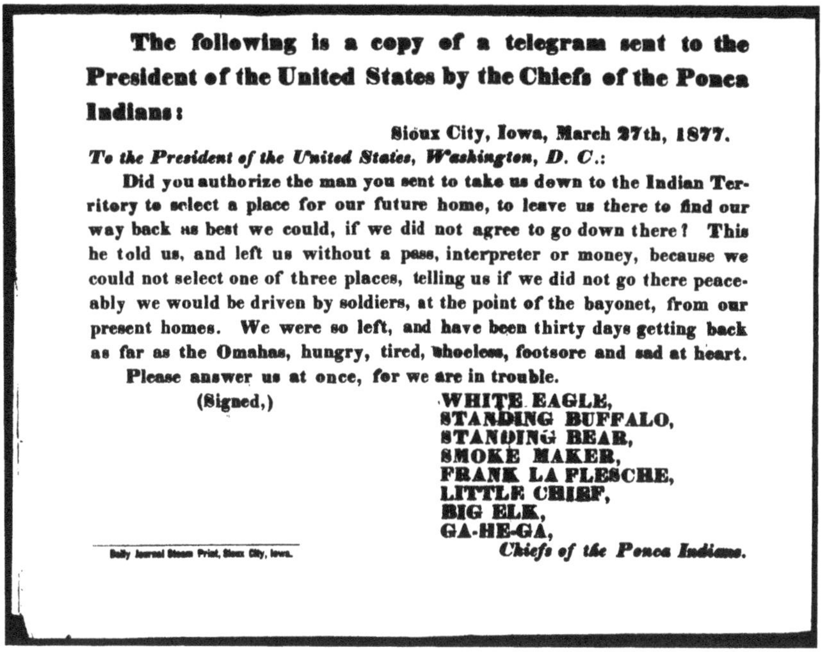
The following is a copy of a telegram sent to the President of the United States by the Chiefs of the Ponca Indians:

Sioux City, Iowa, March 27th, 1877.

To the President of the United States, Washington, D. C.:

Did you authorize the man you sent to take us down to the Indian Territory to select a place for our future home, to leave us there to find our way back as best we could, if we did not agree to go down there? This he told us, and left us without a pass, interpreter or money, because we could not select one of three places, telling us if we did not go there peaceably we would be driven by soldiers, at the point of the bayonet, from our present homes. We were so left, and have been thirty days getting back as far as the Omahas, hungry, tired, shoeless, footsore and sad at heart. Please answer us at once, for we are in trouble.

(Signed,) WHITE EAGLE,
STANDING BUFFALO,
STANDING BEAR,
SMOKE MAKER,
FRANK LA FLESCHE,
LITTLE CHIEF,
BIG ELK,
GA-HE-GA,
Chiefs of the Ponca Indians.

Daily Journal Steam Print, Sioux City, Iowa.

Fig. 45 Ponca Protest, March 27, 1877. From LR, Ponca Agency, 1876–1877. Courtesy of Nebraska State Historical Society, RG 508

their meager possessions to raise eight dollars for the journey, how they walked on worn-out moccasins along the railroad tracks to Wichita, slept in hay stacks, and lived on dried corn. They reached the Otoe Reservation in fifty days, where they were fed and given horses for the remaining miles. Five days later they rode onto the Omaha Reservation. On March 27, at Sioux City, the weary and angry chiefs sent a telegram to President Hayes demanding to know if Kemble had been acting on official orders (fig. 45). They received no answer. Meanwhile, Kemble was railing that they should be arrested "until such times as they show consent to yield obedience to the orders of their agent."[72]

While the chiefs recuperated from their two-month ordeal at the Omaha Reservation, Kemble rushed back to Niobrara and immediately, and forcefully, started the process of removal. Forty troops were brought down from Fort Randall to back him up. Kemble claimed that the Ponca were "divided" over whether to stay or go, with the "more civilized portion," including the mixed-bloods, in favor of moving. John Springer, an Omaha eyewitness to the events, saw it quite differently: none of the Indians wanted to leave and they shut themselves up in their lodges and houses and wailed through the night. When the chiefs returned from the Omaha Reservation, telling of their dissatisfaction with the land in Indian Territory, Kemble told them that they would be shot if they failed to follow his orders. Two of his most vocal critics, Standing Bear and his brother, Big Snake, were arrested and detained at Yankton. Through pressure and threats Kemble induced 170 Ponca, mainly mixed-bloods, to close up their homes at the agency village. On April 11 they crossed the still-icy Niobrara on the first stage of the journey to what became known to the Ponca, all too accurately, as "Death Country."[73]

The ragged procession marched through rain and snow, averaging only eleven miles a day, and reached their new home on the northern Quapaw Reservation on June 12, 1877. The rest of the Ponca joined them there on July 9. They had resolutely resisted the government's efforts to move them, saying that they "preferred to remain and die on their native heath . . . than to die by disease in the unhealthy miasmatic country" of Indian Territory. But at a council held on May 15 their new agent, E. A. Howard, told them categorically that they would go, "either peaceably or by force," and he sent for additional troops from Fort Randall. On the following day the soldiers led the approximately five hundred Ponca across the swollen Niobrara at the start of a fifty-four day nightmare (fig. 43). At least thirty Ponca evaded removal by seeking refuge with the Omaha, Santee, or Yankton. The Indians marched through a season of almost incessant rain, along roads that Howard described as "frightfully bad." They were mired in mud for days on end. Violent thunderstorms, including a tornado that shredded their tents and tossed people three hundred yards, added to the ordeal, as if to confirm in their eyes that it was the wrong step to take. They buried their first dead child on May 19, barely twenty miles out from home, and Standing Bear's daughter, Prairie Flower, died of consumption on June 5. By the time they reached Indian Territory, nine Ponca—all children or old women—had perished.[74]

They found the other Ponca camped to the south of the commissary on the Quapaw Reservation (fig. 43). They set up camp to the north, and animosity between the two Ponca groups seems to have persisted for some time. No serious preparations had been made for their arrival; they would live in porous canvas tipis for more than a year. They had no funds at all, because their former reservation had not been sold, and the eight thousand dollar annuity and the forty thousand dollar removal fund (an additional fifteen thousand dollars was appropriated in 1878) had been spent on the migration. The Ponca would receive no per capita payments at all until 1881. The government provided rations, at considerable expense, but the Ponca started dying at an alarming rate. Influenza, scrofula, dysentery, and, especially, malaria were endemic. The malaria could have been controlled, but the agent lacked the funds for quinine. It is difficult to know how many people died in this uprooting because the Ponca concealed the deaths in order to acquire extra ration cards. But at a minimum, forty-five Ponca died in the first year in Indian Territory. These included the son of Standing Bear, the wife and four children of White Eagle, and almost all of the aged Smoke-Maker's family.[75]

On August 7, then again on August 23, 1877, the Ponca gathered in council and pleaded to be returned to their homes on the Niobrara. This should have been feasible, because Spotted Tail's Dakota had stayed only briefly at the Ponca Agency before withdrawing two hundred miles inland to more familiar country on the White River. But Commissioner Hayt rejected their petitions, pointing out what seemed to him the "obvious unwisdom of removing Indians *from* the Indian Territory." What the government was concerned about, as the Senate investigation revealed, was setting a precedent that other dislocated Indians would try to follow.[76]

The Ponca kept dying through the fall and into the winter of 1877. Entire families were wiped out; children would become ill and die within a day; they died so fast that there was not time to bury them, and they were taken out into the prairie and left. By early 1878 fear and helplessness had given way to anger. Their agent, A. G. Boone, reported that they were becoming "restless," "arrogant," and "destructive." They had selected a site for a new reservation on the Salt Fork River just to the west of the Kansas Agency, but there were no funds to move them there. At a council on January 29, Smoke Maker spoke about how in the old country they had owned stoves and plows and had "milk to put in [their] coffee," and now they had nothing. Boone told them they would have to stay where they were until the government was ready to move them.[77]

In late March, 380 Ponca took it upon themselves to leave for the reservation on the Salt Fork River (fig. 43). In June Congress finally appropriated the money (forty-five thousand dollars) to make the move possible. The official removal took place in late July when Agent Whiteman (Boone having been fired) led the remaining Ponca 185 miles through one-hundred-degree-heat to their new homes. The land was good; the reservation was the best received by any of the relocated Nebraska Indians in Indian Territory. It was well-watered, with fertile soils, and there were substantial stands of timber, though these had been cut into by Kansas settlers. It was too late to put in a crop, so they continued to live (and die) on government rations. Another forty-five Ponca died from July 1878 to July 1879. They still expressed a "strong desire" to return to the Niobrara and lamented that the "Great Father [had] forgotten them."[78]

Standing Bear and thirty Ponca—nine men, the rest women and children—made their own decision to return home that winter. They had saved up their rations over the previous months with this purpose in mind. Whiteman had been aware of their intentions and had monitored their movements, but he did not believe that they would leave in the prevailing snow and cold. On January 1, 1879, the fugitives left, traveling in four wagons and living on one dollar a day and the kindness of settlers. Standing Bear took with him the bones of his dead son to bury in the familiar earth between Ponca Creek and the Niobrara. He considered this return a complete break from his people, an expatriation made mandatory by the need to survive. They reached the Omaha reservation in mid-March, where they were given land and farming implements by their friends. At about the same time Smoke Maker and what remained of his family pulled into the Yankton Agency and asked for permission to stay.[79]

At this point the government once again intervened. Federal troops, led by a sympathetic General George Crook, arrested Standing Bear and his followers with the intention of returning them to Indian Territory. But the plight of the Ponca had caught the public imagination, prompting two prominent Omaha lawyers, A. J. Poppleton and John L. Webster, to secure a writ of *habeas corpus* which permitted Standing Bear to present his case.[80] The writ specifically argued that Standing Bear and his followers had withdrawn from the Ponca and were trying to live "like Whites," without government aid, when they were arrested. The return statement to the writ maintained that these were renegade Ponca who should be returned to their reservation. In the widely publicized case of *Standing Bear v. Crook*, heard in the Omaha circuit court, an overtly supportive Judge Elmer Dundy accepted the writ, ruling that an Indian is indeed a "person" and therefore entitled to petition on these grounds. Dundy also ruled that Standing Bear was within his rights to withdraw from the Ponca and that the United States had no authority to return him to Indian Territory. Dundy then ordered Standing Bear's discharge from custody. No appeals to a higher court were accepted.

Standing Bear, an early media hero, then toured the eastern United States with the Omaha newspaperman and reformer, Thomas Henry Tibbles, arousing support for Indian reform. In the fall of 1879 he settled with his growing band of expatriate Ponca on the old reserve. By the summer of 1880 just over one hundred Ponca (about one-sixth of the total number) were building houses and farming in the crescent of the Niobrara and on an island in the river, just opposite and upstream from the town of the same name (fig. 44).[81]

By 1880, therefore, Ponca society was irrevocably divided into two segments: the Northern and Southern Ponca. In Indian Territory the Ponca were becoming reconciled to their new reservation. Their new agent, William Whiting, described their disposition as "unsettled," and another five families left for the north. But by October the Ponca leaders had decided to stay in Indian Territory: "Our tribe will not be finally settled," they reasoned in a petition to Commissioner Trowbridge, "until we have a title to our present reservation, and we have relinquished all right to our Dakota land." In December the chiefs, led by White Eagle, met with Secretary of the Interior Carl Schurz in Washington, D.C., and stated their intentions to remain in their new homes on the Salt Fork River. Bear Scar put it most succinctly: "I have put a big stone down here, and will sit on it." They had not wanted to come to Indian Territory, but they no longer had the will to leave. Moreover, they believed that they had a better chance to get title to land there than in the disputed corner of the Great Sioux Reservation.[82]

Government commissioners returned with the Ponca chiefs to Indian Territory on January 3, 1881, and got confirmation from the rest of the people that they wanted to stay. The commissioners and a Ponca delegation then traveled to the Niobrara to see if a consensus could be reached on the sale of the old reservation.

They assembled in council in the town of Niobrara on January 11 and 12, 1881, the two groups of Ponca friendly but sitting on opposite sides of the room. More than fifty local settlers were also on hand. The aged Smoke Maker recalled how they had been driven to Indian Territory like "a drove of cattle into a corral to be slaughtered." Standing Bear made a "vehement speech" denying that the Southern Ponca had any right to sell their Niobrara land. He argued that there were now 178 Ponca there, doing well without any government aid. They wanted their share of the annuities and they wanted "white man's houses" that were "full of light." They also needed security of tenure on their lands. When the vote was taken, not a single Northern Ponca agreed to return to Indian Territory or to sell their old reservation.[83] The division of the Ponca was complete, and the government, now apologetic over its recent heavy-handedness, was willing to acknowledge it.

The way for the Northern Ponca to stay on their regained lands was cleared on August 20, 1881, when the chiefs of the Oglala, Brulé, and Standing Rock Dakota recognized the Ponca's right to the "land . . . where they had formerly resided."[84] This clause was part of a larger proposal to break up the Great Sioux Reservation into separate reservations for each Dakota band, with allotments being the ultimate objective. The Northern Ponca would receive 640 acres for each family and eighty acres for each single adult.

It would be another decade, however, before they received allotments. The 1881 agreement stipulated that three-quarters of the adult males in each Dakota band had to consent to the terms, and this was difficult to achieve. The allotment process stalled, but there were no more Dakota raids, and the Ponca, for the first time in more than two decades, felt safe on their Niobrara reservation.

Both segments of the Ponca also had better financial support from the government after 1881, and the Southern Ponca finally acquired a legally purchased reservation. By the act of March 3, 1881, a total of $165,000 was appropriated to compensate the Ponca for their losses and to settle them more comfortably in their new homes. This appropriation was a direct outcome of the scathing report of the investigation commission, which had recommended an "ample and speedy redress of wrongs."[85] A total of fifty thousand dollars was allocated to the Southern Ponca for the purchase of their reservation lands from the Cherokee. In addition, they were given ten thousand dollars for per capita distribution and ten thousand dollars to purchase cattle and draught animals. The Northern Ponca were also given ten thousand dollars for per capita distribution, as well as five thousand dollars for agricultural aid and five thousand dollars for education. The remaining seventy thousand dollars was placed in a treasury account to draw interest (at 5 percent a year) for future per capita payments to both groups of Ponca.

In Indian Territory, despite their good reservation, the Southern Ponca stagnated. Their population, rising and falling with the vicissitudes of life in what was still an unfamiliar country, stayed on a jagged plateau between 580 and 650 until after 1900, before reviving in the twentieth century. The chiefs, especially Standing Buffalo, continued to resist allotments well into the 1890s. Allotments were authorized on September 6, 1890, and the reservation was surveyed accordingly. But even after four years only 420 Ponca had accepted allotments and the remainder, mostly old men, were still refusing to participate. Finally, on August 25, 1894, the commissioner of Indian affairs ordered the remaining allotments to be assigned. A total of 101,051 acres were allotted, leaving no surplus lands for sale.[86]

Despite allotments and the associated fragmentation of the communal society, the Southern Ponca retained many traditions, practicing the Sun Dance, for example, even though their agents tried to suppress it. They also actively incorporated ceremonies from other Indian societies, including the Peyote religion and the Ghost Dance. What was forgotten, however, was their traditional history. Without the familiar landscapes of the Niobrara country, their stories lost their contexts and lapsed when the old people died.[87]

The Northern Ponca continued to thrive during the 1880s on their small holdings in the bend of the Niobrara. They were invariably described favorably in agent reports as "making an honest living" and "getting along very well."[88] Their harvest was so successful in 1885 that they were obliged to store the surplus in their homes, prompting Standing Bear to suggest that the government either provide additional storage facilities or additional houses. They were administered by a superintendent attached to the Santee Agency, and by 1886 there were warehouses, a combined blacksmith-carpenter shop, and dwellings at their subagency. Their population surpassed two hundred in 1888. More than one-quarter were mixed-bloods, possibly representing an infusion of local people of mixed descent who had never left the area. It is even said by Ponca historians that Standing Bear encouraged such intermarriage to swell the population and thus make a stronger claim to their reservation. Because of the high degree of intermarriage, and because their numbers were relatively few and their locations dispersed, the Northern Ponca adopted "citizens' clothing" and other American attributes more rapidly than their southern relatives. However,

Fig. 46. Standing Bear and Family, circa 1870s. Courtesy of Nebraska State Historical Society, 1397:1–2

traditional ceremonies and practices, such as visiting for ceremonies and cele-
brations with the Omaha, Yankton, and Santee, persisted.

On March 2, 1889, the government finally secured the breakup of the Great
Sioux Reservation and so opened the way for allotments for the Northern
Ponca. They were not enthusiastic about this, probably because it signaled the
end of their reservation, a reservation they had fought hard to retain. The
opponents included Standing Bear, who, in a bizarre retracing of steps, left with
sixty others for Indian Territory in the spring of 1890. At least half of them,
including Standing Bear, returned in July and accepted their lands.

By 1891 a total of 27,202 acres had been allotted to 167 heads of families and
single adults in 320-, 160-, and 80-acre portions. As was usual, the government
would hold the titles to the allotments during a twenty-five-year trust period to
prevent immediate, wholesale purchase by settlers. The Ponca chose their lands
mainly on the fertile floodplain and terraces between the Niobrara and Ponca
Creek, the area that had long been their heartland. Standing Bear selected a
family allotment on the Niobrara near the agency (figs. 44 and 46). He lived
there until his death in 1908, when he was buried alongside his ancestors.[89]

The Ponca's title to the remainder of their 96,000-acre reservation was extinguished. By the terms of the 1889 treaty the land would sell for $1.25 an acre
during the first three years and seventy-five cents an acre thereafter. Much of
the land was taken by settlers in 1892–93, although the relinquishment of many
of these claims to other buyers within a year of their entry (that is, before any
payments were due) indicates a high degree of speculation. When the trust
period was over (abbreviated by subsequent legislation) and the Northern
Ponca received their titles of ownership, the land quickly passed into the hands
of Americans. By 1939 only 1,028 acres remained under Ponca control. As in the
past, the Indians were prompted by poverty to sell their primary resource for
short-term income, only now it was individuals, not the people as a whole,
doing the selling. The Ponca scattered, mainly in Nebraska and South Dakota.
On September 5, 1962, in a period of renewed government assault on Indian
societies, they were "terminated" as a tribe.[90] This would not, however, be the
end of this irrepressible people.

Divided But Not Conquered

The Otoe-Missouria sold their unfulfilled Eden on the Big Blue in two stages, in
1876 and 1881, and migrated as a deeply divided people to Indian Territory.
Their removal lacked the drama and tragedy of the Pawnee's and Ponca's final
years in Nebraska; for the Otoe-Missouria it was more a matter of attrition, of
poverty, and of complex, interacting internal and external stresses that precipitated their exodus. Indeed, for some of them, removal was seen as an escape
rather than an imposition. The end result was the same, however, as for the

Pawnee and Ponca: a poor existence in Indian Territory, a population dwin-dling to a dangerous low, and a former Nebraska reservation sold to Americans bent on capitalizing on the Indians' relinquished estate.

Throughout the 1870s, and even after their resettlement in Indian Territory, the Otoe-Missouria remained predominantly traditional. According to their zealous Quaker agent, Jesse Griest (who took over from Albert Green in April 1873), they "resolutely contested" the government's assimilation policy and remained "wedded to the traditions of their ancestors." They continued to rely on their own doctors and to eschew American medicine. They resisted all efforts to convert men into farmers and "stigmatized" any individual who even entertained the idea. They still lived in their conventional earth lodges and tipis, and every earth lodge retained its own medicine bundle. Even as late as 1879 there were only nine frame houses occupied by Indians (mainly mixed-bloods) on the reservation. An impressive and expensive manual-labor school opened in 1875, but fewer than twenty of the almost one hundred school-age children attended. Time-honored practices, such as pipe dancing and sacrificing a horse on the grave of its dead owner, persisted, despite relentless efforts by the agents to suppress them. Griest was forced to admit, as he watched newly built houses be stripped of their boards and freshly cleared prairie become choked with weeds, that the Otoe-Missouria were simply "unwilling to give up the hope that they might return to the unrestrained life of the forefathers."[91]

Some clung to this hope more fervently than others. The Otoe-Missouria had been torn by factionalism since at least the 1830s, but the line between the competing constituencies was drawn more clearly after 1870. The first group—the "stable-faction," Griest called them—paid at least lip service to the civiliza-tion program and were committed to retaining a portion of their Nebraska lands. Griest championed their cause even to the extent of creating chiefs (headed by Big Elk, or Harre-garrow) from the young men in their ranks to replace the recalcitrant hereditary leaders. The second group, christened the "wild party" by Griest, were contemptuous of the agent and his policies, and their abiding goal was to sell the entire reservation and move to Indian Terri-tory. Like the Pawnee, they mistakenly believed that they could continue to live there in the old ways. In this, of course, they were heartily supported by the surrounding settlers. Griest argued that the rebellious Indians were in a minor-ity, accounting for no more than a quarter to a third of the total, but it was in his interest to make this case to his superiors, to try to show that the Quaker policy was working. When the move to Indian Territory was finally made, in 1880 and 1881, it was evident that the society was divided into two camps of approximately equal size. Moreover, because the defiant Indians had the weight of tradition behind them and the leadership of influential hereditary chiefs like Medicine Horse and Ar-ka-ke-ta, their power exceeded their numbers. Antago-nism between the two groups was intense, even to the point of violence: in 1874, for example, a man killed a friend who had mocked him for breaking the prairie to plant crops.[92]

This antagonism was aggravated by the stresses which buffeted the Otoe-Missouria during the 1870s. The first stress was poverty. Their subsistence base crumbled. There was no increase in cultivated acreage over the decade. Where was the sense of putting effort into improving a reservation when it was uncertain that they would be able to keep it? Crops that did get sown frequently (in 1873, 1874, and 1879, for example) fell victim to drought or grasshoppers. It was a rare year (1876 was one) when they harvested more than five thousand bushels of corn or one thousand bushels of wheat, despite the inherent fertility of the land.

Their bison hunts died out by mid-decade. The Otoe-Missouria were permitted to undertake at least one hunt a year until 1875, because the alternative was starvation or subsistence on expensive rations. Griest had to get special permission from the commissioner of Indian affairs for this to happen. Their last successful hunt was in the summer of 1872. They made their final organized hunt in the summer of 1875, 340 men, women, and children moving through settled country, up the Little Blue, down to the Republican and, eventually, out to the headwaters of the Saline (fig. 43). But the herds were so thin and distant by this time, and conflicts with settlers so frequent, that the trip was hardly worth the effort. That same year the government made an emergency appropriation of twelve thousand dollars for the "destitute" Otoe-Missouria. This money was largely spent on rations and the purchase of a large (308-head) cattle herd. By 1877 the starving Indians had eaten most of the cattle. The herd built back up again by 1880, but only because Griest organized a police force of the more conciliatory Indians to protect it.[93]

Nor was there much support from annuities, those diminishing payments for former lands. The annual payment now stood at nine thousand dollars, most of which was put over to agency improvements (including a jail, built in 1879) and agricultural aid. The Indians received biannual per capita payments of only $3.50 in 1873 ($4.00 for the chiefs); after 1875 they were given no cash payments at all. Their combined debt to the trader accumulated to twenty-five hundred dollars. When starvation was imminent and rations were furnished, these, too, were generally paid for from the Indians' own funds. No wonder the chiefs demanded to know from Griest "what [became] of their money." The fact is, most of their money, as much as seven thousand dollars a year after 1875, went to pay a swelling coterie of agency employees. The special funds for these teachers, farmers, blacksmiths, and other workers had expired in 1865. Small amounts of additional income came from the sale of two railroad rights of way, in 1872 and 1879, and from processing bison hides and skins for American hunters, but these hardly kept starvation at bay.[94]

The Otoe-Missouria's population profile during these years mirrored their stagnated, marginal existence (fig. 10). They did not experience the rapid declines of the Ponca and Pawnee; there were no Brulé raids on their reservation or on their hunting parties to cause such demographic disaster. The end of raiding was reflected in a new equal balance between men and women in the population. The Otoe-Missouria started and ended the decade with 434 people, which was the nadir of their numbers in Nebraska. In between, their population rose (but by no more than thirty) and fell from year to year as their misfortunes ameliorated or deepened. Deaths exceeded births in half of the years of the decade. Malaria, tuberculosis, typhoid, and stomach ailments resulting in diarrhea and dehydration were the main killers. As usual, children died in disproportionate numbers. The small family sizes, averaging three to four adults and children, was testimony to the high infant mortality rates and, perhaps, a declining birth rate. The largest annual decline came in 1880 after an exceedingly dry summer in which the creeks dried up and "every" child and adult became ill by drinking from pools of standing water.[95]

A second stress, in addition to poverty, was the increasingly mandatory nature of federal policy and the associated curtailment of the Otoe-Missouria's ability to control their own affairs. Like the other native Nebraskans, the Otoe-Missouria were subjected to stringent pass laws, and this confinement chaffed upon the recently unbridled Indians. They were also subjected to efforts by Griest to fill the manual-labor school through "persuasive or compulsory means," such as the threatened withholding of flour from the families of those children who did not attend and the lure of free meals for the children who did. But the main point of contention was the commissioner's decision in 1873 to terminate cash annuities and to allocate all the funds to agricultural aid and to laboring for a wage.[96] In effect the Indians would be paid for their work out of money that was already theirs. This became the occasion of a heated confrontation in Washington, D.C., between the hereditary chiefs and Commissioner Edward Smith.

A delegation of chiefs, including Medicine Horse, Ar-ka-ke-ta, and Big Bear, had traveled to the nation's capital in October 1873, accompanied by Griest. They paid for the trip with fifteen hundred dollars from their annuities. They met in council with Smith on November 1 and 4 and explained to him their plan to sell the entire reservation and move to Indian Territory. Smith would have nothing to do with the plan, seeing it (probably accurately) as a scheme to delay settling down on allotments. The discussion then moved onto the topic of who controlled the Otoe-Missouria's funds. Medicine Horse insisted that the Otoe-Missouria had the right to sell their own lands and to receive their money in cash. "That is your mistake," Smith replied, and he supported his case by referring to the terms of the 1854 treaty. Smith added that the government had an obligation to "take care of its children." To this Medicine Horse retorted, "There is such a thing as children being whipped to death." Ar-ka-ke-ta, who would not be silenced despite Griest's attempts to pacify him, pointedly asked how it was that the whites had such fine farms on lands that had lately been the Indians', while they, the Otoe-Missouria, lived in poverty? Smith reiterated, "I do not take your money but use it for you." Becoming impatient, he continued, "You do not seem to understand that a change is come over you, and that white people are going to try to teach you how to live." Big Bear, who was as frankly defiant as the other chiefs and not at all intimidated by the "Great Father," replied, "You cannot make white men of us. That is one thing you can't do."[97]

He was correct; these chiefs would die before they agreed to "hang on the plow." But Smith could, and did, stop the cash annuities, channeling the extra into farming (with poor results), buildings, and salaries. He also initiated, through Griest, the policy of working for money, paying one dollar a day for labor in the fields. In 1875 Griest boasted that 130 out of 132 men over the age of thirty were on the payroll. If this was correct, then it did not last long. That same year, Superintendent Barclay White reported that members of the "wild party" (here described as one-third of the people) were refusing to work, to accept any annuities, or to send their children to school, because their money was being allocated without their permission. They camped away from the agency and made a living by selling timber to settlers, another practice that infuriated Griest. They continued this defiance, though it deepened their poverty, even after they left Nebraska. Meanwhile, their goods accumulated in a warehouse at the agency. In the end they prevailed, at least locally, because by 1878 they had convinced all the Indians that they did not have to work for their own money. Still, the government would not pay them their annuities in cash.[98]

The third major stress came from Nebraskans and Kansans who completely surrounded the Otoe-Missouria and who had long believed that the fertile valley of the Big Blue was wasted on Indians (fig. 47). Relations with the settlers were relatively amicable; after all, the Indians provided a captive market for many locally produced products and services. The low point in relations came in July 1871 when the mixed-blood Jim Whitewater killed two settlers in a drunken encounter. A major clash was averted only because the Otoe-Missouria themselves captured Whitewater and delivered him to jail. He would spend the next eighteen years in the state penitentiary. There were also frequent timber thefts (although it was difficult to distinguish between these and sales), as well as horse rustling by whites. Significantly, according to agency police records, after 1879 the new jail filled up with Indians, whereas cases against whites invariably were dismissed for lack of evidence.[99]

But there were many friendly day-to-day exchanges too. On September 16, 1874, for example, the Otoe-Missouria baseball team vied with a team from Hebron for league honors, and on June 26, 1873, the Indians were in Beatrice to dance for the locals. An Italian-American dance troupe was also there, but the Otoe-Missouria drew the larger crowd.[100]

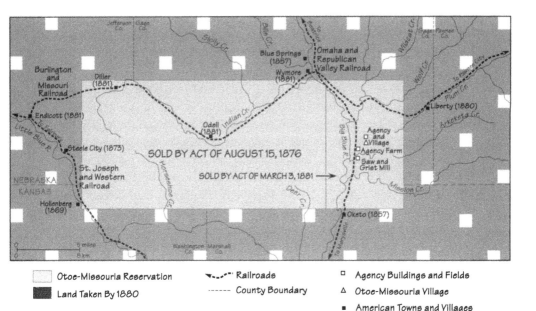

Fig. 47. Otoe-Missouria Reservation and Vicinity, circa 1880

Despite these diversions, however, the overriding objective of the settlers was to get the Indians to sell their reservation. It is not difficult to explain why. In addition to the widely acknowledged fertility of the reservation—it was common practice to describe the tract as the "garden of Nebraska"—it was widely believed that Indian lands could always be acquired cheaply. Even during the economically stagnant 1870s, land values in the counties around the Otoe-Missouria reservation averaged six dollars to eight dollars an acre.[101] This is partly explained by scarcity, because the speculators were still holding on to their vast acreages, waiting for the selling price to rise, which it would, rapidly, in the 1880s. So established settlers who wished to accumulate larger acreages, or newcomers who had only the choice of expensive purchases in improved country or free homesteads on the isolated frontier, looked longingly at the "underutilized" Otoe-Missouria Reservation.

The first serious attempt to sell the Otoe-Missouria lands since Agent Smith's self-serving effort in 1869 came on June 10, 1872, when Congress passed a bill to sell eighty thousand acres of the western part of the reservation. The prevailing rationale, which was frequently reiterated in official correspondence, was that the Otoe-Missouria possessed a "large reservation . . . far beyond the needs of so small a number of Indians."[102] This partial sale was backed by the Quakers, who wanted to use the money to settle the Otoe-Missouria on allotments on the eastern remnant, and by the mixed-bloods (there were between twenty and thirty at this time) who wanted to secure the improvements they had made on their own lands. The bill required the consent of the Indians in open council, and this was not immediately forthcoming.

From 1871 to mid-1873, before Griest launched his aggressive campaign to retain a part of the reservation, the Otoe-Missouria were intent on selling all their lands and relocating in Indian Territory. Green, a more tolerant man than his successor, had even permitted a delegation of chiefs to visit Indian Territory in the spring of 1872 to investigate a potential site for a new reservation near the Osage (the costs of the trip, as usual, were met by taking two hundred dollars from the annuity payments). The chiefs were impressed with what they saw, and Green subsequently reported that it was "the unanimous wish of the tribe to sell out and remove." In September the leading men met in council and rejected the June 10 agreement, insisting that they would sell "all or none" of their lands. In this they were backed by a flurry of settlers' petitions demanding to know why the agents and the Indian Office would not let the Indians go. In one of the petitions settlers claimed, quite disingenuously it seems, that they were only "prompted by impartial motivations."[103]

Soon their political representatives had taken up the call to "permit" the Otoe-Missouria to leave. Senator Phineas Hitchcock introduced a bill in the Senate on December 11, 1872, requesting removal and the sale of the reservation at $1.25 an acre, a price which must have stirred the settlers' hearts. In January 1873 the Nebraska Legislature added its weight in a memorial to Congress which argued that the reservation was in a "wild and uncultivated state, presenting a barrier to the settlement" of that part of Nebraska. Moreover, the memorial held, the Otoe-Missouria wanted to sell it in its entirety.[104]

The Otoe-Missouria avoided making a decision on the June 10 agreement through the latter months of 1872. On April 23, 1873, pressured to act by the newly arrived Griest, they met in council and rejected the plan for a partial sale. Griest claimed that "ruling members" and "scheming white men" had dissuaded the others. Griest kept up his pressure, including threatening to depose the hereditary chiefs, and finally secured consent for the sale on May 25, 1873. In September 1873, 77,174 acres were surveyed into forty-acre segments in anticipation of the sale (fig. 47). But no appraisement or sales were made at this time, and Medicine Horse and his followers continued their active opposition to any deal short of a total purchase.[105]

The year 1874 found the Otoe-Missouria in a "ferment of excitement." Griest had rallied a sizable (but indeterminate) number of Indians to his cause, promising that the sale of the western eighty thousand acres would yield a bonanza of funds for improvements to the eastern remnant of the reservation. The hereditary chiefs, the memory of the unsatisfactory meeting with Commissioner Smith still stinging in their minds, were in no mood for compromise. In the fall, these "refractory Otoes" (White's characterization), led by Medicine Horse and Pipe Stem, made a break from the reservation with the intention of joining the Potawatomie on a bison hunt in southwestern Kansas. The leaders were arrested and held in prison at Fort Hays for a month, while their followers—ninety had gone with them—drifted back to the reservation. The Otoe-Missouria were obliged to make restitution to the War Department by paying one thousand dollars from their annuities. Griest pronounced that the punishment would have a "salutory effect" on the rebels.[106]

Instead, their resistance hardened. On December 8, 1875, the bill to sell the entire reservation was reintroduced in the Senate, and the eastern half of the reservation was surveyed in anticipation of its passage. According to the local newspapers, the bill received the "unanimous support of every citizen" in the surrounding counties. The newspapers called for an investigation of Griest, claiming he had "continually misrepresented" the settlers' views, "stepped beyond the pale of his jurisdiction by removing old and honored chiefs," and ignored the wishes of "nineteen-twentieths" of the Indians. The members of the "wild party," determined to leave, did not even plant their crops in the spring of 1876.[107]

But it was Griest who prevailed, and the bill for removal, after passing in the Senate, was amended in the House to a partial sale of 120,000 acres from the west of the reservation. When the bill was returned to the Senate, Algernon Sidney Paddock, of Nebraska, supported the amendment, saying that it was "the wish of the Quakers and the Indian Office" that the Otoe-Missouria should retain some lands for allotments, and he thought it "best to accede." President Grant, after initial hesitation, signed the amended bill on August 15, 1876.[108]

The terms of the 1876 agreement were these: after appraisal, the land would be sold to settlers in portions not exceeding 160 acres each; payments could be made in cash at the Beatrice land office or in deferred payment over three years at 6 percent interest; the land would be sold at its appraised value and in no case at less than $2.50 an acre; and the proceeds would be held in the United States Treasury to yield 5 percent a year as an annual payment to the Indians. In a strange construction of the agreement, ostensibly to prevent speculation, preference of purchase was given to settlers who had already occupied their chosen tract. All of this was contingent on the Otoe-Missouria's approval, to be granted in open council.[109]

After much disagreement, the Otoe-Missouria gave their consent in council on December 23, 1876. In a poignant resolution, they asked for "good honest men" to be appointed to appraise the tract because, they said, "we do not want to sell it as was done in former times when our old Chiefs sold large tracts of land for very little, and eat up and wasted what little they got."[110] The resolution was signed by Big Elk and the other agent-appointed chiefs; Medicine Horse and his followers did not give their consent.

The appraisal was completed in July 1877. It is significant that the entire reservation, not just the 120,000 acres, was appraised, much to the alarm of Griest and his supporters. The tract to be sold—officially, 119,846 acres—was valued at $427,091, or $3.56 an acre.[111] The terms of the agreement may well have been devised to discourage speculation by preventing the accumulation of large acreages (which had recently happened with the sale of the Pawnee Reservation), but the results were disappointing for the Otoe-Missouria. First, with no competitive bidding, it was guaranteed that each tract would sell only at, or near, the appraised value: on average about one-half the prevailing rate for lands in the surrounding area. Indeed, the average price the Indians received was $3.85 an acre, just above the appraised value. Second, because of the occupancy preference, squatters overran the tract with no intention of producing the payment. Some stayed only long enough to strip the timber. The deferred payments were deferred indefinitely. In 1878 Griest lamented that the Otoe-Missouria had "realized nothing from the intended sale," despite the fact that the land was settled, towns platted, and a trade store opened. In 1879 only $18,745 had accumulated in the treasury account, yielding an interest payment of a meager $967. By 1882, $184,737 had been collected and interest payments had risen to $9,237 a year. But even in 1887, ten years after the sale, the total amount had not been received.[112]

After the 1876 sale, events quickly moved toward the Indians' complete relinquishment of the reservation and removal to Indian Territory. In petition after petition, Big Elk and his party (with the backing of Griest) pleaded in vain for an audience with the commissioner of Indian affairs, while Medicine Horse and the other hereditary chiefs (heartily supported by local settlers) demanded to be allowed to move to Indian Territory. The balance was swinging toward a total sale of the reservation. A discouraged Griest acknowledged in his 1879 report that the "prevailing belief" among the Indians was that they would leave. The failure to reap any benefits from the 1876 sale, the "constant depredations" being committed on the eastern remnant of the reservation (particularly following the construction of the railroad through the agency in 1880), and the ongoing "schisms, jealousies, inconfidence, [and] dissatisfaction," persuaded all but the most ardent Quaker supporters that the Indians' future lay to the south.[113]

In council on May 3, 1880, the government-appointed inspector, William J. Pollock, invited the Otoe-Missouria to tell him "all their troubles." They did this so convincingly that the following day Pollock sent a telegraph to the secretary of the interior, saying, "With one voice they ask to go to Indian Territory. All efforts to dissuade them seem unavailing. Many have already sold dishes, etc., preparing for journey."[114] Even before the council had been held, thirty Otoe-Missouria had left for Indian Territory; on May 18 another 160 joined them in their new location on the Cimmarron, just to the west of the

Sauk and Fox Reservation (fig. 43). These of course were the wild party, led by Medicine Horse, Little Pipe, and Pipe Stem. No mixed-bloods went with them. Characteristically, they chose a country rich in game and poor for farming. The commissioner of Indian affairs threatened to withhold their rations, but this was an idle threat because they had been refusing to accept them for years.[115]

The remainder of the Otoe-Missouria left Nebraska in the fall of 1881, following the act of March 3, 1881, whereby the last forty-two thousand acres of their lands were sold to the United States. The Indians gave their consent to the sale on May 4, 1881. Their new agent, Lewellyn Woodin, started south with their 224 head of cattle on September 22, and the Indians left with seventy wagons and two hundred horses on October 5. By late October they were erecting their tipis on a new 129,113-acre reservation located between the recently established Ponca and Pawnee agencies (fig. 43). The reservation was purchased with an advance from the delayed proceeds of the 1876 sale. Medicine Horse and the other defiant Indians had no say in the selection of this location, and they chose to stay out on the Cimmarron, seething with anger at their kinfolk.[116]

The remaining Otoe-Missouria Reservation lands, embracing the fertile valley of the Big Blue, were reappraised in late 1882 and offered for sale in 160-acre tracts at auction on May 1, 1883. Prices were borne up on a tide of speculative bidding. Land that had been appraised at an average of $6.08 an acre brought an average selling price of $12.22 an acre, the highest per-acre payment awarded to any Indians on the Great Plains in the nineteenth century. The bidding process was rife with speculation and fraud, and many of the initial purchasers defaulted, resulting in a second sale in December 1883. Many local settlers felt cheated because they had not been able to get the coveted land at appraised values. But the party that was really cheated was the Otoe-Missouria, because the purchasers of their lands were given repeated extensions on their deferred payments through the 1880s and 1890s. In 1899 there were still 124 delinquent purchasers and the Otoe-Missouria were owed $270,000. The following year they accepted a compromise which reduced the debt by $168,784.[117] They had come to the realization that this was the only way they would receive any money at all.

In Indian Territory, the division in Otoe-Missouria society persisted. The new reservation was a poor substitute for the old lands of the Otoe-Missouria: the soils were infertile, and good timber and water were scarce. They were administered as part of the Pawnee, Ponca, and Otoe Agency, and in their agent's opinion they were the "least satisfactory" of the three peoples. They were described as "retrograding," "lazy," and "shiftless," living only for the day when their money from the sale of their Nebraska lands would deliver them from poverty. But by the time the interest payments from the 1876 sale had begun to accumulate, the annuities from the 1854 treaty had diminished to only five thousand dollars a year, and both sets of funds were spent for them by the

Indian Office rather than by them in ways of their own choosing. They remained defiantly traditional, practicing the Sun Dance and what Agent John Scott called "other heathenish customs." The agents tried to stamp these out, and once again they replaced the chiefs with more compliant men.[118]

Meanwhile, fifty miles to the south on the Deep Fork tributary of the Canadian, Medicine Horse and more than two hundred Otoe-Missourias—officially known as the "Absentee Otoes"—lived a "precarious" but independent existence near the Iowa and Sauk and Fox. Gradually the wound in the society healed, as past affronts faded from memory. More and more of the Absentee Otoes reestablished connections with their kin. Their numbers diminished to 125 in 1886, and by 1890, when the Iowa took out allotments, at least the geographical dimension of the division had disappeared. In that year there were only 358 Otoe-Missouria left. Their population would drop to an absolute low of 340 in 1894 before beginning a hesitant recovery.[119]

Even in the 1890s, when extinction loomed as a possible fate, the Otoe-Missouria remained resistant to American policies and dictates. It was not until 1899 that they were finally compelled to accept allotments. In that year 65,000 acres were allotted to 441 heads of families and single adults, leaving 63,400 acres of surplus lands. But, with typical determination, the Otoe-Missouria refused to sanction the sale of the excess lands, forcing the government to capitulate and, in 1907, to enlarge the size of each allotment to 280 acres. All the reservation was retained. The forces of dispossession were not to weaken however, especially after the discovery of oil on the reservation in 1912. By the time the expedited trust period had ended in 1920, fully 90 percent of their lands had passed out of their control.[120]

The Long Road to Allotments

Of the original Nebraska Indians, only the Omaha were able to completely withstand the forces of removal and to preserve their reservation, more or less intact, until allotments were made. They were able to do this for two related reasons. First, they were a success, at least in American eyes, because they were good farmers and because the progressive contingent among them—possibly one-third of the population—had made considerable strides along the path marked out for them by government authorities: "No tribe of Indians in this superintendency," Barclay White wrote to Commissioner Edward Smith in 1875, "is making the advance and progress in agriculture that the Omahas now are."[121] Second, and probably also connected to their good reputation and their approachability, the Omaha gained the support of influential Americans who aided them in their drive to secure their lands. There was the eccentric activist Thomas Henry Tibbles, impresario for the Ponca's cause and particularly involved with the Omaha after his marriage to Susette La Flesche (Joseph's daughter) in 1881; there was James Owen Dorsey, former minister to the Ponca and resident ethnographer among the Omaha from 1878 to 1880; and, most crucially, there was the indefatigable anthropologist Alice Fletcher, who labored from 1881 to 1884 in Washington, D.C., and on the reservation to get the Omaha legal titles to their allotments.

By comparison with the other Nebraska Indians during the 1870s, the Omaha were prosperous. In only one year from 1870 to 1884—the grasshopper year of 1876—did they produce less than twenty thousand bushels of corn. In most years they harvested more than thirty thousand bushels, averaging about thirty-five bushels per acre. Increasingly the surplus was stored in above-ground granaries rather than caches, which cut down on spoilage. Each year large amounts of corn (as well as timber and furs) were sold in the new towns that had sprung up around the reservation (fig. 48). The American market had, in effect, come to them. In addition to the corn, the Omaha raised considerable amounts of wheat (the agents' preferred crop), potatoes, and many other vegetables; they started fruit orchards, cut hay, and owned more than one thousand horses, six hundred cattle, and one thousand hogs.[122]

By 1880 much of this agricultural production came from individual farms which were worked by both men and women. These were the allotments that had slowly been taken following the survey of the reservation in 1867 (and in compliance with Article 4 of the 1865 treaty). They were located in the eastern third of the reservation, particularly along the wooded valleys that bordered the streams. From 1873 to 1876 Big Village, that bastion of communal living, literally emptied out onto the allotments. The leading chief, Two Crows (Kah-a-num-ha), for example, had eighteen acres under cultivation, not including his hay lands. He and his family of six (including two wives) lived on North Blackbird Creek in a frame house, built at their own expense (fig. 48). Joseph La Flesche, back on the reservation after his brief exile and, though no longer a chief, still an influential man in Omaha affairs, farmed forty-five acres just south of the mission and lived in a government-built frame house. Altogether, by 1880, there were about one hundred frame houses on the reservation. Many less-powerful families also lived on their own lands, but their dwelling place was more likely to be a dugout or a tipi. Often families camped in the shelter of the woods in winter and moved their tipis onto the fields in summer.[123]

There was also some lingering success from the bison hunts. The Omaha made at least one large-scale hunt every year until 1876. This was permitted, as their agent, Theodore Gillingham, explained in 1874, because it was the only way to get enough meat.[124] Typically the hunts involved about three hundred Omaha, chaperoned by an American or mixed-blood whose job it was to prevent friction with settlers or strife with other Indians. The hunts were drawn-out affairs, because the bison had been pushed back to the upper reaches of the Republican, Saline, and Solomon rivers. Generally the results did not justify the

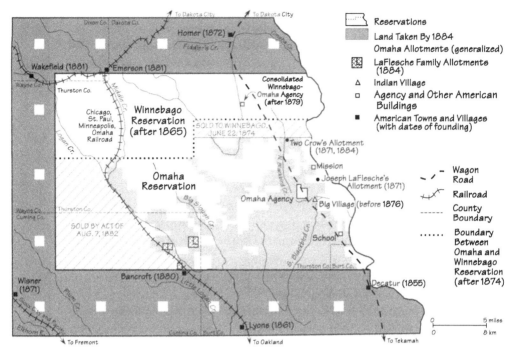

Fig. 48. Omaha Reservation and Vicinity, circa 1880

effort in terms of food or robes, though any bison meat was a boon for ceremonial purposes. The winter hunt of 1870–71 was, however, most successful,
and it must have been a scene of great celebration when the hunters returned, as
in days gone by, with the meat and robes of more than one thousand bison, as
well as large quantities of deer and elk.

Annuity payments were still coming in from the 1854 sale of land. The
Omaha received twenty thousand dollars a year in money, goods, and services
until 1882, which left twelve installments of ten thousand dollars a year until
1894 to complete the obligations of the treaty. This was roughly twice the
amount that the Ponca and Otoe-Missouria received during the same years
(table 6). The agents budgeted the annuity on a quarterly basis. In the fourth
quarter of 1871, for example, $2,502 was paid in cash, in return for labor in
building houses, bridges, and roads. The remainder of the $6,207 payment went
mainly to pay the engineer, blacksmith, miller, farmer, and interpreter (of
whom only the last was an Omaha), to repair the still-decrepit steam mill, and
to support the schools. Chiefs were paid a "small compensation," and a twenty-
seven-man police force was also funded from the annuities.[125]

By any standard other than comparison with the Ponca, Pawnee, and Otoe-
Missouria, however, the Omaha lived a marginal existence. Their population

total even fell from 1870 to 1874, before beginning a sustained recovery until 1884 (fig. 9). Painter reported "much sickness and death" from malaria in the fall of 1871, and sixty-seven children lost to a measles epidemic in 1873–74.[126] Official statistics show that about one-quarter of the people contracted some type of severe infectious disease each year. Tuberculosis and pneumonia were the main causes of death. The Omaha continued to put their faith in their own doctors. A large infirmary was built in 1875–76, using Omaha funds, but they preferred to care for their own sick, and the building was used as an industrial boarding school after 1879.

Two Crows, at least, believed that the extent of poverty among his people was being covered up. The agents "tell great lies," he wrote to Tibbles, when they reported that the Omaha were doing well.[127] Two Crows and Joseph La Flesche both believed that Omaha women were increasingly becoming sterile and Omaha children were dying more frequently at an early age because of poor living conditions. The 1886 census displayed graphically on a population pyramid (fig. 49) shows that large numbers of children were still being born, but also that many perished before they were fifteen. Girls died in greater numbers than boys. Despite the presence in the population of three old men and one old woman in

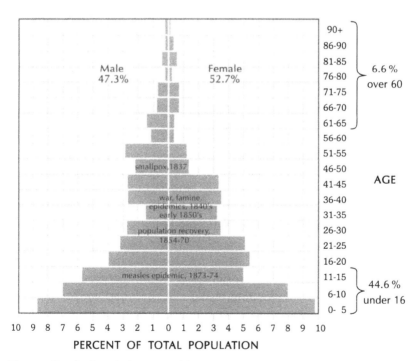

Fig. 49. Omaha Population Pyramid, 1886. Compiled from Census Records, 1885–1917. Nebraska State Historical Society, RG 508

their nineties (they had been born when Spain ruled Louisiana), the rapid narrowing of the pyramid at the top reveals that relatively few Omaha lived past the age of sixty. In fact, survival beyond the age of forty-five was not common for Omaha women, probably the result of frequent child-bearing and constant hard work. The pyramid also reveals the earlier nineteenth-century experience of the Omaha—the pinching of the age-groups in past periods of disease, famine, and war, and the general rebuilding of population after 1854.

The Omaha who lived to an advanced age, who could remember the unfettered days before the reservation when the land was still theirs, were particularly shaken by the jarring pace of change in their lives. Joseph La Flesche, speaking in 1882, recalled a time when he used to see Indians and "think they were the only people." But then Americans came "just as the blackbirds do, and spread over the country."[128] As the land filled with Americans, it was emptied out of animals. Paradoxically it was the "emptiness" of the fully settled country—this lack of living creatures other than Americans—that made the old chief, White Horse, feel an "unspeakable sadness," a loneliness so heavy that he felt that he would suffocate under its weight.[129]

The year 1876 was a particularly significant turning point in Omaha history.[130] In December of that year they made their final bison hunt, six hundred Indians moving southwest to the Platte, Republican, Solomon, Saline, and Smoky Hill rivers until, finally, they located a small herd on White Woman's Creek in Wichita County, Kansas (fig. 43). They garnered very little meat and were reduced to subsisting on emergency rations issued by the military at Fort Hays. It was a severe disillusionment for a people who had believed that the "moving herds" would always be there, provided by Wakonda. They tried to adjust, substituting beef from purchased cattle as offerings in their ceremonies but they could not regain their lost universe.

Many adult Omaha were unwilling, or unable, to adjust to the new order, though most understood that this was the world that their children would inherit: "They often express hope for the future of their children," Agent Gillingham reported in 1875, "but frequently say that they (the older ones) cannot become white men."[131] The schools remained the main contexts for acculturation. After the government withdrew its support for the Presbyterian mission boarding school in 1869 (at the request of Quaker agent Painter) three day-schools served to introduce the children to English, arithmetic, geography, and manual skills such as farming (for boys) and sewing (for girls). The schools were financed partly by the government and partly from the Omaha's annuities. In addition, the Quakers donated clothes, shoes, and supplies. One of the schools was in Furnas's old blockhouse near the agency, another was two and a half miles to the northeast, and the third was located in the southeastern part of the reservation (fig. 48). Some parents even moved their tipis to the vicinities of the schools to facilitate attendance. The northernmost school closed in 1875 because few Omaha had taken out allotments in that area. Average attendance at the two day-schools was sixty-five in 1875, from more than two hundred eligible children.

By the late 1870s, however, Two Crows and other influential progressives were campaigning for the reopening of the mission boarding school. Two Crows explained in a letter to the Reverend John Lowrie of the Presbyterian Board of Foreign Missions, that the standard of education had deteriorated since the Quakers took over.[132] In 1879 the mission school was resurrected and operated with funds provided by the government and the Presbyterians. After 1883 the school accepted only girls. The government also funded the new industrial boarding school in the infirmary building after 1879. The day-school to the southeast of the agency remained in operation.

By the early 1880s, as a result of increasingly forceful attendance policies, agents were claiming that more than two hundred Omaha children could speak English, which must have widened the cultural gap between them and their monolingual parents. The most promising students (Susette La Flesche, for example) were sent to off-reservation boarding schools like the Elizabeth Institute (New Jersey), Carlisle (Pennsylvania), and Genoa (on the old Pawnee reservation). The children were generally away for years, and when they returned they were often estranged from the life they had left behind and ignored by the authorities who had given them the training. In addition, the absence of as many as seventy students from the reservation posed a serious labor problem for families who were trying to improve their allotments.

There were also drastic changes in the political organization of the Omaha during these years, the end result of persistent attempts by agents to create their own puppet government. The division between the conservatives and modernizers had been widening since the early days on the reservation, and by the 1870s the polarization was complete. On one side of the gulf stood the "chiefs party," determined to hold onto traditional lifestyles and their own power; on the other side was the "young men's party," leading the drive for American education and allotments, though still generally reverent concerning their traditions. The Quaker agents considered the old chiefs to be "arrogant and authoritarian" and opposed to the allotment process because it would lead to the waning of their power. Agent Jacob Vore, in particular, wanted to abolish the entire system of hereditary chieftainship and to encourage the "more intelligent and thrifty members of the tribe" to make an accommodation with Quaker policy.[133]

By the time that Vore, the last Quaker agent, had left the reservation in 1880, he had accomplished his goal. In March of that year a committee of chiefs was elected by the Omaha. A council of seven, and later ten, chiefs became the new government. Representation was equally divided between members of the two opposing political parties, with a third group of nonaligned chiefs. This may well have been democratic, but it was engineered by Vore, and the significant outcome, according to Fletcher and La Flesche, was that "all governing power [became] centered in the United States Indian Agent."[134] The suppression of the Omaha's independence, a process which had commenced with the fur traders and the appointment of the first agent in the 1820s, was virtually complete.

The changes went even deeper than this, cutting to the very heart of the Omaha's identity. From 1884 to 1898 their most treasured possessions, the contents of the three sacred tents, were transmogrified into exhibits in American museums. The first to go were the ceremonial war pipes, the sacred shell, and the cedar pole that had been kept in the tent of war. On June 7, 1884, Alice Fletcher excitedly wrote to Frederic Putnam, director of the Peabody Museum in Cambridge, Massachusetts, that the "entire belongings" of the tent had been presented to her by Mon'hinthinge, their hereditary keeper.[135] The old man solemnly handed them over in the fading light of a late afternoon, saying that he had intended to have the articles buried with him, but instead he would place them in a museum so that future Omaha could view them and "think of the past and the way their fathers walked." He knew that some Omaha would "say hard things" about him for this, but he thought it the best solution now that his people had "chosen a path different from that of their fathers."

The sacred pole and associated bundles followed the contents of the tent of war to the Peabody in 1888. Its last anointing with bison meat had taken place in 1875. Thirteen years later, Francis La Flesche persuaded Yellow Smoke (Shu'de-naci) to part with his sacred charge, saying, "why don't you send the 'Venerable Man' to some eastern city where he could dwell in a great brick house rather than a ragged tent?" When Yellow Smoke gave the sacred pole to Francis La Flesche, it was the first time that it had been touched by anyone other than its hereditary keeper. To many Omaha the death of Joseph La Flesche, Francis's father, only two weeks later, was incontrovertibly linked to this breach of faith.

Francis La Flesche had also hoped to transfer the contents of the third sacred tent, the white buffalo hide, to the Peabody, but its keeper, Wakon'monthin, pleaded to retain it one more season. In 1898 the hide was stolen, eventually to reside in the Academy of Sciences in Chicago. Wakon'monthin, devastated by the loss, died soon after. Only the two sacred pipes, those instruments of unity and symbols of the dual organization of the *hu'thuga,* stayed to guide the Omaha into an uncertain future.

What concerned the Omaha most during these years of frenetic change was their insecure hold on their lands. Every agent reported that this insecurity was sapping their energy and hindering the further development of the reservation. The Omaha watched as first the Pawnee, then the Ponca, and finally the Otoe-Missouria were pressured out of their reservations and dispatched to Indian Territory, and they naturally worried that they would be next. "They are ardently attached to their reservation and homes," Jacob Vore wrote in 1877, "and any intimation of change excites emotions of uneasiness and grief."[136]

They had found out, to their alarm, that the certificates identifing them as owners of their allotments carried no legal weight. The certificates had initially been dispensed by Painter in March of 1871. (Painter had wanted to make "American-style marriage" a prerequisite for obtaining a certificate, but this was unenforceable; even as late as 1886 eleven Omaha men had two wives). Painter observed that the certificates were a "source of great satisfaction" to the Indians.[137] By August 1871 a total of 331 certificates had been handed out, and they continued to be granted over the course of the decade. After witnessing the forced removal of the Ponca in 1877, the Omaha became anxious, and some men took their certificates to local lawyers. The lawyers told them that their certificates were virtually worthless.

The sale, or attempted sale, of different parts of the reservation from 1872 to 1882 was closely connected to the Indians' efforts to gain a secure hold on at least some lands through allotments. Of course, the Quaker agents also pursued this goal. On June 10, 1872, through the same act that provided for sale of portions of the Pawnee and Otoe-Missouria reservations, the secretary of the interior was authorized to arrange the survey and appraisal of fifty thousand acres from the western end of the reservation. The Omaha gave their consent in council on September 26. The act provided for the appointment of a three-man commission (including one Omaha) to make the survey and appraisal for public advertisements of the sale and for purchase through sealed bids, the land going to the highest bidder. The minimum size of a purchase was 160 acres, the minimum selling price $2.50 an acre. The money would be placed in a treasury account to yield semiannual payments at 5 percent a year. The United States reserved the right to use the money for agricultural improvements and schools.[138]

The land was surveyed in the fall of 1872, and the commission made its report on January 10, 1873. The quarter sections were valued at between $1.25 and $5 an acre. In May and June impressive full-page advertisements showing the appraised value of each quarter-section were taken out in newspapers in New York, New Jersey, Ohio, and elsewhere. It all came to nothing, or next to nothing. The country was entering a depression, the area was experiencing repeated droughts, and the appraised prices were high compared to the selling prices of unimproved land in surrounding counties. Only 300.72 acres sold the first year, bringing in a paltry revenue of $702.19. On December 3, 1873, the Indian Office offered an amendment to the act to make purchasing more attractive. Land would be bought for one-quarter down in cash and three annual payments at 6 percent interest. Congress, however, did not approve the amendment. By 1879 only 712 acres had been sold. The land was held in trust by the government until 1882, by which time the railroad had been built along the Logan valley, adding a new premium to its value.[139]

Meanwhile, there was a small boost to the Omaha's income in 1874, when the chiefs reluctantly agreed to sell 12,348 acres to the Wisconsin Winnebago. The chiefs were reluctant for at least two reasons. First, most Omaha were opposed to the sale: they did not get on well with the Winnebago who were already there, and the Wisconsin Winnebago were even more problematic. They were rebellious—they had simply refused to be moved to Indian Territory, and when they arrived in Nebraska, at least one-half of them would not settle down on the designated allotments. In Superintendent White's opinion, at least, they were "surly, defiant and complaining."[140]

The second reason for the sale's unpopularity was that the land lost to the Omaha—a twenty-section strip running back from the Missouri River (fig. 48)—contained the best timber on the reservation. Moreover, seventeen Omaha, including No Knife, had their allotments on this land. According to Agent Gillingham, the sale was eventually made only after he offered the Omaha chiefs a visit to Washington, D.C., as an inducement. Congress recognized the transaction on June 22, 1874. Two months later the chiefs got their trip to Washington.

The act of June 22 specified that $82,000 would be paid to the Omaha (for "purposes of civilization") in exchange for the land. This would have been a fair payment of $6.64 an acre. The government could afford to be generous because the money was actually to be taken from what remained of the Winnebago's 1837 treaty funds. As it turned out, the Omaha probably received only about $32,000 for the cession, or $2.50 an acre. It seems (at least this was the recommendation from Commissioner Smith) that the remaining $50,000 was applied to removal costs for the Winnebago. The deal was consummated at a council held on July 31. The Omaha handed over a deed for 12,348 acres and received a note for $30,800.87 of the money that was owed. Half of it was spent immediately on wagons, harnesses, oxen, plows, and spades.[141]

The Omaha had been correct in believing that there would be friction with the Winnebago. In fact the animosity between the two peoples was the subject of a government investigation in 1881. Inspector C. H. Howard found evidence that 173 Omaha horses had been stolen by Winnebagos from 1871 to 1881. The culprits were the "dancing Winnebagos," traditional Indians who frequently traveled back to visit friends and relatives in Wisconsin. They would swim the Omaha's horses across the Missouri and sell them to settlers all the way across Iowa. The Winnebago's complaint, in return, was that Omaha men harassed their women. The inspector sided with the Omaha, and the Winnebago were docked $5,190 ($30 a horse) from their annuities.[142]

To add insult to injury, the Omaha were slighted—negated, in a sense—in 1879, when their agency was consolidated with that of the Winnebago. The headquarters was placed on the Winnebago reservation, which was distant and in hostile territory as far as the Omaha were concerned. In 1880 Gahige, an old traditional chief, wrote to the commissioner of Indian affairs asking for their separate agency to be restored because he did not want the trouble of going to Winnebago. In the same letter White Horse complained that the Omaha were now ignored because they were "well-behaved," while the Winnebago were "disobedient" and therefore took up all the agent's time. But the consolidation saved the Indian Office money and therefore endured.[143]

The money from the 1874 sale did nothing to alleviate the Omaha's sense of insecurity. Indeed, they would later lodge a complaint with Congress arguing that they were never paid the full compensation for the land from either the 1865 or the 1874 treaty. By the close of the 1870s, with legal control of allotments no closer than at the beginning of the decade, the Omaha (particularly the progressive leaders) were no longer hesitant to express their anger. "You have brought on us great trouble," Joseph La Flesche wrote in angry indictment of Americans in general, and of the president in particular, who was accused of blocking their way to allotments.[144] This message, and many other appeals for action and support in securing allotments, were carried to Washington, D.C., and other eastern cities by the committed emissaries Tibbles and Dorsey. But nothing of substance was accomplished until Alice Fletcher arrived on the reservation in the fall of 1881.

Fletcher quickly became convinced that the Omaha's only salvation—the only way to avert removal—lay in the legal recognition of their allotments. By the end of the year she had written and submitted a petition to Congress to this effect. Fifty-three men signed the petition and made statements describing how long and successfully they had farmed their acreages, how they dreaded removal from their homes, and how they wanted property to hand down to their children: "We are going to ask for our titles," promised Waje'pa (Ezra Fremont), "and we won't stop asking until the government gets tired."[145] The signers of the petition represented only a minority of Omaha families, and some frankly noted in their comments that there were others who did not "care for titles." But the supporters of allotments included influential chiefs, or former chiefs, like Joseph La Flesche, Two Crows, No Knife, Do-uba-moni (Harrison McCauley), Sind-de-haha (William Hamilton), and Shu-shury-ga (Prairie Chicken). With Fletcher on their side this was an indomitable force.

Fletcher followed the petition to Washington, D.C., in February 1882. There she worked effectively through politicians' wives and women's organizations to win over policy makers to her cause. By August she had written, submitted, and virtually single-handedly achieved the passage of an act that at least temporarily secured the Omaha in the possession of their allotments and of most of the reservation. Even Commissioner Hiram Price acknowledged that Fletcher was largely responsible for the enactment of the legislation.[146]

The act of August 7, 1882 provided for the survey, appraisal, and sale of the part of the reservation lying to the west of the railroad right-of-way that had been granted to the Sioux City and Nebraska Railroad Company on April 17,

1880. This railroad, which operated as the Chicago, St. Paul, Minneapolis, and Omaha Railroad, ran alongside Logan Creek (fig. 48). It was the same area that the Omaha had been trying to sell since 1872. The land would be sold in forty, eighty, and 160-acre parcels at appraised prices and not less that $2.50 an acre. Settlers would be allowed to occupy and improve their property for up to a year before paying for it, but the act also left open the possibility of a revised schedule involving deferred payments if the secretary of the interior considered it appropriate. The money from the sale would be deposited in a treasury account to provide interest payments to the Omaha on an annual or semi-annual basis.

East of Logan Creek the reservation was to be divided into allotments, with 160 acres going to every head of family, eighty acres to every single adult or orphan child, and forty acres to each person under the age of eighteen. Selections would be made by heads of families, single adults, or in the case of orphans, by the agent. They could even choose land to the west of the railroad if they so wished. Certificate owners from the previous allotment process would be given preference in the selection of lands, so that they could keep their farms. Each allottee would be issued a patent of ownership, though, as was usual, the title to the land would reside with the government during a twenty-five-year trust period. More fortunate than most Indians, the Omaha were permitted to retain any surplus lands left after the allotments had been assigned. This remaining area would be held by the government on behalf of the Omaha and used as a reserve from which to create additional allotments for children born during the trust period.[147]

Appropriately, the job of overseeing the assignment of allotments was given to Alice Fletcher. She was appointed special agent in March 1883 and by the end of April she was ready to dispense the allotments. Fletcher purposefully set up her headquarters in a tent on the bank of Logan Creek because she considered that vicinity, with its fertile soils, gently rolling prairies, and proximity to the railroad as the best prospect for commercial farming.

With the help of Francis La Flesche, her future collaborator and lifelong companion, she systematically began the allotment process. Her procedure was marked by what she described as "considerable formality." She believed that the almost ceremonial selection process, involving the signing (or marking) of papers in front of witnesses, introduced the Indians to the concept of property ownership and legal protection, lessons of "permanent value" to the Omaha. She made sure that certificate holders were guaranteed continued ownership of their improved lands, and she dealt equitably (by consulting Indian leaders) with disputed claims. In the process, she made the first scientific census of the Omaha, identifying family relations and lines of descent so that the inheriting of allotments would not be disputatious. The Indians' main complaint was that wives did not get separate acreages, a policy that was "contrary to the idea of equal relations in the traditional family." This was rectified on March 3, 1893, by an amendment that granted wives allotments of eighty acres in their own right.[148]

Fletcher's "noble work" (the praise came from Agent George Wilkinson) almost killed her. The hard labor and privations of living on the prairie left her bedridden with inflammatory rheumatism for eight months. She continued to assign allotments from her bed and finalized the work by imposing allotments on the conservative families who had refused to participate. By July 11, 1884, when she submitted the allotment schedule to Commissioner Price, 954 patents, involving 1,194 people and 76,810 acres, had been allocated. This left 55,000 acres to be held in common and diminished as needed by future allotments.[149]

The geography of the reservation was altered almost overnight. About one-third of the allotments were selected in the townships adjoining the railroad (fig. 48). These selections were predominantly made by the progressive Indians, including the La Flesche family, who had followed Fletcher's recommendation that "nearness to market" was the key to future success. Ten allotments, involving 879 acres, were taken to the west of the railroad, prompting Wilkinson to proclaim that these Omaha had "cast their lot directly among the white people."[150] Others who wanted to be near markets (including many mixed-bloods) made their selections along the southern boundary of the reservation, close to the towns of Decatur and Bancroft. Many other Omaha, however, who went largely unnoted in the agents' or Fletcher's reports, were guided by tradition and familiarity and located their allotments on the deeply dissected uplands near the Missouri River, where there was timber. The largest area of unallotted land—the area to be held in common—was in the treeless northwestern part of the reservation. Poorly drained soils on the floodplains of Logan Creek and the Missouri River were also avoided.[151]

The lands to the west of the railroad were thrown open to American settlers on April 30, 1884. In addition, by a clause in section 2 of the 1882 treaty, all lands unallotted by June 1, 1885, in township 24, range 7 east were also made available for purchase. The appraised value of what turned out to be 50,127 acres was $512,670, or just over $10 an acre. This was a fair price in that it matched the average valuation of lands in the counties surrounding the reservation. The lands were taken in a rush between 1885 and 1887, but many settlers had difficulty meeting their payments within the designated year. In 1885, 1888, and then again in 1890, the secretary of the interior exercised his right to extend the period of purchase through deferred payments. No attempt was made to enforce payments. This delayed the Omaha's acquisition of their money, but in the long run it worked to their benefit by adding interest of 5 percent a year to the principal. By 1891, $187,317 had accumulated in their treasury account, yielding an annual payment of $9,366 or about $8 per capita; and by 1914, with almost all the land sold, the proceeds had accumulated to $821,907, which brought the approximately thirteen hundred Omaha an annual interest payment of $41,095 a year, or $32 each. The sum was hardly princely, but it went some distance in replacing the old annuity from the 1854 treaty, the last seven installments of which had been paid in two lump sums of $35,000 in 1888 and 1889, in one more effort to get the allotments going.[152]

When the Omaha took out allotments, they also asked to be released from federal supervision. They wanted to control their own affairs, to enjoy a new independence earned on American terms. Commissioner Price liked the idea, of course, and on September 30, 1884, all agency employees (except the agent himself and the school teachers) were discharged, and the mills, shops, stock, stores, and all other government property were handed over to the Omaha councilmen. Jesse Warner, who took over control of the Omaha-Winnebago agency in 1887, proclaimed that this was an "experimental test of the capabilities of these Indians to take care of themselves."[153]

At first it seemed that the Omaha would fail the test. The transition to allotments was accompanied by declines in both agricultural production and population (fig. 9). The society, even individual families like the La Flesches, continued to be divided over which course to take. But the adjustment was made, and the Omaha's population recovered and continued its slow upward incline, reaching twelve hundred in 1900. Some families successfully farmed their lands; others took the easier way out by leasing their allotments to settlers. By 1896 there were 102 farming and grazing leases on allotted land and thirty on the unallotted land held in common. At the prevailing rates of twenty-five cents an acre per year for grazing privileges and one dollar per acre for farming, this system brought the Omaha some (officially unsanctioned) income.

They began selling their allotments even before the mandated trust period was over, driven by poverty and forced by an aggressive government program which imposed individual ownership. By 1910 fully 50,000 acres of the land base they had fought so hard to preserve had been lost in this manner. By 1955 the figure had risen to 107,297 acres, leaving only 28,405 acres in Omaha hands.[154] They had kept their reservation and dutifully moved onto allotments, but still they were dispossessed.

Twentieth-
Century
Reappraisal

Despite the concerted and protracted efforts of Americans to suppress and transform them, the Nebraska Indians have prevailed and reinforced their shaken tribal identities. Their populations have risen from the depths in the late nineteenth century until now, near the end of the twentieth century, there are approximately fourteen hundred Otoe-Missouria, fifteen hundred Omaha, twenty-three hundred Pawnee, twenty-two hundred Southern Ponca, and in excess of four hundred Northern Ponca.[1] Many of the old traditions have weathered the storm of Americanization, though many others fell by the wayside when the annual cycle of hunting and farming was broken and the Indians' lands were taken from them. The return of skeletal remains from museum shelves to the Pawnee and Omaha and their reburial in native ground, the repatriation of the sacred pole and the white buffalo robe to the Omaha, the purchase of additional land by the Otoe-Missouria, and the restoration of the Northern Ponca to tribal status (after a long uphill battle) are recent victories for the Indians and evidence of the cultural and political resurgence that is now taking place.[2]

One of the main catalysts for this reassertion of rights and identities has been the claims process, whereby the Indians sought a second compensation for lands that had been taken from them without consent, or at an unfair price, in the nineteenth century. This process involves an explicit reevaluation of the government's past dealings with the Indians; as such it yields an official conclusion as to whether the United States, to paraphrase a statement made by Commissioner Edward Smith in 1875, having taken from the Indians the possibility of living in their way, gave them in return a genuine opportunity to live as Americans.[3]

Even before 1920 the Omaha, Pawnee, and Otoe-Missouria had taken their grievances to the courts, and the Pawnee and Omaha had received favorable judgments. In 1918, for example, the Court of Claims awarded the Omaha $94,740 for 783,365 acres of original territory lying north of the Aoway River

Table 9. Awards by the Indian Claims Commission

Indian Group	Docket Number	Time of Taking	Acreage	Original Payment		Fair Market Value		Award (with citation)
				a) Total	b) Per Acre	a) Total	b) Per Acre	
Otoe-Missouria	a) 11A	July 15, 1830	One-quarter share of 10,000,000 acres	Compromise settlement				$1,750,000 (13icc289 [1964])
	b) 11	Sept. 21, 1833 / March 15, 1854	792,000 / 1,087,893	$39,000 / $463,424	4.9 cents / 42.6 cents	$554,590 / $1,087,893	70 cents / $1	$1,156,035 (131Ct.Cl. 593 [1955])
Omaha	a) 138	July 15, 1830	One-quarter share of 10,000 acres	Compromise settlement				$1,750,000 (13icc289 [1964])
	b) Combined 225-A,B,C,D	March 16, 1854	4,982,098	$881,000	19.6 cents	$3,736,573	75 cents	$2,900,000 (8icc407 [1960])
Pawnee	10	a) Oct. 9, 1833	13,074,000	$148,200	1.1 cents	$4,427,700	35 cents	$7,315,800 (157Ct.Cl. 134 [1962])
		b) Aug. 6, 1848	110,419	$2,000	1.8 cents	$97,380	90 cents	
		c) Sept. 24, 1857	9,878,000	$2,144,610	21.7 cents	$4,939,000	50 cents	
		d) March 3, 1875	4,800	$6,000	$1.25	$12,000	$2.50	
Ponca	a) 322	March 2, 1858	2,334,000	$455,500	19.5 cents	$2,334,000	$1	$1,878,500 (26icc217 [1971])
	b) 323	March 16, 1877	96,000	$36,873	38.4 cents	$211,200	$2.20	$1,013,425* (28icc350 [1972])

Note: The award often is not an exact subtraction of the original payment from the fair market value, because gratuitous offsets are also involved. Also, in the cases of Pawnee and the Otoe-Missouria, the total award was changed by appeal to the Court of Claims. In the table icc refers to the Indian Claims Commission and Ct.Cl. to the Court of Claims. Citations are from Indian Claims Commission, *Final Report* (Washington D.C.: Government Printing Office, 1978).

*Includes interest at 5 percent a year from 1877

that had been ceded without compensation in 1854. The Omaha were also allowed interest on this debt, at the rate of 5 percent a year from 1854, so that by the time the payment was made, in 1926, the amount had grown to $374,456.[4]

It was only after 1946, however, with the establishment of the Indian Claims Commission, that the Nebraska Indians were given a full opportunity to seek "belated justice" for the loss of their homelands. The claims process is structured like this: The Indians (the claimants) have first to prove that they are "successors in interest" to those who had lost their lands. They then have to establish that they had title to the land at the time it was taken. This can be achieved by proving "original title"—exclusive possession of a defined territory "since time immemorial"—or "reserved title," whereby the United States had recognized, through treaty or other means, the Indians' right to the land. The size of the defined territory has to be specified to the acre. Once title is established, the focus shifts to the valuation stage, which involves two main steps. First, the "consideration," or what the Indians were originally paid for the land, has to be itemized; second, the "fair market value," or the price an "informed purchaser" might have paid for the land at the time it was taken, is estimated. If it can be convincingly shown that the consideration was "unconscionable" (so low "as to shock the conscience"), or if there had been no payment at all for the land, then the Indians are due an award, or second compensation. The final award is the fair market value minus the consideration and any "gratuitous offsets" (payments by the United States without obligation, as in the case of some rations). The Indian Claims Commission Act also allowed for awards to be made on the basis of "fair and honorable dealings," but this was so narrowly construed by the commission that it rarely entered decisively into the deliberations.[5]

The Indians were given five years after the establishment of the commission to organize and lodge their claims. All four of the Nebraska nations met this deadline and embarked on the lengthy and often frustrating process that would, in the end, result in additional payments for their nineteenth-century cessions.

The Otoe-Missouria were the first to win their case. In 1955 the Court of Claims (the appellate court for the Indian Claims Commission) ruled that the payments for the 1833 and 1854 cessions had indeed been unconscionably low and that the Otoe-Missouria were due an additional payment of $1,156,035 (table 9). Lands had been sold for 4.9 cents an acre in 1833 and 42.6 cents an acre in 1854 should have brought, respectively, 70 cents and $1 an acre. Moreover, the commission also ruled that these cessions had been made "under duress." This was a landmark case which confirmed that the Indian Claims Commission could make awards on the basis of original title. The ruling made it easier for the other Nebraska Indians to prove titles to their ancestral lands, and any disputed boundaries among the four nations were subsequently settled by

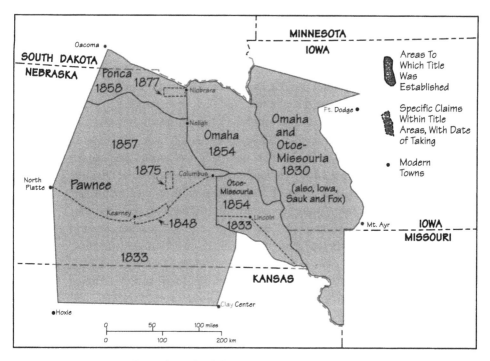

Fig. 50. Traditional Lands of the Nebraska Indians, as Established by the Indian Claims Commission, 1955–1972

stipulation (mutual agreement) so that overlapping claims would not confound the success of each case (fig. 50).[6]

Later, in 1964, the Otoe-Missouria were awarded $1,750,000 for one-fourth share (along with the Omaha, Iowa, and Sauk and Fox) of the vast cession that had been made in 1830 at Prairie du Chien. The award in this instance was the result of a compromise among the interested parties, which obviated the expenses and complexities of the valuation stage. Other Otoe-Missouria claims, involving the 1876 and 1881 sales of their reservation, were dismissed on the grounds that the buying prices had not been unconscionably low and that the Indians had given their consent to the compromise settlement with purchasers in 1899.[7]

In 1964 the Omaha also received compensation of $1,750,000 for their share in the Prairie du Chien treaty cession. Previously, in 1960, they had been awarded $2.9 million to correct the meager payment they had originally been given for their 1854 cession of northeastern Nebraska (table 9, fig. 50). In making this award, the commission ruled that the land would have been worth 75 cents an acre on the open market, not just the 19.6 cents an acre which the Omaha had been paid. The $2.9 million award included a small compromise settlement covering accounting errors, trespass by settlers, and the claim that the payment for the 1865 cession to the Winnebago had also been "grossly inadequate."[8]

In 1963, after a tortuous case that was first rejected by the Indian Claims Commission then resurrected by the Court of Claims, the Pawnee were awarded an additional $7,315,800 in compensation for their nineteenth-century cessions. These included the extensive areas that had been ceded in 1833, 1848, and 1857, as well as the narrow strip of land that had been excluded from their reservation in its initial survey. Like the other Nebraska Indians, the Pawnee were able to prove, through a "preponderance of evidence," that they had original title to their lands at the times they were taken, that the payments they had received for their cessions had been unconscionably low, and that the treaties had been made under duress.[9]

The Ponca did not get satisfaction in their case until 1972. In Docket 322, involving the 1858 cession of their hunting grounds, the Ponca were awarded $1,878,500, representing the difference between what they were originally paid (19.5 cents an acre) and what they should have been paid ($1 an acre) as a fair price for the land. In this instance the Ponca had to fight off an effort by the United States to have $1,056,703 worth of gratuitous offsets deducted from the award. The government claimed that they had paid this much in the form of rations during those years (1861–77) when the Ponca were starving on their reservation; the commission disagreed, pointing out that it was government neglect that had reduced the Ponca to their straitened condition in the first place.

In Docket 323, which covered the 1877 uprooting of the Ponca from their reservation, the commission not only granted the difference between the consideration and the fair market value of the land ($174,327), but allowed 5 percent interest a year on the principal, because the taking had been without the Indians' consent. By the time of the final judgment in 1972 the award had accumulated to $1,013,425.[10]

The claims cases stand as candid and emphatic acknowledgment that the dispossession of the Nebraska Indians had been unjust, that a fair price had not been paid for their lands, and that no genuine effort had been made to give them the means to cope with the conditions that were being imposed upon them. This is hardly surprising, given the prevailing nineteenth-century buying policy, which sought to obtain Indian lands as cheaply as possible. But what if a fair market value had been paid at the times their lands were taken? What if, for example, the Omaha had received the fair market value of $3.7 million for their 1854 cession instead of the actual payment of $881,000? The additional resources would surely have reduced the Indians' suffering at a time when their traditional subsistence base was collapsing. The money would have facilitated the move to allotments and dispensed with the need to sell parts of the reservation to finance the government's policies, or simply to survive. For the United States, paying a fair price for the land would have given some credibility to the proclaimed goal of "expansion with honor" and reduced the gap between the official rhetoric and the hardships of Indian life on the Nebraska frontier.

Yet even with fairer payments and a more honest effort to accommodate the Indians, it is doubtful that a place would have been found for them in the nineteenth-century United States. Frontier expansion was so rapid, and frontier attitudes were so hostile, that it is unlikely that the Indians would ever have been allowed to retain more than a fraction of their lands. Even the fragments of land that they kept as reservations after the 1850s were regarded by Americans as unnecessarily large for their needs. Moreover, any extra monies may well have been absorbed by corrupt suppliers, traders, and agents, or, at the best, spent for the Indians by the government on its Americanization policy. Finally, additional payments would not have solved the Indians' main dilemma: they wanted to keep their lands, their lifestyles, their cultures—to turn back the clock to a time when the land was filled with game, not Americans. When time ran out in the 1870s, with the bison gone and the Indians still resisting change, then change was simply imposed in the form of removal and allotments.

It has been said that Indian land claims indicate an "extraordinary recognition" of the rights of the Indian minority by the white majority, a recognition not usually accorded to a conquered people.[11] Yet in many ways the claims process is less a break from past agendas than a continuation of them. The Indian Claims Commission was an essential backdrop to the termination policies of the 1950s, a "cleaning of the slate" of backlogged claims before the tribes were (or so the plan went) dissolved and the Indians finally eliminated as a "separate factor" in American society. Once an award was accepted, that claim was settled forever. As in the nineteenth-century treaties, the terms of agreement in the claims cases were set by the United States. Return of land was never an issue; the Indian Claims Commission Act expressly excluded this method of repaying historical debts. Estimates of fair market value were made using only American parameters and gave no weight to the value the Indians had put on their homelands. As Thomas LeDuc, the Otoe-Missouria's expert witness on fair market value, put it in 1955, "values cannot be determined on a basis of berries and wild fruits."[12]

Finally, and again as in the nineteenth century, the Indians generally felt obliged to accept the payments offered by the United States, no matter how unsatisfactory. The dealing, once more, was made against a backdrop of poverty. What appear to be substantial awards translate into small per capita payments once the offsets were deducted, the lawyers paid, and the residue divided up. The Otoe-Missouria, for example, received a paltry $581.40 each as their share of the 1955 award; and in 1964, after almost twenty years of litigation, the 1,883 enrolled members of the Pawnee tribe were given $3,530 each in restitution for the loss of a homeland. The lawyers, meanwhile, received $876,897 as their payment.[13] No doubt the awards were a boon in hard times, but like the nineteenth-century treaty payments, they had as much to do with appeasing the American conscience as with fair treatment of the American Indians.

If a statement is needed to bring this study of nineteenth-century Indian dispossession up to date, then this may suffice: by virtually any important socioeconomic indicator (life expectancy, infant mortality rate, per capita income), Thurston County, home to the Omaha and Winnebago, is still by far the poorest place in Nebraska.[14]

Notes

Abbreviations

ARCIA   *Annual Report of the Commissioners of Indian Affairs*

CT.CL.   Court of Claims

ICC   Indian Claims Commission

LR   Letters Received by the Office of Indian Affairs

NA   National Archives

R   Roll

RG   Record Group

Chapter 1. Lands and Lifestyles of the Nebraska Indians

1. "Jefferson's Instructions to Lewis, June 20, 1803," *Letters of the Lewis and Clark Expedition with Related Documents, 1783–1854,* ed. Donald Jackson (Urbana: University of Illinois Press, 1978) 1: 61–66.

2. Gary E. Moulton, ed., *The Journals of the Lewis and Clark Expedition* (Lincoln: University of Nebraska Press, 1987) 3: 388–400. Also, John L. Allen, *Passage Through the Garden: Lewis and Clark and the Image of the American Northwest* (Urbana: University of Illinois Press, 1975) and James Ronda, *Lewis and Clark among the Indians* (Lincoln: University of Nebraska Press, 1984).

3. Reuben G. Thwaites, ed., "The Original Journal of Sergeant Charles Floyd," *The Original Journals of the Lewis and Clark Expedition, 1804–1806* (New York: Arno Press, 1969) 7: 22.

4. The council is described in Moulton, *The Journals of the Lewis and Clark Expedition,* vol. 2, 438–43, and in Ronda, *Lewis and Clark among the Indians* 20–26.

Lewis's speech is reprinted in Donald Jackson, "Lewis and Clark among the Oto," *Nebraska History* 41.3 (1960): 241–46.

5. Milo M. Quaife, ed., *The Journals of Captain Meriwether Lewis and Sergeant John Ordway, 1803–06* (Madison: Wisconsin Historical Society, 1916) 109–10.

6. The second council is described in Moulton, *The Journals of the Lewis and Clark Expedition*, vol. 2, 487–93.

7. Roger T. Grange, *Pawnee and Lower Loup Pottery*, Nebraska State Historical Society Publications in Anthropology, no. 3 (Lincoln: Nebraska State Historical Society, 1968) and "An Archeological View of Pawnee Origins," *Nebraska History* 60.2 (1979): 134–60. Also, Douglas R. Parks, "The Northern Caddoan Languages: Their Subgrouping and Time Depths," *Nebraska History* 60.2 (1979): 197–213, Waldo R. Wedel, *An Introduction to Pawnee Archaeology*, Bulletin of the Bureau of American Ethnology, no. 112 (Washington, D.C.: Government Printing Office, 1936), and John O'Shea, "Pawnee Archaeology," *Central Plains Archaeology* 1.1 (1989): 45–107.

8. George A. Dorsey, *The Pawnee Mythology; Part 1*, Carnegie Institution of Washington Publications, no. 59 (Washington, D.C.: Carnegie Institution, 1906) 8–9.

9. George Bird Grinnell, *Pawnee Hero Stories and Folk Tales* (Lincoln: University of Nebraska Press, 1961) 223–31.

10. Mildred M. Wedel, *The Prehistoric and Historic Habitat of the Missouri and Oto Indians* (New York and London: Garland Publishing Inc., 1974) 25–76.

11. Marcel Giraud, ed., "Etienne Veniard De Bourgmont's Exact Description of Louisiana," *Bulletin, Missouri Historical Society* 15.1 (1958): 16.

12. Edwin James, *An Account of an Expedition from Pittsburgh to the Rocky Mountains*, in Reuben G. Thwaites, ed., *Early Western Travels* (Cleveland: The Arthur H. Clark Company, 1905) 15: 134.

13. Alice C. Fletcher and Francis La Flesche, *The Omaha Tribe* (Lincoln: University of Nebraska Press, 1972) 1: 70–71.

14. For the Omaha, see John M. O'Shea and John Ludwickson, *Archaeology and Ethnohistory of the Omaha Indians: The Big Village Site* (Lincoln: University of Nebraska Press, 1992), G. Hubert Smith, "Notes on Omaha Ethnohistory, 1763–1820," *Plains Anthropologist* 18.62 (1973): 257–70, as well as Fletcher and La Flesche, *The Omaha Tribe* 1:33–87, and James Owen Dorsey, *Omaha Sociology*, Third Annual Report of the Bureau of Ethnology, 1881–2 (Washington, D.C.: Government Printing Office, 1884): 205–370, especially map between pages 212 and 213. For the Ponca, see Joseph Jablow, *Ethnohistory of the Ponca* (New York: Garland Publishing Inc., 1974) and James Howard, *The Ponca Tribe*, Bulletin of the Bureau of American Ethnology, no. 195 (Washington, D.C.: Government Printing Office, 1965). Strictly speaking, from 1867 to 1889 the Ponca were the "Ponca of Dakota," because the boundary between Nebraska and Dakota Territory ran along the Niobrara. But because their Niobrara homeland has been in Nebraska since 1889 and because the Northern Ponca are officially known as the "Ponca of Nebraska," they are included here as Nebraska Indians.

15. James Mackay, "Journal," *Before Lewis and Clark: Documents Illustrating the History of the Missouri, 1783–1804,* ed. Abraham P. Nasatir (St. Louis: St. Louis Historical Documents Foundation, 1952) 2: 489.

16. Moulton, *The Journals of the Lewis and Clark Expedition,* vol. 3, 388–400. Lewis and Clark recorded a range of population in some cases, and in one place (388) Clark (?) noted that the population totals should be reduced by "about ⅓ generally." Because no explanation of this adjustment is provided, and for the sake of consistency, averages are used where ranges are given, and the totals have not been reduced by one-third.

17. For overviews of the impact of epidemics, see Russell Thornton, *American Indian Holocaust and Survival: A Population History since 1492* (Norman and London: University of Oklahoma Press, 1987) and Henry F. Dobyns, *Their Number Become Thinned: Native American Population Dynamics in Eastern North America* (Knoxville: University of Tennessee Press, 1983).

18. Carlos D. Delassus to Casa Calbo, April 3, 1801, in Nasatir, *Before Lewis and Clark,* vol. 2, 631–32.

19. Moulton, *The Journals of the Lewis and Clark Expedition,* vol. 3, 398–99, and Mackay "Journal," in Nasatir, *Before Lewis and Clark,* vol. 1, 358. O'Shea and Ludwickson, in *Archaeology and Ethnohistory of the Omaha Indians* 30–31 and 292–93, argue that the population loss from the 1800–1801 epidemic was much less than Lewis and Clark's figures suggest.

20. Moulton, *The Journals of the Lewis and Clark Expedition* vol. 3, 398–99. For the medical symptoms of malignant smallpox, see *Stedman's Medical Dictionary* (Baltimore: Williams and Wilkins, 1989) 1429.

21. This story is told in Fletcher and La Flesche, *The Omaha Tribe,* vol. 1, 86–87.

22. Moulton, *The Journals of the Lewis and Clark Expedition* vol. 3, 395, 400.

23. Annie H. Abel, ed., *Tabeau's Narrative of Loisel's Expedition of the Upper Missouri* (Norman: University of Oklahoma Press, 1939) 100.

24. John Dougherty to William Clark, Oct. 29, 1831, LR, Upper Missouri Agency, 1824–35.

25. Francis Haines, "The Northward Spread of Horses among the Plains Indians," *American Anthropologist* 40 (1938): 429–37.

26. This is according to Ponca tradition, as told in Fletcher and La Flesche, *The Omaha Tribe,* vol. 1, 79–80.

27. For a disdainful view of Blackbird and his influence on the fur trade, see "Journal of Truteau on the Missouri River, 1794–1795," in Nasatir, *Before Lewis and Clark,* vol. 1, 282–86.

28. Mackay, "Journal," in Nasatir, *Before Lewis and Clark,* vol. 1, 358.

29. Jacques Clamorgan, "Petition," January 15, 1800, in Nasatir, *Before Lewis and Clark,* vol. 2, 608.

30. Abraham P. Nasatir, "Anglo-Spanish Rivalry on the Upper Missouri," *Mississippi Valley Historical Review* 16 (December 1929–March 1930): 359–82, 507–30.

31. Fletcher and La Flesche, *The Omaha Tribe,* vol. 1, 134–37, 198, 206–7, and vol.

2, 597–99. This section relies on Fletcher and La Flesche and simplifies what are controversial issues in Omaha sociology. The other standard source, Dorsey's *Omaha Sociology,* sometimes comes to quite different conclusions. A third source, and the best summary of the conflicting interpretations, is R. H. Barnes, *Two Crows Denies It: A History of Controversy in Omaha Sociology* (Lincoln: University of Nebraska Press, 1984).

32. William Whitman, *The Oto,* Columbia University Contributions in Anthropology, vol. 28 (New York: Columbia University Press, 1937). See also, Richard Shunatona, "Otoe Indian Lore," *Nebraska History* 5.4 (1922): 60–64. For differences between Omaha and Ponca societies and cultures, see Jablow, *Ethnohistory of the Ponca* 57–64.

33. Gene Weltfish, "The Question of Ethnic Identity: An Ethnohistorical Approach," *Ethnohistory* 6.4 (1959): 328.

34. James R. Murie, *Ceremonies of the Pawnee* (Lincoln and London: University of Nebraska Press, 1989) 13–14, 40–46, 201–2.

35. Joseph Epes Brown, "The Roots of Renewal," *Seeing with a Native Eye: Essays on Native American Religion,* ed. Walter H. Capps (New York: Harper and Row, 1976) 28.

36. John Bradbury, *Travels in the Interior of North America in the Years 1809, 1810, and 1811,* in Reuben G. Thwaites, ed., *Early Western Travels, 1748–1846* (Cleveland: Arthur H. Clark, 1904) 5: 89.

37. Moulton, *The Journals of the Lewis and Clark Expedition,* vol. 2, 504–5.

38. Douglas R. Parks and Waldo R. Wedel, "Pawnee Geography: Historical and Sacred," *Great Plains Quarterly* 5.3 (1985) 143–76; Grinnell, *Pawnee Hero Stories and Folk Tales* 98–120, 358–59.

39. Moulton, *The Journals of the Lewis and Clark Expedition,* vol. 3, 394, 396–97, 399.

40. Howard, *The Ponca Tribe* 130–32.

41. Grant Foreman, ed., "Notes of Auguste Chouteau on Boundaries of Various Indian Tribes," *Glimpses of the Past* 7 (1940): 119–40.

42. Fletcher and La Flesche, *The Omaha Tribe,* vol. 1, 88–89; Melvin R. Gilmore, "Indian Tribal Boundary-Lines and Monuments," *Indian Notes* 5.1 (1928): 59–63.

43. Fletcher and La Flesche, *The Omaha Tribe,* vol. 1, 88–89; Wedel, *An Introduction to Pawnee Archaeology* 3–5 and figure 1.

44. Gene Weltfish, *The Lost Universe: Pawnee Life and Culture* (Lincoln: University of Nebraska Press, 1977) 46; Preston Holder, *The Hoe and the Horse on the Plains: A Study of Cultural Development Among North American Indians* (Lincoln: University of Nebraska Press, 1974) 35.

45. Fletcher and La Flesche, *The Omaha Tribe,* vol. 1, 99.

46. Howard, *The Ponca Tribe* 60.

47. Bradbury, *Travels in the Interior,* in Thwaites, *Early Western Travels,* vol. 5, 78–79.

48. David I. Bushnell, Jr., *Villages of the Algonquian, Siouan, and Caddoan Tribes*

West of the Mississippi, Bulletin of the Bureau of American Ethnology, no. 77 (Washington, D.C.: Government Printing Office, 1922) 162. Also, George F. Will and George E. Hyde, *Corn Among the Indians of the Upper Missouri* (Lincoln: University of Nebraska Press, 1964) 50.

49. Melvin R. Gilmore, *Uses of Plants by the Indians of the Missouri River Region* (Lincoln: University of Nebraska Press, 1977) 16, 21, 23. Gilmore's classic work was first published in the Thirty-Third Annual Report of the Bureau of American Ethnology in 1919.

50. Weltfish, *The Lost Universe* 20.

51. Fletcher and La Flesche, *The Omaha Tribe* 140–98, quote 140; Dorsey, *Omaha Sociology* 255–58; Whitman, *Oto* 16; Howard, *The Ponca Tribe* 81–93; and Jablow, *Ethnohistory of the Ponca* 53–56.

52. Murie, *Ceremonies of the Pawnee* 30–42 (especially the table on 34–35); Weltfish, *The Lost Universe* 80–86; Holder, *The Hoe and Horse on the Plains* 42–76.

53. Fletcher and La Flesche, *The Omaha Tribe,* vol. 1, 218. Dorsey, *Omaha Sociology* 234–35.

54. Holder, *The Hoe and the Horse on the Plains* 49; Murie, *Ceremonies of the Pawnee* 11; and Whitman, *Oto* 36. Barnes, in *Two Crows Denies It* (29–49) presents an excellent summary of Omaha chieftainship but is unable to resolve whether the office was attained solely by hereditary right or also through deeds of bravery and generosity. John M. O'Shea and John Ludwickson, in a comprehensive analysis, conclude that Omaha chieftainship was indeed hereditary. See "Omaha Chieftainship in the Nineteenth Century," *Ethnohistory* 39.3 (1992): 316–52.

55. The quotations are from James, *An Account of an Expedition,* in Thwaites, *Early Western Travels,* vol. 17, 160, and John Dunbar, "Journal" (May 23, 1834–May 27, 1835) in W. R. Wedel, ed., *The Dunbar-Allis Letters on the Pawnee* (New York and London: Garland Press, 1985) 611. See also, Charles Augustus Murray, *Travels in North America in the Years 1834, 1835, and 1836* (London: Richard Bently, 1839) vol. 1, 307–16 for the hard work load of the women.

56. Alexis de Tocqueville, *Democracy in America* (New York: Harper and Row, 1966) 576–79; Gerda Lerner, *The Woman in American History* (Menlo Park: Addison Wesley Pub. W., 1971).

57. Traditional activities of Indian men and women are discussed in Whitman, *Oto* 53; Howard, *The Ponca Tribe* 83; Murie, *Ceremonies of the Pawnee* 14, 75–76; Weltfish, *The Lost Universe* 20–21, 95–96, and 382–88; and Fletcher and La Flesche, *The Omaha Tribe,* vol. 2, 325–48. For modern perspectives, see Patricia C. Albers and Beatrice Medicine, *The Hidden Half: Studies of Plains Indian Women* (New York: University Press of America, 1983).

58. Dorsey, *Omaha Sociology* 261–63 and 266–67.

59. James, *An Account of an Expedition from Pittsburgh to the Rocky Mountains,* in Thwaites, *Early Western Travels,* vol. 15, 164.

60. Murie, *Ceremonies of the Pawnee* 11; Weltfish, *The Lost Universe* 18–19, 86, 103; Fletcher and La Flesche, *The Omaha Tribe* 98.

61. Whitman, *Oto* 64. Also, Holder, *The Hoe and the Horse on the Plains* 61–64. For lodge sizes and their populations, see Waldo R. Wedel, "House Floors and Native Settlement Populations in the Central Plains," *Plains Anthropologist* 24 (1979): 85–98.

62. For Pawnee planting ceremonies, see Murie, *Ceremonies of the Pawnee* 72–91 and Weltfish, *The Lost Universe* 95–119. For the Omaha, see Fletcher and La Flesche, *The Omaha Tribe* 1: 261–70.

63. The main source on Indian agriculture is Will and Hyde, *Corn Among the Indians of the Upper Missouri*. See also, Fletcher and La Flesche, *The Omaha Tribe*, vol. 1, 269–70 and vol. 2, 339–42. Weltfish, *The Lost Universe* 95–105, 238–71 and Howard, *The Ponca Tribe* 43–47 are also useful.

64. James, *An Account of an Expedition from Pittsburgh to the Rocky Mountains*, in Thwaites, *Early Western Travels*, vol. 15, 216.

65. Dunbar, "Journal," in Wedel, *The Dunbar-Allis Letters* 604. Dunbar, as a guest, was feted by the Pawnee, but he noted in several places in his journal that there was generally food available for all.

66. Elliot Coues, ed., *The Expeditions of Zebulon Montgomery Pike* (New York: Francis P. Harper, 1895) 2: 533.

67. Gilmore, *Uses of Plants by the Indians of the Missouri River Region*. Contemporary nomenclature for the various plants is taken from Great Plains Flora Association, *Flora of the Great Plains* (Lawrence, Kansas: University Press of Kansas, 1986).

68. On August 15, 1804, William Clark and ten of his men pulled 308 fish out of the Missouri River near the Omaha village using a "brush drag." Moulton, *The Journals of the Lewis and Clark Expedition*, vol. 2, 483.

69. Mackay, "Journal," in Nasatir, *Before Lewis and Clark*, vol. 2, 494.

70. White, *The Roots of Dependency* 178–98.

71. Stephen Long observed that the Pawnee were obliged to undertake the bison hunts not only for food, but also to obtain wood for fuel and forage for their horses. James, *An Account of an Expedition from Pittsburgh to the Rocky Mountains*, in Thwaites, *Early Western Travels*, vol. 15, 215.

72. Weltfish, *The Lost Universe* 141, 205.

73. Fletcher and La Flesche, *The Omaha Tribe*, vol. 2, 356–60; Dorsey, *Omaha Sociology* 282–302.

74. Will and Hyde, *Corn Among the Indians of the Upper Missouri* 59.

75. Samuel Allis to Rev. David Greene, July 14, 1836, in Wedel, *The Dunbar-Allis Letters* 705.

76. Weltfish, *The Lost Universe* 130–36, 175–77; Fletcher and La Flesche, *The Omaha Tribe*, vol. 1, 276–77; Howard, *The Ponca Tribe* 39–40.

77. Fletcher and La Flesche, *The Omaha Tribe*, vol. 1, 283–309; Murie, *Ceremonies of the Pawnee* 95–98.

78. Moulton, *The Journals of Lewis and Clark*, vol. 3, 388–400.

79. Weltfish, *The Lost Universe* 172.

80. Dunbar, "Journal," in Wedel, *The Dunbar-Allis Letters* 608.

81. Weltfish, *The Lost Universe* 140–43, 159, 171–80; Fletcher and La Flesche, *The Omaha Tribe*, vol. 1, 255, 278.

82. Fletcher and La Flesche, *The Omaha Tribe*, vol. 2, 441–46.

83. For example, Allis to Greene, May 12, 1835, in Wedel, *The Dunbar-Allis Letters* 698.

84. There is a good discussion of this subject in White, *The Roots of Dependency* 188, 376. See also, the analysis of reproduction rates in Frank Gilbert Roe, *The North American Buffalo: A Critical Study of the Species in Its Wild State* (Toronto: University of Toronto Press, 1970) 505–6.

85. Dunbar, accompanying the Pawnee on their hunts in 1834 and 1835, traveled four hundred miles the first winter, nine hundred miles the second winter, seven hundred miles the first summer, and eight hundred miles the second summer. John Dunbar, "Missionary to the Indians," Nebraska State Historical Society (Lincoln, Nebraska) 18. Also, Donna C. Roper, "John Dunbar's Journal of the 1834–35 Chaui Winter Hunt and its Implications for Pawnee Archaeology," *Plains Anthropologist* 36 (1991): 193–214.

86. See the list of places and Indians known to the Omaha and Ponca in Fletcher and La Flesche, *The Omaha Tribe*, vol. 1, 89–103, and James O. Dorsey, *Omaha Indian Map* (Lincoln: Nebraska State Historical Society). This map, compiled from 1877 to 1892, was based on the memories of old Indians.

87. Coues, *The Expeditions of Zebulon Montgomery Pike*, vol. 2, 845. On their return to the Pawnee villages the young men were stripped of the medals that President Jefferson had given them and ridiculed as liars. Challenges to the authority of the chiefs were simply not tolerated. See George R. Brooks, ed., "George Sibley's Journal of a Trip to the Salines in 1811," *Missouri Historical Society Bulletin* 21 (1965): 184.

88. This is noted in a speech by Big Elk in Bradbury, *Travels in the Interior,* in Thwaites, *Early Western Travels*, vol. 5, 222–23.

89. Information on trading systems is drawn from John C. Ewers, "The Indian Trade of the Upper Missouri before Lewis and Clark: An Interpretation," *Bulletin, Missouri Historical Society* 10 (1954): 429–46; Joseph Jablow, *The Cheyenne in Plains Indian Trade Relations, 1795–1840,* American Ethnological Society Monographs, no. 19 (New York: J. Austin, 1950); Donald J. Blakeslee, "The Plains Interband Trade System: An Ethnohistoric and Archaeological Investigation," diss., University of Wisconsin-Milwaukee, 1975; and W. Raymond Wood, "Plains Trade in Prehistoric and Protohistoric Intertribal Relations," in Wood and Liberty, *Anthropology on the Great Plains* 98–109.

90. Coues, *Expeditions of Zebulon Montgomery Pike*, vol. 2, 535.

91. See the discussion in Will and Hyde, *Corn Among the Indians of the Upper Missouri* 190–91.

92. Bradbury, *Travels in the Interior,* in Thwaites, *Early Western Travels*, vol. 5, 87.

93. Coues, *Expeditions of Zebulon Montgomery Pike*, vol. 2, 590.

94. Fletcher and La Flesche, *The Omaha Tribe*, vol. 2, 406.

95. Coues, *Expeditions of Zebulon Montgomery Pike*, vol. 2, 544.

96. Abel, *Tabeau's Narrative* 72; Moulton, *The Journals of the Lewis and Clark Expedition*, vol. 3, 390, 484.

97. Moulton, *The Journals of the Lewis and Clark Expedition*, vol. 3, 485.

98. For the calumet ceremony among the Pawnee, see Alice Fletcher, *The Hako: A Pawnee Ceremony*, Bureau of American Ethnology, Annual Report No. 22, Pt. 2 (Washington, D.C.: Government Printing Office, 1904) and Weltfish, *The Lost Universe* 175–77. For the details of the Omaha ceremony, see Fletcher and La Flesche, *The Omaha Tribe*, vol. 2, 376–401.

99. Background information on warfare is drawn from Bernard Mishkin, *Rank and Warfare Among the Plains Indians*. Monographs of the American Ethnological Society, no. 3 (New York: J. J. Augustin, 1940); Frank Raymond Secoy, *Changing Military Patterns on the Great Plains*, Monographs of the American Ethnological Society, no. 21 (New York: J. J. Augustin, 1953); and Holder, *The Hoe and the Horse on the Plains*.

100. Grinnell, *Pawnee Hero Stories and Folk Tales* 46. Lone Chief went on to be a great warrior who was most celebrated for making peace between the Pawnee and Wichita.

101. Moulton, *The Journals of the Lewis and Clark Expedition*, vol. 3, 388–400.

102. Fletcher and La Flesche, *The Omaha Tribe*, vol. 2, 408. Unless otherwise noted, the remaining description of raiding and related ceremonies is drawn from this source, 402–58.

103. Coues, *The Expeditions of Zebulon Montgomery Pike*, vol. 2, 535.

104. Holder, *The Hoe and the Horse on the Plains* 131.

105. Fletcher and La Flesche, *The Omaha Tribe*, vol. 1, 82–83 and "Journal of Truteau on the Missouri River," in Nasatir, *Before Lewis and Clark*, vol. 1, 282–85.

106. Whitman, *The Oto* 2.

107. Fletcher and La Flesche, *The Omaha Tribe*, vol. 2, 596.

Chapter 2. Forces of Intervention

1. Reuben G. Thwaites, ed., *Original Journals of the Lewis and Clark Expedition, 1804–1806* (New York: Arno Press, 1969) 5: 370–85.

2. Meriwether Lewis to President Thomas Jefferson, Sept. 23, 1806, in Thwaites, *Original Journals of the Lewis and Clark Expedition*, vol. 7, 335. Rumors of this rich beaver country had been circulating in St. Louis for at least ten years before Lewis and Clark's return. See "Trudeau's Description of the Upper Missouri," in Nasatir, *Before Lewis and Clark*, vol. 2, 381.

3. For an overview of the fur trade, see David J. Wishart, *The Fur Trade of the American West, 1807–40: A Geographical Synthesis* (Lincoln: University of Nebraska Press, 1979) and John E. Sunder, *The Fur Trade on the Upper Missouri, 1840–1865* (Norman: University of Oklahoma Press, 1965). Biographies of individual traders

are found in LeRoy R. Hafen, *The Mountain Men and the Fur Trade of the Far West,* 10 vols. (Glendale, California: Arthur H. Clark Co., 1965).

4. Hiram Martin Chittenden, in his classic work on the American fur trade, estimated that at least twenty posts were built between Council Bluffs and Bellevue from 1804–54. See *American Fur Trade of the Far West* (New York: Francis P. Harper, 1902) 3: 949.

5. Dougherty to Lewis Cass, Nov. 19, 1831, LR, Upper Missouri Agency 1824–35.

6. Richard E. Oglesby, "The Fur Trade as Business," in John F. McDermott, ed., *The Frontier Re-examined* (Urbana: University of Illinois Press, 1967) 111–27.

7. William Gordon to William Clark, Oct. 17, 1831, *Fur Trade Envelope* (St. Louis: Missouri Historical Society).

8. The best contemporary analyses of the fur trade, and especially of its impact on the Indians, are Dougherty to Cass, Nov. 19, 1831, LR, Upper Missouri Agency, 1824–35, and Thomas Forsyth to Cass, Oct. 24, 1831, *Forsyth's Letter Book, 1822–33* (Madison: Wisconsin State Historical Society). Forsyth's letter is reprinted in Chittenden, *American Fur Trade of the Far West,* vol. 3, 926–38.

9. Preston Holder, "The Fur Trade as Seen from the Indian Point of View," in John F. McDermott, ed., *The Frontier Re-examined* (Urbana: University of Illinois Press, 1967) 129–39.

10. Maximilian, Prince of Wied, *Travels in the Interior of North America, 1832–1834,* in Reuben G. Thwaites, ed., *Early Western Travels, 1748–1846* (Cleveland: The Arthur H. Clark Co., 1906): 22, 284.

11. Maximilian, *Travels in the Interior of North America,* in Thwaites, *Early Western Travels,* vol. 22, 266–67, 272–73.

12. John C. Ewers, "Mothers of the Mixed Bloods: The Marginal Women in the History of the Upper Missouri," *Probing the American Past: Papers from the Santa Fe Conference,* ed. K. Ross Toole, John A. Carroll, Robert M. Utley, and A. R. Mortensen (Santa Fe: Museum of New Mexico Press, 1962) 62–70. For the motivations of Indian women and traders, see J. N. B. Hewitt, ed., *Journal of Rudolf Friederich Kurz,* Bureau of American Ethnology, Bulletin 115 (Washington, D.C.: Government Printing Office, 1937) 155–56.

13. Fletcher and La Flesche, *The Omaha Tribe,* vol. 2, 626, 631–34. These questions of descent among the Omaha are controversial, even through to the present. For details, see Barnes, *Two Crows Denies It* 22–28 and 237, note 10.

14. Francis P. Prucha, *The Great Father: The United States Government and the American Indian* (Lincoln: University of Nebraska Press, 1984) 1: 89–114, 293–302. The 1834 act defined "Indian Country" mainly as that part of the United States west of the Mississippi, except for Missouri and Louisiana.

15. Dunbar, "Journal," July 21, 1835, in Wedel, *The Dunbar-Allis Letters* 588–89.

16. Allis to Greene, May 12, 1835, in Wedel, *The Dunbar-Allis Letters* 699–70. See also, White, *The Roots of Dependency,* 190–92, on this subject.

17. Dougherty to James Barbour, July 1, 1827, LR, Upper Missouri Agency, 1824–35.

18. See, for example, Allis to Greene, May 12, 1835, in Wedel, *The Dunbar-Allis Letters* 69–70. A strong case for explaining Indian drinking as a response to Americans' drinking habits is made in Craig MacAndrew and Robert B. Edgerton, *Drunken Comportment: As Social Explanation* (Chicago: Aldine Publishing Co., 1969) 100–163.

19. Merrill Mattes, "Joseph Robideaux," in Hafen, *The Mountain Men and the Fur Trade of the Far West*, vol. 8, 287–314, and "Jean Baptiste Roy—St. Louis Fur Trader," *Bulletin of the Missouri Historical Society* 3.3 (1947): 85–93.

20. Moses Merrill, *Diary*, Nov. 1832–May 14, 1834 (Lincoln: Nebraska State Historical Society), entry May 13, 1834, ms. 480.

21. John Barrow, "Report," ARCIA, *1849*, 139. See also, Sunder, *The Fur Trade on the Upper Missouri, 1840–1865*, 117–22.

22. Fletcher and La Flesche, *The Omaha Tribe*, vol. 2, 613–20.

23. David Miller to David Mitchell, Jan. 25, 1844, LR, Council Bluffs Agency, 1836–43.

24. Maximilian, *Travels in the Interior of North America*, in Thwaites, *Early Western Travels*, vol. 22, 260.

25. Paul Wilhelm, *Travels* 310. Duke of Wurttemberg, *Travels in North America, 1822–1824* (Norman: University of Oklahoma Press, 1973) 310.

26. Dougherty to Clark, Jan. 30, 1830 and July 16, 1835, LR, Upper Missouri Agency, 1824–35. It is also possible that disease, spread from American stock, caused the depletion of the bison herds. For this, see Dan Flores, "Bison Ecology and Bison Diplomacy: The Southern Plains, 1800–1850," *The Journal of American History* 78 (1991): 465–85.

27. "Speech of Big Elk," June 25, 1828, in Clark to Peter B. Porter, Aug. 4, 1828, LR, Upper Missouri Agency, 1824–35.

28. Dougherty to Clark, Sept. 20, 1832, LR, Upper Missouri Agency, 1824–35.

29. Dale L. Morgan and Eleanor Towles Harris, eds., *The Rocky Mountain Journals of William Marshall Anderson: The West in 1834* (San Marino, California: The Huntington Library, 1967) 178.

30. Paul Wilhelm, *Travels* 338.

31. The larger context of missionary activity is presented in Robert F. Berkhofer, Jr., *Salvation and the Savage: An Analysis of Protestant Missions and American Indian Response, 1781–1862* (New York: Atheneum, 1972) and Francis Paul Prucha, *The Great Father: The United States Government and the American Indian* (Lincoln: University of Nebraska Press, 1984) vol. 1, 135–58.

32. Merrill, *Diary*, and "Extracts from the Diary of Rev. Moses Merrill, A Missionary to the Otoe Indians from 1832–40." *Transactions of the Nebraska State Historical Society* 4 (1892): 157–91. Edmund McKinney, *Papers, 1847–1916* (Topeka: Kansas State Historical Society) ms. 4179. The missionaries' journals and letters generally refer to the wives formally—Mrs. Merrill, for example—so their first names are not always apparent.

33. Wedel, *The Dunbar-Allis Letters* 647. Also, Samuel Allis, *Manuscript* ms. 2628,

and John Dunbar, "Records of the Pawnee Mission Church" (Lincoln: Nebraska State Historical Society) ms. 480. The experiences of the Ranneys are recounted in "Letters from the Past," *Vermont Quarterly* 21 (1953): 118–27, 200–10, 279–88 and vol. 22 (1954): 42–51, 212–22.

34. Dunbar, "Journal," in Wedel, *The Dunbar-Allis Letters* 616–18.

35. Ranney, "Letters from the Past," vol. 21, 210; Dunbar, "Records of the Pawnee Mission Church," n.p.

36. Dunbar to Greene, May 5, 1836, and Aug. 18, 1845, in Wedel, *The Dunbar-Allis Letters* 622, 677; Merrill, *Diary*, entries Mar. 12, 1834 and Mar. 12, 1837.

37. Dunbar, "Journal," entry Jan. 25, 1835, in Wedel, *The Dunbar-Allis Letters* 608; McKinney to Rev. Moderator Presbytery of Carlisle, 1847 (?) *Papers*, n. pag.

38. Allis to Greene, May 12, 1835, and Dunbar to Greene, June 8, 1838, in Wedel, *The Dunbar-Allis Letters* 629, 701.

39. McKinney to Rev. Moderator, Presbytery of Carlisle, Pennsylvania 1847 (?) *Papers*, n. pag.

40. Paul Wilhelm, *Travels* 394–95.

41. Merrill, *Diary*, entries Feb. 23 and Mar. 8, 1834.

42. Edmund McKinney, Report no. 3–A, in ARCIA, 1849–1850, 141–42.

43. Dunbar to Greene, July 10, 1843, in Wedel, *The Dunbar-Allis Letters* 652 and Merrill, "Extracts from the Diary," Aug. 24, 1837 (184).

44. Dunbar to Greene, July 10, 1843, in Wedel, *The Dunbar-Allis Letters* 652.

45. Dunbar to Greene, July 10, 1843, in Wedel, *The Dunbar-Allis Letters* 653.

46. Merrill, *Diary*, entry Feb. 15, 1834.

47. Allis to Greene, Dec. 17, 1838, in Wedel, *The Dunbar-Allis Letters* 717.

48. Dunbar to Greene, Jan. 25, 1845, in Wedel, *The Dunbar-Allis Letters* 672–76.

49. J. Henry Carleton, *The Prairie Logbooks: Dragoon Campaigns to the Pawnee Villages in 1844 and to the Rocky Mountains in 1845* (Lincoln: University of Nebraska Press, 1983) 95–99. Ed. Louis Peltzer.

50. Baptist General Convention, *The Baptist Missionary Magazine* 16 (1836): 129–30.

51. Dunbar to Greene, Oct. 9, 1844, in Wedel, *The Dunbar-Allis Letters* 668–71.

52. Merrill, "Extracts from the Diary," Sept. 15, 1838 and May 30, 1839, 189–91.

53. Dunbar to Greene, June 30, 1846, in Wedel, *The Dunbar-Allis Letters* 683–86.

54. Robert M. Kvasnicka and Herman J. Viola, eds, *The Commissioners of Indian Affairs, 1824–1977* (Lincoln: University of Nebraska Press, 1979) and Edward E. Hill, *The Office of Indian Affairs, 1824–1880: Historical Sketches* (New York: Clearwater Publishing Company, Inc., 1974).

55. For attitudes of Americans toward Indians see Roy Harvey Pearce, *Savagism and Civilization: A Study of the Indian and the American Mind* (Baltimore: The Johns Hopkins Press, 1965) and Brian W. Dippie, *The Vanishing American: White Attitudes and the U.S. Indian Policy* (Middletown, Connecticut: Wesleyan University Press, 1982).

56. "Extracts from Minutes of a Treaty held at Prairie du Chien, July 7, 1830," in

Documents Relating to the Negotiation of Ratified and Unratified Treaties with the Various Tribes of Indians, 1801–1869, NA, RG75, R2, 1827–33.

57. Clark to Cass, Dec. 7, 1831, *Clark Papers* (Topeka: Kansas State Historical Society) vol. 4; *Letterbook,* Jan. 15, 1829–Aug. 24, 1837, ms. 94.

58. Dougherty's ambitions were not achieved. When Clark died in 1838, Joshua Pilcher was appointed superintendent, with the background aid of the American Fur Company. Pilcher had also loudly criticized Dougherty for his absenteeism from Bellevue. Pilcher's attack on Dougherty was made in a letter to William Clark in 1832 (no exact date), in LR, Upper Missouri Agency, 1824–35. Dougherty responded in a letter to Cass, March 9, 1832, *Dougherty Papers* (Topeka: Kansas State Historical Society) ms. 48740.

59. Joseph Hamilton to Joshua Pilcher, Oct. 4, 1839, in LR, Council Bluffs Agency, 1836–43.

60. John Miller to Thomas Harvey, Sept. 10, 1847. LR, Council Bluffs Agency, 1847–51.

61. William T. Hagan, *American Indians* (Chicago: University of Chicago Press, 1961) and R. F. Berkhofer, Jr., *The White Man's Indian: Images of the American Indian from Columbus to the Present* (New York: Alfred A. Knopf, 1978).

62. Dougherty to Thomas Hart Benton, Jan. 20, 1829. LR, Upper Missouri Agency, 1824–35. For other early references to the need to place the adult Indians on allotments and Indian children in manual labor schools, see reports of commissioners McKenney and T. H. Crawford, *ARCIA, 1826,* Sen. Ex. Doc. 1, 19th Cong., 1st Sess., SN144, 507–10, and *ARCIA, 1839,* Sen. Ex. Doc. 1, 26th Cong., 1st Sess., SN354, 327.

63. For an analysis of this process on the Great Plains, see David J. Wishart, "Compensation for Dispossession: Payments to the Indians for their Lands on the Central and Northern Great Plains in the Nineteenth Century," *National Geographic Research* 6.1 (1990): 94–109.

64. Felix S. Cohen, "Original Indian Title," *Minnesota Law Review* 47 (1947): 28–49; Charles F. Wilkinson, *American Indians, Time, and the Law* (New Haven: Yale University Press, 1987); and Robert A. Williams, Jr., *The American Indian in Western Legal Thought: The Discourses of Conquest* (New York: Oxford University Press, 1990).

65. "Extracts from the Minutes of a Treaty Held at Prairie du Chien," in *Documents Relating to the Negotiation of Ratified and Unratified Treaties,* R2. Unless otherwise stated, the following section is drawn from this source.

66. Clark to Thomas McKenney, July 23, 1830, in *Documents Relating to the Negotiation of Ratified and Unratified Treaties,* R2.

67. Dougherty to Carey Harris, Dec. 6, 1837, LR, Council Bluffs Agency, 1836–43.

68. Charles J. Kappler, *Indian Affairs: Laws and Treaties,* 5 vols. (Washington, D.C.: Government Printing Office, 1903–1938) 2: 305–10, 479–81, 557–60. See also, Berlin Basil Chapman, *The Otoes and Missourias: A Study of Indian Removal and the Legal Aftermath* (Oklahoma City: Times Journal Pub. Co., 1965) 1–21, 29–33.

69. Kappler, *Indian Affairs,* vol. 2, 307–8; Chapman, *The Otoes and Missourias* 15–

16, 51–83; Maximilian, *Travels in the Interior,* in Thwaites, *Early Western Travels,* vol. 22, 259–60; *Half-Breed Tract,* ms. 726 (Lincoln: Nebraska State Historical Society).

70. The description is from John T. Irving, Jr., *Indian Sketches Taken During an Expedition to the Pawnee Tribes* (Philadelphia: Carey, Lea and Blanchard, 1835) vol. 1, 170–237. The details of the Otoe-Missouria, Pawnee, and Fort Leavenworth councils are from *Documents Relating to the Negotiation of Ratified and Unratified Treaties with the Indians,* R2.

71. Kappler, *Indian Affairs,* vol. 2, 400–401.

72. Estimates of acreage are taken from the findings of the Indian Claims Commission, which convened from 1946 to 1978 to consider the claims of Indians for second awards for their lands. See *Otoe and Missouria Tribe of Indians v. United States* 2 ICC 335 (1953).

73. Big Elk and other Omaha chiefs, "Petition," in Henry Ellsworth to Elbert Herring, Oct. 4, 1833, in *Documents Relating to the Negotiation of Ratified and Unratified Treaties with the Indians,* R2.

74. Dougherty to Clark, Oct. 29, 1831, LR, Upper Missouri Agency, 1824–35.

75. "Council Minutes," in *Documents Relating to the Negotiation of Ratified and Unratified Treaties with the Indians,* R2.

76. Irving, *Indian Sketches,* vol. 2, 85.

77. Kappler, *Indian Affairs,* vol. 2, 416–18.

78. *Pawnee Tribe of Oklahoma v. United States,* 5 ICC 224 (1957); Henry Ellsworth to Elbert Herring, Oct. 4, 1833, in *Documents Relating to the Negotiation of Ratified and Unratified Treaties with the Indians,* R2.

79. "Grand Council for Making Peace, Nov. 8, 1833," in *Documents Relating to the Negotiation of Ratified and Unratified Treaties with the Indians,* R2.

80. John D. Unruh, Jr., *The Plains Across: The Overland Emigrants and the Trans-Mississippi West, 1840–60* (Urbana: University of Illinois Press, 1979), 119–20, 156–85.

81. David Miller to David Mitchell, July 1 and Dec. 28, 1843, LR, Council Bluffs Agency, 1844–46.

82. Thomas Harvey to Harley Crawford, Sept. 10, 1845, in ARCIA, 1845–1846, 84–91, and Harvey to William Medill, Sept. 5, 1846, ARCIA, 1846–47, 70–76.

83. D. P. Woodbury to Col. Joseph G. Tottem, Mar. 30, 1847, in *Field Notes, Fort Kearny, 1839–83,* ms. 1046 (Topeka: Kansas State Historical Society).

84. Kappler, *Indian Affairs,* vol. 2, 571–72.

85. John Miller to Thomas Harvey, Mar. 20, 1848, LR, Council Bluffs Agency, 1847–51.

86. *Pawnee Indians v. United States* 5 ICC 224 (1957).

87. John Miller to Thomas Harvey, June 17, 1848, LR, Council Bluffs Agency 1847–51.

88. "Speech of Big Elk, Council with the Omahas, Oct. 3, 1833," in *Documents Relating to the Negotiation of Ratified and Unratified Treaties with the Indians,* R2.

89. Harvey to William Medill, Feb. 4, 1847, LR, Council Bluffs Agency, 1847–51.

90. "Speeches of the Chiefs of the Otoes and Missouris and of the Pawnees and of

the Omahaw Nations of Indians whilst receiving their annuities for the year 1834," in Dougherty to Clark, Oct. 20, 1834, LR, Upper Missouri Agency, 1824–35.

91. Miller to Harvey, Sept. 10, 1847, LR, Council Bluffs Agency, 1847–51.

92. Miller to Harvey, Sept. 10, 1847, LR, Council Bluffs Agency, 1847–51. This letter also includes the reference to the butchered stock.

93. Allis to Greene, July 10, 1839, in Wedel, *The Dunbar-Allis Letters* 719.

94. "Speeches of Chiefs . . . for the year 1834," in Dougherty to Clark, Oct. 20, 1834, LR, Upper Missouri Agency, 1824–35.

95. Mitchell to Lea, Oct. 17, 1852, *ARCIA, 1852*, 62–68.

96. Lea, "Report," *ARCIA, 1852*, 4.

97. Brown, "Report," *ARCIA, 1849*, 11–12.

98. Lea, "Report," *ARCIA, 1850*, 3–4. See also on this subject, James Malin, *Indian Policy and Westward Expansion* (Lawrence, Kansas, 1921) and Robert A. Trennert, Jr., *Alternative to Extinction: Federal Indian Policy and the Beginnings of the Reservation System* (Philadelphia: Temple University Press, 1975).

Chapter 3. Twilight of Independence

1. For general historical demography, see Edward A. Wrigley, *Population and History* (New York and Toronto: McGraw Hill Book Company, 1969). Many less-developed countries in the late twentieth century have doubling rates—the predicted time it takes for a population to double in size—of twenty to twenty-five years.

2. John B. Dunbar, "The Pawnee Indians: Their History and Ethnology," *Magazine of American History* 4.4 (1880): 242–79 (Rpt. ts., Nebraska State Historical Society), and Dorsey, *Omaha Sociology* 264.

3. Moulton, *The Journals of the Lewis and Clark Expedition*, vol. 3, 394, 396; Bradbury, *Travels in the Interior*, in Thwaites, *Early Western Travels*, vol. 5, 90; Henry Marie Brackenridge, *Views of Louisiana, Together with a Journal of a Voyage up the Missouri River, in 1811* (Chicago: Quadrangle Books, Inc., 1962) 76. For the Pawnee see also, Brooks, "George Sibley's Journal," 183.

4. William Clark, "Names of Tribes and Numbers of Each in the St. Louis Superintendency, Nov. 4, 1816," in *Letters Received by the Office of the Secretary of War Relating to Indian Affairs, 1800–1823*, NA, RG75, 1800–16; "Henry Atkinson to Col. W. S. Hamilton, Dec. 21, 1825," *Nebraska History* 5.1 (1922): 9–11; Benjamin O'Fallon to Peter Wilson, Oct. 19, 1824, LR, Upper Missouri Agency, 1824–35. It is possible, but unlikely, that the Pawnee population reached 20,000 in the 1820s. According to Wedel, probably the person best qualified to judge, 10,000 to 12,500 is a more likely number (Wedel, personal communication, March 6, 1981).

5. Peter Wilson to Benjamin O'Fallon, Oct. 24, 1824, LR, Upper Missouri Agency, 1824–35.

6. Kappler, *Indian Affairs*, vol. 2, 225–27. Also see James Howard, "Known Village Sites of the Ponca," *Plains Anthropologist* 15 (1970): 128–29.

7. Maximilian, *Travels in the Interior,* in Thwaites, *Early Western Travels,* vol. 22, 266. It is more than possible that the Ponca dispersed to avoid epidemics, which ran rampant through crowded villages.

8. Dougherty to Clark, Nov. 12, 1834, LR, Upper Missouri Agency, 1824–35.

9. Joshua Pilcher to Clark, Aug. 26, 1835, LR, Upper Missouri Agency, 1824–35; Pilcher to Clark, Sept. 15, 1838, LR, 1836–51. The Ponca continued to obtain corn by trade from the Omaha.

10. Pilcher, "Statistical Return for the Upper Missouri Agency, Sept. 30, 1837," LR, Upper Missouri Agency, 1836–51. For other estimates, see George Catlin, *Letters and Notes on the Manners, Customs, and Condition of the North American Indians* (New York: Wiley and Putnam, 1841) 1: 212; Isaac McCoy, *The Annual Register of Indian Affairs within the Indian (or Western) Territory* (Shawnee Baptist Mission: J. Meeker, 1836) 4; and Mitchell, "Report," *ARCIA, 1842,* Sen. Ex. Doc. 1, 27th Cong., 3rd Sess., SN413, 431–35.

11. Dougherty to Thomas McKenney, Sept. 14, 1827, LR, Upper Missouri Agency, 1824–35.

12. For hunting patterns see Henry Ellsworth to Elbert Herring, Oct. 4, 1833, in *Documents Relating to the Negotiation of Ratified and Unratified Treaties with the Indians,* R2. For farming near Bellevue see Dougherty, "Report," *ARCIA, 1836,* Sen. Ex. Doc. 1, 25th Cong., 2nd Sess., SN314, 547–49, and Dougherty, "Report," *ARCIA, 1837,* SDI, 25th Cong., 3rd Sess., SN338, 503–5.

13. Dougherty to Clark, Sept. 30, 1832, LR, Upper Missouri Agency, 1824–35.

14. Maximilian, *Travels in the Interior,* in Thwaites, *Early Western Travels,* vol. 22, 227.

15. Paul Wilhelm, *Travels* 338; Henry Ellsworth to Elbert Herring, Oct. 4, 1833, in *Documents Relating to the Negotiation of Ratified and Unratified Treaties with the Indians,* R2; McCoy, *The Annual Register* 4.

16. "Speech of Big Elk, Council with the Omahas, Oct. 3, 1833," in *Documents Relating to the Negotiation of Ratified and Unratified Treaties with the Indians,* R2. The dates of Big Elk's chieftainship are from Barnes, *Two Crows Denies It* 41.

17. Fletcher and La Flesche, *The Omaha Tribe,* vol. 1, 84; Ellsworth to Elbert Herring, Oct. 4, 1833, in *Documents Relating to the Negotiation of Ratified and Unratified Treaties with the Indians,* R2. Pilcher, "Report," *ARCIA, 1840,* Sen. Ex. Doc. 1, 25th Cong., 2nd Sess., SN314, 316–17; Paul Wilhelm, *Travels* 396.

18. Dougherty, "Report," *ARCIA, 1837,* Sen. Ex. Doc. 1, 25th Cong., 2nd Sess., SN314, 547–49.

19. Merrill, "Extracts from the Diary," July 26, Aug. 6, Aug. 14, 1837 (175–76).

20. Clark, "Names of Tribes and Numbers of Each in the St. Louis Superintendency, Nov. 4, 1816"; Dougherty, "Statistical Return, Sept. 30, 1836," LR, Upper Missouri Agency, 1836–51; Joseph Hamilton, "Report," *ARCIA, 1840,* Sen. Ex. Doc. 1, 26th Cong., 2nd Sess., SN375, 318–19. Another indication of population numbers is provided by Merrill in "Extracts from the Diary, May 26, 1837" (183). Witnessing the delivery of annuities, Merrill counted 190 married men. Considering that there were

more women than men in the population, and that almost half the population were children, this could translate into a total number of about nine hundred to one thousand. Catlin's estimate of twelve hundred Otoe-Missouria in 1832 and McCoy's figure of sixteen hundred for 1836 are unlikely. See Catlin, *Letters and Notes*, vol. 2, 25–26 and McCoy, *The Annual Register* 16.

21. John Gray to Joseph Hamilton, Oct. 24, 1839, LR, Upper Missouri Agency, 1836–51. The first shipment of government-issued vaccine did not work, and a new batch had to be sent.

22. James, *An Account of an Expedition from Pittsburgh to the Rocky Mountains*, in Thwaites, *Early Western Travels*, vol. 14, 239.

23. Merrill, "Extracts from the Diary," Apr. 28 and Apr. 29, 1837; Feb. 11, 1839 (180–82, 189).

24. Paul Wilhelm, *Travels* 388–40.

25. Merrill, "Extracts from the Diary," Apr. 28 and Apr. 29, 1837 (180–82).

26. Dougherty to James Barbour, June 28, 1827, LR, Upper Missouri Agency, 1824–35; Joseph Vizcarra to Alexander McNair, Sept. 8, 1823, in James W. Covington, ed., "Correspondence Between Mexican Officials at Santa Fe and Officials in Missouri, 1823–1825," *Bulletin of the Missouri Historical Society* 16 (1959): 20–32; Dougherty to Clark, Nov. 4, 1828, LR, Upper Missouri Agency, 1824–35; Paul Wilhelm, *Travels* 389. Wilhelm also noted (389) that the Pawnee were waging "a relentless war of extermination" against the Spaniards and Mexicans.

27. Dougherty to Clark, Oct. 29, 1831, LR, Upper Missouri Agency, 1824–35. Catlin's claim that the Pawnee were reduced from between twenty and twenty-four thousand to between ten and twelve thousand in 1831–32 is, like many of his claims, erroneous. See Catlin, *Letters and Notes*, vol. 2, 25–26. For an overview of Pawnee population and social change, see Benjamin R. Kracht, *The Effects of Disease and Warfare on Pawnee Social Organization, 1830–59: An Ethnohistorical Approach*. Master's thesis, University of Nebraska-Lincoln, 1982.

28. Dougherty to Clark, Nov. 29, 1832, LR, Upper Missouri Agency, 1824–35.

29. Dunbar, "Journal," entry Oct. 27, 1835, in Wedel, *The Dunbar-Allis Letters* 602.

30. Dougherty to Clark, June 8, 1836, LR, UMA, 1824–25.

31. Dougherty, "Report," *ARCIA, 1838*, Sen. Ex. Doc. 1, 25th Cong., 3rd Sess., SN338, 503–5; Dougherty to Clark, June 8, 1836, LR, Upper Missouri Agency, 1824–25; also White, "The Winning of the West" 337–38.

32. Dunbar to Greene, June 8, 1838, in Wedel, *The Dunbar-Allis Letters* 628–29.

33. John Gray to Joseph Hamilton, Oct. 24, 1839, LR, Upper Missouri Agency, 1836–51.

34. Allis to Greene, May 12, 1835, Dunbar to Greene, Oct. 1, 1839, and July 13, 1840, in Wedel, *The Dunbar-Allis Letters* 640–42, 700. Dougherty's estimate of ten thousand in 1836, which was also echoed by McCoy, is probably too high. See Dougherty, "Statistical Report, Sept. 30, 1836," LR, Upper Missouri Agency, 1824–35, and McCoy, *The Annual Register* 16.

35. Dunbar, "Journal," entry Mar. 2, 1836, in Wedel, *The Dunbar-Allis Letters* 612;

and *Speeches of the Chiefs . . . for the Year 1834,* in Dougherty to Clark, Oct. 20, 1834, LR, Upper Missouri Agency, 1824–35.

36. Dunbar to Joseph Hamilton, Oct. ? 1839, LR, Upper Missouri Agency, 1836–51; James, *An Account of an Expedition from Pittsburgh to the Rocky Mountains,* in Thwaites, *Early Western Travels,* vol. 14, 205–10, and Irving, *Indian Sketches,* vol. 2, 85.

37. McKinney to Rev. Moderator, Presbytery of Carlisle, Pennsylvania, 1847 (?), *Papers,* n. pag.

38. Even the meticulous Jablow, in his *Ethnohistory of the Ponca,* could find relatively little to say about Ponca life in the 1840s.

39. Hiram Martin Chittenden and Alfred Talbot Richardson, eds., *Life, Letters and Travels of Father Pierre-Jean De Smet* (New York: F. P. Harper, 1905) 4: 625–28.

40. The Indians complained about the profligate bison tongue trade to Superintendent Harvey in 1846. Harvey sympathetically passed on their concerns to Commissioner Medill with this observation: "Notwithstanding that the Indians kill great numbers of the buffalo, they do not kill them wastefully. . . . Not so with the white man; he kills for the sake of killing." T. Harvey, "Report," *ARCIA, 1846–47,* 70–76. For numbers of robes traded in the Upper Missouri Agency, see W. S. Hatton, "Report," *ARCIA, 1850,* 43, J. A. Norwood, "Report," *ARCIA, 1852,* 69–70, and A. J. Vaughn, "Report," *ARCIA, 1852,* 112–13.

41. David D. Mitchell, "Report," *ARCIA, 1842,* Sen. Ex. Doc. 1, 27th Cong., 3rd Sess., SN413, 631–35. Also Howard, "Known Village Sites of the Ponca" 126–27.

42. Chittenden and Richardson, eds., *Life, Letters and Travels of Father Pierre Jean De Smet,* vol. 4, 627; Daniel Miller, "Report," in *ARCIA, 1843,* Sen. Ex. Doc. 1, 28th Cong., 1st Sess., SN431, 398–404.

43. Dunbar to Greene, Apr. 29, 1844 and Aug. 18, 1845, in Wedel, *The Dunbar-Allis Letters* 664, 679–80.

44. Chittenden and Richardson, eds., *Life, Letters and Travels of Father Pierre-Jean De Smet,* vol. 4, 625.

45. T. P. Moore, "Report," *ARCIA, 1846–47,* 83, and Edwin A. Fry, "Mormons on the Niobrara," *Nebraska History* 5.1 (1922): 4–6.

46. Chittenden and Richardson, eds., *Life, Letters and Travels of Father Pierre-Jean De Smet,* vol. 4, 625; John Miller to T. Harvey, Apr. 1, 1848, LR, Council Bluffs Agency, 1847–51.

47. Charles Larpenteur, *Forty Years a Fur Trader on the Upper Missouri* (New York: F. P. Harper, 1898) vol. 2, 299–301. Ed. Elliot Coues.

48. Miller, "Report," *ARCIA, 1842,* Sen. Ex. Doc. 1, 27th Cong., 3rd Sess., SN413, 437–40.

49. For village site, see Edmund McKinney to Rev. David McKinney, Sept. 13, 1848, *Papers,* n. pag. For state of health and drinking, see McKinney to Rev. Moderator, 1847 (?), *Papers,* n. pag., and John Miller to Thomas Harvey, Sept. 10, 1847, LR, Council Bluffs Agency, 1847–51. For the land dispute, see Harvey, "Report," *ARCIA, 1846–47,* 70–76, and Harvey to William Medill, Feb. 4, 1847, LR, Council Bluffs Agency, 1847–51.

50. Mitchell, "Report," *ARCIA, 1843*, Sen. Ex. Doc. 1, 28th Cong., 1st Sess., SN431, 387–88.

51. The description is Joshua Pilcher's, in his "Report," *ARCIA, 1840*, Sen. Ex. Doc. 1, 26th Cong., 2nd Sess., SN375, 316. Daniel Miller described the Omaha as "rather docile Indians" and reported the Dakota alliance in "Report," *ARCIA, 1844*, Sen. Ex. Doc. 1, 28th Cong., 2nd Sess., SN449, 440–44. The hunt with the Skiri is noted in Miller, "Report," *ARCIA, 1842*, Sen. Ex. Doc. 1, 27th Cong., 3rd Sess., SN413, 437–40. Unlike the other Nebraska Indians, the Omaha did not have a specific treaty stipulation that the United States would protect them, but judging by the experiences of the Otoe-Missouria, Ponca, and Pawnee, this guarantee was in any case an empty gesture.

52. Jonathan Bean to Thomas Harvey, Dec. 31, 1845, LR, Council Bluffs Agency, 1844–46. For other indications of the Omaha's distress, see McKinney to Rev. Moderator, 1847 (?) *Papers*, n. pag.; Miller to Harvey, Sept. 10, 1847, LR, Council Bluffs Agency, 1847–51; Harvey "Report," *ARCIA, 1847*, 70–76.

53. For the connection between disease, infecundity, and infertility, see David E. Stannard, "Disease and Infertility: A New Look at the Demographic Collapse of Native Populations in the Wake of Western Contact," *Journal of American Studies* 24.3 (1990): 325–50; and Gregory R. Campbell, "Changing Patterns of Health and Effective Fertility Among the Northern Cheyenne of Montana, 1886–1903," *The American Indian Quarterly* 15 (1991): 339–58. There is also a good discussion of this in Thornton, *American Indian Holocaust and Survival* 53–54 and elsewhere.

54. Miller to David Mitchell, Feb. 9, 1844, LR, Council Bluffs Agency, 1844–46, and Harvey, "Report," *ARCIA, 1845*, 12–13.

55. Gatewood, "Report," *ARCIA, 1853*, 105–10.

56. Fletcher and La Flesche, *The Omaha Tribe*, vol. 1, 83–84.

57. Harvey, "Report," *ARCIA, 1845*, 12–13.

58. Carlton, *The Prairie Logbooks* 122; and Miller, "Report," *ARCIA, 1844*, Sen. Ex. Doc. 1, 28th Cong., 2nd Sess., SN449, 441.

59. Mitchell, "Report," *ARCIA, 1843*, Sen. Ex. Doc. 1, 28th Cong., 1st Sess., SN431, 386–88.

60. McKinney to Rev. Moderator, 1847 (?), *Papers*, n. pag.

61. Miller to Mitchell, Apr. 5, 1842, LR, Council Bluffs Agency, 1836–43; and Miller, "Report," *ARCIA, 1842*, Sen. Ex. Doc. 1, 27th Cong., 3rd Sess., SN413, 437–40.

62. See virtually any agent's report for evidence of these conditions, including Miller's 1842 report, quoted in the above footnote, Miller's report in *ARCIA, 1843*, Sen. Ex. Doc. 1, 28th Cong., 1st Sess., SN431, 398–404, and Superintendent Harvey's report in *ARCIA, 1846–47*, 70–76.

63. In addition to Miller's reports for 1842 and 1843, see Miller to David Mitchell, Dec. 27, 1842, LR, Council Bluffs Agency, 1836–43.

64. Gatewood, "Report," *ARCIA, 1853*, 105.

65. Harvey, "Report," *ARCIA, 1845*, 12–13.

66. Miller to Thomas Harvey, Sept. 10, 1847, LR, Council Bluffs Agency, 1847–51.

67. Gatewood, "Report," *ARCIA, 1853*, 106–7.

68. There is a good description of the rapid settlement of the country to the east of the Missouri in Gottlieb F. Oehler and David Z. Smith, *Description of a Journey and Visit to the Pawnee Indians . . . April 22–May 18, 1851*, Moravian Church Miscellany, 1851–52, 3–7.

69. "Extract of a Letter from Capt. H. Wharton, June 10, 1852, in LR, Council Bluffs Agency, 1852–57. For general discussion of Pawnee-emigrant clashes, see Unruh, *The Plains Across* 171–73.

70. For complaints about Siracherish (or Cross Chief) see Alexander McElroy to John Miller, May 17, 1847 and Harvey to William Medill, June 5, 1847, in LR, Council Bluffs Agency, 1847–51. Harvey considered Siracherish to be "very impertinent" and wanted permission to burn his village.

71. Dunbar to Greene, June 30, 1846, in Wedel, *The Dunbar-Allis Letters* 685–86.

72. Wild Warrior made this speech in a council with Capt. Henry Wharton in 1844. Recorded in Carlton, *The Prairie Logbooks* 128.

73. Miller, "Report," *ARCIA, 1844*, Sen. Ex. Doc. 1, 28th Cong., 2nd Sess., SN449, 440–44.

74. Dunbar to Greene, June 30, 1846, in Wedel, *The Dunbar-Allis Letters* 686.

75. For information on locations, see Dunbar to Greene, Apr. 26, 1842, Apr. 24, 1844, and Apr. 29, 1844, in Wedel, *The Dunbar-Allis Letters* 648–50, 662–65, and 664–65. Also, Wedel, *An Introduction to Pawnee Archaeology* 23–38 and Grange, *Pawnee and Lower Loup Pottery* 22–23.

76. The best description of the massacre is in Dunbar to Greene, July 10, 1843, in Wedel, *The Dunbar-Allis Letters* 656–58. Carlton, in *The Prairie Logbooks* (107–9), also gives a detailed account, as told to him by an eyewitness.

77. Carlton, *The Prairie Logbooks* 109; Dunbar to Greene, Nov. 14, 1843, in Wedel, *The Dunbar-Allis Letters* 659.

78. Oehler and Smith, *Description of a Journey* 16–23, 27; Grange, *Pawnee and Lower Loup Pottery* 19, 24–25; and Wedel, *An Introduction to Pawnee Archaeology* 28, 31.

79. Information on this succession of disasters is from Miller to Harvey, March 20, 1848, in LR, Council Bluffs Agency, 1847–51; Barrow, "Report," *ARCIA, 1849–50*, 137–40; and Miller, "Report," *ARCIA, 1850*, 16–18.

80. Carlton, *The Prairie Logbooks* 68–77.

81. Barrow, "Report," *ARCIA, 1850*, 41; Oehler and Smith, *Description of a Journey* 20.

82. Weltfish, *The Lost Universe* 3.

83. Carlton, *The Prairie Logbooks* 88–89.

84. Information on material changes is drawn from Wedel, *An Introduction to Pawnee Archaeology* 62–74; Grange, *Pawnee and Lower Loup Pottery* 121, 132; Weltfish, *The Lost Universe* 137–38, 140, 363–64; Howard, *The Ponca Tribe* 51–56; O'Shea and Ludwickson, *Archaeology and Ethnohistory of the Omaha Indians* 157–220; and especially, Fletcher and La Flesche, *The Omaha Tribe*, vol. 2, 341, 359, and 613–20. See

also, Edward H. Spicer, "Types of Contact and Processes of Change," *Perspectives on American Indian Culture Change*, ed. Edward H. Spicer (Chicago: University of Chicago Press, 1961) 517–44.

85. Carlton, *The Prairie Logbooks* 65.

86. Theoretical aspects of the effects of depopulation on social organization are given in Elman R. Service, *Primitive Social Organization* (New York: Random House, 1971), especially pages 123–26.

87. Kracht, in *The Effects of Disease and Warfare on Pawnee Social Organization*, has covered this topic well.

88. Weltfish, *The Lost Universe* 20.

89. Dunbar to Joseph Hamilton, Oct. (?), 1839, LR, Council Bluffs Agency, 1836–43; Oehler and Smith, *Description of a Journey* 15–16.

90. Carlton, *The Prairie Logbooks* 89.

91. Harvey, "Report," ARCIA, *1845*, 12–13; Harvey to William Medill, Feb. 4, 1847, LR, Council Bluffs Agency, 1847–51.

92. Carlton, *The Prairie Logbooks* 80.

93. Murie, *Ceremonies of the Pawnee* 113–46 and Weltfish, *The Lost Universe* 106–18. Grinnell, in *Pawnee Hero Stories and Folk Tales* 362–68, maintains that Morning Star sacrifices may have taken place secretly after 1838.

94. Murie, *Ceremonies of the Pawnee* 77–82, 179 (note 28).

95. Fletcher and La Flesche, *The Omaha Tribe* 202–3, 486–87, 495–96.

96. Edward E. Bruner, "Mandan," in *Perspectives on American Indian Culture Change* 187–277 and John C. Ewers, "The Influence of Epidemics on the Indian Population and Cultures of Texas," *Plains Anthropologist* 18 (1973): 104–15.

97. McKinney, "Report," ARCIA, *1851*, 95–97; See also, Berkhofer, *Salvation and the Savage* 16–43.

98. Miller, "Report," ARCIA, *1842*, Sen. Ex. Doc. 1, 27th Cong., 3rd Sess., SN415, 437–40 and Mitchell, "Report," ARCIA, *1851*, 60–64.

99. Carlton, *The Prairie Logbooks* 89.

Chapter 4. Restriction to Reservations

1. James Malin, *The Nebraska Question, 1852–1854* (Ann Arbor: Edward Bros., 1953).

2. *St. Joseph Gazette*, June 8, 1853; John Allen, "The Garden-Desert Continuum: Competing Views of the Great Plains in the Nineteenth Century," *Great Plains Quarterly* 5 (1985): 207–20.

3. *St. Joseph Gazette*, June 29, 1853.

4. Manypenny to Robert McClelland, Nov. 9, 1853, Sen. Ex. Doc. 1, 33rd Cong., 1st Sess., 1853–54, 269–76. See also, Manypenny's retrospective on Indian affairs, written in 1880: *Our Indian Wards* (New York: Da Capo Press, 1972), especially pages 116–20.

5. Manypenny, "Report," ARCIA, *1854*, 5–6.

6. Greenwood, "Report," ARCIA, 1859, 5 and Manypenny, "Report," ARCIA, 1854, 5–6.

7. Mitchell, "Report," ARCIA, 1851, 61; Cuming, "Report," ARCIA, 1857, 117–22; and *St. Joseph Gazette*, Oct. 26, 1853.

8. Kappler, *Indian Affairs*, vol. 2, 603–14, 764–67, and 772–75. In a period of two months in the spring of 1854, Manypenny negotiated nine treaties with Indian nations of eastern Nebraska and Kansas, resulting in the acquisition of about fourteen million acres for the public domain.

9. Manypenny, "Report," ARCIA, 1855, 18.

10. Denver, "Report," ARCIA, 1857, 1–12; Manypenny, "Report," ARCIA, 1854, 3–23; Robert M. Kvasnicka, "George W. Manypenny 1853–57," and Donald Chaput, "James W. Denver, 1857, 1858–59," in *The Commissioners of Indian Affairs* 57–75.

11. Addison E. Sheldon, *Land Systems and Land Policies in Nebraska*, Publications of the Nebraska State Historical Society (Lincoln: Nebraska State Historical Society, 1936) 22: 25–73, 160–62. The Preemption Act stipulated occupancy on the 160 acres and payment of the two hundred dollars within twelve months. Many settlers took out a claim, and then left to work in the towns. Military-bounty land warrants were issued to veterans, but could be transferred to others for a price. In 1860 the going price was about fifty cents an acre, which allowed speculators to accumulate large amounts of land. These lands were often sold as values rose, which they did rapidly in frontier Nebraska.

12. United States Bureau of the Census, *Eighth Census, 1860, Population of the United States in 1860* (Washington, D.C.: Government Printing Office, 1864) 1: 558–61 and John C. Hudson, "Who was 'Forest Man'? Sources of Migration to the Plains," *Great Plains Quarterly* 6 (1986): 69–83.

13. Charles Howard Richardson, *Early Settlement of Eastern Nebraska Territory: A Geographical Study Based on the Original Land Survey*, diss., University of Nebraska-Lincoln, 1968.

14. *The Nebraskian* (Omaha City), Nov. 25, 1856; on attitudes to annuities, see *Nebraska Palladium* (Bellevue), Feb. 28, 1855.

15. Augustus Ford Harvey, *Field Notes* (Topeka: Kansas State Historical Society) ms. 1046.

16. Dennison, "Report," ARCIA, 1858, 102–4.

17. Robinson to Greenwood, July 26, 1859, LR, Pawnee Agency, 1859–62.

18. Manypenny, "Report," ARCIA, 1855, 4.

19. *United States Land Survey*, T12N, R10E, Apr. 18–June 9, 1856; T12N, R13E, July 17–28, 1856; T9N, R14E, Dec. 18, 1855–Apr. 7, 1856; Richardson, *Early Settlement of Nebraska Territory*, Append. E.

20. Kappler, *Indian Affairs*, vol. 2, 608.

21. Hepner to Cuming, Oct. 23, 1854, LR, Council Bluffs Agency, 1852–57.

22. Kappler, *Indian Affairs*, vol. 2, 661–62.

23. *United States Land Survey Field Notes*, 1875 Survey of the Otoe-Missouria

Reservation in Nebraska and Kansas, Book 135 (T1N, R7E and T2N, R7E) and Book 136 (T1N, R8, and T2N, R8E).

24. Information on settlement is taken from the *United States Land Survey General Land Office Records*; Hugh J. Dobbs, *History of Gage County* (Lincoln: Western Publishing and Engraving, 1918); Emma E. Porter, *History of Marshall County, Kansas* (Indianapolis: B. F. Brown, 1917); and Marshall County and Washington County *Clippings* (Topeka: Kansas State Historical Society).

25. Albert L. Green, *Papers* (Lincoln: Nebraska State Historical Society) ms. 2800 and Hugh J. Dobbs, *History of Gage County* 55–110. The village was approximately on the site of present-day Barneston, Nebraska.

26. Cuming to Manypenny, Dec. 27, 1853, LR, Council Bluffs Agency, 1852–57; *The Nebraskan*, Feb. 6, 1856.

27. Daniel Vanderslice to Cuming, June 23, 1856, LR, Council Bluffs Agency, 1852–57.

28. "Petition," Otoe Indians to Manypenny, March 3, 1857, LR, Otoe Agency, 1856–60; Dennison to Robinson, Jan 21, 1859, LR, Otoe Agency, 1856–60.

29. Dennison, "Report," ARCIA, *1860*, 96–99.

30. Dennison to Robinson, July 14, 1859, LR, Otoe Agency, 1856–60.

31. Dennison, "Report," ARCIA, *1859*, 140.

32. Murdock, "Report," ARCIA, *1857*, 155; Dennison, "Report," ARCIA, *1858*, 102.

33. Dennison to Robinson, Feb. 3, 1860, LR, Otoe Agency, 1856–60. Prucha, *The Great Father* 312–14, 334, 653–55.

34. Dennison, "Report," ARCIA, *1858*, 102–4 and Dennison to Mix, Sept. 6, 1858, LR, Otoe Agency, 1856–60.

35. Murdock, "Report," ARCIA, *1857*, 155.

36. ARCIA, *1861*, Entry no. 88, 213–14. The annuity rolls in 1859 had listed 845 people (257 men, 318 women, 145 boys, and 125 girls), but there are indications that there were generally more names on the rolls than there were Otoe-Missouria. Hepner, in his 1856 report (ARCIA, *1856*, 86) had noted this discrepancy, which may be accounted for by the ingratiation of traders into Indian families, and the uncertain status of mixed-bloods.

37. Dennison, "Report," ARCIA, *1860*, 96–99 and Dennison to Robinson, Aug. 27, 1860, LR, Otoe Agency, 1856–60.

38. For example, J. V. Dodge to McClelland, June 2, 1854, and H. D. Johnson to Manypenny, Apr. 17, 1855, LR, Council Bluffs Agency, 1852–57.

39. Hepner to Cuming, Nov. 12, 1854, and Apr. 1, 1855, LR, Council Bluffs Agency, 1852–57.

40. The murder took place in northern Boone County (T21N, R7W). See Fletcher and La Flesche, *The Omaha Tribe*, vol. 1, 100–101 and Manypenny's and Hepner's reports in ARCIA, *1855*, 1–12, 85–87.

41. Hepner, "Report," ARCIA, *1855*, 86.

42. Irish to Branch, Sept. 19, 1862, LR, Omaha Agency, 1856–63. The map, "Omaha Indian Reservation" is kept in the National Archives, RG75, no. 342. See also Fletcher

and La Flesche, *The Omaha Tribe,* vol. 2, 629–34, and United States Land Survey plats of the reservation, 1867.

43. Wilson, "Report," ARCIA, *1858,* 100–102; Moore to Robinson, Jan. 13, 1860, LR, Omaha Agency, 1856–63; and *The Omaha Arrow,* Sept. 29 and Oct. 6, 1854.

44. Specific locations, taken from *United States Land Survey* plats and other primary sources, are as follows: mission (T25N, R9E, section 12); La Flesche's village (T25N, R9E, sections 12 and 13); agency (T25N, R9E, section 24); and Big Village (T25N; R10E, section 30). See also Francis La Flesche, *The Middle Five* (Lincoln: University of Nebraska Press, 1963) xix–xx.

45. Robertson, "Report," ARCIA, *1856,* 103–5 and "Report," ARCIA, *1857,* 149–50; Irish, "Report," ARCIA, *1861,* 62–65.

46. "Council of Indian Chiefs on Disbursement of Annuities," in Graff to Branch, LR, Omaha Agency, 1856–63; Irish to Branch, Sept. 13, 1862, LR, Omaha Agency, 1856–63; Sturgis, "Report," ARCIA, *1857,* 151–52.

47. For the case against Hepner, see "Claims against the Omahas and Otoe-Missouria, 1855–57," Special File No. 109, R87, Agency Files, Box 5 (Lincoln: Nebraska State Historical Society); *The Nebraskian* (Omaha City), Feb. 6, 1856; and Omaha v. United States, 53 Ct. Cls. 549 (1917–18). On Wilson, see Omaha Chiefs, "Petition," June 11, 1859, LR, Omaha Agency, 1856–63. On Hamilton, see La Flesche to Wilson, Jan. 14, 1859, and Wilson to Mix, Jan. 19, 1859, LR, Omaha Agency, 1856–63.

48. "Proceedings of a Council of the Omaha Indians, Jan. 20, 1860" and Graff to Robinson, Dec. 13, 1860, LR, Omaha Agency, 1856–63.

49. This retrospective on Joseph La Flesche was given to Alice Fletcher and Francis La Flesche (Joseph's son) by Wa'thishnade shortly before his death. See Fletcher and La Flesche, *The Omaha Tribe,* vol. 2, 630–34, 638, and plate 29.

50. On the alcohol issue, see Hepner, "Report," ARCIA, *1855,* 86–87, and Susan La Flesche, *Papers* (Lincoln: Nebraska State Historical Society) ms. 2026; for the police force, see Burtt to Walter Lowie, June 6, 1860 and July 18, 1861, *Presbyterian Missionary Letters Relating to the American Indians in Nebraska Country* (Philadelphia: Presbyterian Historical Society). Also, La Flesche to Denver, Feb. 5, 1858; Moore to Robinson, Jan. 13, 1860; and Graff to Robinson, July 22, 1860, LR, Omaha Agency, 1856–63.

51. Graff to Robinson, Dec. 13, 1860, LR, Omaha Agency, 1856–63; and Irish, "Report," ARCIA, *1861,* 63.

52. Moore to Robinson, Jan. 13, 1860, LR, Omaha Agency, 1856–63; and Burtt to Lowie, July 18, 1861, in *Presbyterian Missionary Letters,* n. pag.

53. Burtt to Lowie, March 22, 1861 and June 20, 1861, in *Presbyterian Missionary Letters,* n. pag.

54. Fletcher and La Flesche, *The Omaha Tribe,* vol. 2, 630.

55. Allis to Cuming, Oct. 28, 1856, LR, Otoe Agency, 1856–60; and DePuy to Dole, July 2, 1861, LR, Pawnee Agency, 1859–62; Hepner, "Report," ARCIA, *1855,* 85–87.

56. Allis, "Report," ARCIA, *1856,* 106; Settlers' "Petition" to Manypenny, Dec. 1,

1856; Dennison to Cuming, May 5, 1857, including "Proceedings of a Council" held Apr. 21, 1857; from LR, Otoe Agency, 1856–60.

57. See the *Nebraska Advertiser* (Brownville), Nov. 29, 1856 and Apr. 20, 1857; *The Nebraskian* (Omaha), Nov. 25, 1856; and the *Bellevue Gazette*, Apr. 16 and Oct. 22, 1857. The Davis incident is detailed in Dennison to Cuming, May 5, 1857, LR, Otoe Agency, 1856–60.

58. "Proceedings of a Council," in Dennison to Cuming, May 5, 1857, LR, Otoe Agency, 1856–60. For breakdown of annuities, see DePuy to Dole, Nov. 20, 1861, LR, Pawnee Agency, 1859–62. On the Pawnee's reluctance to move back to the Loup, see Robinson, "Report," *ARCIA, 1859*, 112–15.

59. Dennison, "Report," *ARCIA, 1858*, 102–4, and Dennison to William West (territorial marshall), Nov. 1, 1858, LR, Otoe Agency, 1856–60.

60. Sterling Morton to President James Buchanan, July 7, 1859; P. F. Wilson to Buchanan, July 7, 1859, and Gillis to Alfred B. Greenwood, Feb. 6, 1860, all in LR, Pawnee Agency, 1859–62.

61. Dennison to Henry Hudson (secretary of the Genoa Agricultural Association), Feb. 16, 1859, LR, Otoe Agency, 1856–60, and B. D. Holbrook to Gillis, Nov. 18, 1859, LR, Pawnee Agency, 1859–62. Holbrook was the surveyor of the reservation.

62. DePuy to Branch, July 30, 1861, LR, Pawnee Agency, 1859–62.

63. Gillis to Greenwood, June 22, July 5, July 12, Sept. 1, and Sept. 13, 1860, and Gillis to Robinson, Oct. 25, 1860, LR, Pawnee Agency, 1859–62. See also, Gillis, "Report," *ARCIA, 1860*, 92–95.

64. DePuy to Dole, July 5, 10, and Dec. 29, 1861, LR, Pawnee Agency, 1859–62.

65. R. B. Gillis (agency farmer), "Report," *ARCIA, 1860*, 95.

66. Gillis, "Report," *ARCIA, 1860*, 92–95, and DePuy to Dole, Nov. 20, 1861, LR, Pawnee Agency, 1859–62.

67. David Collins to Dole, Oct. 29, 1861; DePuy to Branch, Nov. 23, 1861; Branch to Dole, Apr. 18, 1862, LR, Pawnee Agency, 1859–62.

68. Robertson to Cuming, May 22, 1857, LR, Omaha Agency, 1856–63.

69. Robertson to Mix, Mar. 14, 1858, LR, Omaha Agency, 1856–63.

70. Robertson to Cuming, May 22, 1857; R. R. Cowan to B. B. Chapman, June 9, 1857; and "Petition" to Denver, June 30, 1857, all in LR, Omaha Agency, 1856–63. See also, Howard, "Known Village Sites of the Ponca" 123–24.

71. Manypenny, "Report," *ARCIA, 1855*, 5; Redfield, "Report"; and Robertson, "Report," *ARCIA, 1857*, 149–50.

72. *Documents Relating to the Negotiation of Ratified and Unratified Treaties with the Indians*, Ratified Treaty, no. 306, R6.

73. Robinson to Mix, Mar. 14, 1858, LR, Omaha Agency, 1856–63.

74. Gregory to Wilson, July 20, 1858, and Gregory to Mix, Mar. 23, 1859, LR, Omaha Agency, 1856–63.

75. Gregory to Mix, Mar. 23, 1859, LR, Omaha Agency, 1856–63.

76. Gregory to Mix, Aug. 27, 1859, and Gregory to Greenwood, Mar. 27, 1860, LR, Ponca Agency, 1859–63.

77. "Speech by Wah-ga-sap-pi (The Whip)," in Gregory to Mix, Aug. 27, 1859, LR, Ponca Agency, 1859–63.

78. Gregory to Mix, Sept. 15, 1859; Gregory to Robinson, Jan. 3, 1860; and Sergeant John Munroe, Order 161, Sept. 23, 1859, LR, Ponca Agency, 1859–63.

79. Stone's report and Gregory's reaction are in Gregory to Robinson, July 3, 1860, LR, Ponca Agency, 1859–63.

80. "Minutes of a Council, Feb. 3, 1860," in Gregory to Greenwood, Apr. 10, 1860, LR, Ponca Agency, 1859–63.

81. Gregory to Robinson, June 26, 1860, LR, Ponca Agency, 1859–63.

82. Joshua Hoffman to Branch, June 11, 1861, LR, Ponca Agency, 1859–63.

83. Gregory to Robinson, Nov. 15, 1860, LR, Ponca Agency, 1859–63.

84. "Minutes of a Council, Nov. 29, 1860," in Gregory to Robinson, Dec. 5, 1860, LR, Ponca Agency, 1859–63.

85. Hoffman to Branch, June 11, 1861, LR, Ponca Agency, 1859–63.

86. Hoffman to Branch, July 17, 1861, and Hoffman to Mix, Oct. 1, 1861, LR, Ponca Agency, 1859–63.

87. "Census Roll, July 6, 1860," in Gregory to Mix, Aug. 25, 1860, and "Statistical Report, June 30, 1861," LR, Ponca Agency, 1859–63.

Chapter 5. Life on the Reservations

1. Mix, "Report," *ARCIA, 1867,* 1.

2. Allis, *Manuscript* 58.

3. Parker, "Report," *ARCIA, 1869,* 4–5. The vaunted "Peace-Policy," which was initiated during the term of Commissioner Nathaniel Green Taylor (1867–69) under the influence of humanitarian reformers, was only a more enlightened version of the old reservation idea. The principal components of the policy were education, allotments, and concentration of the Indians within a single "large reservation" (in practice, Indian Territory) until the individualization process could be completed. The Quakers were part of this policy but were not always in agreement with it, particularly over the question of removal. See Prucha, *The Great Father,* vol. 1, 479–606 and the annual reports of the commissioners of Indian affairs from 1868 through the 1870s.

4. *Report of the Joint Delegation of Baltimore, Philadelphia and New York Annual Meetings in their Visit to the Northern Superintendency, 7th and 8th Months, 1869* (Baltimore: J. Jones, 1869) 34; Clyde A. Milner II, *With Good Intentions: Quaker Work Among the Pawnees, Otoes, and Omahas in the 1870s* (Lincoln: University of Nebraska Press, 1982).

5. Sheldon, *Land Systems and Land Policies in Nebraska* 75–93 and S. J. Bellovich, *A Geographic Appraisal of Settlement within the Union Pacific Land Grant in Eastern Nebraska, 1869–1890,* diss. University of Nebraska, 1974.

6. *ARCIA, 1863,* 3–4; *ARCIA, 1867,* 19–20; *ARCIA, 1868,* 2; Kvasnicka and Viola, eds., *The Commissioners of Indian Affairs, 1824–1977,* 89–133.

7. *The Congressional Globe,* 41st Congress, 2nd Sess. (1870), 4080–81.

8. There is a brief biography of Turner in Margaret Curry, *The History of Platte County, Nebraska* (Culver City, California: Murray and Gee, 1950) 920.

9. Hoffman to Dole, Nov. 1, 1862, LR, Ponca Agency, 1859–63.

10. The Whip, "Council Speech, Aug. 31, 1865," in Joint Special Committee, *Condition of the Indian Tribes* (Washington, D.C.: Government Printing Office, 1867) 400–401; Hoffman, "Report," ARCIA, *1862,* 181–89.

11. Hoffman to Jayne, Sept. 18, 1862, LR, Ponca Agency, 1859–63; Potter, "Report," ARCIA, *1865,* 216–17.

12. Hoffman, "Report," ARCIA, *1864,* 265–69.

13. Hoffman, "Report," ARCIA, *1862,* 181–89 and "Statistical Table," ARCIA, *1865,* 580–84.

14. Dole, "Report," ARCIA, *1864,* 37 and Edmunds to Dole, Jan. 28, 1865, LR, Ponca Agency, 1864–70.

15. Kappler, *Indian Affairs,* vol. 2, 875–76; Faulk to Mix, Oct. 15, 1867, LR, Ponca Agency, 1864–70.

16. The agency and village were in section 21 of township 33 north, range 7 west. This was close to the sites of known historical Ponca villages, including Farming Ground village, Húbdon (Fish-Smell) village, and Kúhe-wadè (Scary Creek) village. The smaller Ponca village in 1869 may have been at the site of Wáin-xúde (Grey Blanket) village. All of these villages were within a few miles of each other. See Howard, "Known Village Sites of the Ponca" 110–11, 123–26.

17. Potter, "Report," ARCIA, *1866,* 186–87; Potter to Cooley, Jan. 8 and Sept. 30, 1866, LR, Ponca Agency, 1864–70.

18. Hugo, "Report," ARCIA, *1869,* 309–11; Potter to Faulk, Jan. 23, 1869, LR, Ponca Agency, 1864–70.

19. Hugo to Parker, Nov. 13, 1869, LR, Ponca Agency, 1864–70 and Hugo, "Report," ARCIA, *1870,* 216–17.

20. Standing Buffalo, "Council Speech, Aug. 9, 1870," in Burbank to Parker, Aug. 13, 1870, LR, Ponca Agency, 1864–70.

21. Burbank to Parker, June 27, 1870, LR, Ponca Agency, 1864–70.

22. "Minutes of a Council, Jan. 13, 1870," LR, Ponca Agency, 1864–70; Burbank to Parker, Sept. 9, 1870, LR, Ponca Agency, 1864–70.

23. Hoffman to Jayne, Apr. 26, 1862, and Hoffman to Hutchinson, Sept. 10, 1863, LR, Ponca Agency, 1859–63.

24. Hoffman to Jayne, Sept. 18 and Nov. 17, 1862, LR, Ponca Agency, 1859–63; Hoffman to Edmunds, July 11, 1864, LR, Ponca Agency, 1864–70.

25. Edmunds to Dole, June 23, 1864, LR, Ponca Agency, 1864–70.

26. Hoffman, "Report," ARCIA, *1864,* 265–69. Helen Hunt Jackson used Hoffman's report to convey the story to a much wider audience in her chapter on the Ponca in her influential book, *A Century of Dishonor* (Boston: Roberts Brothers, 1885) 193–94. Hoffman went into even greater detail in a letter to Governor Newton Edmunds, dated Dec. 27, 1864, which includes statements by Indians who witnessed

the atrocity (LR, Ponca Agency, 1864–70). Huddleston's farm was in section 15 of township 32 north, range 6 west.

27. Edmunds to McKean, Jan. 11, 1864, LR, Ponca Agency, 1864–70; Joint Special Committee, *Condition of the Indian Tribes* 401; J. M. Rubles, *ARCIA, 1862*, 191–92.

28. Edmunds to Dole, Jan. 11, 1864; McKean to Edmunds, Jan. 13, 1864; and Hoffman to Edmunds, Apr. 11, 1864, all in LR, Ponca Agency, 1864–70. Also, Cooley, "Report," *ARCIA, 1865*, 26.

29. Kappler, *Indian Affairs*, vol. 2, 998–1007 and Royce, *Indian Land Cessions* 848–49 and plate cxviii.

30. Callon, "Report," *ARCIA, 1868*, 240–41.

31. Furnas to Taylor, Dec. 15, 1865, LR, Omaha Agency, 1864–70; Furnas, "Report," *ARCIA, 1865*, 403–5; Burtt to Lowrie, Nov. 7, 1863, *Omaha Mission School Letters*; Irish to Branch, Sept. 13, 1862, LR, Omaha Agency, 1856–63; and Callon to Denman, June 30, 1868, LR, Omaha Agency, 1864–70.

32. Painter to Janney, Aug. 16, 1869, LR, Omaha Agency, 1864–70; Callon to Denman, Dec. 17, 1867, LR, Northern Superintendency, 1867.

33. Furnas submitted a detailed map of his defense plan to Superintendent Albin on October 25, 1864 (LR, Omaha Agency, 1864–70); for a good description of conditions on the reservation in the late 1860s, see Hamilton to Lowrie, Feb. 1, 1868, *Presbyterian Missionary Letters*, n. pag.

34. Furnas to Taylor, Oct. 24, 1865, LR, Omaha Agency, 1864–70, Furnas to Dole, June 21, 1865, LR, Omaha Agency, 1864–70; Painter to Janney, July 7, 1870, LR, Northern Superintendency, 1870–71.

35. Irish to Branch, Sept. 11, Sept. 24, and Oct. 5, 1863, LR, Omaha Agency, 1856–63.

36. Furnas to Albin, July 28, 1864, LR, Omaha Agency, 1864–70; Furnas, "Report," *ARCIA, 1864*, 355–56; Burtt to Lowrie, June 21, 1864, *Presbyterian Missionary Letters*, n. pag.

37. Furnas, "Report," *ARCIA, 1866*, 215; Omaha Chiefs "Petition," Aug. 28, 1866," LR, Omaha Agency, 1864–70; Donald F. Danker, ed., *Man of the Plains: Recollections of Luther North, 1856–1882* (Lincoln: University of Nebraska Press, 1961) 278–79.

38. Furnas, "Report," *ARCIA, 1864*, 349–52.

39. Painter to Janney, May 17, Oct. 14, 21, and 31, 1870, LR, Omaha Agency, 1864–70.

40. Callon to Denman, Mar. 1, 1869, LR, Omaha Agency, 1864–70. Agricultural output is detailed in the agents' reports and in the tables at the end of each volume of the annual reports of the commissioner of Indian affairs.

41. Callon to Denman, Dec. 2, 1867 and Omaha chiefs, "Petition," Aug. 28, 1866, LR, Omaha Agency, 1864–70.

42. Furnas to Taylor, Dec. 3, 1865, LR, Omaha Agency, 1864–70; Furnas, "Report," *ARCIA, 1864*, 349–52; Callon to Denman, June 30, 1868, LR, Omaha Agency, 1864–70.

43. Furnas to Dole, May 3, 1864, LR, Omaha Agency, 1864–70; La Flesche to Graff, Apr. 30, 1864, in *Furnas Papers, 1844–1905* (Lincoln: Nebraska State Historical Society).

44. Kappler, *Indian Affairs*, vol. 2, 872–73; Furnas, "Memoranda on Trip to Wash-

ington, February–March 1865," *Furnas Papers*, n. pag.; Robert C. Farb, "Robert W. Furnas as Omaha Indian Agent, 1864–1866," *Nebraska History* 32.3 (1951): 186–203, and 32.4 (1951): 268–83; Callon to Denman, May 9, 1868, and Denman to Mix, May 27, 1868, LR, Omaha Agency, 1864–70.

45. Denman to Bogey, Feb. 4, 1867; Furnas to Taylor, Sept. 28, 1866; Doane to Bogey, Nov. 19, 1866, LR, Omaha Agency, 1864–70.

46. Callon, "Report," *ARCIA, 1868*, 240–41; Ellick to Mix, Oct. 14, 1867, and Denman to Bogey, Feb. 4, 1867, LR, Omaha Agency, 1864–70.

47. Denman to Mix, Sept. 14, 1867, LR, Omaha Agency, 1864–70.

48. Omaha chiefs, "Petition," Feb. 8, 1868, LR, Omaha Agency, 1864–70; Denman, "Report," *ARCIA, 1868*, 225–31.

49. Painter to Janney, Aug. 16, 1870 and Omaha chiefs "Petition," Nov. 8, 1870, LR, Omaha Agency, 1864–70; Omaha chiefs "Petition," May 17, 1870; Painter to Janney, June 23 and Oct. 31, 1870, LR, Northern Superintendency, 1870–71.

50. Irish to Branch, Oct. 5, 1863, LR, Omaha Agency, 1856–63 and Irish "Report," *ARCIA, 1863*, 240–42; Dorsey, *Omaha Sociology* 358.

51. Furnas to Albin, Jan. 15, 1865, LR, Omaha Agency, 1864–70; Furnas to Harlan, Aug. 14, 1865, LR, Omaha Agency, 1864–70.

52. Furnas to La Flesche, June 3, 1864, Dole to Furnas, June 16, 1864, Cooley to Taylor, Apr. 4, 1866, all in *Furnas Papers*, n. pag. Callon to Denman, June 30, 1868, Furnas to Lowry, June 29, 1866, and Burtt to Lowrie, April 16, 1866, all in *Presbyterian Missionary Letters*, n. pag., and Furnas to Taylor, Dec. 3, 1865, Feb. 28, 1866, and Sept. 28, 1866, in LR, Omaha Agency, 1864–70.

53. Fletcher and La Flesche, *The Omaha Tribe*, vol. 1, 244. See also vol. 2, 481 and 486–87.

54. Painter to Janney, Sept. 16, 1870, LR, Northern Superintendency, 1870–71; Fletcher and La Flesche, *The Omaha Tribe*, vol. 2, 480–87.

55. Cooley, "Report," *ARCIA, 1866*, 43; Mix, "Report," *ARCIA, 1867*, 19; Janney, "Report," *ARCIA, 1869*, 337–38.

56. Baker to Dole, Nov. 20 and 28, 1862, LR, Otoe Agency, 1861–67, Green to Janney, June 30, 1869, LR, Otoe Agency, 1868–71. Other statistics are from the tables at the end of each *ARCIA* from 1862 to 1870.

57. Smith to Denman, Apr. 27, 1867 and Aug. 11, 1868; Janney to Parker, June 5, 1869, LR, Otoe Agency, 1868–71.

58. Population figures are from the agents' reports for each year, *ARCIA, 1864–70*; also, Janney to Parker, June 5, 1869, LR, Otoe Agency, 1868–71. There were an estimated eighty Missouria among the Otoe in 1869.

59. For example, Denman to Taylor, June 12, 1868, LR, Otoe Agency, 1868–71.

60. Green to "Dear Ones at Home," June 12 and July 1, 1869, in *Green Papers*, n. pag.

61. Baker to Branch, May 1, 1861; Gregory to Robinson, Mar. 13, 1861; Branch to Dole, Aug. 1, 1861; and "Petition," Otoe-Missouria chiefs, Jan. 12, 1861, all in LR, Otoe Agency, 1861–67.

62. "Petition," Otoe-Missouria chiefs, June 11, 1861, and Baker to Dole, Jan. 6, 1863, LR, Otoe Agency 1861–67.

63. "Petition," Otoe-Missouria chiefs, Mar. 17, 1865; Daily to Dole, July 25, 1864; and Harlan to Cooley, Jan. 2, 1866, all in LR, Otoe Agency, 1861–67.

64. Smith to Denman, Feb. 1, 1867, LR, Otoe Agency, 1861–67.

65. Baker to Dole, Sept. 6, 1862; Daily to Dole, July 25, 1864; "Petition," Otoe-Missouria chiefs, Mar. 17, 1865; Denman to Taylor, Apr. 27, 1867, all in LR, Otoe Agency, 1861–67.

66. "Petition," Otoe-Missouria chiefs, Mar. 22, 1871, and Green to Janney, Mar. 23, 1871, LR, Otoe Agency, 1868–71.

67. Yasudo Okada, *Public Lands and Pioneer Farmers: Gage County, Nebraska* (Tokyo: Keio Economic Society, 1971), especially figure 1, page 17; Richard D. Brown, "The Agricultural Land Grant in Kansas—Selection and Disposal," *Agricultural History* 37.2 (1963): 94–102.

68. Denman to Taylor, June 12, 1868, LR, Otoe Agency, 1868–71.

69. Green to Janney, July 8, 1869; Denman to Taylor, June 12, 1868; Green to Janney, Apr. 13, 1870, all in LR, Otoe Agency, 1868–71.

70. Smith to Denman, Feb. 1, 1867 and Denman to Taylor, Apr. 27, 1867, LR, Otoe Agency, 1861–67; Smith to Denman, Dec. 31, 1867 and Denman to Taylor, June 12, 1868, LR, Otoe Agency, 1868–71. See also, Smith, "Report," ARCIA, 1867, 271–72 and 342–45. It should be noted that the Otoe-Missouria knowledgeably referred back to Article 6 of the 1854 treaty in insisting that any land sales would come from the west of the Big Blue and that any allotments would be taken to the east of that river. See Kappler, *Indian Affairs*, vol. 2, 609.

71. "Treaty Between the United States and the Otoe and Missouria Tribe of Indians, Feb. 13, 1869," in *Documents Relating to the Negotiations of Ratified and Unratified Treaties with the Various Indian Tribes*, R10. Also, Chapman, *The Otoes and Missourias* 84–92.

72. "Petition," Otoe-Missouria chiefs, Feb. 3, 1870, and Janney to Parker, Feb. 5, 1870, LR, Otoe Agency, 1868–71.

73. Green to Janney, Sept. 6, 1871, LR, Otoe Agency, 1868–71 and Benjamin Hallowell, "Views of the Delegation of the Friends," Oct. 30, 1869, in ARCIA, 1869, 119–20.

74. This overview of Otoe-Missouria life in 1869–70 is drawn from the *Green Papers*, especially "Reminiscences, Remembrances, Observations, and Occurrences that may have some Historical Value to a future History of Gage County," and "Therapeutics Among the Otoes." See also, "Narrative of Major Albert Lamborn Green," in Dobbs, *History of Gage County* 89–110.

75. Dennison to Greenwood, June 22, 1860, LR, Otoe Agency, 1856–60.

76. Lushbaugh, "Report," ARCIA, 1862, 122–24.

77. Branch to Dole, Apr. 18, 1862, LR, Pawnee Agency, 1859–62.

78. This section on population change and living conditions is drawn from agents' reports to the commissioner of Indian affairs for each year from 1862 to 1870 and from letters sent from the agency.

79. Lushbaugh to Albin, Sept. 30, 1864, LR, Pawnee Agency, 1863–69.

80. Wheeler to Taylor, Sept. 15, 1865, LR, Pawnee Agency, 1863–69 and Lushbaugh to Dole, Jan. 13, 1863, LR, Pawnee Agency, 1863–69. It might be noted that the Pawnee still receive their perpetual annuity, which in 1990 amounted to about twenty dollars per person. This is noted in Martha Royce Blaine, *Pawnee Passage, 1870–1875* (Norman: University of Oklahoma Press, 1990) 201.

81. *The Platte Journal* (Columbus), July 6, 1870; Wheeler to Taylor, Sept. 15, 1866, LR, Pawnee Agency, 1863–69.

82. Whaley to Denman, July 6, 1867.

83. Lushbaugh, "Report," ARCIA, 1863, 247.

84. Taylor to Mix, Aug. 10, 1866; Wheeler to Mix, Sept. 16, 1866, LR, Pawnee Agency, 1863–69.

85. John Williamson, "History of the Pawnee Indians," in *Williamson Papers* (Lincoln: Nebraska State Historical Society) ms. 2710; Whaley to Denman, June 26, 1867, LR, Northern Superintendency, 1867; *Report of the Joint Delegation* 7–8. Archaeologists Wedel (*An Introduction to Pawnee Archaeology* 29) and Grange (*Pawnee and Lower Loup Pottery* 21–22) maintain that there was only one village, with the Skiri occupying the western neighborhood and the other three bands the remainder, but the Quakers noted two villages separated by a mile. On the general continuance of traditional Pawnee life, see Weltfish's vivid recreation of a hypothetical year in the late 1860s in *The Lost Universe*.

86. Wheeler to Taylor, Sept. 15, 1865, and Wheeler to Turner, Dec. 16, 1865, LR, Pawnee Agency, 1863–69; Platt, "Reports," ARCIA, 1862, 124, ARCIA, 1863, 249–50, ARCIA, 1868, 236–37, and ARCIA, 1869, 351–53; Maxfield, "Reports," ARCIA, 1864, 383–84 and ARCIA, 1865, 423–25; Denman, "Report," ARCIA, 1868, 249; Janney, "Report," ARCIA, 1870, 227–33; Blaine, *Pawnee Passage* 163–69.

87. Lushbaugh to Dole, June 24, 1863, Whaley to Albin, Sept. 26, 1864, Janney to Parker, Sept. 28, 1869, all in LR, Pawnee Agency, 1863–69; Wheeler, "Report," ARCIA, 1865, 420–23.

88. Lushbaugh to Dole, Apr. 1, 1863, LR, Pawnee Agency, 1863–69 and Troth, "Report," ARCIA, 1870, 242–44; James Mead, *Hunting and Trading on the Great Plains, 1859–1875* (Norman: University of Oklahoma Press, 1986) 182–91. Ed. Schuyler Jones.

89. Taylor to Mix, Aug. 10, 1866, LR, Pawnee Agency, 1863–69 and O. G. Hammond to adjutant general, June 27, 1870, LR, Pawnee Agency, 1870–72; Thomas W. Dunlay, *Wolves For the Blue Soldiers: Indian Scouts and Auxiliaries with the United States Army, 1860–90* (Lincoln: University of Nebraska Press, 1982) especially 147–64.

90. Janney to Parker, June 22, 1870 and Feb. 17, 1870, LR, Pawnee Agency, 1870–72.

91. It is worth noting that by the terms of the 1868 Treaty of Fort Laramie, the eight bands of the Teton Dakota and the Yankton, Yanktonai, Santee, Cheyenne, and Arapahoe had been given explicit permission to hunt in these areas "so long as the buffalo may range in such numbers as to justify the chase." Kappler, *Indian Affairs,* vol. 2, 998–1007, 1012–15 (quote from 1002).

92. The Brulé numbered about sixteen hundred in 1867–68, according to official statistics (*ARCIA, 1867,* 352), but other estimates indicate a much higher population, and in any case they often amalgamated with other Dakota to raid the Pawnee. Other figures are given in John C. Ewers, *Teton Dakota: Ethnology and History* (Berkeley: National Parks Service, 1938) iv.

93. Lushbaugh to Dole, Jan. 19 and June 2, 1863, Lushbaugh to Albin, Sept. 30, 1864, Albin to Dole, June 15, 1865, Lushbaugh to Dole, Feb. 11, 1865, Wheeler to Taylor, Sept. 15, 1865 and July 6, 1866, all in LR, Pawnee Agency, 1863–69. See also, Whaley to Denman, June 22, 1867, LR, Northern Superintendency, 1867.

94. Troth to Janney, July 30, 1870, LR, Northern Superintendency, 1870.

95. Janney, "Report," *ARCIA, 1870,* 227–33 and Troth to Janney, Oct. 6, 1870, LR, Pawnee Agency, 1870–72.

96. Denman to Taylor, Feb. 19, 1869, LR, Pawnee Agency, 1863–69.

97. Whaley to Denman, Mar. 22, 1869, LR, Pawnee Agency, 1863–69; James Riding In, "Six Pawnee Crania: Historical and Contemporary Issues Associated with the Massacre and Decapitation of Pawnee Indians in 1869," *American Indian Culture and Research Journal* 16.2 (1992): 101–20.

98. "Proceedings of the United States District Court in the McMurty Murder Case, Nov. 5, 6, 1869," LR, Pawnee Agency, 1870–72; Janney to Parker, July 4, 5, and 15, Aug. 3, Sept. 1, and Nov. 10, 1869, all in LR, Pawnee Agency, 1863–69; Janney to Parker, May 19 and Nov. 1, 1870, LR, Pawnee Agency, 1870–72. Blaine, in *Pawnee Passage* 17–23, also pays considerable attention to the McMurty case. McMurty's eighty-acre homestead was in section 22 township 16 north, range 1 west of the 6th principal meridian.

99. The jurisdictional dispute centered around whether crimes supposedly committed by Indians off the reservation should be tried by federal authorities (as were any reservation matters) or by state authorities. On May 4, 1870, the decision was made that the U.S. district court had no authority in the case. See the discussion, sympathetic to the Indians, in the *Omaha Daily Herald,* May 5, 1870.

100. Danker, *Man of the Plains* 129–30.

101. Troth to Janney, May 31 and June 30, 1870.

102. Pa:haku was homesteaded by a Mr. William McCowin.

Chapter 6. Hemmed In and Forced Out

1. Hayt, "Report," *ARCIA, 1879,* iii.

2. Charles B. McIntosh, "Use and Abuse of the Timber Culture Act," *Annals, Association of American Geographers* 65.3 (1975): 347–62.

3. David Butler, *Biennial Message to the Legislature of Nebraska 1871* (Des Moines: Mills & Co., 1871) 23–24 and Robert W. Furnas, *Inaugural Address* (Lincoln: Journal Co., 1873) 13–14.

4. Walker, "Report," *ARCIA, 1872,* 4.

5. The population statistics for each year are found in the annual reports of the

commissioner of Indian affairs, both in the superintendents' and agents' reports, or in the statistical tables. For the raid on the Cheyenne, see *Proceedings of the Council,* Nov. 1 and Nov. 15, 1871.

6. Burgess to White, White to Smith, and Williamson to Burgess, Aug. 9, 11, and 12, 1873, LR, Pawnee Agency, 1873; Blaine, *Pawnee Exodus* 134–39 and P. D. Riley, "The Battle of Massacre Canyon," *Nebraska History* 54 (1973): 221–50.

7. *Proceedings of the Council,* Feb. 2, 1874; ARCIA, *1876,* 290; Blaine, "Interview," KUON-TV, Lincoln, Nebraska, Oct. 1977.

8. White to Clum, Oct. 27, 1871, LR, Pawnee Agency, 1870–72 and *Proceedings of the Council,* Oct. 18, 1873.

9. Estes to Howard, Aug. 6, 1873, LR, Pawnee Agency, 1873; Clum to White, Dec. 2, 1873, LR, Pawnee Agency, 1873.

10. Troth, "Report," ARCIA, *1871,* 651–53; Janney to Parker, May 3, 1871, LR, Pawnee Agency 1870–72; Walker, "Report" and Troth, "Report," ARCIA, *1872,* 28, 221–24; Drummond to Smith, Sept. 5, 1873, LR, Pawnee Agency, 1873.

11. *Proceedings of the Council,* Mar. 27, 1871 and Apr. 20, 1871; Janney to Parker, Feb. 23, 1871, LR, Pawnee Agency, 1870–72.

12. *The Platte Journal,* Jan. 10, 1872.

13. Troth to Janney, Oct. 29, 1872, White to Walker, Nov. 2, 1872, and White to Smith, June 11, 1873, all in LR, Pawnee Agency, 1870–72.

14. I. N. Taylor, *History of Platte County, Nebraska* (Columbus: Columbus Republican Print, 1876) 6; *The Platte Journal,* July 6, 1870.

15. *The Platte Journal,* Sept. 2, 1874.

16. Jane G. Swisshelm, *The Platte Journal,* Sept. 10, 1873.

17. "Petition," Settlers of Platte County, Mar. 29, 1873 and W. J. Haddock, special agent, "Investigation of Charges against W. Burgess," May 20, 1873, LR, Pawnee Agency, 1873.

18. Lester Platt, husband of Pawnee teacher Elvira Platt, and Delane Willard ran trading posts just off the eastern edge of the reservation.

19. *Proceedings of the Council,* Oct. 8, 1874, and Burgess, "Report," ARCIA, *1875,* 322.

20. W. F. Schmidt, ed., "The Letters of Charles and Helen Wooster: The Problems of Settlement," *Nebraska History* 46 (1965): 121–38 and D. K. Watkins, ed., "A Dane's Views on Frontier Culture: Notes on a Stay in the United States," *Nebraska History* 55 (1974): 265–89.

21. Troth to White, Nov. 2, 1872, and White to Walker, Nov. 11, 1872 and Dec. 26, 1872, LR, Pawnee Agency, 1870–72.

22. Burgess to White, Jan. 9, 1874, and White to Smith, Jan. 12, 1874, LR, Pawnee Agency, 1874–75.

23. *The Platte Journal,* Jan. 28, 1874. Also, White to Smith, Dec. 18, 1874, LR, Pawnee Agency, 1874–75.

24. *Proceedings of the Council,* Oct. 16, 1871, and Sept. 27, 1872; White to Clum, Oct. 27, 1871, LR, Pawnee Agency, 1870–72.

25. Troth to White, July 18, 1872, LR, Pawnee Agency, 1870–72 and *Proceedings of the Council,* Feb. 15, 1873.

26. *Proceedings of the Council,* June 8, 1872, June 14, 1873, and Oct. 6, 1873.

27. *Proceedings of the Council,* May 2, June 14, Oct. 6, 1873; White, "Report," ARCIA, *1872,* 214.

28. *Proceedings of the Council,* Oct. 18, 1873.

29. *Proceedings of the Council,* June 1, 1871.

30. *Proceedings of the Council,* July 7, 1871.

31. Pe-ta-na-sharo, "Speech," in White to Clum, Feb. 22, 1873, LR, Pawnee Agency, 1873.

32. *Proceedings of the Council,* Jan. 1 and 24, 1873.

33. White, "Report," ARCIA, *1873,* 187 and White to Clum, Feb. 22, 1873, LR, Pawnee Agency, 1873.

34. Troth, "Report"; White, "Report," ARCIA, *1873,* 651–53; and ARCIA, *1872,* 212–17 and 221–24. The Dakota tried to raid in the spring of 1872, but the first party went out too early and their horses could not be subsisted all the way to the Pawnee reservation. The second raiding party was diverted from the Pawnee by the cavalry, so they struck the Ponca instead, killing a leading doctor.

35. White to Clum, Feb. 22, 1873, LR, Pawnee Agency, 1873.

36. White to Smith, July 28, 1873, LR, Pawnee Agency, 1873.

37. Grinnell, *Pawnee Hero Stories and Folk Tales* 389–97; also, White, "Report," ARCIA, *1874,* 199–202.

38. *Proceedings of the Council,* Oct. 18, 1873; Burgess to White, Oct. 30 and White to Smith, Nov. 1, 1873, LR, Pawnee Agency, 1873.

39. Burgess to White, Oct. 30, 1873, LR, Pawnee Agency, 1873 and *Proceedings of the Council,* Mar. 16, 1874.

40. Burgess, "Report," ARCIA, *1874,* 207–8, and Williamson, "The Moving of the Pawnee," *Williamson Papers* 40.

41. "Petition," Pawnee chiefs, Aug. 21, 1874, and Burgess to White, Sept. 15, 1874, LR, Pawnee Agency, 1874–75.

42. Williamson, "Autobiography," *Williamson Papers,* n. pag.

43. *Proceedings of the Council,* Oct. 8, 1874; Burgess, "Report," ARCIA, *1875,* 321–22; White to Smith, Oct. 9, 1874, LR, Pawnee Agency, 1874–75; and *The Columbus Journal,* Nov. 18, 1874.

44. "Petition," Pawnee chiefs, Aug. 21, 1874, LR, Pawnee Agency, 1874–75.

45. Williamson, "The Moving of the Pawnee," *Williamson Papers;* Burgess, "Report" and White, "Report," ARCIA, *1875,* 311–14 and 321–22; *Proceedings of the Council,* Nov. 1, 1874, and Mar. 18, 1875; White to Smith, Oct. 9, 1874, LR, Pawnee Agency, 1874–75; Blaine, *Pawnee Passage* 214–92.

46. Kappler, *Indian Affairs,* vol. 1, 159–61.

47. *Proceedings of the Council,* Nov. 1, 1874.

48. Burgess, "Report," ARCIA, *1875,* 321–22.

49. Scott, "Report," ARCIA, *1885,* 94.

50. Murie, *Ceremonies of the Pawnee* 21, 107, 111.

51. Grinnell, *Pawnee Hero Stories and Folk Tales* 360–61.

52. Woolsey, "Report," ARCIA, *1894*, 248; Kappler, *Indian Affairs*, vol. 1, 496–98; 56 Ct. Cl., 1920–21, 1–15, whereby the Pawnee were awarded the original total ($132,916.71) plus interest at five percent a year from 1893 to 1920, for an award of $325,777.03.

53. Historical population figures are from the annual reports of the commissioner of Indian affairs. It should be cautioned, however, that twentieth-century population totals reflect not only natural increase, but also legal definitions of who constitutes an Indian. Definitions vary from tribe to tribe.

54. Kappler, *Indian Affairs*, vol. 1, 159–61; Sheldon, *Land Systems* 204–7, 332; Stephen L. Egbert, *The Resettlement of Nance County: Land Alienation Patterns, 1878–1913*, Unpublished master's thesis, University of Nebraska-Lincoln, 1983.

55. *Proceedings of the Council*, Mar. 18 and 22, 1878; Grinnell, *Pawnee Hero Stories and Folk Tales* 401; "Statement of Trust Funds," ARCIA, *1889*, 53.

56. Charles P. Birkett, "Report," ARCIA, *1873*, 239–43; Birkett to Smith, Nov. 19, 1874, LR, Ponca Agency, 1874–75; and Fletcher and La Flesche, *The Omaha Tribe*, vol. 1, 51.

57. J. Orwen Dorsey, "Ponka Mission," May 6, 1872, and Martin E. Hogan to William Welsh, Aug. 30, 1872, LR, Ponca Agency, 1871–73.

58. The environmental disasters are noted in every annual report; see, for example, Birkett, "Report," ARCIA, *1873*, 239–43.

59. Birkett, "Report," ARCIA, *1873*, 243; Birkett to Smith, Sept. 2, 1873, LR, Ponca Agency, 1871–73.

60. Gregory to Parker, Dec. 23, 1870 and Dorsey, "Ponka Mission," May 6, 1872, LR, Ponca Agency, 1871–73; James Lawrence, "Report," ARCIA, *1875*, 32.

61. Birkett to Smith, June 9, 1873, LR, Ponca Agency, 1871–73 and Birkett, "Report," ARCIA, *1873*, 239–43.

62. A. J. Carrier, "Report," ARCIA, *1875*, 248–50; Dorsey, "Ponka Mission," May 6, 1872; Birkett to Smith, Jan. 13, 1873; and Capt. C. A. Webb to Birkett, Aug. 10, 1873, all in LR, Ponca Agency, 1871–73.

63. "Petition," Ponca chiefs, in Alfred L. Riggs to Joseph Webster, Sept. 19, 1871, LR, Ponca Agency, 1871–73.

64. Carrier, "Report," ARCIA, *1875*, 248–50 and Carrier to Smith, June 18 and Nov. 11, 1875, LR, Ponca Agency, 1874–75.

65. "Statistics Relating to Population," ARCIA, *1876*, 208–14; Birkett to Smith, Sept. 2, 1873, LR, Ponca Agency, 1871–73.

66. "Petition," citizens of Verdigre Creek to secretary of war, Mar. 9, 1872, LR, Ponca Agency, 1871–73 and Birkett to U.S. Marshall Burdick, Mar. 12, 1874, LR, Ponca Agency, 1874–75.

67. Birkett to Smith, Nov. 3, 1873, LR, Ponca Agency, 1871–73; E. P. Smith, "Report," ARCIA, *1874*, 47–48; "Report," ARCIA, *1875*, 24; and J. Q. Smith, "Report," ARCIA, *1876*, xvi–xvii. Kappler, *Indian Affairs*, vol. 1, 166–67.

68. Carrier to Smith, Feb. 5, June 18, and Nov. 17, 1875, LR, Ponca Agency 1874–75.

69. "Petition," Ponca chiefs, Sept. 23, 1875, LR, Ponca Agency, 1874–75 and James Lawrence to J. Q. Smith, Aug. 26, 1876, LR, Ponca Agency, 1876–77.

70. William Whiteman, "Report," ARCIA, 1879, 72–75; Sen. Rep. 610, 46th Cong., 3rd Sess. (1879–80), SN1898; "Removal and Situation of the Ponca Indians," Misc. Doc. 49, 46th Cong., 3rd Sess. (1880), SN1944; and "Report of the Commission to Ascertain the Fact in Regard to the Removal of the Ponca Indians," Ex. Doc. 30, 46th Cong., 3rd Sess. (1881) SN1941.

71. This, and the following quotations are from Sen. Rep. 670, vii–xii and 16.

72. Sen. Rep. 670, x and 6–7. Also, see Standing Bear's own account in Thomas H. Tibbles, The Ponca Chiefs (Lincoln: University of Nebraska Press, 1972) 7–9.

73. Sen. Rep. 670, xii–xiii; Hayt, "Report," ARCIA, 1877 1–27; and Alfred Riggs to Carl Schurz, Mar. 19, 1877, LR, Ponca Agency, 1876–77.

74. Howard, "Report," ARCIA, 1877, 96–102.

75. Sen. Rep. 670, xii–xvi; Howard, "Report," ARCIA, 1877, 99–100; Whiteman, "Report," ARCIA, 1878, 64–65; "Statement of Amounts Paid . . . to the Poncas," July 27, 1882, in Sen. Ex. Doc. 192, 47th Cong., 1st Sess., SN1991; H. Price, "Report," ARCIA, 1881, xlii. "Petition," Ponca chiefs, Mar. 27, 1878, and Whiteman to Hayt, July 29, Aug. 20, 1878, LR, Ponca Agency, 1878.

76. Sen. Rep. 670, xvii; and Hayt, "Report," ARCIA, 1877, 23; Howard to Hayt, Aug. 7, 1877, and Nicholson to Smith, Aug. 23, 1877, LR, Ponca Agency, 1876–77.

77. "Memorandum of Council," Jan. 19, 1878, and Boone to Hayt, Feb. 7 and 22, 1878, LR, Ponca Agency, 1878; and Tibbles, The Ponca Chiefs 14–15.

78. Boone to Hayt, Apr. 4, 1878, Schurz to Hayt, May 23, 1878, and Whiteman to Hayt, July 29, 1878, all in LR, Ponca Agency, 1878; also, Whiteman, "Report," ARCIA, 1878, 64; Kappler, Indian Affairs, vol. 1, 175.

79. Tibbles, The Ponca Chiefs 15–17, 85–90; Sen. Rep. 670, 16–18; Whiteman to Hayt, Jan. 8, Mar. 15, and Mar. 17, 1879, and John Douglas (Yankton agent) to Hayt, Mar. 12, 1879, all in LR, Ponca Agency, 1878–79.

80. Standing Bear v. Crook, 25 Nebraska Federal District Court 695 (1879) 695–701. The testimony is as reported daily by Henry Tibbles in The Omaha Herald during April 1879 and subsequently widely publicized in his book, The Ponca Chiefs (first published in 1880). The Ponca's ordeal was also recounted in Helen Hunt Jackson's influential book, A Century of Dishonor, 186–217 and Appendix II.

81. Isaiah Lightner (Santee agent), "Report," ARCIA, 1880, 122.

82. Whiting to Trowbridge, Apr. 15, 1880, and "Petition," Ponca chiefs, Oct. 25, 1880, in LR, Ponca Agency, 1880. Also, Sen. Misc. Doc. 49, 80–81, and "Report of Special Commission to the Poncas," ARCIA, 1881, 217–25.

83. Sen. Misc. Doc. 49 and Sen. Ex. Doc. 30.

84. H. Price, "Report," ARCIA, 1881, xlvii–xlix and "Report," ARCIA, 1882, lxv–lxvi.

85. Sen. Ex. Doc. 30, and "Report of the Special Commission to the Poncas," ARCIA, 1881, 218; Kappler, Indian Affairs, vol. 1, 191; ARCIA, 1881, 229.

86. D. M. Browning (commissioner), "Report," ARCIA, 1894, 22; J. P. Woolsey

(agent), "Report," ARCIA, 1895, 259; Klein, *Reference Encyclopedia of the American Indian* 66; National Native American Cooperative, *Native American Dictionary* 158–66.

87. Howard, *The Ponca Tribe* 156–65.

88. Lightner, "Reports," ARCIA, 1883, 107–10, ARCIA, 1884, 125, ARCIA, 1885, 136–40 and 329; "Statistics Relating to Population," ARCIA, 1886, 402.

89. Kappler, *Indian Affairs*, vol. 1, 328–39, 946–48; Smith, "Reports," ARCIA, 1889, 247 and ARCIA, 1890, 146–47. The details on allotments are given in ARCIA, 1891, 41 and ARCIA, 1893, 603; Oliver Fröehling, "Allotment in Severalty on the Northern Ponca Reservation: The Geography of Dispossession," Master's thesis, University of Nebraska-Lincoln, 1993.

90. Kappler, *Indian Affairs*, vol. 6, 967–68 and vol. 7, 1555, 1561; Elizabeth Grobsmith, *The Ponca Tribe of Nebraska: History, Socio-Economic Status and Current Efforts to Obtain Restoration of Tribal Status* (Lincoln, Nebraska, 1990). The 1939 figure is from U.S. Department of the Interior, *Statistical Supplement of the Annual Report of the Commissioner of Indian Affairs* (Washington, D.C., 1939) Table IX.

91. Griest, "Report," ARCIA, 1876, 98–101, ARCIA, 1877, 145–46, ARCIA, 1878, 95–98, and ARCIA, 1879, 103–4; on the continued practice of sacrificing horses, see the eyewitness account, "Otoe Agency," *Gage County Democrat*, Jan. 2, 1880.

92. Griest, "Report," ARCIA, 1878, 95–98; Milner, *With Good Intentions*, 117–52; Chapman, *The Otoes and Missourias* 92–154.

93. The year-to-year data are from the agents' reports and the statistical tables in each ARCIA for the decade. In addition, see Griest to White, Nov. 16, 1874; White to Smith, July 2, 1875, 1872–76; Griest to Smith, Feb. 23, 1875, LR, Otoe Agency, 1872–76; and Batiste Barneby and Batiste Derin to Green on Dec. 12, 1871, and Jan. 27, 1872, respectively, *Green Papers*, n. pag.

94. Green to White, Feb. 26, 1872; "Report of a Council between the Otoe-Missouria and The Commissioner of Indian Affairs," Nov. 1 and 4, 1873; and White to Smith, April 21, 1875, all in LR, Otoe Agency, 1872–76. Also, Daniel Warren Overton, *A Historical Geography of the Eastern Remnant of the Otoe-Missouria Reservation on the Big Blue River,* Master's thesis, University of Nebraska-Lincoln, 1991.

95. W. C. Boteler (doctor) and R. Pickering (clerk), "Report," ARCIA, 1880, 118–20. Population figures are from the commissioners' reports during the 1870s, and family sizes are from a census taken in 1879 in connection with payments for the granting of a railroad right of way, in "Omaha and Republican Valley Railroad," Oct. 13, 1879, *Union Pacific Railroad Collection*, Nebraska State Historical Society, ms. 3761.

96. Smith, "Report," ARCIA, 1874, 34–35, and Griest, "Report," ARCIA, 1875, 313.

97. "Report of a Council," Nov. 1 and 4, 1873, LR, Otoe Agency, 1872–76.

98. Griest, "Reports," ARCIA, 1874, 203–5, ARCIA, 1875, 319–20, and ARCIA, 1878, 103–4; White to Smith, Apr. 21, 1875, and Griest to Smith, Feb. 7, 1876, LR, Otoe Agency, 1872–6; Griest to Hayt, Jan. 1, 1879, LR, Nebraska Agencies, 1879.

99. "Reminiscences, Remembrances, Observations, and Occurrences," and "Nee-

Scaw, the Fugitive," *Green Papers*, n. pag. Whitewater to Green, Mar. 16, 1873, in *Green Papers* and White to Walker, Apr. 29, 1872, LR, Otoe Agency, 1872–76; Richard Lumbard to Griest, Jan. 15, 1879, and Feb. 28, 1880, LR, Nebraska Agencies, 1879–80.

100. *Beatrice Express*, June 26, 1873, and Sept. 16, 1875.

101. *Beatrice Express*, Apr. 5, 1877; Eleanor H. Hinman, *History of Farm Land Prices in Eleven Nebraska Counties, 1873–1933*. University of Nebraska Agricultural Experiment Station Research Bulletin, no. 72 (Lincoln, 1934); and Sheldon, *Land Systems and Land Policies* 94–142.

102. O. H. Browning (secretary of the interior) to Mix, Dec. 12, 1867, in House Ex. Doc. 38, 40th Cong., 2nd Sess., SN1330; Kappler, *Indian Affairs*, vol. 1, 138–40. The mixed-blood figure is from the statistical tables in the commissioners' reports.

103. Green to White, Sept. 4, 1872; White to Walker, Dec. 19, 1872; and Settlers' "Petition," Aug. 4, 1872, all in LR, Otoe Agency, 1872–76.

104. *Senate Bills and Joint Resolutions*, 42nd Cong., 3rd Sess. SN1235 and "Memorial of the Legislature of Nebraska," Jan. 26, 1873, 42nd Cong., 3rd Sess., Sen. Misc. Doc. 61, SN1546.

105. Griest, "Report," ARCIA, *1873*, 196–98 and Smith, "Report," ARCIA, *1874*, 34–35. The survey is recorded in the *Original Government Survey Plats*, R79–33–7.

106. Griest, "Report," ARCIA, *1874*, 205, White, "Report," ARCIA, *1875*, 313, and White to Smith, Oct. 21, 1874, all in LR, Otoe Agency, 1872–76.

107. White, "Report," ARCIA, *1875*, 313 and the *Beatrice Express*, July 13, 1876.

108. *Congressional Record*, 44th Cong., 1st Sess., 4517–18, 5336, 5664, and 5696.

109. Kappler, *Indian Affairs*, vol. 1, 166–67, 176–77.

110. Griest to Smith, Dec. 26, 1876, LR, Nebraska Agencies, 1876–80.

111. Hayt, "Report," ARCIA, *1877*, 25–26; "Petition," Otoe-Missouria chiefs, Apr. 16, 1877, LR, Nebraska Agencies, 1877.

112. Griest, "Report," ARCIA, *1878*, 95–98, ARCIA, *1879*, 211, ARCIA, *1882*, 234, and ARCIA, *1887*, 290.

113. Griest, "Reports," ARCIA, *1878*, 95–98 and ARCIA, *1879*, 103–4; Boteler and Pickering, "Report," ARCIA, *1880*, 118–20.

114. "Confederated Otoe-Missouria Reservation," House Rep. 31, 46th Cong., 3rd Sess., SN1982.

115. Marble, "Report," ARCIA, *1880*, xliii; Boteler and Pickering, "Report," ARCIA, *1880*, 118–20 and Griest to Trowbridge, Apr. 8 and May 18, 1880, LR, Nebraska Agencies, 1880.

116. Kappler, *Indian Affairs*, vol. 1, 190–91; Woodin, "Report," ARCIA, *1882*, 79–80.

117. Overton, *A Historical Geography of the Eastern Remnant*, 100–182.

118. Woodin, "Report," ARCIA, *1883*, 75–79; John W. Scott, "Reports," ARCIA, *1884*, 84–90 and ARCIA, *1885*, 96–98; and E. C. Osborne, "Report," ARCIA, *1886*, 138–44.

119. Population figures are from statistical tables in each commissioner's report.

120. R. David Edmunds, *The Otoe-Missouria People* (Phoenix: Indian Tribal Series, 1976) 72–87.

121. White to Smith, July 22, 1875, LR, Omaha Agency, 1871–76.

122. Statistics on agricultural production are drawn from the tables in each annual report of the commissioner of Indian affairs from 1870 to 1884. For the failure of the crops in 1876 see Vore to Smith, Nov. 5, 1876, LR, Nebraska Agencies, 1876.

123. George Wilkinson, "Report," ARCIA, 1883, 105–7; List of Land Allotments, 1871 Box 7, R120 (Nebraska State Historical Society); White, "Report," ARCIA, 1875, 312; Gillingham to Smith, July 20, 1875, LR, Omaha Agency, 1871–76; "Memorial of the Members of the Omaha Tribe of Indians for a Grant of Land in Severalty," Sen. Misc. Doc. 31, 47th Cong., 1st Sess. (1879–80) SN1993; Mark J. Swetland, "Aspects of Omaha Land Allotments, 1855–1910," Unpublished Seminar Paper, Dept. of Geography, University of Nebraska, Spring 1992.

124. Gillingham, "Report," ARCIA, 1874, 203–4, White to Hiram Chase, July 9, 1873, and Painter to Janney, Feb. 1, 1871, LR, Omaha Agency, 1871–76.

125. "Estimate of Funds for 4th Quarter, 1871," LR, Omaha Agency, 1871–76.

126. Painter to White, Oct. 1, 1871, LR, Omaha Agency, 1871–76; Gillingham, "Report," ARCIA, 1874, 203–4; White to Smith, July 7, 1873, and Gillingham to Smith, Sept. 17, 1875, LR, Omaha Agency, 1871–76; and Alice C. Fletcher, *Historical Sketch of the Omaha Tribe of Indians in Nebraska* (Washington, D.C.: Bureau of Indian Affairs, 1885) 10.

127. "Several Omahas" to T. H. Tibbles, Oct. 22, 1879, in James Owen Dorsey, *Omaha and Ponca Letters* (Washington, D.C.: Government Printing Office, 1891) 20–33; Omaha Census, Sept. 24, 1886, R121 (Nebraska State Historical Society).

128. "Memorial of the Members of the Omaha Tribe of Indians for a Grant of Land in Severalty," 11.

129. Melvin Gilmore, *Prairie Smoke* 11.

130. Melvin R. Gilmore, "Methods of Indian Buffalo Hunts, with the Itinerary of the Last Tribal Hunt of the Omaha," *Papers of the Michigan Academy of Science, Arts and Letters*, vol. 16, 17–32; chief clerk, War Department to secretary of the interior, Jan. 29 and Mar. 29, 1877, LR, Nebraska Agencies, 1877; Fletcher and La Flesche, *The Omaha Tribe*, vol. 1, 244–45 and vol. 2, 634–35; Gillingham to Smith, July 20, 1875, LR, Omaha Agency 1871–76.

131. Gillingham, "Report," ARCIA, 1875, 318; Hamilton, "Report," ARCIA, 1871, 610; White, "Report," ARCIA, 1879, 106–9; Painter to White, Feb. 1, 1873 and Gillingham to Smith, Oct. 27, 1875, LR, Omaha Agency, 1871–76; Milner, *With Good Intentions* 169–71.

132. Two Crows (and "others") to Rev. John C. Lowrie, Sept. 16, 1879, in Dorsey, *Omaha and Ponca Letters* 34–36; Francis La Flesche, *The Middle Five: Indian Schoolboys of the Omaha Tribe* (Lincoln: University of Nebraska Press, 1963); Norma Kidd Green, *Iron Eye's Family* (Lincoln: Johnsen Press, 1969) 47–55; Fletcher, *Historical Sketch of the Omaha Tribe* 11.

133. Vore, "Reports," ARCIA, 1877, 143–45 and ARCIA, 1878, 95; Fontenelle to Hayt, Jan. 16, 1879, LR, Nebraska Agencies, 1879. Also, Dorsey, *Omaha Sociology* 357–58; Fletcher and La Flesche, *The Omaha Tribe*, vol. 2, 635; and Barnes, *Two Crows Denies It* 39–40.

134. Fletcher and La Flesche, *The Omaha Tribe*, vol. 2, 635.

135. Fletcher to Putnam, June 7, 1884, in *Fletcher Papers* (Lincoln: Nebraska State Historical Society) R3, ms. 2728; Fletcher and La Flesche, *The Omaha Tribe*, vol. 1, 243–51, 283–84, and vol. 2, 452–58, 634–35.

136. Vore, "Report," ARCIA, *1877*, 144.

137. Painter to Janney, Dec. 27, 1870, Feb. 1, 1871, Mar. 2, 1871, and Mar. 8, 1871, LR, Omaha Agency, 1871–76; Gillingham to Smith, June 4, 1875, Omaha Agency, 1871–76.

138. Kappler, *Indian Affairs*, vol. 1, 138–39; "Action in Regard to Indian Lands," ARCIA, *1873*, 20; and "Petition," Omaha chiefs, Oct. 27, 1871, LR, Omaha Agency, 1871–76.

139. "Action in Regard to Indian Lands," ARCIA, *1873*, 20 and ARCIA, *1879*, 213; "Legislation Recommended," ARCIA, *1874*, 20; Sheldon, *Land Systems and Land Policies in Nebraska* 338–39.

140. White to Smith, July 3, 1874, LR, Omaha Agency, 1871–76; also, Gillingham to White, Dec. 13, 1873, White to Smith, Dec. 18, 1873, Smith to Delano, Jan. 29, 1874, and Delano to House of Representatives, Feb. 4, 1874, all in House Ex. Doc. 109, 43rd Cong., 1st Sess. (1874) SN1607.

141. Kappler, *Indian Affairs*, vol. 1, 153; White to Smith, Aug. 3, 1874, and Gillingham to White, Sept. 3, 1874, LR, Omaha Agency, 1871–76.

142. Sen. Misc. Doc. 78, 47th Cong., 1st Sess. (1879–80), SN1993, and House Rep. 1530, 47th Cong., 1st Sess. (1881–82) SN2069.

143. Omaha chiefs to R. E. Trowbridge, Mar. 18, 1880, in Dorsey, *Omaha and Ponca Letters* 82–85.

144. Several Omaha to T. H. Tibbles, Oct. 22, 1879, in Dorsey, *Omaha and Ponca Letters* 20–33; Sen. Misc. Doc. 78, 47th Cong., 1st Sess. (1879–80) SN1933.

145. "Memorial of the Omaha Tribe of Indians for a Grant of Land in Severalty" (quotes from pages 4 and 11); Joan Mark, *A Stranger in Her Native Land: Alice Fletcher and the American Indians* (Lincoln: University of Nebraska Press, 1988).

146. Price, "Report," ARCIA, *1883*, lxiii; Mark, *A Stranger in Her Native Land* 70–77; Fletcher and La Flesche, *The Omaha Tribe*, vol. 2, 639.

147. Kappler, *Indian Affairs*, vol. 1, 212–14.

148. Fletcher to Price, June (?), 1884, in *Fletcher Papers* and Alice Fletcher, "Lands in Severalty to Indians; Illustrated by Experiences with the Omaha Tribe," *Proceedings of the American Association for the Advancement of Science* 33 (1885): 654–65; Mark, *A Stranger in Her Native Land* 88–94; Kappler, *Indian Affairs*, vol. 1, 486.

149. Wilkinson, "Report," ARCIA, *1884*, 117–20 and "Sale of Omaha Lands in Nebraska and Allotment of Lands in Severalty of Omaha Indians," ARCIA, *1884*, xlviii–l.

150. Wilkinson, "Report," ARCIA, *1883*, 105–7 and Fletcher, "Lands in Severalty to Indians."

151. "Map of the Omaha Indian Reservation, Nebraska" NA, RG75, Map no. 1236; Price, "Report," ARCIA, *1884*, xlviii–l and Atkins, "Report," ARCIA, *1885*, lxii.

152. Kappler, *Indian Affairs*, vol. 1, 231, 270, and 263; Sheldon, *Land Systems and Land Policies in Nebraska* 333. "Relief of Omaha Indians," Sen. Ex. Doc. 90, 49th Cong., 1st Sess. (1885–86) SN2339.

153. Warner, "Report," ARCIA, *1887*, 152; Potter, "Report," ARCIA, *1886*, 186–88; and Price, "Report," ARCIA, *1884*, xlvii–l.

154. A. R. Longwell, *Lands of the Omaha Indians*, Master's thesis, University of Nebraska-Lincoln, 1961; Janet A. McDonnell, "Land Policy on the Omaha Reservation: Competency Commissions and Forced Fee Patents," *Nebraska History* 63.2 (1982): 399–411.

Postscript

1. National Native Co-operative, *Native American Directory* 158–66; Confederation of American Indians, *Indian Reservations: A State and Federal Handbook* 135–36, 233, 236–237; Klein, *Reference Encyclopedia of the American Indian* 90, 96.

2. Robin Riddington, "Omaha Survival: A Vanishing Indian Tribe that would not Vanish," *American Indian Quarterly* 11 (1987): 37–49; Elizabeth Grobsmith and Beth R. Ritter, "The Ponca Tribe of Nebraska: The Process of Restoration of a Federally Terminated Tribe," *Human Organization* 51 (1992): 1–16; Edmunds, *The Otoe-Missouria People* 87–91; Legislative Bill 340 (approved May 2, 1989), in *Laws of Nebraska*, 91st Legis., 1st Sess. (1989) 1291–99.

3. Smith, "Report," ARCIA, *1875*, 24.

4. Omaha v. United States, 53 Ct. Cl. 549 (1917–18); Pawnee v. United States, 56 Ct. Cl. 1 (1920–21); and the Otoe and Missouria Tribe v. United States, 52 Ct. Cl. 424 (1916–17).

5. Wilcomb E. Washburn, ed., *The American Indian and the United States: A Documentary History* (New York: Random House, 1973) 3: 2218–27; Imre Sutton, ed., *Irredeemable America: The Indians' Estate and Land Claims* (Albuquerque: University of New Mexico Press, 1985); and Susan Danforth, "Repaying Historical Debts: The Indian Claims Commission," *North Dakota Law Review* 49 (1973): 359–403.

6. Otoe and Missouria Tribe v. United States, 2 ICC 500 (1953) and 131 Ct. Cl. 593 (1955); Chapman, *The Otoe and Missourias* 223–89.

7. Iowa, Omaha, Sac and Fox, and Otoe and Missouria v. United States, 13 ICC 272 (1964).

8. Omaha v. United States, 4 ICC 627 (1957) and 8 ICC 392 (1960).

9. Pawnee v. United States, 9 ICC 94 (1961) and 157 Ct. Cl. 134 (1962). Also, Wishart, "The Pawnee Claims Case, 1947–64," *Irredeemable America* 157–86.

10. Ponca v. United States, 26 ICC 203 (1971), 24 ICC 339 (1970), and 197 Ct. Cl. 1065 (1972).

11. Wilcomb E. Washburn, "Land Claims in the Mainstream of Indian/White Land History," *Irredeemable America* 21–33, quote from 22–23.

12. Otoe and Missouria Tribe v. United States, 131 Ct. Cl. 593 (1955).

13. Chapman, *The Otoes and Missourias,* 270 and Wishart, "The Pawnee Claims Case," *Irredeemable America* 182–83.

14. For example, the average per capita income for Thurston County in 1990 was $10,670 compared to the state average of $17,490, From *The Lincoln Star,* May 6, 1992, 16.

Selected
Bibliography

Manuscripts

Allis, Samuel. *Manuscript*. Ms. 2628. Nebraska State Historical Society, Lincoln.

Clark, William. *Papers*. Ms. 94. Kansas State Historical Society, Topeka.

Documents Relating to the Negotiation of Ratified and Unratified Treaties with the Various Indian Tribes, 1801–1869. RG75, R494. National Archives, Washington, D.C.

Dunbar, John. *Records of the Pawnee Mission Church*. Ms. 480. Nebraska State Historical Society, Lincoln.

Dougherty, John. *Papers*. Ms. 48740. Kansas State Historical Society, Topeka.

Fletcher, Alice. *Papers*. Ms. 2728. Nebraska State Historical Society, Lincoln.

Field Notes, Fort Kearney, 1839–83. Ms. 1046. Kansas State Historical Society, Topeka.

Furnas, Robert. *Papers*. Ms. RG1510. Nebraska State Historical Society, Lincoln.

Green, Albert L. *Papers*. Ms. 2800. Nebraska State Historical Society, Lincoln.

Harvey, Augustus Ford. *Field Notes*. Ms. 1046. Kansas State Historical Society, Topeka.

La Flesche, Susan. *Papers*. Ms. 2026. Nebraska State Historical Society, Lincoln.

McKinney, Edmund. *Papers*. Ms. 4179. Nebraska State Historical Society, Lincoln.

Merrill, Moses. *Diary*. Ms. 480. Nebraska State Historical Society, Lincoln.

Pawnee Tribe, *Proceedings of the Council*. Oklahoma Historical Society, Oklahoma City.

Presbyterian Missionary Letters Relating to the American Indians in Nebraska Country. Presbyterian Historical Society, Philadelphia.

Letters Received, Office of Indian Affairs, 1824–1881. RG75, microfilm 234. National Archives, Washington, D.C.

Central Superintendency, 1851–65. Rolls 55–58.

Council Bluffs Agency, 1836–57. Rolls 215–18.

Dakota Superintendency, 1861–70. Rolls 250–251.

Nebraska Agencies, 1876–80. Rolls 519–29.

Northern Superintendency, 1865–76. Rolls 599–600.

Omaha Agency, 1856–76. Rolls 604–606.

Otoe Agency, 1856–76. Rolls 652–655.

Pawnee Agency, 1859–80. Rolls 659–668.

Ponca Agency, 1859–80. Rolls 670–677.

St. Louis Superintendency, 1824–51. Rolls 747–756.

Upper Missouri Agency, 1824–59. Rolls 883–885.

Union Pacific Railroad Collection. Ms. 3761. Nebraska State Historical Society, Lincoln.

United States General Land Office. Township Plats and Field Notes. Nebraska State Historical Society, Lincoln.

——. Land Tract Books. Nebraska State Historical Society, Lincoln.

Williamson, John. Papers. Ms. 2710. Nebraska State Historical Society, Lincoln.

Published Sources

Albers, Patricia C., and Medicine, Beatrice. The Hidden Half: Studies of Plains Indian Women. New York: The University Press of America, 1983.

Banforth, Douglas B. "Historical Documents and Bison Ecology in the Great Plains." Plains Anthropologist 32 (1987): 1–16.

Barnes, R. H. Two Crows Denies It: A History of Controversy in Omaha Sociology. Lincoln: University of Nebraska Press, 1984.

Blaine, Martha Royce. Pawnee Passage: 1870–1875. Norman: University of Oklahoma Press, 1990.

Bradbury, John. Travels in the Interior of North America in the Years 1809, 1810, and 1811. Cleveland: The Arthur H. Clark Company, 1904. Vol. 5 of Early Western Travels, 1748–1846. Ed. Reuben G. Thwaites. 39 vols. 1904–7.

Carlton, J. Henry. The Prairie Logbooks: Dragoon Campaigns to the Pawnee Villages in 1844 and to the Rocky Mountains in 1845. Lincoln: University of Nebraska Press, 1983. Ed. Louis Peltzer.

Chapman, Berlin, B. The Otoes and Missourias: A Study of Indian Removal and the Legal Aftermath. Oklahoma City: Times-Journal Publishing Co., 1965.

Coues, Elliot, ed. The Expeditions of Zebulan Montgomery Pike. New York: Francis P. Harper, 1895.

Danforth, Susan. "Repaying Historical Debts: The Indian Claims Commission." North Dakota Law Review 49 (1973): 359–403.

Dorsey, James Owen. Omaha Sociology. Third Annual Report of the Bureau of American Ethnology, 1881–82. Washington, D.C.: Government Printing Office, 1884.

——. Omaha and Ponca Letters. Washington, D.C.: Government Printing Office, 1891.

Dunbar, John B. "The Pawnee Indians: Their History and Ethnology." Magazine of American History 4.4 (1880): 242–79.

Echo-Hawk, Roger C. "Pawnee Mortuary Traditions." *American Indian Culture and Research Journal* 16.2 (1992): 77–99.

Forb, Robert. "Robert W. Furnas as Omaha Indian Agent, 1864–1866." *Nebraska History* 32 (1951): 186–203 and 268–83.

Fletcher, Alice C. *Historical Sketch of the Omaha Tribe of Indians in Nebraska.* Washington, D.C.: Bureau of Indian Affairs, 1885.

——. "Lands of Severalty to Indians: Illustrated by Experiences with the Omaha Tribe." *Proceedings of the American Association for the Advancement of Science* 33 (1885): 654–65.

Gilmore, Melvin R. "Methods of Indian Buffalo Hunts, with the Itinerary of the Last Tribal Hunt of the Omaha." *Papers of the Michigan Academy of Science, Arts and Letters* 16 (1931): 17–32.

——. *Uses of Plants by the Indians of the Missouri River Region.* Lincoln: University of Nebraska Press, 1977.

Grange, Roger. *Pawnee and Lower Loup Pottery.* Nebraska State Historical Society Publications in Anthropology, no. 3. Lincoln: Nebraska Historical Society, 1968.

Grinnell, George Bird, *Pawnee Hero Stories and Folk Tales.* Lincoln: University of Nebraska Press, 1961.

Grobsmith, Elizabeth, and Ritter, Beth R. "The Ponca Tribe of Nebraska: The Process of Restoration of a Federally Terminated Tribe," *Human Organization* 51 (1992): 1–16.

Hill, Edward E. *The Office of Indian Affairs, 1824–1880: Historical Sketches.* New York: Clearwater Publishing Company, Inc., 1974.

Hinman, Eleanor H. *History of Farm Land Prices in Eleven Nebraska Counties, 1873–1933.* University of Nebraska Agricultural Experiment Station Research Bulletin, no. 72. Lincoln, 1934.

Holder, Preston. *The Hoe and the Horse on the Plains: A Study of Cultural Development Among North American Indians.* Lincoln: University of Nebraska Press, 1974.

Howard, James. *The Ponca Tribe.* Bulletin of the Bureau of American Ethnology, no. 195. Washington, D.C.: Government Printing Office, 1965.

——. "Known Village Sites of the Ponca." *Plains Anthropologist* 15 (1970): 109–34.

Indian Claims Commission, *Final Report.* Washington, D.C.: Government Printing Office, 1978.

Irving, John T. Jr. *Indian Sketches Taken During an Expedition to the Pawnee Tribes.* Philadelphia: Carey, Lea, and Blanchard, 1835.

Jablow, Joseph. *Ethnohistory of the Ponca.* New York: Garland Publishing, 1974.

Jackson, Helen Hunt. *A Century of Dishonor.* Boston: Roberts Brothers, 1885.

James, Edwin. *An Account of an Expedition from Pittsburgh to the Rocky Mountains.* Cleveland: The Arthur H. Clark Company, 1905. Vols. 14–17 of *Early Western Travels.* Ed. Reuben G. Thwaites. 39 vols. 1904–7.

Kappler, Charles J. *Indian Affairs: Laws and Treaties.* Washington, D.C.: Government Printing Office, 1903–1938.

Kvasnicka, Robert M., and Viola, Herman J., eds. *The Commissioners of Indian Affairs, 1824–1977*. Lincoln: University of Nebraska Press, 1979.

La Flesche, Francis. *The Middle Five*. Lincoln: University of Nebraska Press, 1963.

Malin, James. *Indian Policy and Westward Expansion*. Lawrence, Kansas: published by author, 1921.

Mark, Joan. *A Stranger in Her Native Land: Alice Fletcher and the American Indians*. Lincoln: University of Nebraska Press, 1988.

Maximilian, Prince of Wied. *Travels in the Interior of North America, 1832–1834*. Cleveland: The Arthur H. Clark Company, 1906. Vols. 22–25 of *Early Western Travels, 1748–1846*. Ed. Reuben G. Thwaites. 39 vols. 1904–7.

Merrill, Moses. "Extracts from the Diary of Rev. Moses Merrill, A Missionary to the Otoe Indians from 1832–40." *Transactions of the Nebraska State Historical Society* 4 (1892): 157–91.

Milner, Clyde A. II. *With Good Intentions: Quaker Work Among the Pawnees, Otos, and Omahas in the 1870s*. Lincoln: University of Nebraska Press, 1982.

Moulton, Gary E., ed. *The Journals of the Lewis and Clark Expedition*. Lincoln: University of Nebraska Press, 1986–87.

Murie, James R. *Ceremonies of the Pawnee*. Ed. Douglas Parks. Lincoln: University of Nebraska Press, 1989.

O'Shea, John M., and Ludwickson, John. *Archaeology and Ethnohistory of the Omaha Indians: The Big Village Site*. Lincoln: University of Nebraska Press, 1992.

——. "Omaha Chieftanship in the Nineteenth Century." *Ethnohistory* 39.3 (1992): 316–52.

Nasatir, Abraham P. *Before Lewis and Clark: Documents Illustrating the History of the Missouri, 1783–1804*. St. Louis: St. Louis Historical Documents Foundation, 1952.

Oehler, Gottlieb F., and Smith, David Z. *Description of a Journey and Visit to the Pawnee Indians. . . .* Moravian Church Miscellany, 1851–52.

Paul Wilhelm, Duke of Wurttemberg. *Travels in North America, 1822–1824*. Ed. Savoie Lottinville. Norman: University of Oklahoma Press, 1973.

Okada, Yasuo. *Public Lands and Pioneer Farmers: Gage County, Nebraska*. Tokyo: Keiv Economic Society, 1971.

Parks, Douglas R., and Wedel, Waldo R. "Pawnee Geography: Historical and Sacred." *Great Plains Quarterly* 5.3 (1985): 143–76.

Prucha, Francis P. *The Great Father: The United States Government and the American Indian*. Lincoln: University of Nebraska Press, 1984.

Ranney, Timothy. "Letters from the Past." *Vermont Quarterly* 21 (1953): 118–27, 200–10, 279–88 and vol. 22 (1954): 42–51, 212–22.

Report of the Joint Delegation of Baltimore, Philadelphia and New York Annual Meetings in their Visit to the Northern Superintendency, 7th and 8th Months, 1869. Baltimore: J. Jones, 1869.

Riddington, Robin. "Omaha Survival: A Vanishing Tribe that would not Vanish." *American Indian Quarterly* 1 (1987): 37–49.

Riding In, James. "Six Pawnee Crania: Historical and Contemporary Issues Associated with the Massacre and Decapitation of Pawnee Indians in 1869." *American Indian Culture and Research Journal* 16.2 (1992): 101–20.

Royce, Charles C. *Indian Land Cessions in the United States,* Eighteenth Annual Report, Bureau of American Ethnography, 1896–1897. Washington, D.C.: Government Printing Office, 1899.

Sheldon, Addison E. *Land Systems and Land Policies in Nebraska.* Publications of the Nebraska State Historical Society, vol. 22. Lincoln: Nebraska State Historical Society, 1936.

Shunatona, Richard. "Otoe Indian Lore." *Nebraska History* 5.4 (1922): 60–64.

Stannard, David E. "Disease Infertility: A New Look at the Demographic Collapse of Native Populations in the Wake of Western Contact." *Journal of American Studies* 24.3 (1990): 325–50.

Sutton, Imre, ed., *Irredeemable America: The Indians' Estate and Land Claims.* Albuquerque: University of New Mexico Press, 1985.

United States Department of the Interior. *Reports of the Commissioner of Indian Affairs.* Washington, D.C.: various publishers, 1845–1900.

Wedel, Waldo. *An Introduction to Pawnee Archaeology.* Bulletin of the Bureau of American Ethnology, no. 112. Washington, D.C.: Government Printing Office, 1936.

——. *The Dunbar-Allis Letters on the Pawnee.* New York: Garland Press, 1985.

Weltfish, Gene. *The Lost Universe: Pawnee Life and Culture.* Lincoln: University of Nebraska Press, 1977.

White, Richard. *The Roots of Dependency: Subsistence, Environment, and Social Change among the Choctaws, Pawnees, and Navajos.* Lincoln: University of Nebraska Press, 1983.

Whitman, William. *The Oto.* Columbia University Contributions in Anthropology, vol. 28. New York: Columbia University Press, 1937.

Wishart, David J. *The Fur Trade of the American West, 1807–40: A Geographical Synthesis.* Lincoln: University of Nebraska Press, 1979.

——. "The Pawnee Claims Case, 1947–64," *Irredeemable America: The Indians' Estate and Land Claims.* Ed. Imre Sutton. Albuquerque: University of New Mexico Press, 1985.

——. "Compensation for Dispossession: Payments to the Indians for their Lands on the Central and Northern Great Plains in the 19th Century." *National Geographic Research* 6.1 (1990): 94–109.

Unpublished Works

Collister, R. Paul. "An Early Stage in Decline: The Pawnees as Seen through Indian Office Correspondence, 1824–1835." Master's thesis, University of Nebraska-Lincoln, 1985.

Egbert, Stephen L., "The Resettlement of Nance County: Land Alienation Patterns, 1878–1913," Master's thesis. University of Nebraska-Lincoln, 1983.

Fröehling, Oliver. "Allotment in Severalty on the Northern Ponca Reservation: The Geography of Dispossession." Master's thesis, University of Nebraska-Lincoln, 1993.

Kracht, Benjamin R. "The Effects of Disease and Warfare on Pawnee Social Organization, 1830–59: An Ethnohistorical Approach." Master's thesis, University of Nebraska-Lincoln, 1982.

Longwell, A. R. "Lands of the Omaha Indians." Master's thesis, University of Nebraska-Lincoln, 1961.

Overton, Daniel Warren. "A Historical Geography of the Eastern Remnant of the Otoe-Missouria Reservation on the Big Blue River." Master's thesis, University of Nebraska-Lincoln, 1991.

Richardson, Charles Howard. "Early Settlement of Eastern Nebraska Territory: A Geographical Study Based on the Original Land Survey." Diss. University of Nebraska-Lincoln, 1968.

Riding In, James. "Keepers of Tirawahut's Covenant: The Development and Destruction of Pawnee Culture." Diss. University of California, Los Angeles, 1991.

Swetland, Mark J. "Aspects of Omaha Allotments, 1855–1910." Unpublished paper, University of Nebraska-Lincoln, 1992.

Index

Page numbers in bold refer to figures and tables.

Ar-ka-ke-ta (Stay By It), 116, 167, **172**, 217, 219–20; Americanization resisted by, 173–74, 219

Armstrong, Major, 152

Ashley, William, 64

Assimilation program. *See* Civilization program

Assiniboine, 30

Atchison and Nebraska Railroad, 170

Atkinson, Henry, 75

Baker, John, 166, 167

Barneby, Batiste, 170, 172

Barrow, John, 93

Bear Scar, 212–13

Becker, John, 177

Bellevue, **44**, 45, 46, 56

Bennett, Gideon, 113

Benton, Thomas Hart, 57, 101–2

Bernard Pratte and Company, 41

Big Axe, 91, 92, 98

Big Bear, 219, 220

Big Eagle, 177

Big Elk (chief of the Omaha), 30, 44, 59, 100, 123; and farming by the Omaha, 62–63; on the fur traders, 47–48; and the government, 66, 68, 78; leadership of, 78, 88, 97

Big Elk (son of Big Elk), 80, 88, 97, 123

Big Elk (Harre-garrow of the Otoe-Missouria), 217, 223, 224

Big Horse, 3, 4

Big Kaw, 62, 90

Big Snake, 210

Big Soldier, 206

Big Spotted Horse, 189, 196, 197

Birkett, Charles, 203, 204, 205, 206, 207

Bison: and the Dakota, 28, 47, 181; disappearance from Nebraska of, 47–48, 187, 256 n.25; hunts (*see* Bison hunts); killed by Americans for tongues only, 84, 263 n.40; materials supplied by, 23, 25, 26, 30; and the

Omaha, 11, 26–27, 28, 77, 84, 87, 153, 157, **158**, 158, 181, 227, 228, 230; and the Otoe-Missouria, 11, 47, 78, 79, 84, 181; and the Ponca, 11, 36, 48, 76, 84, 181; and the Pawnee, 48; in religion, 11, 18, 25–26, 27, 29, 98; scarcity of, 84, 98, 141, 144, 181, 196, 218

Bison hunts, 16, 17, 25–29, 91, 94; and the Cherokee, 36; and the Dakota, 77, 146, 276 n.91; danger of, by 1860s, 146–47, 190, 204; discouraged by U.S. government, 133, 157, 164, 197, 204; last made in early 1870s, 187, 204; and the Omaha, 15, 27, 47, 48, 60, 61, 77; and the Otoe-Missouria, 27, 60, 61, 102, 218; and the Pawnee, 15, 26, 27, 28–29, 81, 93, 102, 181, 196–97, 253 n.85; and the Ponca, 27; and religion, 25–26, 27, 37, 98; traditions weakened by emphasis on, 46–47; villages abandoned during, 23, 25; women's work during, 21, 26, 28, 29

Blackbird, 8–9, 35–36

Blackfeet, 29, 41, 84

Blaine, Garland, 191

Blue Hawk, 184, 277 n.99

Board of Indian Commissioners, 204

Bohemian Settlement Association, 161

Boone, A. G., 211

Brackenridge, Henry, 73

Bradbury, John, 12, 17, 31, 73, 113

Branch, Harrison, 118, 129, 139, 174

British, 9, 58, 59

Brulé, 102, 130, 134, 146 (*see also* Dakota); and the Omaha, 73, 77, 87, 102, 123, 135, 138, 155, 157, 180; and the Otoe-Missouria, 102, 113; and the Pawnee, 80, 102, 128, 130–32, 135, 138, 174, 175, 180–81, 182, 191, 219, 277 n.92; and the Ponca, 73, 76, 102, 133, 134, 135, 136–37, 138, 145, 180, 203, 204, 205, 213, 219

Buffalo Chief (Tcha-wan-na-ga-he), 170

Dakota (*cont.*)

purchased from, 153; and the Omaha, 6, 33, 64, 76, 77, 84, 86, 87, 97, 102, 117, 121, 122–23, 135, 138, 155, 157, 180, 264 n.51; and the Otoe-Missouria, 5, 64, 78, 89, 90, 102, 113, 165; and the Otoe, 5; and the Pawnee, 49, 53, 54, 63, 64–65, 76, 80, 81, 82, 84, 85, 90–92, 102, 124, 126, 127, 128, 130–32, 135, 138, 144, 149, 156, 174, 175, 180–81, 182, 185, 190–91, 192–93, 194, 195, 196, 197, 199, 205, 210, 212, 215, 219, 277 n.92, 279 n.34; and the Pitahawirata, 53; and the Ponca, 6, 8, 27, 33, 43, 53, 54, 64, 73, 75, 76, 80, 84, 85, 86, 90, 93, 102, 133, 134, 135, 136–37, 138, 139, 145, 148, 149, 153, 156, 180, 200, 202, 203, 204, 205, 207, 208, 210, 211, 212, 213, 215, 219, 279 n.34; rations received by, 204; and the Skiri, 53, 54, 80, 92, 93, 192, 199, 200; territory claimed by, 13, 59, 134, 276 n.91; and the U.S. Army, 64, 180–81; war of intended extermination waged by, 37, 86

Dakota Territory, 147, 149, 151, 153, 207

Dawes Act of 1887, 58

De Bourgmong, Etienne Veniard, 5

Delaware, 64, 81; and the Pawnee, 61, 63

Denman, Superintendent, 169, 182

Dennison, William, 111, 114–15, 116–17, 126–27, 128; Otoe-Missouria money stolen by, 166

Denver, John, 105

DePuy, Henry, 129, 132, 174, 177

Deroin, Batiste, 170, 172

De Smet, Pierre-Jean, 84, 85

Diet, 23–25 (*see also* Bison; Corn)

Dineson, Wilhelm, 194

Diphtheria: among the Pawnee, 174, 180

Dirty Face (In-da-ma-sha-da), 151, 152

Disease, 35, 36, 45, 46, 77 (*see also* Cholera; Diphtheria; Malaria; Measles; Smallpox)

Doctrine of Discovery, 58–59

Dole, Commissioner, 152, 156, 157, 160, 167

Dorion, Pierre, 1

Dorsey, James Owen, 21, 164; Omaha assisted by, 227, 235; and the Ponca, 204, 205

Do-uba-moni (Harrison McCauley), 235

Dougherty, John, 45, 47, 258 n.58; on the civilization program, 57, 104; as Indian agent, 56, 258 n.58; and the Omaha, 56, 59, 60–61, 76; and the Otoe-Missouria, 56, 59, 60–61, 62, 79; and the Pawnee, 8, 56, 80, 81, 82, 98, 262 n.34; and the Ponca, 56, 76, 80

Drouillard, George, 1, 3

Drum, The, 86, 133, 140

Dunbar, Reverend John, 45, 52, 55, 85; amalgamation of nations promoted by, 97; and the Pawnee, 19, 23, 28, 49, 50, 53–54, 80, 81, 82, 90, 91, 92, 190, 253 n.85; viewed by Indians, 53, 54

Dundy, Elmer, 212

Dysentery, 174, 210

Eagle, 170, 171

Eagle Chief, 192, 196, 200

Eastman, Seth, 111, 117

Edmunds, Newton, 151, 152

Education, 55, 59; impact on Indian culture of, 99; and the Omaha, 121, 122, 123, 159, 164, 230–31; and the Otoe-Missouria, 114, 115–16, 172, 173, 219, 220; and the Pawnee, 130, 132, **176**, 177–79, 180, 195, 197; and the Ponca, 206, 214; strategy of acculturation through, 142, 178, 271 n.3

Ellick, Frank, 161

Ellsworth, Henry L., 61–64

Farming, 21, 22; discontinued due to fur trading, 36; and federal Indian pol-

Harvey, Thomas (*cont.*)
  promoted by, 97; and the Omaha, 66,
    87–88
Haxti, 98
Hayes, President, 209
Hayt, Commissioner, 187, 211
Hepner, George, 112–13, 114, 117, 268
  n.36
Herring, Elbert, 55
Hitchcock, Phineas, 222
Hoffman, Joshua, 139, 140, 145, 146–47,
  150–51; on U.S. Army massacre of
  Ponca, 151, 152, 153
Hogan, Martin E., 204
Holder, Preston, 35
Hollis, James, 132
Homestead Act of 1862, 109, 142
Horr, Chauncey, 120
Horse Driver, 184, 277 n.99
Horses, 25, 33, 35, 95; and the bison
  hunts, 23, 26, 28, 29, 85; and the Da-
  kota, 8, 191; and the discontinuation
  of farming, 23, 36; and the Omaha, 8,
  45, 87, **147**, 157, 227, 234; and the
  Otoe-Missouria, 45, 89, **147**, 166, 173;
  and the Pawnee, 8, 25, 30, 31, 43, 80,
  92, 124, **147**, 159, 180, 191; and the
  Ponca, 8, 146, **147**, 148, 157, 204; used
  in trade, 8, 30, 45
Howard, C. H., 234
Howard, E. A., 210
Howard, James, 13, 17
Hudson's Bay Company, 42
Hugo, William, 149
Hunting. *See* Bison hunting

Ietan, 46, 56, 62, 80, 90; death of, 79, 88,
  89; and Otoe annuities, 59, 60
Immigrants. *See* Settlers
Indian agents, 39 (*see also* Indian Office); and the Cheyenne, 56; and the
  Crow, 83; and the Dakota, 56, 57, 83,
  207, 208; duties charged with, 55, 56;

inter-tribal conflicts intensified by,
  97; missionaries appointed as 55; and
  the Omaha, 56, 57, 114, 142, 164, 230,
  231–32, 233 (*see also* Indian Office,
  and the Omaha); and the Otoe-
  Missouria, 56, 57, 112, 114–15, 142, 144,
  166–67, 168, 172, 173, 177, 217, 221–22,
  223, 224, 225–26 (*see also* Indian Office, and the Otoe-Missouria); and
  the Pawnee, 56, 57, 114–15, 126, 142,
  177, 182, 184, 195, 197, 198, 276 n.85 (*see
  also* Indian Office, and the Pawnee);
  and the Ponca, 56, 83, 142, 145, 205–6
  (*see also* Indian Office, and the
  Ponca); Quaker (*see* Quaker agents)
Indian Claims Commission, 241, 243,
  244, 259 n.72
Indian Claims Commission Act, 241, 244
Indian Office, 111; administrative hierarchy of, 55–56; agents of (*see* Indian
  agents); amalgamation of nations
  promoted by, 97, 104; assimilation
  policy of (*see* Civilization program);
  coalescence of nations promoted by,
  97; criticism of previous policies of,
  by current commissioners, 103; and
  the Dakota, 56, 57, 64, 83, 207, 208;
  funding of, 58; and the Kansa, 97;
  and the Omaha, 69, 88, 97, 104, 117,
  121–22, 123, 153, 156, 159, 161, 233, 234–
  35 (*see also* Indian agents, and the
  Omaha); and the Otoe-Missouria,
  61, 69, 79, 104, 111, 114, 115, 166, 167,
  169–70, 219, 221–22, 224–25, 226 (*see
  also* Indian agents, and the Otoe-
  Missouria); and the Pawnee, 61, 69,
  104, 127, 191, 193–94, 195–96, 197, 198,
  199 (*see also* Indian agents, and the
  Pawnee); and the Ponca, 69, 97, 104,
  133, 137, 147, 207–8 (*see also* Indian
  agents, and the Ponca); Quakers in
  charge of, 177; reservation policy of,
  69, 103–5, 107, 109, 141, 143; and the

Sauk, 59, 64, 113, 199; compensation sought for land taken from, 242; and the Omaha, 77, 165; and the Otoe-Missouria, 5–6, 8, 226

Sauk and Fox Reservation, 225

Schak-ru-leschar, 80

Schurz, Carl, 212

Scott, John, 226

Scrofula, 197, 204, 210

Settlers, 101; annuities viewed by, 110; and the Cheyenne, 165; Indian lands coveted by, 143, 144, 153, 161, 163, 188, 193–94, 220, 221, 244; Indians of Nebraska viewed by, 88, 110–11, 113, 117, 122, 124, 125, 126–27, 145, 151, 153, **162, 163**, 165, 181, 182, 193, 194, 225, 226, 264 n.51; location of, **108**, 109–10; origins of, 109; and the Omaha, 117, 118, 120, 142, 153, 155–56, 159, 227, 237; and the Otoe-Missouria, 206, 217, 218, 220, 221, 222; and the Otoe-Missouria reservation, 113, 142, 168–69; and the Pawnee, 64, 65, 80, 110–11, 125, 126–27, 128, 132, 174, 182, 183–85, **192**, 193–95, 206, 277 n.99; and the Ponca, 133, 135, 206–7; speculation by, 109, 113, 142, 169, 187–88, 221, 267 n.11; timber of Pawnee stolen by, 182, 194–95, 199

Shah-re-tah-riche, 63

Shu-shury-ga (Prairie Chicken), 235

Shawnee, 45, 64

Sheldon, Addison, 109

Sh-laa-wa-te-de, 127

Shooting Star, 185

Shudegacheh, 43

Shu-de-gah-he. *See* Smoke Maker

Shu-kah-bi (Heavy Chief), 135, 136

Shunatana, Richard, 11

Sind-de-haha (William Hamilton), 235

Sioux. *See* Dakota

Sioux City and Nebraska Railroad Company, 235–36

Siracherish, 90, 265 n.70

Siskatuppe, 96

Sisseton, 59 (*see also* Dakota)

Skiri, 26, 82, 91, 92, 96 (*see also* Pawnee); Allis among, 29, 49; bison hunting range of, 27; and the fur trade, **31**; in Indian Territory, 201; missionaries among, 49; offshoots of, 5 (*see also* Kawarahki); and the Oglala, 81; and the Omaha, 87; origins of, 4, 5; on the Pawnee reservation, 129, 177, 197, 276 n.85; population of, **82, 190**; traditions and ceremonies of, 12, 98, 201, 266 n.93

Sky Chief, 191, 196

Smallpox, 6–7, 24, 46, 71; and the Chaui, 63; and the Mandan, 99; and the Omaha, 7–8, 36, 77, 87; and the Otoe-Missouria, 8, 78, 79, 89; and the Pawnee, 8, 63, 80, 81, 93; and the Ponca, 8, 76; and the Skiri, 81, 98; vaccination for, 76, 79, 262 n.21

Smith, David, 92, 93, 96

Smith, Edward, 199, 207, 226, 234, 239; and mandatory federal policy, 204, 219–20; and Otoe-Missouria, 219–20, 222

Smith, John, 167, 169, 170, 221

Smith, John Q., 208

Smoke Maker, 75, 208, 211, 213

South Bands, 5, 27, 91 (*see also* Chaui; Kitkahahki; Pitahawirata)

Spanish, 3, 4, 9, 16, 58; horses provided by, 35; and the Pawnee, 31, 262 n.26

Spotted Tail, 192–93, 207, 208, 211

Springer, John, 209

Standing Bear, 202, 203, 210, 213, 214, **215**, 216; deposed by Agent Carrier, 206; return to Niobrara homeland of, 202, 211–12; testimony of, in Senate investigation, 202, 208, 209

Standing Bear vs. Crook, 212

Standing Buffalo, 133, 148, 149, 206, 214

Standing Hawk, 154, 160
Stone, Thomas J., 137
Strong Walker, 133, 134
Sully, Alfred, 131, 150
Sun Dance, 11, 214, 226

Tabeau, Pierre, 8
Taylor, Nathaniel, 164, 169, 178, 181, 271
  n.3; and reservation policy, 143
Te-ra-eta-its, 127
Ter-re-kaw-wah (Pawnee Chief), 184, 197
Thief, The, 62
Threatening Clouds, 133
Tibbles, Thomas Henry, 212, 226, 235
Timber Culture Act, 187
Tipton, Thomas W., 143–44
Trade, fur. See Fur trade
Treaty of Prairie du Chien, 59, **60**, 60–
  61, 62, 68
Troth, Jacob, 177, 184, 196; and the
  Pawnee reservation, 192, 194, 195
Trowbridge, Commissioner, 212
Truteau, Jean Baptiste, 35
Tuberculosis; among the Omaha, 153,
  229; among the Otoe-Missouria, 166,
  219; among the Ponca, 149
Turner, Moses K., 144, 194
Two Crows (Kah-a-num-ha), 227, 229,
  231, 235
Typhoid; among the Otoe-Missouria,
  219; among the Pawnee, 197

Union Pacific, 142, 181, 185
United States Army, 59, 64; assisted by
  Pawnee against Dakota and Cheyenne, 180–81; and the Dakota, 64,
  150, 180–81; massacre of Poncas by,
  151–53, 156; murder of Omaha
  women by, 156; Omahas promised
  protection by, 87, 264 n.51; Otoe-
  Missouria promised protection by,
  264 n.51; Pawnees promised protection by, 64–65, 180, 181, 191, 264 n.51;

Pawnees attacked by, 182, 183; Poncas
  promised protection by, 150–51, 205,
  208, 264 n.51
United States Congress: absolute power
  over Indians of, 58–59; annuities
  given by, 60, 137, 179; and the Morrill
  Act, 142; petitioned for legal recognition of the Omaha allotments, 235;
  and the relocation of the Pawnee in
  Indian Territory, 199; and the removal of Ponca to Indian Territory,
  207, 208, 211; and the sale of the
  Omaha Reservation, 233, 234, 235;
  and the sale of the Otoe-Missouria
  Reservation, 221, 222
United States Court of Claims, 201, 243
United States government, 3; civilization policy of (see Civilization program); dependence of Indians on,
  66, 89–90, 105, 107; guns given to Indians by, 63, 64, 66, 130, 136, 191, 205;
  and mixed-blood marriages, 44–45;
  purchase of Indian land by, 16, 37,
  58–59, **60**, 60–64, 66 (see also individual nations, lands purchased
  from); rituals of Indians suppressed
  by, 98; roles of Indian men and
  women changed by, 19; treatment of
  Indians by, xiv, 57, 134, 144, 150, 153,
  202, 204, 207, 239, 243–45; vaccination efforts of, 76
Union Pacific, 193, 196
United States Senate, 144, 223; investigation of, into removal of Ponca to Indian Territory, 208, 211, 213
Upper Missouri Indian Agency, 43, 56,
  83, 84
Ute, 31

Vaughan, A. J., 84
Village life, 16–18, 21–25; changes in
  19th century in, 35–37; and class
  structure, 21–22; gender and respon-

sibilities in, 19, **20**, 20–21; social structure of, 36

Vore, Jacob, 231, 232

Wahpeton, 59

Waje'pa (Ezra Fremont), 235

Wakon'monthin, 232

Walker, Francis, 188

Wa-non-ki-ga (Noise), 154

Warfare, 42, 45, 50 (*see also* Raiding); as means of spreading subsistence base, 85; and the Otoe-Missouria, 33; and the Pawnee, 33, 262 n.26; and religion, 33

Warinase, 51

Warner, Jesse, 238

War of 1812, 41, 48

Wa'thishnade, 269 n.49

Wea, 64

Webster, John L., 212

Welsh, William, 204

Weltfish, 94, 96

Whaley, Charles, 177, 182, 184

Wharton, Major Clifton, 54, 92, 94

Wheeler, Daniel, 177, 178, 179

Whip, The, 86, 136, 137, 140, 145; and Ponca land sales, 133, 134

Whiskey. *See* Alcohol

White, Barclay, 191, 220, 223, 226, 234; and the Pawnee, 193, 196–97

White, Frank, 197

White Bird (Wah-zhing-gah-skah), 149

White Eagle, 203, 204, 208, 211, 212

White Horse, 230, 235

Whiteman, William, 207–8, 211

Whitewater, Jim, 172, 220

Whiting, William, 212

Whitman, William, 11, 18

Whooping cough, 71, 81

Wichita: and the Pawnee, 5, 31, 33, 189, 197, 198, 199

Wichita Agency, 189, 197, 199

Wilcox, Captain, 152

Wild Warrior, 91

Wilhelm, Paul. *See* Wurttemberg, Duke of

Wilkinson, George, 237

Willard, Delane, 194, 198, 202, 278 n.18

Williamson, John, 198, 199

Wilson, Peter, 75

Wilson, William, 135

Winnebago, 59, 234; and the Omaha, 147, 153, 159–60, 234–35, 243; and the Otoe-Missouria, 97; poverty of, 245, 287 n.14

Women, Indian: and bison hunts, 21, 26, 28, 29, 97; chores and responsibilities of, 8, 19, **20**, 20–21, 22, 23, 24; Euro-American perceptions of, 18–19, 21; and the fur trade, 19, 42, 47, 97; land ownership of, 19, 22; marriage to traders of, 43, 44–45; of the Omaha, 154, 229, 230; of the Otoe-Missouria, 21; of the Pawnee, 19, 97, **178**, 182; and raiding, 33; and religion, 19, **20**, 21

Woodbury, D. P., 65

Woodin, Lewellyn, 225

Woolsey, J. P., 201

Wooster, Charles, 194

Wurttemberg, Duke of, 47, 48, 51, 79, 80

Yankton, 39, **67** (*see also* Dakota); bison hunting by, 146; homeland for mixed-bloods of, given to, 61; and the Omaha, 33, 77, 87; and the Pawnee, 174, 181; and the Ponca, 33, 149, 205, 210, 212, 216; territory claimed by, 59, 276 n.91

Yanktonai, 276 n.91

Yellow Smoke (Shu'de-naci), 232

Yellow Sun, 184

Lightning Source UK Ltd.
Milton Keynes UK
UKHW011240290821
389562UK00009B/351